For you, dear reader.

TruthNotes
Press

truth
notes

A Devotional of
Timeless Truth in
a Changing World

RUTH E. MEYER

Table of Contents

March

April

May

November

December

Author's Note

Welcome, dear friend! I'm so glad you're joining me for this journey through my past blog posts, plus a few new ones. When I began compiling this book, I thought it would be easier than my other books. Boy, was I wrong about that! If anything, this book proved to be *more* challenging than starting from scratch. Yes, many of the posts were written, but as I went through the process of copying and pasting them, I came to a sobering realization. Over the course of six years, I repeated myself quite a bit. Some posts, written four or five years apart, were nearly identical. I also discovered I'd used a number of Bible passages multiple times throughout my blogging history. So a good portion of assembling this book was editing out redundant posts and changing Scripture passages.

At first, this was discouraging. Was I *that* unoriginal? But then I remembered the subtitle of my blog: Timeless Truth in a Changing World. The message never changes. God's Word is always the same. While the world around us is constantly changing, the message of the cross never will. So why shouldn't there be some overlap in my posts over the years?

What you have before you is the "best of" my blog posts in one handy book. You don't need to wade through my entire blog online to find a certain post. I have included a Scripture index and topical index so you can find posts for specific topics or Bible verses as situations arise in your own life.

How you use this book is up to you. Rather than list my posts in a strictly chronological fashion, I decided to group them together by month, so you can follow along throughout the year if you wish. There's not a post for every day of the year, but many of the posts in any given month are seasonal. If you wish to read a post every other day or so, go for it! If you prefer to read the entire thing all at once, that's fine too. Or if you have specific concerns on your mind, you can use the topical index to start with posts pertaining to that issue. There's no right or wrong way to read this book!

I pray that these posts will bless you, my friend. May you find strength and courage in God's Word, which never changes.

In Christ,

Ruth Meyer

The grass withers, and the flower falls, but the Word of the Lord remains forever.

1 Peter 1:24-25

January

This is the Year

January 1, 2018

This is the year I stick to my diet.

This year I'm gonna get into an exercise routine.

This is the year I finally lose those extra pounds.

Most people start a new year off with high hopes and good resolutions, and many resolutions center around one's health. Gyms do their best business around the end of December and beginning of January, because so many people join as motivation for a New Year's resolution. This is all fine and good. There's nothing wrong with committing to a healthier lifestyle. But what if we took our spiritual health as seriously as we take our physical health? What might those resolutions look like?

1. Healthy diet

What we put into our bodies directly impacts our health and the way we feel, not to mention our weight. But your spiritual diet is far more important than your physical one. Jesus quotes Deuteronomy 8:3 when He says, "Man shall not live by bread alone, but by every word that comes from the mouth of God" (Matthew 4:4). So what does your spiritual diet look like? Are you feeding yourself junk food, just reading shallow religious snippets on occasion? Or are you getting a steady diet of God's Word and His body and blood in Holy Communion? Those are His means of grace—the way He promises to sustain you in the faith and in holy living. If you aren't getting His pure Word and Sacraments, you aren't nourishing yourself spiritually. Jesus calls Himself the "bread of life" in John 6:48, and goes on to say that "if anyone eats of this bread, he will live forever" (John 6:51). So make time each day to read the Bible. Set aside Sunday mornings for worship. God will feed you and strengthen you through it.

2. Exercise regularly

It's no coincidence that our faith life is often called a faith walk. The Bible also likens the Christian life to a race. "Let us throw off everything that hinders and the sin that so easily entangles. And let us run with perseverance the race marked out for us," Hebrews 12:1b (NIV) exhorts us. We are running a long-distance race toward the finish line of heaven, fixing our eyes on Jesus. As we do so, we "throw off everything that hinders." We pray that God would help us exercise self-control and exhibit the fruit of the Spirit in our lives. Prayer is an excellent (and underutilized!) exercise in and of itself. So is fasting, a practice that has largely fallen out of usage in our society, but which can be helpful in the life of a

Christian. Pray Luther's Morning Prayer when you wake up and the Evening Prayer and Lord's Prayer before you go to bed. Make a list of people to pray for. Get in the habit of confessing your sins to God and praying for strength and wisdom. James 5:16 tells us that "the prayer of a righteous person is powerful and effective" (NIV). Trust that God will hear and answer your prayers as you run your race.

3. Lose weight

You may be carrying around extra baggage without even realizing it. Do you bear a grudge? Are you weighed down with shame or guilt over past mistakes? Be rid of it all. Let go of any grudges you may have. Pray that God will fill you with His peace and forgiveness rather than the bitterness you now feel. Pray for strength to reconcile with someone you have wronged or who has wronged you. Perhaps you're carrying around guilt and regret. If so, bring it to Jesus' cross and leave it there. He has fully atoned for your sins—all of them—by His death and resurrection. He doesn't want you to carry the burden of your sin around any longer, for He has already borne that burden for you. You are forgiven. You are free.

So yes, face this new year with anticipation and high hopes. It's time to maintain a healthy diet, exercise regularly, and lose weight. Now is the time to get in shape.

This is the year.

Beginning with the End

January 4, 2016

I have a bona fide obsession. Actually, it's probably more like an addiction. I cannot stop writing. I find this odd, since I didn't grow up hoping to write a book someday. It was never even on my radar. But suddenly, all I want to do is write. Once I started, I couldn't stop. In the past half year, I've written two manuscripts for novels, and I'm a third of the way done with another. Plus, I just came up with an idea for a new book series, and have written a handful of scenes for those as well. I talk about my characters as if they were real people. I've laughed through chapters and sobbed while writing others. And I don't know how other authors write their books, but in my case I've found a pattern. I have to write the end first.

Writing a novel is a journey unlike any other. I've found that in order to make the whole thing tie together, I have to know how it's going to end before I even start. I need to know where I'm going in order to get there. And knowing how the story ends helps me fashion the events leading up to that finale. If I don't have a clear idea of where I'm going, the story itself is kind of pointless.

You're on a journey too, you know. It's called life. And believe it or not, you already know the ending. No, you don't know how or when you'll die, but you know that at some point, you *will* die. But even that's not the end of the story. Those who believe in Jesus will spend eternity with Him. Talk about a happy ending!

So how does knowing the ending affect how you plan your journey? Keep that ending in mind as you go through your daily life. Tell others about Jesus and the happy ending awaiting you. You'll have good scenes and bad scenes in this thing called life, but remember that eventually you'll make it to the end. And God's already written the final chapter. You, me, and all the saints in heaven will be together for all eternity.

And we'll all live happily ever after.

Broken Resolutions

January 7, 2019

I broke my New Year's resolution on January 2. It was my daughter's birthday, and with everything else going on that day, I just didn't get in the thirty minutes of decluttering that I'd vowed to do each day. Understandable, sure, but what a downer all the same. I didn't even make it two days into the new year before I broke my resolution. So much for a fresh start.

People love a fresh start, and January is a perfect time for one. A new year brings the promise of a new beginning; the potential for change. People make resolutions about exercise, diet, better sleep, time management, and more. But all too often, New Year's resolutions fall by the wayside. New habits are hard to establish, and old ones difficult to break. We're barely a week into January, and many people have already broken their resolutions.

But why wait for January 1 to make a fresh start? A resolution for a new year is a fine idea, but also very daunting. Very few people will actually be able to keep a resolution for an entire year. Why not make small changes weekly or monthly? And even if you do break a resolution, that doesn't have to be the end. Just because I missed a day of decluttering doesn't mean I have to give up. In fact, I made it up the next day by doing two thirty-minute increments then.

Regardless of where you stand with your New Year's resolution—even if you didn't bother to make one—there's one area where you are guaranteed a fresh start each and every day. No matter how badly you've messed up, no matter how many times you've already failed in the past, God is all about new beginnings and fresh starts. He daily forgives your sins and clothes you with Christ's robe of righteousness.

The Bible is full of references to God's abundant forgiveness. Lamentations 3:22-23 assures us, "The steadfast love of the Lord never ceases; His mercies never come to an end; they are new every morning; great is Your faithfulness." God promises in Isaiah 43:25, "I, I am He who blots out your transgressions for My own sake, and I will not remember your sins." So completely has He forgiven us that "As far as the east is from the west, so far does He remove our transgressions from us," Psalm 103:12 promises.

That's a pretty impressive fresh start, and it's yours, dear child of God. Confess your sins to God and trust that He has indeed removed them from you. Every day is a fresh start, no matter what happened the previous day. Whether you've kept your New Year's resolution or not, trust that God has resolved to forgive and redeem you, and *that's* a resolution that will never be broken.

Raising the Standard

Bonus Post

It's amazing what you can learn from windows. Our church has a stained glass window with a picture of a lamb, who is sitting on a book with seven seals. Behind him is a river flowing, and the lamb is holding a banner. The Bible reference is Revelation 5, the chapter about the Lamb of God (Jesus) and the seven seals. But there's no mention of a banner in that chapter. To find the answer to that, we need to look to the Old Testament.

Revelation 5:5 refers to Jesus as "the Lion of the tribe of Judah, the Root of David, [who] has conquered, so that He can open the scroll and its seven seals." Jesse was King David's father, so Jesus is called either the "root of David" or the "root of Jesse." Isaiah 11 is a beautiful description and prophecy of the coming Messiah and His reign. Right away in verse 1, he says, "There shall come forth a shoot from the stump of Jesse…" When the two kingdoms of Israel were taken into captivity, the Davidic line seemed to be snuffed out. It was dead, like a tree stump. But lo and behold, Jesus was born of the line of David (and hence, Jesse). Jesus is that living shoot coming forth from the dead stump.

Isaiah 11 goes on to give details about the Messiah's ministry, as well as the final (heavenly) establishment of His kingdom. We read in verse 10: "In that day, the root of Jesse, who shall stand as a signal for the peoples—of Him shall the nations inquire, and His resting place shall be glorious." This "root of Jesse" is to stand as a "signal" for the people, but what does it mean by "signal"? The Hebrew word is *nēs,* which can be translated as a flag or flagstaff, banner, pole, sail, ensign, or standard. Aha! This is a banner, like troops use in battle as a rallying point.

Jesus' cross is our banner, our emblem, our signal or standard. What unites us as Christians is the cross. Jesus didn't come to be an earthly king with great pomp and power. Rather, He came in weakness and humility. He came to die. We rally to the cross.

But the story doesn't end at the cross. That Lamb of God who came to die came to life again three days later. We do not worship a dead Savior, but a living one! And the standard that He bears isn't just a national flag for one race or people. The cross is for all peoples of all times and all places. Jesus' standard goes far beyond national loyalties. It stretches to eternity.

Why Me?

January 13, 2020

Life is hard.

I have a friend who started her second round of chemo treatments last week. An adolescent from our church was hit by a truck over the weekend and is in the hospital for the foreseeable future. One of my friends was abused as a child and still carries those scars. People struggle with addiction, health problems, persecution, accidents, natural disasters, financial troubles, relationship problems... The list goes on and on. And the natural inclination when trouble strikes is to ask God, *Why me?*

Why indeed? This question has plagued mankind since the beginning. Job is a fine example of this. Yes, he's held up as a righteous example of perseverance. Yes, he keeps his faith. But in his lowest moments, he pictures God as his enemy. He sees God as a wrathful tyrant seeking to punish. "For the arrows of the Almighty are in me," he says in Job 6:4, "the terrors of God are arrayed against me." In 9:17, he argues, "For [God] crushes me with a tempest and multiplies my wounds without cause." These are words spoken in distress and anguish. Elsewhere in the book, Job does speak words of confidence and hope. But not now. The pain is too raw.

When talking about suffering, you'd be hard pressed to find someone who suffered more than Job. He lost all his livestock and wealth, his children all died, and he was covered in nasty, blistering sores from head to foot. All this happened within a very short time frame. This poor guy just couldn't catch a break. But here's the interesting plot twist: While Satan is the one to afflict Job, *God* is actually the one to suggest Job to Satan in the first place.

When Satan presents himself before God, God asks him where he has come from, to which Satan answers, "From going to and fro on the earth, and from walking up and down on it" (Job 1:7). Then God says, "Have you considered My servant Job, that there is none like him on the earth, a blameless and upright man, who fears God and turns away from evil?" (Job 1:9). Satan shoots back a spiteful answer, implying that Job is only faithful because he has such a good life. God then gives Satan permission to oppress Job: "Behold, all that he has is in your hand. Only against him do not stretch out your hand" (Job 1:12).

Are you uncomfortable with that thought? I am! To think that God would offer one of His children to be tested in such a terrible way is disconcerting. I can't help but wonder if similar "bargains" between God and Satan still take place today, such as those that took place in Job 1-2. I'd like to think not, but I can neither confirm nor deny it from Scripture. Regardless, while the reader of Job is aware of this background, Job himself is not. He only knows that he is in torment, and wonders why God has turned against him.

But look at God's words to Satan once more. He calls Job "My servant," which is a title of honor and of possession. God has already claimed Job as His own. God also praises Job's faithfulness. There is "none like him on the face of the earth." God has a deep love for and confidence in Job. He knows Job can and will endure whatever hardships Satan throws at him. It's paradoxical to human reason, but can it be that God allows trials and difficulties to come our way *because* He loves us?

Like Job's friends, we are often tempted to think that when things are going well, God is happy with us. Too often we fall for the lie that if we live in a way that honors God, He will bless us with prosperity, peace, and good health. But the book of Job, along with many other places in the Bible, shows us differently.

Although it might make us bristle, the Bible often commends suffering. Romans 5:3-5 says, "...we also glory in our sufferings, because we know that suffering produces perseverance; perseverance, character; and character, hope. And hope does not put us to shame, because God's love has been poured out into our hearts through the Holy Spirit, who has been given to us" (NIV). Later in the book, we read, "I consider that our present sufferings are not worth comparing with the glory that will be revealed in us" (Romans 8:18, NIV).

Life on this earth is hard, yes. Sin has ruined the perfect creation God made. But take heart, dear friend. You aren't made for this earth. You are made for heaven. We are "strangers and exiles" on this earth, as Hebrews 11:13 reminds us. Or, as Romans 8:22-23 says, "We know that the whole creation has been groaning as in the pains of childbirth right up to the present time. Not only so, but we ourselves, who have the firstfruits of the Spirit, groan inwardly as we wait eagerly for our adoption to sonship, the redemption of our bodies" (NIV).

Whatever you are struggling with or suffering today, remember that God is with you and for you. This side of heaven, you may never understand why He allows your particular suffering, but He is working in you to prepare you for something far better: eternal life with Him, where "He will wipe away every tear from [your] eyes, and death shall be no more, neither shall there be mourning, nor crying, nor pain anymore, for the former things have passed away" (Revelation 21:4). Life may be hard here, but it won't be that way forever. In heaven, your life will be absolutely perfect.

Pushing the Limit

January 14, 2019

This weekend I watched the movie *Silence*. It takes place in 17th-century Japan, when there was heavy persecution of Christians. The story follows two Jesuit priests who are seeking their mentor, who has reportedly committed apostasy and denied the faith. It is an intense movie, and disturbing on many levels. I was drawn into the conflict the characters faced, wondering how I would respond under similar circumstances. Many were strong even in the face of death. But there is one character in particular whose weakness was all too apparent, to the point that I got irritated with him. It was difficult to tell whether he was sincere or not, as he repeated the same mistake over and over. At one point, the priest asks himself, "How can Jesus love such a wretch as this man?"

The question stuck with me. Yes, this character annoyed me. He repented and then turned around and did the same thing all over again. At times he was even flippant about confession, asking jauntily, "Padre, can God forgive me this time? Even me?" I grew tired of him. It was easy to identify his hypocrisy. It was as if he was deliberately pushing the limit, testing the bounds of forgiveness and mercy. But his character was perhaps one of the most realistic in the movie, for whether we care to admit it or not, we are often no different.

How often have you confessed the same sin to God, vowing to do better, only to give in to the exact same temptation later that day? Have you ever felt like you were pushing the limit, asking for pardon one time too many? Or perhaps you've gotten to the point where you don't bother to fight the temptation at all, reasoning that God will forgive you anyhow. Maybe your confession to God is as flippant as the movie character's: *God, can You still forgive me this time?*

True, we ought not take God's grace lightly. God has promised to forgive us, but that's not a license to sin freely. If you're to the point where you're comfortable in your sin, pray for God's Spirit to convict you and change your heart to see your sin for what it really is: something that could separate you eternally from God.

If, however, you're discouraged because you just keep repeating the same sin over and over, remember that God's forgiveness is not like our forgiveness. The priest in the movie struggled to proclaim absolution to the man who could not seem to turn from his ways. God forgives freely, without limitation. When Peter asked Jesus how often he should forgive a brother who sins against him, Jesus replied, "I do not say to you seven times, but seventy times seven" (Matthew 18:22). He places no restrictions on forgiveness.

Furthermore, God promises in 2 Chronicles 7:14, "If My people who are called by My name humble themselves, and pray and seek My face and turn from their wicked ways, then I will hear from heaven and will forgive their sin and heal their land." Note that God here defines what true repentance looks like: "humble...pray...seek...turn." And His response to repentance is that He will "hear...forgive...and heal." Every time. Without limit.

When You Don't Get Anything
out of Church

January 15, 2018

"I didn't get a thing out of that."

These words were spoken by a resident of a nursing home some years ago when I was in college. A group of students went to a local nursing home once a week to sing with the residents and lead them in a short devotional time. One week after the Bible message, a man who was hard of hearing turned to his neighbor and announced rather loudly, "I didn't get a thing out of that!" We laughed about it then, and it still brings a smile to my face now. But have you ever felt that way after church or a devotion, like you didn't get anything of substance out of it? And that begs the question, is it even worth it?

The other day I read an amazing devotion on Hebrews. I've never really understood the whole order of Melchizedek thing, but this devotion explained it really well, and it was an "aha" moment for me. I love it when that happens. Whether it's a great sermon in church or an insightful Bible study or even a study note at the bottom of the page, I love those light bulb moments. Some years ago, I read a commentary of Leviticus like that. (Yes, Leviticus!) It explored the details and significance of all those Old Testament sacrifices and tied them to Jesus' ultimate once-for-all sacrifice. It was fascinating. I looked forward to my devotional time while I was working through Leviticus. It's exciting and invigorating to have moments of insight.

But…

More often than not, my devotions aren't filled with "aha" moments. As bad as it sounds to say it, sometimes my devotions can be rather mundane. Tedious, even. As wonderful as it would be to have amazing devotions all the time or mountaintop experiences every Sunday in church, the simple fact is that that won't always happen. Sometimes you might feel like you're plodding through devotions; like they're just one more thing to cross off your to-do list. Some Sundays you'll think you didn't get anything out of church. Maybe you're already upset about something and your kids are whining and fighting through the service and you barely hear a word of the sermon. Maybe you leave church mad at your entire family and thinking it would have been better had you just stayed home. (Trust me, I've been there!) What then?

The good news is that it's not about you or how you're feeling at any particular time. The results are up to God, not you. His Word is not dependent upon your emotions. His Word has *power*. God promises that "it will not return to Me empty, but will accomplish what I desire and achieve the purpose for which I sent it" (Isaiah 55:11, NIV). Hebrews 4:12 says, "For the Word of God is living and active, sharper than any two-edged sword, piercing to the division of soul and of spirit, of joints and of marrow, and discerning the thoughts and intentions of the heart." Now *that's* power. When we read the Bible or hear it proclaimed, we reap the benefits of that power in our own lives, whether we feel it or not.

Many people make the mistake of thinking that we have to get some sort of emotional response out of church or it's not worth it. They may argue that they can't recall the Bible readings or sermons from weeks past, so it's a waste of time. So let's look at this another way. What did you have for Christmas dinner? Chances are, it was something pretty special. You likely had multiple side dishes and a fancy main course. It was probably fairly memorable. But what about dinner two Thursdays ago? How about last August? Can you recall? Probably not, but it's a safe bet that it wasn't nearly as spectacular as Christmas dinner. Yet it still nourished your body. Maybe meatloaf and baked potatoes aren't as exciting as a ham dinner with all the fixings, but your body was fed nonetheless. Even though you can't recall what you ate a month ago, it still accomplished the purpose of nourishing you. If this is true of something as mundane as food, how much more so does it apply to God's Word, food for your soul?

The next time you read a devotion that sort of seems to fall flat, flip to Isaiah 55:11 and Hebrews 4:12. Remind yourself of God's unfailing promise. The next time you come home from church feeling defeated and frustrated, remember that you *did* get something out of church. You received the forgiveness of sins. God's Word was read and proclaimed, even if you didn't hear much of it. If it was a communion Sunday, you received the body and blood of Christ for the strengthening of your faith and for forgiveness. Turns out, you got quite the outpouring of gifts from God.

Even when you feel like you didn't get a thing out of that.

What is Truth?

January 16, 2014
(Initial post for the entire blog!)

People have been asking the question since Pontius Pilate threw it at Jesus, and it's just as relevant today as it was then. Our society places a great amount of importance on the simple word "truth." As parents we ask our kids to tell us the truth. We are required when giving testimony in court to tell "the truth, the whole truth, and nothing but the truth." We lose respect for public figures who lie to us. We believe we have the right to know the truth behind news stories.

But who decides what is true? Facts can easily be twisted to support a certain agenda. And many people believe that truth is relative—"Whatever you believe is true for you, and whatever I believe is true for me. Neither of us is wrong." But by definition that cannot be true. Yet that is what we are conditioned, from a very young age, to believe, especially in matters of religion. "You have your own belief system and I have mine. Both are correct." Again, though, a lie. So how do we know where to find real truth? The answer is very easy: Jesus.

John's Gospel in particular places a strong emphasis on truth. Read through the book of John and count how many times the word "truth" or a close derivative ("true" or "truly") is used. It's everywhere. Jesus often begins His statements with "Truly, truly, I say to you…" I personally like the Good News Translation, which says, "I am telling you the truth." Jesus wants to assure us that here is where we can find real truth—in Him. John 14:6 tells us, "Jesus said to him, 'I am the way, and the truth, and the life. No one comes to the Father except through Me.'" Not only can we count on Jesus to reveal the truth to us, but by believing that truth we have eternal life. Eternal life in heaven with Him! He is the *way* to heaven, the One who speaks the *truth*, and the only One who gives eternal *life*.

So what does Jesus teach His followers about truth? In John 8:31-32, He says, "'If you abide in My word, you are truly My disciples, and you will know the truth, and the truth will set you free.'" Three uses of "truth" and "truly" in that one sentence. Obviously this is something pretty important. The Jews listening to Him ask what He means about being free, since they aren't slaves of anyone. Jesus tells them, "'Truly, truly, I say to you, everyone who commits sin is a slave to sin. The slave does not remain in the house forever; the son remains forever. So if the Son sets you free, you will be free indeed'" (John 8:34-36).

Have you ever sinned? Of course you have. So has every single person who has ever lived on the face of this earth, except for the notable exception of Jesus. We sin multiple times a day. We can't help ourselves. That's why Jesus tells us we are slaves to sin. We serve our sinful nature like, well, slaves. We are constantly tempted to gossip or lie or cheat or think evil thoughts, and like slaves, we obey. But thanks be to God we aren't doomed to remain a slave to sin. Jesus set us free from that. Those of us who believe in Him are not in slavery anymore. Jesus is telling us the truth. Will we still sin? Yes. But when we do, Jesus will forgive us. We are His now. The devil cannot claim us anymore. We belong to Jesus, the truth.

Fast forward a few chapters in the Bible to John 18. Jesus is standing before Pilate, who is trying to decide if there is just reason to condemn Him to crucifixion. An interesting conversation ensues between Jesus and Pilate. Pilate seems intent on getting Jesus to admit that He is a king. If Jesus does say He is a king, Pilate has an easy way out. He can condemn Jesus for political insurrection against Caesar. But Jesus doesn't play that game with Pilate. He tells Pilate His "kingdom" is not of this world. Then He says, "'I was born and came into the world for this one purpose, to speak about the truth'" (John 18:37, GNT).

So *that* was Jesus' purpose for coming to earth—to "speak about the truth"? Yes, because Jesus *is* the truth. He came to reveal God's beautiful plan of salvation to us. But Pilate doesn't understand any of that. Instead, he throws in one last little dig at Jesus by asking, "'What is truth?'" (John 18:38). Interestingly, Jesus doesn't answer this. Pilate asks this derisively, dismissively. He doesn't realize that Jesus, the Truth, is standing right in front of him. Jesus doesn't answer Pilate because Pilate isn't seeking an answer.

Sadly, many people today are just like Pilate 2,000 years ago. "You Christians know the truth, huh? How arrogant to think you're the only ones who are right!" Well, yes, in one sense that's true. It is arrogant for any one person to assert such a thing.

But that's the beauty of it. We aren't inventing a truth from our own imaginations. We have this truth given to us by Jesus Himself. Just think about God's plan for salvation. We honestly believe that *God* died and rose for us? And to get to heaven we don't have to earn it? We only have to believe in Jesus? Logically that makes absolutely no sense. To our finite minds, this is absurd. We must have to do something, *anything*, to merit heaven. But we don't. And that's why I believe through faith that Jesus is indeed telling the truth. If some small group of men sat down to decide to invent a religion, there's no way they would come up with a plan like this. Who would believe it? If any one person or group of people tried to invent a religion, they would make up something much more logical. But thank God for this plan that to human reason is "illogical."

His plan is perfect. His plan is absolute. His plan, dear one, is *truth*.

How Not to Pray

January 21, 2019

Mary was in a delicate position. She was at a wedding, and they had run out of wine. This would be a huge embarrassment for the bride and groom. Wedding celebrations in those times ran for days, and running out of wine early meant the party would have to be cut short. Mary knew her Son could help. As His mother, she could have pulled the "parent" card and told Him what to do. But this wasn't your typical mother/son relationship. Her Son was God, and she knew her place. The way she handled the situation was diplomatic and wise, and it can teach us a thing or two about prayer.

The well-known story of Jesus changing water into wine in John 2:1-11 isn't a text on prayer, per se. But Mary is talking to Jesus, and when we pray we talk to Jesus too. So let's take a lesson from the woman who knew Jesus as well as anyone can.

1. *Don't tell God how to answer your prayers.* When Mary goes to Jesus to tell Him about the situation, all she does is present the problem to Him. "They have no wine" (v 2). That's it. She doesn't ask Him to do anything. She doesn't suggest a way for Him to remedy it. She doesn't give her own opinion at all. All she does is present the problem to the Son of God.

2. *Don't get discouraged if He doesn't answer right away.* At first Jesus seems to mildly rebuke her. "Woman, what does this have to do with Me? My hour has not yet come" (v 4). Mary is undeterred. She doesn't argue with Him or plead her cause. She doesn't get mad or impatient. In fact, the Bible doesn't record that she even responds to Jesus' statement directly.

3. *Don't second-guess His answer.* After Jesus' somewhat ambiguous response, Mary tells the servants, "Do whatever He tells you." She's presented the problem, and she trusts that Jesus will do what needs to be done. She doesn't know *how* He'll fix the problem, but she knows He *will.*

So what about you, dear child of God? What problems do you face in your life right now? Have you been trying to "help" God solve them? Have you taken matters into your own hands, rather than waiting on God's timing? Do you pour out your troubles to God but try to tell Him how He should fix them? I've certainly done so before. I think I know the perfect solution, and I tell God what He needs to do. But that's not acting in faith. Simply present your problem to God, wait patiently for Him to act, and trust that His answer will be just right.

In fact, you may even witness a miracle.

How Do You Smell?

January 22, 2018

Every house has a unique smell, and ours is no different. Most of the time you don't notice the particular scent of your own house, but the past few days that hasn't been the case here. I noticed a distinctly awful smell that wasn't going away. I pulled out my air purifier, I sprayed air freshener, I washed towels and washcloths, all to no avail. The smell was still there, underneath it all. So I decided to sniff out the source. Shockingly, it wasn't the bathroom this time. It was definitely emanating from the kitchen. My journey took me to many exotic places until I came to a remote one I'd never before visited—under the oven. I tugged it out of its place and was shocked at the abject squalor I found there. Months (years?) of neglect had taken its toll. Who knows what had long since spilled and been forgotten? Even the sides of the oven were dirty from food drippings and crumbs brushed aside. It was disgusting, but once it was scrubbed clean and everything put back into its place, the smell was gone. I'd gotten to the source.

If you've ever tried to get rid of a bad smell, you know how difficult it can be. Sometimes it's easier to cover it up rather than take the time to find it and clean it. Throw on some deodorant or perfume when you don't have time to take a shower, gargle some mouthwash on the go, or spray air fresheners into a room to cover up the unpleasant odor for a while. And sometimes that works. But eventually, you'll have to take care of the problem at its source. You'll have to take a shower or brush your teeth or pull out the couch to clean the spilled and spoiled milk underneath. We've all been there at one time or another. Especially when it comes to our sin.

Try as we might, we can't cover up the stench of our sin on our own. Sure, we might try to cover it for a while. We might do lots of good works, we might put on our best face in public, we might give money to charity, but underneath it all, at the very source, we are still poor, miserable sinners. Not a pretty thought. Isaiah 64:6a tells us that "All of us have become like one who is unclean, and all our righteous acts are like filthy rags" (NIV). That's the nice version. "Filthy rags" actually refers to menstrual cloths, which are about as nasty (and smelly!) as you can get. And that's our "righteous acts." We may be able to fool others, but we can't fool God.

It doesn't take long to uncover the source of our sin—the heart. "For out of the heart come evil thoughts, murder, adultery, sexual immorality, theft, false testimony, slander. These are what defile a person,'" Jesus reminds us in Matthew 15:19-20. You know what's in your own heart, and so does God. And no matter how hard you try to cover it up, you can't. You need another source: Jesus, the "source of eternal salvation for all who obey Him" (Hebrews 5:9). Through His sacrificial death and His glorious resurrection, He has earned heaven for you. And this Jesus, true man but also true God, is in the business of heart transplants. "I will give you a new heart and put a new spirit in you; I will remove from you your heart of stone and give you a heart of flesh," He promises in Ezekiel 36:26 (NIV). (He makes the same promise in Ezekiel 11:19.)

What does this new heart look like? It is a heart filled with the peace and knowledge of sins forgiven; a heart belonging to Jesus. "For with the heart one believes and is justified, and with the mouth one confesses and is saved," Romans 10:10 tells us. As a result of this new heart, we know the stench of our sin has been replaced with something else. "But thanks be to God, who in Christ always leads us in triumphal procession, and through us spreads the fragrance of the knowledge of Him everywhere. For we are the aroma of Christ to God among those who are being saved..." we rejoice with Paul in 2 Corinthians 2:14-15.

Now *that's* a pleasant aroma. I'll take that any day. No matter what my house smells like.

One Thing Needful

January 25, 2014

Hello, dear friend. Let me introduce myself. My name is Martha. I have a sister named Mary and a brother named Lazarus. We are good friends of Jesus of Nazareth and His disciples. I'm sure you know us well. Yes, my brother was the one whom Jesus raised from the dead. It was amazing. Words just cannot describe that scene. Shortly after Lazarus came back to life, my sister Mary anointed Jesus' feet with expensive perfume as an expression of deep gratitude. And what is recorded about me? You know the story well. It's recorded in Luke 10:38-42. Yes, that's me, complaining about my sister not helping me enough. What a legacy.

Of my whole life, that *one* incident is the thing most people remember about me, and I must say, I really get the short end of the stick. I mean, come on. My sister was just sitting there—*sitting down* while there were more than a dozen men in our house. We would have been rude not to serve them a meal, and we were happy to do so, but there was no take out or frozen pizza back then. Everything was from scratch, and Mary had left me to do this meal all by myself!

Do you realize how infuriating this was? Has anything like that ever happened to you? Haven't you ever asked in frustration, "Am I the only one in this household who ever cleans?" If so, you know exactly how I felt that day. People have said that I whined to Jesus about Mary. I've even heard the word "tattle" used. Was it childish? Perhaps so. But you have an advantage over me on that one. Your childish comments aren't recorded in the Bible for everyone to read and dissect. It's very easy to read that one account and assume that I was uptight and missed the entire meaning of Jesus' coming to earth. That is not true.

Far fewer people realize that *I* was the one who, when Jesus came to town after Lazarus had been dead for four days, had a conversation with the Master that included some of the most well-known and comforting passages used at many funerals still today. I believed in Jesus, make no mistake about it. I told Him that if He had been there, Lazarus would not have died. I knew He had the power over sickness and death. Then Jesus told me that Lazarus would rise again, and what did I say? "I know that he will rise again in the resurrection on the last day" (John 11:24).

I hadn't missed all of Jesus' teachings. I wasn't rushing around ignoring Him every time He came to our house. I knew about eternal life. I knew about the resurrection of the saints. I knew that someday in heaven I would indeed see Lazarus again. Then Jesus said words that have comforted Christians ever since: "'I am the resurrection and the life. Whoever believes in Me, though he die, yet shall he live, and everyone who lives and believes in Me shall never die'" (John 11:25-26).

But Jesus wasn't content to leave it there. He then asked me if I believed that statement. My words then have been repeated ever since and are among the great confessions of the Bible. "'Yes, Lord, I believe that You are the Christ, the Son of God, who is coming into the world'" (John 11:27). I knew exactly who Jesus was.

The world has changed a lot since Jesus came into our home some 2,000 years ago. In many ways your lives today are easier than life in biblical times. You have ovens and stoves and indoor lights and running water (with water heaters) and washing machines and microwaves and cars and so many inventions that make daily tasks easier.

Yet you also have it more difficult than we did back then. Along with these inventions that make life easier, your schedules have become far more complicated than ours were. We pretty much had the same schedule week to week. We had different chores for different days but daily chores took so much time that there wasn't room for other things. We rose early in the morning to bake bread rather than running to the store for a few loaves. We washed our clothes by hand instead of throwing them into the washing machine as we ran out the door. In our day, it was expected that we more or less stayed home and worked on the tasks required for daily living.

Now you have work schedules and sports schedules and lessons and recitals and working out at the gym and carpools and volunteering and meetings and duties at church and more. It makes my head spin. I can't even comprehend that way of life. Your world is so fast-paced. Technology is advancing every day, and much of your lives now revolve around computers and iPhones and gaming systems and TV that I don't even know how you do it all. I'm sure many of you wonder the same thing. *How do I fit everything into my life?*

Learn from me. What was Jesus' response to my complaints about Mary? He said, "'Martha, Martha, you are anxious and troubled about many things, but one thing is necessary. Mary has chosen the good portion, which will not be taken away from her'" (Luke 10:41-42).

Friend, if you are too busy for devotions, Bible study, prayer, and worship, then you are too busy. Evaluate the activities in which you participate. What can you cut out? Step back from any activities or obligations that you do only out of guilt. Do a "time audit" of a typical day or week in your life. I'll bet you'd be surprised to see just how much time you waste. How often do you get on Facebook for a quick peek only to realize an hour later that you're still on? How much TV do you watch on a typical night? How often do you start one task, get distracted, and move on to other things only to realize at the end of the day that you never really finished any of the things you started?

Maybe it's time to turn those things around. Remember, the one thing, the *only* thing needed in the end is your relationship with Jesus. Yes, you do have worldly duties. You have to buy groceries, make meals, and do household chores. These things must be factored into your daily life, but they cannot be allowed to take over. Set aside a certain time each day for your own devotional and prayer time. Try getting up fifteen minutes early so it's the first thing you do each day. Or do it in the evening before you go to bed. What better way to end your day than in prayer and reading the Bible? Maybe you could have your devotional time on your lunch break or while your kids are napping or in school. Get recharged in the middle of the day when you need the encouragement. The point is, schedule it into your day. Because remember, daily tasks will eventually cease, but your relationship with Jesus will last for all eternity.

Puppy Love

January 25, 2016

I'm not exactly sure when I lost my sanity. It was a gradual process, I think, but somewhere over the last decade I managed to completely lose my senses. We have five children, a homeschooling schedule to keep up, a house that is never clean, and a dog who will probably never be completely trained. Yet despite all this, we took in another puppy this weekend. A mutt. Emaciated, shivering, and scared. For all we knew, the thing had fleas and worms. So what in the world possessed us to take in a stray under such circumstances? The answer is quite simple. He needed us.

When I read in the Bible that I am "adopted" as God's child, this is how I picture the adoption. God didn't choose me because I was so good or so loyal or so faithful. No, He picked me because I desperately needed Him. I was like that poor, pathetic, starving, terrified dog with nowhere to turn and no hope for the future. Without God's intervention, all I had to look forward to was death. Eternal death, mind you. Not a pretty picture.

Romans 5:6 tells us that "at just the right time, when we were still powerless, Christ died for the ungodly" (NIV). And a few verses later we read that "while we were still sinners, Christ died for us" (Romans 5:8). Jesus died for us when we were powerless. We had no hope of saving ourselves. The action is solely God's, from beginning to end. He's the One who sent Jesus to die for us and rise again, He's the One who calls us His own, and He's the One who now feeds and nourishes us through His holy Word and Sacraments. He brings us into His family, and He's responsible for keeping us there.

Right now, our new dog is in terrible condition. You can see his ribs and spine, and his shoulder blades stick out when he walks. It's almost painful to look at him. But with proper nourishment, time, and love, we just might have a healthy, happy dog. And who knows? Maybe at some point along the way, I'll even find my sanity again.

Guilty Consciences

January 26, 2015

Mornings are usually pretty awful in our household as we complete the mad dash to get ready and out the door on time for school. Just the other day, it was one of *those* mornings where the kids were bickering, whining, ignoring me, and generally behaving badly. Finally I'd had enough. I slammed down the brush I was using for my daughter's hair and yelled at them all. Okay, "yelled" might be a slight understatement. But it got their attention. And as so often happens when tempers are high and sanity is low, the things I yelled at them were not pretty. We all stormed out to the car with me still fuming and wondering why I ever thought motherhood was for me. I slammed the door shut behind me and started the car as the kids sat there in silence.

But then I realized this wasn't how I wanted them to go off to school. I shut off the car and sat there silently for a few moments trying to gain back a modicum of composure. I took deep breaths. And then, with a concerted effort, I apologized. I told them I didn't want us to start our morning in this way, so we said a prayer for God to forgive all of us and to help us put it behind us and make a new start for the day. Then we went on our way.

I'd love to say all was forgotten, but I was honestly still pretty mad at them. Not to mention disappointed in myself for the poor way I had handled things. Even after praying for forgiveness and asking God to give us a fresh start, I still felt a keen sense of failure. As the day went on, I kept praying about that same incident over and over. I had failed again, and I couldn't shake the feelings of guilt.

So what is it that makes you feel guilty? Do you beat yourself up over something you did long ago (or maybe not so long ago)? Maybe you've prayed for forgiveness, and you know God has forgiven you, but you can't quite bring yourself to believe that. That's nothing new. The apostle Paul addresses this very issue.

If anyone had cause for a guilty conscience, it was Paul. Formerly known as Saul, this guy was a persecutor extraordinaire. He was trying his best to stamp out those pesky Christians, and was on his way to Damascus to arrest more of them when Jesus literally stopped him in his tracks and changed the entire course of his life. Now a Christian himself, Paul had every reason to feel guilty about the fact that he had once violently opposed Christianity. Yet look at his words in Philippians 3:13-14: "But one thing I do: forgetting what lies behind and straining forward to what lies ahead, I press on toward the goal for the prize of the upward call of God in Christ Jesus."

Forgetting what is behind. That doesn't mean Paul is trying to gloss over anything or deny his past. But he knows he has already been forgiven, and he takes God at His Word. The Bible is full of assurances of God's forgiveness. He promises us in Isaiah 44:22, "I have swept away your offenses like a cloud, your sins like the morning mist..." (NIV).

You see, God forgives and forgets. Jesus already paid for your sins. All of them. Even the "big" ones. Trust Him that He really has forgiven you. (Side note: if you have a recurring sin that is harming others or yourself, like alcoholism or abusive behaviors, you need to seek help. Don't fall into the trap of such sins and then use the excuse, "Well, I'm forgiven," all the while continuing in that sin. That's a very dangerous path.)

So like Paul, take God at His Word and know that you are forgiven. Forgetting your past sins and trusting in God's forgiveness gives God the proper glory for Jesus' sacrifice. You are forgiven. God has forgotten. Even something like a ruined morning.

A Slap in the Face

January 28, 2015

I don't want to boast or anything, but I make a mean batch of chocolate chip cookies. Ever since I learned the secret of adding a box of instant vanilla pudding to the dough, my cookies have been nice and soft, even a day or two later, if any happen to make it that long. So a number of years ago when we had new neighbors move in across the street, I whipped up a batch of my cookies and took them over as a welcoming gift. The wife made a comment about how soft they were, and I proudly let her in on my little secret. Then her husband informed me that since his mother burned everything while he was growing up, he got used to burned cookies and actually preferred them. Oh. Um, thank you?

Has anything like that ever happened to you? Have you ever given a gift only to have the recipient make some thoughtless comment? That hurts. It's a slap in the face when someone rejects a gift, especially one you worked hard to find or make.

Let's talk about another gift. It comes from Jesus. It's not something you asked for, either. In fact, had it been up to you, you wouldn't have asked for anything at all. But Jesus loves you so much He gave it freely, of His own accord. That gift is, of course, forgiveness. He knows there was no possible way you could ever have repaid the debt you owed because of your sin. So He came down to this earth as a human being, lived a perfect life in your place, and then He died for you. His gift to you cost Him His entire life. But He didn't *stay* dead. He rose three days later to assure you that He's defeated death for you. His gift is forgiveness and eternal life. And not just for you but for everyone else on the face of this earth. What an amazing gift!

Sadly, though, not everyone sees this as a wonderful gift. Some people flat-out reject the gift. They think they don't need it, or that it's just a fairy tale, or some such excuse. Do not underestimate how dangerous this is. John 3:36 tells us that "Whoever believes in the Son has eternal life, but whoever rejects the Son will not see life, for God's wrath remains on him" (NIV). Ouch. Rejecting Jesus' gift has a deadly cost—one's eternal salvation. Those who reject Jesus on this earth finally get what they want when they die—an eternity without Him. And that's tragic. The gift is yours. He gives it freely. There's no need to reject it.

For the record, the couple I spoke of in the opening paragraph became good friends of ours. The husband hadn't meant any harm by his comment to me about my cookies. And there are truly no hard feelings on my part. The story serves merely as an example. But the gifts of forgiveness and salvation offered by Jesus are no trifling matter. Tell everyone you can about those amazing gifts. They are worth far more and last far longer than any other gift on this earth—even a mean batch of chocolate chip cookies.

Nowhere to Hide

January 28, 2019

I never clean more thoroughly than when the exterminator comes. He's coming today, and all day yesterday I was preparing for him. I clean closets, vacuum the rooms, clean under the beds, scrub the bathrooms, sweep and steam mop, and pull out the couch to clean underneath it. You'd think I was preparing for royalty. And all this for a visit that takes less than half an hour.

The reason I go to so much trouble for our exterminator is simple: he goes *everywhere*. He sprays around as many baseboards as he can, and that includes dark and messy places like closets, where cockroaches love to hide. I pull away furniture from the walls so he can spray behind it, but that always reveals junk that's been pushed underneath or dust bunnies that have accumulated. It's like he searches for the dirtiest places in the house. There's nowhere to hide last-minute junk. He sees it all.

As daunting as it is to have a practical stranger coming into every room and closet, it's much more intimidating to have someone know and see your every thought and desire. We hide our deep dark secrets and thoughts from those around us, but we can't fool God. He sees it all.

We read in Job 34:21-22, "For His eyes are on the ways of a man, and He sees all his steps. There is no gloom or deep darkness where evildoers may hide themselves." Hebrews 4:13 takes that a step further. "And no creature is hidden from His sight, but all are naked and exposed to the eyes of Him to whom we must give account." Yikes. That's pretty uncomfortable language. "Naked and exposed"? Couldn't the author of Hebrews have picked a slightly less vivid description? And yet, before God, that's how vulnerable we are. We can't hide anything.

To unbelievers, that thought *should* be scary and intimidating. It's all Law, reminding them that they will have to give an account to God, their Judge, for their thoughts, words, and deeds. But for the believer, the verses above are actually Gospel. God knows all our shortcomings and yet stands ready to help us in our need. The verse from Hebrews is followed by a beautiful assurance: "For we do not have a high priest who is unable to sympathize with our weaknesses, but one who in every respect has been tempted as we are, yet without sin. Let us then with confidence draw near to the throne of grace, that we may receive mercy and find grace to help in time of need" (Hebrews 4:15-16).

We can approach God with *confidence,* trusting in His mercy and grace. Even though He knows our every thought, He still loves us and accepts us as His own. What a comforting thought. We don't need to hide anything from Him; we couldn't anyway. Instead, He stands ready to clean all those dark corners of your heart. We can pray with the psalmist, "Create in me a clean heart, O God, and renew a right spirit within me" (Psalm 51:10).

My house isn't going to be spotless when the exterminator gets here, even though I've been preparing all weekend. Neither could I ever cleanse my heart by myself. But I don't have to. God has already done that for me. Thank God that I can't hide anything from Him.

The Accidental Author

January 29, 2017

I became an author quite by accident. I didn't take a single English class in college. I was a music major, after all, and for years after graduating, my focus was still music. Writing wasn't even on my radar. I played the organ for church, directed a few choirs over the years, and had no intention of becoming an author. But then a student of the week project for my second-grade son gave me an idea that eventually became the book *Our Faith From A to Z*. Now, that's the sort of book I can handle. There were specific parameters under which I had to operate—one word for each letter of the alphabet, each verse had to fit the meter of the poem, and I had to write an explanatory paragraph for each of the twenty-six words or concepts. I could do that.

Fiction, on the other hand, is an entirely different sort of beast. You can pretty much go anywhere and do anything in your writing, so long as it's interesting enough to capture people's attention. It's sort of daunting for someone like me who likes specific boundaries. I even told my best friend once, "I have no desire whatsoever to venture into fiction." And that should have been the end of it. Because once I did try fiction, I did everything wrong.

Many people who aspire to be authors attend writing workshops and/or belong to peer editing groups. Not me. And since I hadn't taken college writing classes, that meant my last official instruction in English had been in high school, many moons ago. Not exactly a resumé to catch the eye. But it gets worse. When I sent my original manuscript to my editor for her to read, it was 35,000 words short of what a novel ought to be. Oops. I waffled back and forth between third person omniscient and third person limited, and didn't even use third person limited properly half the time. The original attempt left a lot of room for improvement. Were it not for the patience and kindness of an editor who saw through these rough edges and helped smooth them over, I never would have become an author at all.

By all rights, I shouldn't be a Christian either. Nor should you. We did everything wrong. Just look at the laundry list of our sinful condition as spelled out for us in Romans 3:10-18: No one is righteous, we have all turned aside, our throats are open graves, our tongues deceitful, under our lips is the "venom of asps," our mouths are full of bitterness and curses, we rush to shed blood, in our paths are ruin and misery, and there is no fear of God in our eyes. Not a terribly inspiring resumé, is it? And that really should have been the end of the story.

But it's not.

Despite all our shortcomings, God sent Jesus to live a perfect life for us and die in our place. It wasn't because of any intrinsic worth in me that He did so. Quite the opposite, actually. I had no worth; nothing at all to offer God. God didn't see worth and potential in me—He *gave* me worth because of the sacrifice of His Son. And because of that, I have a pretty impressive resumé after all—I have Jesus' righteousness credited to my account.

And *that's* no accident.

Exposed by the Light

January 29, 2018

It is a beautiful sunny morning today; a welcome relief from the gray days we've had recently. So I opened the blinds to let in the light. That was a mistake. We have tile floors through much of the house, and the natural light that brightened the day also illuminated the dirt and crumbs on the floor. Every. Single. Particle. It looked awful. Without the natural light, I could almost fool myself into believing that the floor was clean enough, but once the light was shining on it, that illusion was gone. There was no other way around it. My floor was dirty.

We've all seen this phenomenon before. Whether it's dust particles in a ray of sunlight, complexion flaws made worse by fluorescent light, or a cavity made visible by the dentist's special light, the simple fact is that light exposes flaws or dirt. And perhaps that's why so many people try to stay out of *the* Light. People prefer to flounder in the darkness of sin, fooling themselves into believing they are good enough on their own, rather than be exposed as sinners by the Light of the world.

"You have set our iniquities before You, our secret sins in the light of Your presence," Psalm 90:8 says. When we think that we're doing a good job keeping the Commandments, God shines His light into our hearts to reveal secret sins we thought we'd buried. His Law points out every single way we break His commands every day. And it's hard to admit how bad we really are. It's easier to avoid that hard truth. "The light has come into the world, and people loved the darkness rather than the light because their works were evil. For everyone who does wicked things hates the light and does not come to the light, lest his works should be exposed," we read in John 3:19-20.

But unlike the dirt on my floor that I have to sweep, it's not up to me to take care of my problem with sin. Jesus did that for me. "I have come into the world as light, so that whoever believes in Me may not remain in darkness," He promises in John 12:46-47. "I did not come to judge the world, but to save the world."

You see, the purpose of God's light is two-fold: to expose our sins, yes, but also to point to Jesus. Without knowing we are sinners, we have no need for a Savior. Don't stumble around in darkness anymore. Confess your sins to God and trust that He forgives you in Christ. For "if we walk in the light, as He is in the light, we have fellowship with one another, and the blood of Jesus His Son cleanses us from all our sins," 1 John 1:7 promises. Spread that beautiful news to others who need the Light. Because Jesus is the Light for you, for me, and for everyone else in the world. Even people who have dirty floors.

February

The Desire of Your Heart

February 2, 2015

I was a sap in college. I was cheerful and bubbly, naïve and overly optimistic. Quite frankly, my thirty-something self cringes and rolls her eyes at my college self. *She doesn't know anything about real life. She has a real shock coming to her when she gets out in the "real" world.* I even read the Bible from this cheesy perspective. I cringe to read some of the notes I wrote in my Bible from those days, and alas, they're written in pen so I can't just erase them.

Psalm 37:4 is a lovely verse that says, "Delight yourself in the Lord, and He will give you the desires of your heart." Next to it I wrote the following (and please don't judge me—remember, I was still a teenager at this point…): "Just trust in God and serve Him, and He will work everything out in your life!" I nailed that one, didn't I? I truly believed that if I trusted God and served Him well enough, I would have a great life with very few problems. Is that really how it works? Hardly. Any Christian who's a bit more experienced than a college student can tell you that the Christian life is anything but easy. Oftentimes it may even be harder than a non-Christian's life.

Of course, the devil *wants* you to think it's not worth it. He wants you to think the wicked are indeed prospering, and that you may as well just give up on a God who would dare to allow suffering in your life. *Who wants to serve such a God, anyhow?* the devil cunningly asks. Don't fall for his lies.

Look with me at another Bible passage, Isaiah 43:1-2: "But now thus says the Lord, He who created you, O Jacob, He who formed you, O Israel: 'Fear not, for I have redeemed you; I have called you by name, you are Mine. When you pass through the waters, I will be with you; and through the rivers, they shall not overwhelm you; when you walk through fire you shall not be burned, and the flame shall not consume you.'"

What does God promise? His people *will* face trials. "*When* you pass through the waters…*when* you walk through fire…" This is a certainty, not an "if." These are very real dangers God is talking about. Fire and water are scary. But you are not alone. God is with you every step of the way, and He will protect you. That doesn't mean you won't get hurt on this earth, but He will keep you safe *in your faith*. He will not allow troubles to overwhelm His children to the point that they give up their faith. Rest secure—your future is safe with your Father in heaven.

When reading verses like Psalm 37:4, remember that there's a difference between the desires of your *heart* and the desires of your *flesh*. That's where I went wrong back in college. I was thinking in earthly terms, as in the desires of the flesh—for an easy, happy-go-lucky life. Now that I'm older and have a better perspective, I'm glad I haven't had a smooth way of it all along. Some of my times of greatest growth have occurred during very difficult times. God has used those times to work in me in ways I could never have imagined.

So what is the "desire of your heart"? To be with your Lord and Savior. And indeed, dear child of God, most assuredly you will get exactly what your heart desires. For all eternity.

Just You Wait

February 3, 2014

I vividly remember the day our college band director dropped the bombshell on us. It was nearing the end of the semester and we were all freaking out about how much we had to do—finals, term papers, juries, projects… We were *so* busy and we were all sure we'd never make it through. For a while our director just sat there, listening with a bemused smile on his face. After we'd all whined for a while, he said, "You know, you guys have more time now to practice your instruments than you will ever have again."

You should have heard the hoots and howls coming from the band room after that statement. "Yeah, right! You have *no* idea the kind of pressure we're under! We can barely squeeze time in *now* to practice!" Looking back, I blush to think of how clueless we were. We truly believed that this professor, in his mid-thirties with two kids, had it easier than us poor stressed-out college kids. If only. And rather than try to argue his point, he merely smiled and said, "Just you wait."

It turns out our band professor knew exactly what he was talking about. I practiced two hours a day when I was in college—one on flute and one on organ. I could never swing that now. Add a husband, four kids, meals to make and clean up, chores, activities, a job, etc, and I'm lucky if I get two hours a *week* to practice! (And this is even from a paid church musician!) But from the perspective of our college band members, we were busier at that point in our lives than we ever had been before and simply couldn't comprehend life a decade down the road.

Just you wait. It's often said with a touch of derision, much as one would say, "I told you so." It implies that the person to whom it is said has no idea what he or she is talking about. And that might be true, but it's not entirely helpful.

But there's a positive aspect to the phrase as well. The Bible tells us, in essence, "Just you wait. You have no idea what's in store for you in eternity." Paul encourages the Corinthians, "For this light momentary affliction is preparing for us an eternal weight of glory beyond all comparison, as we look not to the things that are seen but to the things that are unseen. For the things that are seen are transient, but the things that are unseen are eternal" (2 Corinthians 4:17-18).

Paul's not talking about being swamped with homework in college or the challenges of having young children in the house when he refers to "light momentary affliction." He means the afflictions we face as a result of our devotion to Christ. Paul faced persecution and danger like you would not believe. He was beaten three times with rods, given "forty lashes less one" five times, stoned, shipwrecked multiple times, in danger on his missionary journeys, imprisoned many times, given "countless beatings, and often near death." Check out his impressive list in 2 Corinthians 11:23-29. Yet he wrote just a few chapters earlier that the "light momentary affliction" is preparing us for the eternal glory of heaven, which is beyond comparison. If Paul called his sufferings "light momentary afflictions," he must have had quite the perspective!

But his perspective is ours, too, dear Christian. We know that someday, we will be in heaven eternally. We won't look back at our lives and say, "Boy, I sure had it rough on earth." We won't even remember the hardships. Keep the eternal perspective. For Jesus' words to His disciples in John 14:2-3 are for you also. "'In My Father's house are many rooms. If it were not so, would I have told you that I go to prepare a place for you? And if I go and prepare a place for you, I will come again and will take you to Myself, that where I am you may be also.'"

Jesus has a room prepared for you in heaven. We have no idea what joy is in store for us there. When you get overwhelmed by the duties and tasks of this life, close your eyes and quote those words from John 14:2-3. Picture Jesus saying those words directly to you. It's as if He is saying, *Dear child, I know you're going through a tough time now, but I promise you, your room here is ready. You have no idea what I've prepared for you. Just you wait.*

Tried and Found Wanting

February 4, 2019

Looking at my friend's list of goals for the week, I felt rather unambitious. She and I are accountability partners, so we check in every week to report progress and set new goals. It's a lovely arrangement, but last week she sent me her list that included seven items, many of them multi-faceted. My list had all of two things on it, both related to writing. I told her my goals looked completely lame in comparison, and she laughed and said, "I was thinking *my* goals were lame! You're writing a book, and all I'm doing is finding people to fix stuff around our house!" Then she reminded me of a saying someone had once told her: "To compare is to despair."

It's so hard *not* to compare ourselves to those around us, especially when it comes to social media. I see pictures of other moms making adorable handmade Pinterest-worthy Valentines with their kids, while I get store-bought ones and make my kids do them on their own. Friends post family pictures taken by real photographers, while our last professional picture is from six years ago, before our youngest was even born. Other people's houses often look neater or classier than our own. It's easy to feel discouraged when I compare myself to others. My own inner failings and shortcomings can never compare to someone else's best foot forward.

What is it about human nature that we so often judge ourselves by unfair comparisons? Perhaps we hope to feel better about ourselves, but usually we end up feeling worse. We think other people have better jobs, better marriages, better-behaved children, better bodies, better time management, better _____. I find this especially holds true for people of similar vocations. I'm most tempted to compare myself to other writers, and I get jealous when fellow authors have better book sales, better reviews, more widely-read blogs… So instead of thinking I'm doing a great job with the talents and abilities God has given me, I am easily led to despair.

The comparison game is a dangerous one when we compare ourselves to the accomplishments of others, but there is one area where comparison is a good thing: when we measure ourselves against God's Law. Make no mistake, it certainly holds true that to compare is to despair, but in this case, that's a *good* thing. We must utterly despair of ourselves and our own abilities before God can work the healing balm of the Gospel in our hearts.

You might think you're a pretty good person morally and religiously. You go to church every week, you do personal devotions every day, you haven't committed any major crimes, you aren't throwing wild parties like the neighbors down the street…This is one area where you actually feel pretty good about yourself.

But read what Jesus says in His Sermon on the Mount. "You have heard that it was said to those of old, 'You shall not murder; and whoever murders will be liable to judgment.' But I say to you that everyone who is angry with his brother will be liable to judgment; whoever insults his brother will be liable to the council; and whoever says, 'You fool!' will be liable to the hell of fire" (Matthew 5:21-22). Ouch. If that's the case, I *have* committed murder in my heart against a great many people. (And let's not even get into His definition of adultery a few verses later…)

The comparison of our sinfulness to God's holiness led the psalmist to ask rhetorically, "If You, Lord, kept a record of sins, Lord, who could stand?" (Psalm 130:3). The answer, of course, is no one. Not one of us could stand before the Lord with our sins. It's like the message God sent King Belshazzar in Daniel 5:27: "You have been weighed in the balances and found wanting."

That's where Jesus steps in. Unlike you and me, Jesus didn't fall short. He kept the Law perfectly in our place. "Do not think that I have come to abolish the Law or the Prophets," He says in Matthew 5:17. "I have not come to abolish them but to fulfill them." Jesus measured up to those impossibly high standards of the Law. And the incredible thing is that Jesus gives *us* the benefits of His obedience. 1 Peter 2:24 asserts, "He Himself bore our sins in His body on the tree, that we might die to sin and live to righteousness. By His wounds you have been healed."

So go ahead. Compare your thoughts, motives, and actions with the strict demands of God's Law. Despair of earning God's favor by your own strength. Repent of those sins and leave them at the foot of Jesus' cross, knowing that He has taken them from you and clothed you in His robe of righteousness. When the devil tries to lead you to despair, pointing out all your sins, point him to Jesus, who took them from you. Thanks to Him, you don't fall short after all.

What Does This Mean?
(Beyond Confirmation Class)

February 5, 2018

I can practically sing "Phantom of the Opera" in my sleep. My son is in the marching band, and their program was "Phantom" this year. Besides the fact that he practiced it at home, we also have the advantage of living two blocks from the school, and therefore we can hear the band when they practice outside. We heard "Phantom" every school morning, every Monday night when they had three-hour clinics, every halftime show for home games, and every weekend in October for competition.

But here's the thing—the harder the competitions got, the more they practiced. You'd think by the time they'd done it a few times, they had the thing pretty well under their belts, but no. They worked on fine tuning the performance, sometimes quite literally. They held chords to figure out which instrument was out of tune. They played the same sixteen measures over and over to make sure everyone was stepping exactly where they ought. They needed to know every single detail about their part, and know it well. It was inspiring to observe their focus and dedication. And it's a good lesson on what it means to live as Christians in the world.

Think back to your middle school days. If you're Lutheran, you were probably required to memorize much of the Small Catechism, as well as key Bible passages for confirmation class. This is certainly a good thing. But then what? Unfortunately, many people view confirmation as a graduation of sorts. *Whew, that's over! I don't have to remember all that stuff anymore!* one may think with relief, much as one would think of a final exam. But that's entirely backwards. Looking back to the marching band's first performance of "Phantom" at a halftime show, it was fairly rough around the edges. The students knew their music and steps for the most part, but a few kids stepped the wrong way or missed a note here and there. They weren't nearly as precise as they were when marching for the competition by the end of October. Those extra weeks of practicing ad nauseum paid off. By then, the kids *knew* their parts.

Is not the same true of growing in the Christian faith? We wouldn't say that an eighth grader knows everything he or she needs to know for math or English, but too often that's the attitude we have toward confirmation. Friends, the catechism isn't a one-time deal. It's something that grows with the Christian and takes on deeper meaning throughout one's life. An eighth grader may be able to quote the sixth commandment, but it's probably not an issue she's grappled with at that point in her life. It becomes much more pertinent as she hits high school, college, and starts considering marriage. A confirmation student can probably quote the meaning of the second article of the Apostles' Creed, but will he be able to recall it when his college roommate asks him what he believes about Jesus? It is simply folly to relegate the catechism to a couple of years of confirmation class in middle school. The catechism is a tool for us to use all our lives through, with deepening understanding as we do so.

So what does this look like? To start, test your own memory on the Ten Commandments, Apostles' Creed, and the Lord's Prayer. If you can't quote them all, this is a great place to begin. Make it a family affair if you have kids, learning one portion of the catechism at a time. This can easily be done at or after mealtime. Work your way around the table so everyone gets a chance to quote a section of the catechism each evening. Sprinkle a good dose of Bible verses along with the catechism selections. In Deuteronomy 6:7, Moses commands the people to teach God's Word "diligently" to their children. The Hebrew word used here is "shanan," which is used elsewhere in the Old Testament to refer to "sharp" arrows or "whetting" a sword. Sharpen your childrens' faith by teaching them God's Word.

But don't stop with teaching your kids. Just as my son's band practiced more in earnest as they got further along in the competition, so we as Christians need to prepare ourselves spiritually the older we get and the more temptations we face. Work through the explanation of the Small Catechism, where Luther asks and answers questions about the six chief parts and lists Bible passages that are pertinent. Read faithful commentaries on Scripture or work through solid Bible studies.

A year from now, my son may still be able to play his part of "Phantom" for memory. He may remember some of the steps. But he won't remember it nearly as well as he does now. Ten years from now, he won't remember his steps at all. In his adult years, he may even struggle to remember the name of the program they played this year. Do not allow the same thing to happen in your faith walk.

If you are not immersed in the Word, participating in worship services regularly, and studying the basics of the Christian faith, you leave yourself vulnerable to the attacks of Satan and the world, who will try to snatch that faith from you. Don't allow that to happen. Rather, bask in the treasures God is waiting to give you as you read and study His Word. It doesn't even matter how long ago you took confirmation.

Daily Bread

February 6, 2015

I'm glad I didn't live in the Old Testament days of wandering in the wilderness with the Israelites. I can't imagine how difficult that lifestyle would have been. Nor can I see eating the same thing for every meal—manna and quail. I'm sorry, but that would get old pretty fast. (On the other hand, at least it took the guesswork out of what to make for dinner every night...) Still, I have to admit that this manna phenomenon was pretty amazing. Every morning God provided for His people, and they always had just the right amount of food. No leftovers (unless it was the sixth day and they gathered some for the Sabbath), and no one went away hungry. Incredible. But it also taught the people a valuable lesson— God provided for them one day at a time. They learned to trust Him that He would indeed provide for them the following day.

Trust is so difficult sometimes, isn't it? To trust someone else, we have to believe they'll do what they said they would do. We become vulnerable to a degree because we aren't doing it ourselves. We have to trust that they'll keep their word. It intrigues me that in the Lord's Prayer we ask God to give us *"this day* our *daily* bread"* (emphasis mine). We aren't asking God to give us a storehouse or to stockpile everything we need for the rest of our lives. No, instead we ask that He give us what we need for today. That's it. And that's hard. Whether it's food, money, or even intangible things like emotional strength, God gives us what we need one day at a time. Sure, you may have money in the bank and food in the fridge, but you use those things one day at a time. Each day we trust that God will give us what we need for that day.

In His Sermon on the Mount, Jesus tells us, "Do not be anxious about your life, what you will eat or what you will drink, nor about your body, what you will put on. Is not life more than food, and the body worth more than clothing? Look at the birds of the air: they neither sow nor reap nor gather into barns, and yet your Heavenly Father feeds them. Are you not of more value than they?" (Mathew 6:25-26). He goes on to give the example of flowers clothed in great splendor even though they put forth no effort. So if God provides for birds and flowers, can't He be trusted to provide for His dear children?

What do you need today, dear one? Do you need emotional strength to get through the day? Perhaps physical strength? Has your paycheck run out too soon? Are you wondering how to stretch the food in the pantry through the weekend? Take it one day at a time. Don't look at the big picture and get overwhelmed. Trust that your Father in heaven will indeed give you just what you need for this day. And that's enough.

Keeping House

Just once I'd like to prove myself wrong. I have this theory that housecleaning is always a humbling and usually disgusting experience. I have yet to disprove that by my own experiences. With five children and two dogs, my house will never pass a white-glove inspection. This weekend, I steam-mopped the house, and even though I had done so the previous week, I went through multiple mop pads, and every one of them was black afterwards. The stuff I swept up beforehand was pretty significant too. And my baby crawls on this every day? I could clean my bathrooms three times a day and they'd still have toothpaste in the sink and who-knows-what on the floor. No matter how I try to keep a counter clear of clutter, it seems like I turn around and there's a mound of stuff. Just once, can't I prove myself wrong?

As I groused about this today, I realized something. The same principle applies to my own life. No matter how many times I repent, I always return to the same old sins. No matter how many times I am washed clean by God's forgiveness, somehow I always manage to get dirty again. And it doesn't take very long, either. I could confess my sins three times a day and still carry with me the stench of sin. It's discouraging, isn't it?

The apostle Paul wrote of this struggle in Romans 7. After his discourse on "I do not do the good I want to do" in verses 15-20, he concludes in verses 21-25 like this:

So I find it to be a law that when I want to do right, evil lies close at hand. For I delight in the law of God, in my inner being, but I see in my members another law waging war against the law of my mind and making me captive to the law of sin that dwells in my members. Wretched man that I am! Who will deliver me from this body of death? Thanks be to God through Jesus Christ our Lord! So then, I myself serve the law of God with my mind, but with my flesh I serve the law of sin.

What an apt picture of the life of a Christian. With our minds we serve the law of God, but with our bodies, the law of sin. That is the constant tension for a believer. We may strive valiantly to rid ourselves of sin, but we will never achieve this. And that's good in one sense. It stops us from relying on ourselves. Paul asks longingly, "Who will deliver me from this body of death?" And the answer, of course, is Jesus.

No, we can't stop sinning. Like my newly-mopped floor that gets dirty within minutes, so it is with us. We confess our sins and then turn right around and yell at our spouse or kids. But don't despair. In God's eyes, you are already clean. The action is all on God, as the words of Psalm 51:7 show: "Purge me with hyssop, and I shall be clean; wash me, and I shall be whiter than snow." 1 John 1:7b tells us that "the blood of Jesus His Son cleanses us from all sin." And *that's* one cleaning that will stay clean, not just for a few hours, but forever.

The Final Countdown

February 9, 2015

It could happen any day now. My due date looms less than a week away, and I live with the constant expectation that any moment my water could break or I could start contractions. And as such, I plan accordingly. I don't venture more than a half mile radius from the house for walks. I don't plan any road trips or shopping expeditions that would take me further from the hospital and my obstetrician. My suitcase is packed for the hospital and I have the baby's clothes neatly tucked into the diaper bag. The infant car seat is in the van. I make mostly Crock Pot meals in case I have to leave while the kids are in school and the babysitter needs to feed them supper. I know that the baby *is* coming, I just don't know *when*. And even though my body is the one that will determine the time for labor and delivery, I have no control over the timing at all. Now all I can do is wait in expectation. It's the final countdown.

Waiting in the final days for the birth of our baby reminds me very much of waiting for the return of Jesus. We know that Jesus *will* come, but we don't know *when*. And let's be honest—most of us probably aren't waking up every morning wondering, "Will today be the day Jesus returns?" We've largely become indifferent to the whole thing. Sure, we know Jesus is coming again, but we really don't think it'll happen any time soon. We tend to think we're in the "first trimester," so to speak. When I was only two months pregnant, my bags certainly weren't packed. I could have made a visit across the world without giving it a second thought. I didn't live with the knowledge that the baby could be born any day. But as my due date gets closer and closer, that thought process changes and I make sure I'm ready at a moment's notice for the big event.

What does the Bible tell us about the Last Day? Paul tells us in 1 Thessalonians 5:2-3 that "the day of the Lord will come like a thief in the night. While people are saying, 'There is peace and security,' then sudden destruction will come upon them as labor pains come upon a pregnant woman, and they will not escape." (Ah, I *knew* the pregnancy illustration sounded familiar!)

Whenever Jesus returns, it will be a shock to everyone. Keeping with the pregnancy theme, it's sort of like a preemie birth. When a woman's water breaks in her sixth month, she isn't expecting it. It's not normal, and there's no way she could have anticipated such an early labor or delivery. So it will be with Jesus' return—totally unexpected, catching people off guard. And yet the Bible warns us to always be ready. We learn from the parable of the wise and foolish virgins in Matthew 25 to keep our lamps trimmed and burning. We are told in Luke 12:38 that it will be good for the master who finds his servants prepared in the second and third watches of the night.

The early church possessed a sense of urgency in spreading the Gospel that we no longer have. After all, if He hasn't returned yet, what's the hurry? We have time, right? And yet Paul tells us in 2 Corinthians 6:2 that "*Now* is the time of God's favor, *now* is the day of salvation" (NIV, emphasis added). This idea is reinforced in Romans 13:11, where Paul says, "The hour has come for you to wake from sleep. For salvation is nearer to us now than when we first believed." He's speaking, of course, about Jesus' second coming, when we will experience the full extent of our salvation in heaven. And each day brings us closer to the Last Day.

So what would it look like if we lived every day as if we expected Jesus to return any moment? First of all, don't stray too far. From God's Word, that is. I think if we knew Jesus was coming sometime this year, a whole lot of people would be digging into their Bibles in much more depth than usual. We wouldn't waste our time on frivolous things like questionable movies or sitcoms with loose morals. We would get off our iPhones and social media and read our Bibles and commentaries instead. We would stay "close to home" with the Lord.

Next, pack. No, not earthly possessions. Everyone knows that "You can't take it with you." I'm talking about souls. It's true that only God can create saving faith in someone else's heart, but He uses us as His vessels to share the Word. If you knew Jesus would return within the month, with whom would you share your faith? You would take every opportunity to make sure your kids were secure in their faith, but wouldn't you tell your neighbors about Jesus too? What about the UPS delivery guy? The lady in the checkout aisle at the grocery store? There are tons of people in this world who still need to hear the message of salvation. Share it freely, even recklessly.

Lastly, simplify and take it easy. My Crock Pot meal strategy has greatly improved my efficiency. Over the past few weeks I've even doubled most of the recipes to stick an extra meal in the freezer for the chaos of the first few weeks of a newborn in the house. But look what the unintended side effects have been— I've been able to have dinner ready and the prep work cleaned up by mid-morning. When the kids get home from school I have time to actually spend with them, playing outside or working on homework or just talking. I don't have to do the mad dash of dinner crunch time as I search through the pantry for available ingredients.

In a similar fashion, take stock of your life and see where you can simplify. Cut out activities that take your time and attention away from your family and from God. Are your kids involved in sports that meet on Sunday mornings? Do you work yourself so hard you don't have time for devotions at the end of the day or church on weekends? How can you change that? Simplify where you can in order to make room for the things in life that really matter—eternally.

So get ready. Whether my bags are packed or not, this baby is coming soon. And whether you're prepared or not, Jesus will return one day when you're least expecting it. Don't stray too far from home, pack those bags, and simplify. It's the final countdown.

Seeing God's Back

February 10, 2020

Moses had a daunting task. He'd already been through a lot, and he was at least eighty years old. He probably preferred to just retire, but that wasn't God's plan for him. He'd grown up in Pharaoh's household before spending forty years in the wilderness as a shepherd, and then he was called to go back to Egypt, lead his people out of slavery and into the Promised Land. Talk about an overwhelming calling. And scarcely had the novelty of the plagues and God parting the Red Sea worn off when the whining began. The water was bitter. There was nothing to eat. We should have stayed in Egypt. Sigh. And there were forty more years of this to look forward to?

The Israelites did have moments of integrity, when they did the right thing. After God gave the Ten Commandments, they confirmed the covenant and promised, "All the words that the Lord has spoken we will do" (Exodus 24:3). But they also fell into doubt and unbelief. While Moses was literally having a mountaintop experience, they grew impatient and built the golden calf. Moses was so angry he broke the tablets God had given him, ground the golden calf into powder, scattered it on the water, and made the people drink it. He rallied the Levites and went through the camp killing those who had committed idolatry. But that was nothing compared to the consequence from God. He told the Israelites He would no longer accompany them.

The Israelites then repented of their sin, and Moses pleaded with God to forgive them and asked Him to be present with them after all. God listened to Moses and agreed. Then Moses had an interesting request. He asked God to show him His glory. I suppose in his shoes, I'd want some sort of visible sign myself. And really, haven't we all asked God for a visible sign at one time or another? Wouldn't it be great to say, "God, if it's Your will for me to do this, please let me see a shooting star tonight"? How much easier that would make things!

But look at God's response. He tells Moses, "You shall see My back, but My face shall not be seen" (Exodus 33:23). We can only see God by where He's been and what He's done in the past. His face is yet to be revealed. We can't find God outside the places He's promised we will find Him: His Word and Sacraments. And even there, we don't find God the way our human minds think we should. God reveals Himself more fully by taking on frail human flesh. Jesus' greatest glory was the cross. God's plan looks foolish to the world. "For the foolishness of God is wiser than human wisdom, and the weakness of God is stronger than human strength," 1 Corinthians 1:25 tells us (NIV).

We may want God to reveal Himself in power and strength, but that's not how He chooses to show Himself. Instead of beholding Him face to face, we see

His back. The next time you face a daunting task and you ask God to reveal His will to you, look no further than the Scriptures. Look to Jesus on the cross. There is no more glorious way for God to reveal Himself to us.

Basking in the Son

February 11, 2019

Jesus' Transfiguration must have been an impressive sight. His face "shone like the sun" (Matthew 17:2), and His clothes became "as bright as a flash of lightning" (Luke 9:29, NIV), "intensely white, as no one on earth could bleach them" (Mark 9:3). The disciples weren't even seeing Jesus in all His glory, because no sinful human can do that and live, but they saw Him in a more glorified state than anyone else had. It's interesting that Moses was there, because He was another person who had not only seen God's glory, but had also been "transfigured," in a sense. When He came down Mount Sinai after being in God's presence, his face was radiant as well, similar to the way Jesus' face shone on the Mount of Transfiguration.

Impressive as that might be, it might surprise you to learn that *you* are in the process of being transfigured as well.

Romans 12:2 urges us, "Do not be conformed to this world, but be transformed by the renewal of your mind." Paul is referring to the ongoing process of sanctification in the life of a believer when he admonishes us to "be transformed." The same word is used in 2 Corinthians 3:18, when he says, "And we, who with unveiled faces all reflect the Lord's glory, are being transformed into His likeness with ever-increasing glory, which comes from the Lord, who is the Spirit" (NIV). In both of these verses, the Greek word that is used for "being transformed," is the same word used in Jesus' Transfiguration account. In other words, we are "being *transfigured* into His likeness with ever-increasing glory."

I don't know about you, but I sure don't feel like I reflect God's glory very often or very well. I am acutely aware of my shortcomings and failures. How can I ever shine God's light to those around me when I'm so sinful? The answer is that it doesn't depend on me. If it did, I would never be able to reflect His glory. Instead, it's God's action within me that causes me to be transformed. As 2 Corinthians reminds us, the glory comes "from the Lord."

Consider Moses. When did his face shine? After he'd been in the presence of God. He came away from those encounters with a radiant face. But it wasn't a one-time deal. He didn't go up on Mount Sinai and come back with a face forever glowing. Rather, as he wore the veil, his face slowly faded and returned to normal until the next time he was in God's presence.

So it is with us. Sanctification is a lifelong process rather than a one-time thing. As we spend time in God's presence—in the Word, in prayer, in divine worship—God is working on our hearts. We come away from those encounters with radiant faces, reflecting God's glory, as we are "being transformed into His likeness." True, we may not feel like that's the case. Moses didn't realize his face was radiant. You probably won't finish your devotion thinking, "I'm sure reflecting God's glory now! I bet my family can tell I've been in the presence of God!" But trust God when He says it is so.

The process of sanctification is a gradual one, similar to physical growth. You don't notice your kids getting taller because you see them every day. But people who haven't seen them for a year can tell right away that they've grown. Same thing with sanctification—it happens slowly and gradually. You won't read one chapter of the Bible and become instantly more patient, more kind, more generous, etc. But every day you spend in the Word, every time you pray, every time you participate in corporate worship and partake of His body and blood, God is working in you and giving you His glory to reflect to those around you.

Take the time every day to spend time in the presence of the Son. You can't help but reflect His glory when you're in His presence. Pray that He continues the work of sanctification in your life, and trust that He will answer that prayer. Then go forth into the world transfigured, ready to shine His light.

Growing Out of Faith

February 12, 2018

This morning I dropped my daughters off at school and they both walked in without looking back. This is quite a change from the beginning of the year, when my kindergartner would cling to me for dear life before I left. I had to walk her down to her classroom, help her put her backpack in her cubby, and give her a dozen hugs before leaving. After a few days of that routine, we shortened it so that her big sister walked her to the classroom, so long as I stood in the entryway where she could see me until she got to her classroom. Then when she got more comfortable with school and more self-reliant, I was able to wave at her from the doorway when she turned the corner to go to her classroom. And now she doesn't even bother to look back. She's on her own.

This is a bittersweet aspect of parenting, but a necessary one. After all, it would be weird to walk hand-in-hand with a high schooler to his classroom and give him a hug and kiss before leaving. Part of our goal as parents is to shape our children into self-reliant, responsible citizens who can function independently and contribute to the overall well-being of society. We parent our children knowing eventually they will not need us anymore.

The same is not true of children of the Heavenly Father. All too often, people view religion as something to "grow out of." Oh, it's nice to send kids off to Sunday School and watch them in the children's Christmas program. Sure, it's a good idea to send them to confirmation class, but as they get older and obtain more "knowledge," they'll come to see that they don't need God as much or at all. It's like believing in Santa Claus too long—childish and naive. Self-sufficient and independent adults don't need God. They're on their own.

This line of thinking is entirely wrong. If anything, I need God *more* as an adult than I ever did as a child. When I was growing up, my parents saw to it that I had food and clothes and a house in which to live. They provided for me and helped me make decisions. But now that I'm an adult and have my own children to provide for and my own decisions to make, I know it's not nearly as easy or as fun as I'd thought it would be. I need God's Word to guide, correct, and strengthen me, and to reassure me when I'm feeling guilty or discouraged.

I may buy clothes for my kids and make meals for them, but God gives them life and breath. He keeps their hearts beating and their brains functioning. He blesses my husband and me with the means to provide for them. God blesses the earth with rain and sun in season, so that the plants grow. He maintains all of creation. Without Him, life would cease to exist. And this almighty God doesn't stop there. He has provided for an even bigger need. More than food and clothes and good health, we need salvation. God sent Jesus to this sinful earth as true God and true man to live a perfect life in our stead, to die for our sins, and to rise victorious from the grave. Because of Jesus' saving actions on our behalf, our eternity is secure.

Romans 8:15 explains our relationship with God as one of children to a Father. "You have received the Spirit of adoption as sons, by whom we cry, 'Abba! Father!'" What a beautiful picture. God has chosen us; adopted us into His family. *Abba* is Aramaic for "Father," and conveys an intimate and childlike relationship, much like a young child calling his father "Daddy." *That's* the type of relationship God desires with us. A childlike confidence that our Daddy will always provide for us, that we can ask anything of Him in prayer and He will answer. It's a relationship that grows and deepens as we get older. In other words, we can never grow out of it. We'll never be on our own. Our *Abba* is always with us.

A Light in the Closet

February 13, 2014

Instead of a nightlight, I turn on the closet light for my children at bedtime. At first, when our eyes are used to the brightness of the rest of the house, this is a tough adjustment. Even with the door wide open, the light seems dim. But as our eyes adjust, that light which once appeared so dim is now way too bright. So every night I go into their rooms and close the closet door. That light is still shining as brightly as it was before, but now it is contained. Light seeps out around the cracks and underneath the bottom, so it's enough to comfort them if they wake up, but it's not enough to offend the eyes if they awaken from a deep sleep.

Matthew 5:14-16 has much to say about light. This section of Scripture is part of Jesus' Sermon on the Mount, and He speaks of Christians as "salt" and "light" in the world. His followers are the light of the world and are instructed to "let your light shine before others, so that they may see your good works and give glory to your Father who is in heaven."

But wait. *We* are the light of the world? In John 8:12 Jesus claims that *He* is the light of the world. So which is it? Both. Jesus is, of course, *the* light of the world. He came into this sin-darkened world to shine the light of mercy and forgiveness. His Gospel message shines in stark contrast to the darkness of sin and condemnation under the Law. He is the source of this light, and we are merely the reflectors. Much as the moon reflects the light of the sun, yet has no light of its own, so we of our own accord do not have "light" to shine; we merely reflect the light of Jesus.

Are you reflecting that light? Are you the city on a hill that cannot be hidden, or do you try to hide that lamp under the basket? Do your coworkers, friends, neighbors, and fellow soccer moms know that you are a Christian? If not, it's time to change that.

Read James 2:14-26, and keep in mind that James is *not* speaking about earning heaven with works. He's talking about sanctification. Consider verses 15-17 in the context of your own life: "If a brother or sister is poorly clothed and lacking in daily food, and one of you says to them, 'Go in peace, be warmed and filled,' without giving them the things needed for the body, what good is that? So also faith by itself, if it does not have works, is dead."

I'm convicted. How many times have I told someone struggling through a tough time, "I'm praying for you," and left it at that? Yes, it's good to pray for someone, but sometimes that's not enough. If your neighbor is going through a tough time financially, show up at her door with a few freezer meals. Spearhead a fundraiser for someone racking up medical bills. Volunteer at a soup kitchen or have your kids make cards for children in the hospital. The point is to *do* something. Live that faith. Others will see you doing those things and wonder why.

But it can't stop there. I think a lot of us (myself included) tend to use "witnessing by actions" as a cop out. We figure just living a Christian life is enough of a witness. If someone wants to ask us why we live the way we do, then great! But no one has *ever* come up to me to say, "I sense there's something different about the way you live your life. What's your secret?" Yes, actions do speak loudly, but they aren't specific enough for the kind of witness we need to have.

We read in Romans 10:14 and 17, "How then will they call on Him in whom they have not believed? And how are they to believe in Him of whom they have never heard? And how are they to hear without someone preaching? ... So faith comes from hearing, and hearing through the word of Christ." People will not know what you believe only by how you act. Paul says faith comes from *hearing*, not through observation. It's time to get out of our comfort zone. Work up the courage to tell someone what you believe, to invite them to church with you, to ask if you can pray with them.

Think back to my light analogy. When does the closet light shine brightest? When it's darkest outside and in the house. In the middle of the night when our eyes are adjusted to the dark and our pupils are dilated, any light at all blazes forth. But if I turn on a closet light when other lights are on, it's hardly even noticeable. Those who most need to hear the Gospel message are those in the darkness of sin, despair, and hopelessness. Those who are living in some sort of artificial light have no need for this Gospel light. The Pharisees of Jesus' day thought they *were* walking in the light. They had no need for Jesus' message because they thought they had it all figured out. I'm sure you know people like that. Pray that God humbles them and gives them a reason to need the light.

But the people who most desperately need to hear about Jesus are those broken and in despair. The friend who just lost a family member, the neighbor whose son is in jail, the coworker who just learned his daughter is on drugs—*these* are the people who need the light. Invite them for coffee and let them share what's on their mind. Then ask if you may share your faith with them. They may say no. But you've opened the door a crack and they can glimpse the light. It's not up to us to convince anyone. That's the Holy Spirit's work. You are merely the instrument, always ready to share "the reason for the hope that is in you," as 1 Peter 3:15 says, and we do so "with gentleness and respect." Don't worry that you may not have all the answers or that you aren't eloquent enough. If God could use stuttering Moses, He can surely use you.

So how will you reflect God's light to those He puts in your path today? The devil will tempt you with all his might to be a closet Christian. He wants the light to stay shut up tightly because he is the prince of darkness. But remember, Jesus has already defeated him. Jesus will empower you to shine your light, because really, that light is *His* light. Don't be afraid. Open that closet door and let His light pour out for all to see.

All You Need is Love

February 13, 2015

Our world, and Christianity in particular, is obsessed with the concept of love. A loving God wouldn't condemn anyone to hell, now would He? Nor would a loving Christian condemn homosexuality, because, after all, love is love, right? A Christian wouldn't speak against people living together before marriage, because who are we to judge others? "Christians should be loving," we are told, which really means, "Christians should be tolerant and accept everything without question." But that's completely false.

What does Jesus say about love? In John 13:34-35 He says, "'A new commandment I give to you, that you love one another: just as I have loved you, you also are to love one another. By this all people will know that you are My disciples, if you have love for one another.'" Ah, see? There you go! Love is the defining mark of a Christian! "They'll know we are Christians by our love," right?

No, actually. Don't gloss over Jesus' words right before the last phrase—*"just as I have loved you,* you also are to love one another." And how exactly did Jesus love us? "In this is love, not that we have loved God but that He loved us and sent His Son to be the propitiation for our sins," 1 John 4:10 tells us. You see, Jesus didn't look the other way when confronted with sin. Jesus didn't tolerate it or allow people to continue indulging in their pet sins. He *died* for those sins. That's how seriously He takes sin. And that's how seriously He loves us. Love doesn't excuse sin or condone it. Love confronts sin and points to the solution—Jesus.

So what defines a Christian, if not love? Jesus says, "'If you abide in My word, you are truly My disciples, and you will know the truth, and the truth will set you free'" (John 8:31-32). *That's* the defining mark of a Christian—one who abides in God's Word, one who knows the truth as *Jesus* has revealed it. We don't make up our own truth; it isn't subjective. Truth is revealed in God's Word, whether it makes you feel good or not. Jesus' true disciples are known by their adherence to His Word or truth. And as Ephesians 4:15 says, we then "speak the truth in love."

So yes, dear Christian, love one another by all means. But understand what "love" really means. We don't need to blindly tolerate and accept lifestyles and teachings which are contrary to the Bible. To truly love someone, share with them the truths of God's Word. Share with them the full extent of Jesus' love for them—the love that drove Him to the cross. For them. For you. For everyone. Now *that's* true love.

It's About More Than Jesus' Death

February 16, 2015

It's that time of the year again, where we transition from the happy and joyful seasons of Christmas and Epiphany into the long, somber season of Lent. There are no more alleluias for six weeks. The hymns are more solemn. Midweek services are reflective. Our focus is on the cross at the end, on Good Friday, where it all culminates. But don't just focus on His death. Yes, Jesus died for you, but He also *lived* for you.

By all means, there *should* be an emphasis on Jesus' atoning sacrifice. By His death and resurrection, He paid for the sins of everyone on this earth. But His death would have meant nothing had He not lived the perfect life for us as well. God demands absolute perfection, and since all of us fall far short of that standard, we needed someone to live that sinless life in our place. That someone was none other than Jesus, "who in every respect has been tempted as we are, yet [was] without sin," as Hebrews 4:15 reminds us.

Jesus began His saving work right from conception. Psalm 51:5 states, "Surely I was sinful at birth, sinful from the time my mother conceived me" (NIV). Since we were sinful from conception, Jesus had to take our place from this point and pass through all stages of human development. He entered this world as a single cell in Mary's womb, sinless from the very start. He lived the perfect childhood, adolescence, and adult years.

Matthew records one account of Jesus' temptation, and says that He was "led by the Spirit into the wilderness to be tempted by the devil" (Matthew 4:1). These temptations were actually willed *by God*. He knew that only a flawless Lamb could be offered in our place, so He made sure there was no question that Jesus was that sinless Lamb of God. The wilderness was a place associated with demons and barrenness. No one would want to spend time there, but Jesus did, and even fasted during that time. I can't even skip dinner without being ravenously hungry by breakfast time, so I can't begin to fathom going without food for forty days. And when those forty days were spent, Jesus was understandably hungry. That crafty devil used His hunger to tempt Him, but that didn't work. Satan even used Scripture to tempt Jesus, although he twisted the meaning. Jesus saw through his tactics and countered them with correct use of Scripture.

Jesus' temptation in the wilderness wasn't the only time Satan attacked Him. Satan even used Peter, one of Jesus' own disciples, to tempt Him away from the cross. More than anything, Satan wanted to bring down the Son of God, and he would stop at nothing. When Jesus revealed the plan for His suffering and death, Peter rebuked Him. Jesus recognized this as an attack by the devil and said so in no uncertain terms—"Get behind Me, Satan!" (Matthew 16:23). He didn't need the devil tempting Him away from His plan of salvation for the entire world.

Jesus was tempted throughout His entire earthly ministry, especially in Gethsemane. But He withstood every attack by the devil and remained sinless. He offered that sinless life for you. "You were washed, you were sanctified, you were justified in the name of the Lord Jesus Christ and by the Spirit of our God," 1 Corinthians 6:11 states. That is possible only because of Jesus' perfect, sinless life. Yes, Jesus died for you. But never forget that He *lived* for you as well.

The Secret to Church Growth

February 17, 2014

My family is unusual because we're so, well…normal. Take my dad's side of the family. He is one of six children. That generation married and had kids, so my cousins and siblings and I total eighteen. Now our generation is getting married and having kids, and so far there are thirty and counting in the next generation. And of all of us, there are no black sheep, no rebels, no skeletons in the closet, and all of us get along. Furthermore, we are all actively living out our Christian faith.

Now imagine what would have happened had my grandparents *not* raised their children to know Jesus. What would have happened if they hadn't made faith a priority, both on Sundays and at home throughout the week? Think of the difference they made in the lives of generations to follow. Counting spouses, that's roughly seventy people so far. If my grandparents hadn't passed on their faith, that's seventy less people active in the kingdom of God.

Parents, take note! You are affecting countless future generations by your example (or lack thereof) in teaching the Christian faith. Yes, children can grow up and decide to leave the church. I know people whose adult children have done just that. It grieves them to no end. But that's on their children, not on them. In the meantime, parents, teach and live the faith while your kids are at home. Make it so natural that they continue in their own faith when they leave home.

So the secret of church growth is none other than the family. Not flashy enough? Maybe not, but it's true. Think back to your confirmation class. How many of those classmates are still active in church today? To the best of my knowledge, eighty percent of my classmates no longer regularly attend church, and probably haven't for years. I'd bet the statistics from your class are similar. Consider how much bigger the church would be if those confirmands who vowed in front of the entire congregation to remain faithful unto death actually meant those vows.

Sadly, most of those who have fallen away were those whose parents dropped them off each week for catechism class but never actually went to church themselves. This is serious business, fellow parents. Do not expect the church to do in an hour a week what you refuse to do in the remaining 167 hours. Kids learn more about the faith by watching you than they will during church or Sunday School. That's not to say the church is irrelevant. Not at all. But *you*, parents, have the biggest impact. If church isn't a priority for you, it won't be for them either. If you go to church casually and do little at home to pray, learn Bible stories, memorize Bible verses and the catechism, chances are they'll follow suit.

What's a parent to do? Teach your kids Bible stories from the time they are babies. Read age-appropriate devotions with them. Ask them for prayer requests and pray with them often. Teach the catechism so that when they get to confirmation class the memory portion is review. We used to go around the table each night and my brothers and I took turns quoting the Ten Commandments and meanings after dinner. It was invaluable.

Teach your kids from the very start. Remember, your faith isn't just about you. It's about the next generation, and the next, and all those following. Do everything in your power (with God's help, of course) to see that the faith doesn't stop with you. *This* is the kind of church growth that produces solid, mature Christians. It's a huge responsibility, but God is by your side the whole way, nurturing each precious soul to grow His Church.

Change of Plans

February 23, 2015

I had this all planned out. My mother was to arrive the day before my due date. I would go into labor the morning of my due date, just as I did with my last baby. Then I'd be in the hospital for the weekend and get out Sunday evening or Monday morning. I would be able to adjust to life with a new baby during a school week when the house was a bit quieter than normal, and everything would be just right. But as it turns out, that's not even close to what happened.

In reality, my due date passed with nary an incident. No contractions, no water breaking, nothing. One day turned into two and then three, and my doctor's appointment showed I was no closer to delivering than I had been the past two weeks. People kept asking me why I was still around. Any woman who has gone past her due date can tell you how frustrating it is. I felt aimless and depressed.

I finally went ahead with an induction so we could have a week to settle in before our families started arriving for the baptism. Even the labor and delivery itself didn't go according to plan. And don't even get me started on our homecoming. Two of our children were home sick from school and by the next evening the other two had fallen ill as well. The baby and I went into hiding in our room, trying desperately to keep him from getting sick too. So much for my original plans.

I'm sure you can relate. Everyone has times in their lives when they've planned something only to have things turn out completely differently. Maybe you have a day of errands or appointments coordinated perfectly only to wake up to a sick child who has to stay home from school. Maybe you were climbing the corporate ladder and doing really well until your company had to declare bankruptcy and suddenly you found yourself out of a job. Whatever the situation, it's a sinking feeling when you realize how little you can actually control.

Even Jesus' friends and disciples grappled with this. Consider their expectations for the Messiah. He was to be their liberator, one who would free them from the reign of the cruel Romans. Most people were looking for a hero to come and save them with brute force, amassing an army against those Romans and breaking free from them once and for all. But that's not what happened at all.

Jesus, the true Messiah, didn't come with a show of might. He didn't march against the Romans to defeat them. He battled much more deadly enemies, ones we could never defeat by ourselves—sin, death, and the devil. And He did battle in the most unlikely way possible, by offering His own life as a sacrifice in our place. When Jesus rode into Jerusalem on Palm Sunday, His followers must have been ecstatic. *Look at all these followers! Look at the support Jesus has! Now He's finally going to do it! He's going to march against the Romans and deliver us! This is so exciting!*

Imagine, then, their disappointment when Jesus didn't proceed to decimate the Romans. Think of their dismay when, instead, He allowed Himself to be captured, beaten, and crucified. Imagine their shattered hopes as they watched Him die an agonizing death. Imagine how aimless and depressed they felt that Friday evening, the entire long Sabbath Saturday, and waking up Sunday morning. That's not how this was supposed to be.

But then came Sunday. The discovery at the tomb changed everything. Jesus wasn't there. He had risen from the dead. Now, to be sure, Jesus had raised people from the dead during His earthly ministry, but to raise *Himself* from the dead? Inconceivable! Yet that's exactly what happened. And in doing so He triumphed over sin and Satan and even death. The tide had turned. The devil was now and forever defeated by this Messiah who had come to do far more than break the tyranny of the Romans on earth. He had broken for all time the claim of Satan on humanity. Jesus was the only Messiah needed, for all people of all times.

I don't know what your "change of plans" is in your life, and I can't promise that it'll turn out better than you imagined. What I *can* promise you is what God promises in His Word: "We know that for those who love God all things work together for good, for those who are called according to His purpose" (Romans 8:28). Perhaps things haven't gone according to *your* plans in life, but you can be sure that they are no surprise to *God*. His plans for your life are perfect, working for your good. Your *eternal* good, that is. Whatever happens to you on this earth, nothing can take away the future Jesus has already secured for you in heaven.

Remember that when you find yourself facing a change of plans. Jesus' followers faced the same thing, but what He accomplished was far greater than their earthly expectations ever could have imagined. And *your* future in heaven is greater than anything you can ever imagine, thanks be to God.

What Prayer Isn't

February 24, 2020

Prayer is hard for me. I've been struggling for years to establish a schedule for daily prayer, but it just isn't happening. I even had a wonderful friend share with me her prayer journaling plan, complete with different prayer categories for different days. That helped, because it gave me some structure, but if you look at my entries you'll see I'm still very sporadic. I was doing pretty well for about a week, with entries on January 2, 3, 4, 5, and 7, but then there's a huge gap until the 27th. The same pattern holds true for February. I'm so much better at sticking with a devotional or Bible reading plan. Working through a Bible study or reading through the Bible is tangible. But prayer isn't like that. I can't update my progress or gauge how far I've come. I need to think of prayer differently. So I find it helpful to keep in mind a few things about prayer. Specifically, here are some examples of what prayer *isn't*.

A quick fix. I'm sure you've heard stories about the amazing power of prayer. Someone was having a hard time in life, they prayed about it, and boom! Suddenly their life turned around, they got a new job, their marriage improved, or their illness magically went away. Now, that *can* happen, and sometimes it does, but we dare not think it always works this way. In fact, I often find that when I'm praying for something, it usually gets *worse* before it gets better. Let's say I'm praying for my children to be kind to one another. Usually, they get even meaner or more snarky toward one another, leaving me wondering if my prayers are being answered at all. When you pray, you've gotta be in it for the long haul, because very seldom is prayer a quick fix.

Tangible. This is another hard one for me. I like to see results. I like seeing my progress bar move up each time I update my page number for a book on Goodreads. But prayer is almost impossible to measure results. If I'm praying for more patience, how on earth can I measure progress? Is my prayer *not* being answered if I yell at my kids three times in one day, or should I be grateful that there was one time that day I was able to control my temper? Should I be discouraged that my kids still argue and call each other names even after I've been praying for months that they learn to get along, or is my prayer being answered when they all laugh together at the dinner table? We have to believe by faith that God is answering our prayers in His time and in the way He sees fit, and in ways only He may ever be able to tell. We must trust that God is working on our own hearts and attitudes, as well as those for whom we pray, even when we can't see it.

Easy. It's easy to say a quick prayer. Anyone can scroll through Facebook and see a prayer request, pause, rattle off a ten-second prayer, and move on without giving the prayer request a second thought. What isn't easy is committing to pray for a situation, checking back in with people we add to our prayer lists, or even keeping a prayer list in the first place! It's so much easier for me to say, "Lord, please bless my family" than it is to sit down and pray individually for each one of them, bringing concerns before Almighty God. Prayer is rightly called a spiritual "discipline," because it is a training for the Christian, an "activity, exercise, or regimen that develops or improves a skill," as *discipline* can be defined. One must be disciplined in order to develop a regular prayer life. It doesn't just happen. In a world of constant distractions, it takes focus and a great deal of personal discipline to shut out those distractions and pray.

One-size-fits-all. My prayer life will look different from yours, and that's another struggle for me. I'm really, really good at following directions or a specific method, like the one-year Bible plans. Give me an exercise program to use, and I'll follow it to the letter, but if you tell me to come up with my own exercise regimen, I'm clueless. It's the same principle for prayer. Everyone has different prayer requests. Maybe you pray first thing in the morning, or maybe you pray right before you go to bed. I tried that, but found that by the end of the day, I was usually too tired, or at least I was more likely to make excuses at the end of the day, so now I try to do my prayer time in the mornings. If you struggle to maintain focus, you might find the open-ended nature of prayer a bit unnerving, so perhaps setting a timer helps you stay focused during that time. Whatever you find works for you, do that. It's customizable to your own needs and schedule.

Law. All this talk about prayer might lead one to despair. *I'm not praying well enough,* you might think. *I'm not a good enough Christian.* That sort of doubt is from the devil. He *wants* to discourage you. But as in any area of the Christian life, you will fall short. You will fail. You might go through three weeks of little to no prayer at all. Don't despair. While prayer *should* be part of every Christian's life, it's Gospel rather than Law. God gives us prayer as a tool in our Christian walk. It is a gift. Once we start making this gift into a "must do," we are turning it into Law. Yes, strive to maintain a regular prayer life, but once you turn it into Law, you might become resentful of the gift in the first place. Remember that this is a gift from a gracious God, who promises to answer prayer and strengthen your faith in the process.

Prayer is still difficult for me. I will probably struggle with a prayer schedule my entire life. But I won't give up. God is growing me through the process. I have already seen many prayers answered in my life, and I look forward to seeing how God answers my prayers in the future. I pray the same holds true for you.

The Diagnosis That Saved my Husband's Life

February 25, 2019

It's been a crazy week. My husband came home early in the week with chills, fever, and aches, and I immediately quarantined him in our room, certain he had the flu. It's been going around our town, to the extent that they canceled school for two days because twenty percent of the school district was out sick. But it soon became apparent that my husband had something worse. After a few days of worsening health, he went to the hospital, where they determined he had MRSA, a bad staph infection. They got him on strong antibiotics to fight the infection, because his body can't fight it on its own. One medical worker told him if he hadn't sought medical help, he likely would have been dead in three more days. It's that serious. You don't want to mess around.

Before my husband could get better, he had to know what was wrong with him. Fighting an illness with the wrong kind of medicine or the wrong dose of the right medicine can be deadly. Nor could his body fight MRSA on its own. He needed outside intervention. Hearing an official diagnosis of a staph infection was a bit scary, but at the same time it was a relief. Once they knew what was wrong, they were able to treat it properly.

This principle is true for spiritual healing as well. The Law gets sort of a bad rap in today's society. We're afraid to offend people by speaking too harshly about sin, and heaven forbid we insinuate that someone else is wrong in his beliefs or lifestyle. Yet the Law is a gift. Without it, we wouldn't even know we were sick. If not for the impossibly high standard set by the Law, we might be tempted to think we're pretty good on our own. The Law diagnoses us for what we truly are—poor, miserable sinners. Psalm 38:3 says, "There is no soundness in my flesh because of Your indignation; there is no health in my bones because of my sin."

What is the ultimate result of this sin? Left untreated, it leads inevitably to death. Spiritual death. Romans 6:23 doesn't mince words. "The wages of sin is death," it bluntly states. Yes, sin really is that serious. You don't want to mess around.

Hearing a diagnosis of spiritual sin-sickness is no different from getting a doctor's diagnosis for a treatable condition. Sin *does* have a cure, but it's something that requires outside intervention. You can't heal yourself, but you don't have to. Your Great Physician did that for you. He took your sickness upon Himself and suffered the death that should have been yours. "He himself bore our sins in His body on the tree, that we might die to sin and live to righteousness. By His wounds you have been healed," 1 Peter 2:24 assures us. And continuing with Romans 6:23, yes, the wages of sin is death, "but the free gift of God is eternal life in Christ Jesus our Lord."

You have a clean bill of health. You are healed completely, and it doesn't cost you anything. There's no deductible or copayment or prescription costs. Jesus gives it to you for free. Don't be afraid of the grim diagnosis. The Great Physician has the cure. And while you're at it, go ahead and share this wonderful news with others. It's one diagnosis that has the power to save lives.

Wrestling With God

February 26, 2018

Have you ever wrestled with God? Jacob did. Literally. He wrestled with God all night long the night before he met Esau again after years away. In the morning, the man (God) touched Jacob's hip socket and put it out of joint, showing how powerful He really was. He could easily have disabled Jacob from the beginning, yet He chose to engage the patriarch in a familiar and personal way. We see that God's ultimate purpose of struggling with Jacob was not to defeat him, but to bless him. Now, I doubt you've wrestled with God quite like that, but perhaps you've wrestled with Him in a different way—in prayer.

Wouldn't it be great if God answered every prayer right away, just the way you wanted Him to? To read certain prayer books, one might get the impression that prayer is just that. One such book I read said that one woman who prayed for her husband to be relieved of his depression noticed an immediate difference every time she prayed, as did he. That's nice. But if you expect an answer like that, you're setting yourself up for disappointment. Not that God can't answer prayer like that, but He rarely chooses to do so. Prayer is more than a quick, "Lord, bless me." It's not a magic fix. Prayer should be more like wrestling with God; really struggling with Him against problems and sins that assail you; reminding Him again and again of His promises to hear and answer your pleas.

It's no coincidence that the one-year lectionary pairs the Old Testament lesson of Jacob wrestling with God and the Gospel reading of Matthew 15:21-28, the faith of a Canaanite woman. Like Jacob, this Canaanite woman wrestled with God, although not in a physical sense. She wrestled with Him spiritually. This is an incredibly accurate account of prayer. So often it appears that Jesus isn't even listening, and that the more fervently I plead, the less of an answer I get. Sometimes it feels like I'm *worse* off after praying than I was before. I pray for patience with my kids, and an hour later I completely lose it with them. Then, on top of impatience, now I struggle with guilt too.

But the Canaanite woman didn't give up, even when Jesus told her He was sent only to the lost sheep of Israel. (Interesting side note here: the Greek word for "only" actually means "first," rather than "exclusively.") She kneels before Him and presents her request yet again. (Also, the Greek for "kneels" connotes a deep worship.) When Jesus seems to call her a dog, she takes it with humility and returns, "Yes, Lord, but even the dogs eat the crumbs that fall from their master's table." She knows the "crumbs" of the Gospel are more than enough for her. She clings to God's Word even when it seems Jesus won't answer. And miraculously, Jesus grants her request and heals her daughter. She has wrestled with God and won. Jesus has taught her valuable lessons in persistence, faith, and the power of prayer. He does the same for you.

In other words, wrestle away.

March

Travel Expenses

March 2, 2015

Since moving here three months ago, my parents and my in-laws have each come to visit twice. Now, please understand that this isn't a half-hour drive. We are 1300 and 1750 miles away from them, respectively. So coming here is no small task. It requires either a two- to three-day drive or an airplane flight. There may be a rental car and hotel stay involved. It requires planning ahead and making arrangements for being away, sometimes taking time off work and losing income while one is away. It's not at all convenient, and it's expensive. But both our families have already made the trip twice, and my dear friend, who has a broken leg, just made the trip with her family, braving bad weather and treacherous roads to serve as godparents for our newest child's baptism.

Love can cause people to go to great lengths for others. And those great lengths don't always make sense on paper. It may seem that "it's not worth it" when you look purely at the facts. But when you truly love someone you know better. You know that it *is* worth it. The costs involved and the sacrifices made are worth it for the chance to spend time with those you love.

Let's talk about another trip with an expensive price tag. Jesus left His home in heaven to come down to this sinful world. For thirty-three years He gave up His throne, where He was worshiped and glorified by the saints and angels in heaven. And what did He get in exchange? He was tempted while fasting in the wilderness for forty days. He was mocked and doubted, even when He performed miracles. He was rejected. He was beaten, crucified as a criminal, and killed. Not exactly sounding like a pleasant trip, is it? Sounds more like a waste of time... or was it?

You see, my friend, Jesus knew the cost beforehand. He knew, and yet He came. Joyfully. Hebrews 12:2 says, "for the joy set before Him [He] endured the cross, scorning its shame, and sat down at the right hand of the throne of God" (NIV). The *joy* set before Him? Coming to earth to die for a bunch of sinners? That's *joy*? Dear one, *you* are His joy. He came to this earth for *you*. He knew what this trip would cost Him, but it was worth it because He knew in dying for you He would also live forever in heaven with you. That's how much He loves you.

So the next time you're planning a trip or having visitors come see you, don't dwell on the costs. Instead, thank God for the opportunity to see your loved ones. And thank Him as well that you have Someone who loves you enough to make the most costly trip ever, just to be with you forever.

The Beauty of Brokenness

March 3, 2014

My daughter's room has a blackout shade that has a tear in it, which of course means light seeps in through the crack. One's eye can't help but be drawn to that flaw in the blind. Forget the rest of the pristine white canvas, it's the tear that draws attention. I find this to be a fitting description of life as well. The "broken" parts of your life are the ones that people notice.

Do you feel broken or torn, my friend? Has your life turned out exactly the way you envisioned it? Mine sure hasn't. My reality is a far cry from the perfect life I hoped for when I was in college. As I've entered the adult world, one thing that constantly hits me is how *hard* life is. I had a normal, stable, perhaps even sheltered childhood. My parents gave us the gift of childhood in all its innocence. But my adult years thus far have shocked me with the harsh realities of life. Everyone has some burden to bear, some part of their life that's broken.

Quite honestly, had someone told me back in college what my life would look like now, I might well have said, "No, thanks. I'll pass. Let me choose another path." At that point I wasn't ready to even comprehend the difficulties I would face. But through our hardships, I've discovered something. I'm stronger than I thought I was.

No, correct that. My *God* is stronger than I realized. *Much* stronger.

He has sustained me through the good days and the crummy days alike. He has given me strength for each day. God has a way of using human weakness to proclaim His power. Remember Paul, pleading with God to take away the thorn in his flesh? What does God say? "My grace is sufficient for you, for My power is made perfect in weakness" (2 Corinthians 12:9).

Think about that. God's *power* is made perfect in…*weakness?* Indeed. Take Job as an example. We don't remember him and set aside a book of the Bible for his narrative because he was so rich and powerful. We remember him sitting in dust and ashes, his children dead, his flocks and cattle destroyed, sores festering on his body, enduring pious speeches from his friends, while still proclaiming, "I know that my Redeemer lives, and at the last He will stand upon the earth" (Job 19:25). *That,* my friends, is where God's light shines through—in Job's darkest hour.

Recall with me another dark hour, *the* darkest hour of all. When Jesus hung upon that cross, it looked as if all was lost. Humanly speaking, it was a display of utter weakness and brokenness. But God's power was shown in this weakness, for Christ emerged victorious from that tomb on a bright Easter morning, changing history forever. His weakness upon the cross was for *you.* His victory over death is yours as well. Make Paul's words your own, as he continues in 2 Corinthians

12:9b-10: "Therefore I will boast all the more gladly of my weaknesses, so that the power of Christ may rest upon me. For the sake of Christ, then, I am content with weaknesses, insults, hardships, persecutions, and calamities. For when I am weak, then I am strong."

Don't be ashamed of the jagged tears and brokenness in your life. It just may be that God is using those to let *His* light shine through.

Three Types of Editing You Need
(Even if You Aren't an Author)

March 4, 2019

One of the more tedious parts of being a writer is the editing phase. When you proudly send off a manuscript and get it back with over a thousand suggestions, it's pretty discouraging. But once you get the nerve to start looking at those suggestions, you find that most of them make sense and do indeed improve the flow of the story. You make the changes, knowing that the story is better as a result. But in the vast majority of cases, one round of edits isn't enough. Most writers go through at least three rounds of edits before they reach a final manuscript. So once you've sent back the revised manuscript implementing the suggested changes, know that you aren't done. You can expect to receive yet another marked-up manuscript. And another…

In the writing world, there are different phases of editing. Three of the most common are developmental, copy-editing, and proofreading. Each of these gets progressively more focused. In a developmental edit, the editor looks at the big picture: what are you trying to say, and are you telling your story effectively? The editor points out plot holes and inconsistencies with characters or setting. The main goal is to make everything flow as well as possible.

Once the developmental edit is done, it's time for copy-editing. Now the focus is a bit more narrow. The editor is looking for inconsistencies with smaller details. She checks facts to make sure the writer isn't misrepresenting anything, like using an iPhone in the 1990's. This is the time to alert the writer to possible legal problems, such as quoting lyrics to a copyrighted song. Copy-editing takes what happened in the developmental edit and ensures the story flows.

And then comes proofreading. This is the most focused type of editing. Proofreaders get into the nitty-gritty. Should this be a comma or a semicolon? Does this need to be hyphenated? The proofreader looks at tricky rules that are hard to remember like "lay/lie/laid." Proofreading is the final step before the manuscript goes off to formatting and printing.

Admittedly, it's easy to get defensive when you're in the middle of editing. Sometimes those suggestions from your editor feel more like an attack. But it's important to remember that you and your editor are on the same side. You have the same goal in mind, which is to make the best book possible.

So what phase of editing are you in? I'm not talking about a written manuscript; I'm talking about your life. You've probably already been through a couple phases of developmental edits growing up, as your parents strove to help you see the bigger picture and how your life relates to those around you. They pointed out inconsistencies where your behavior didn't match your family's morals and beliefs. This is where you developed your character.

As you get older, maybe you find yourself in the copy-editing phase. You're translating what you learned from the developmental edit into your life now, making sure it's in line with who you want to be. You're checking your sources and facts. You look to the Bible to be sure your actions aren't misrepresenting your Lord. You pray with the psalmist, "Put false ways far from me and graciously teach me Your law" (Psalm 119:29). The Bible itself serves as an "editor," after a fashion, correcting you where you are wrong.

Or perhaps you need some proofreading. You need to know how to apply what you've learned to specific situations, rather than just an overall worldview. You search the Bible for passages that pertain to your current experience, praying for God's wisdom in that particular instance.

In life editing, these phases aren't as neatly defined as they are in editing a manuscript. Once I'm done with proofreading a manuscript, I won't go back for another round of developmental editing. But in life, things aren't that tidy. You may feel like you're stuck in continuous rounds of developmental editing, and that can get cumbersome. It's easy to get discouraged and even resentful of the impossibly high standard God sets in the Bible. But as with a human editor, it's important to remember that you're on the same side. God has your best interests in mind, and His goal is to mold and shape you into His own image, so you reflect Him to others.

Editing can be discouraging at times, but there is encouragement along the way. Periodically throughout my manuscript, a comment will pop up—"Great paragraph!"—or some such compliment that warms my heart and reminds me of why I started writing in the first place. And at the final sentence of my manuscript, a one-word comment makes it all worthwhile: *Perfect.*

Likewise, there is encouragement along the way in our "life editing." Periodically throughout our lives, we have the opportunity to draw strength from God's Word with fellow believers in corporate worship. We are reminded in countless Bible verses of God's grace and mercy. We don't have to be perfect. Jesus did that for us. We read God's words to us—"There is therefore now no condemnation for those who are in Christ Jesus" (Romans 8:1). His promises encourage us in our walk of faith. And when we draw our final breath and the last chapter of our life comes to a close, God will welcome us into His presence with the verdict Christ has earned for us:

Perfect.

Are We Failing Our Kids?

Behind every good kid is a mom who's pretty sure she's screwing it all up.

I saw the meme on a friend's Facebook page, and my first thought was, "If that's true, my kids are gonna turn out awesome, because I'm pretty sure I'm completely failing at parenting." What is it about raising kids that makes me so vulnerable, so self-conscious, so quick to believe I'm failing? I worry that I'm letting my kids have too much processed food, that I'm disciplining them wrong, that I let them have too much screen time, that I don't assign enough chores, that I don't spend enough quality time with them, that I don't…The list goes on. Parenting books often make me feel guilty that I'm already messing up my kids by doing things wrong.

There seems to be a general sense that the current generation of parents in America is failing their children. We aren't preparing our kids for adulthood or teaching them life and social skills they need to know. Kids are spending far too much time on screens, doing poorly in school, and aren't developing appropriate social skills. As they get older, many seem to have a poor work ethic and a sense of entitlement, having been raised in a consumerist society. Kids are in something of a crisis, growing up not knowing how to be grown up. And let's face it—that's a valid concern. Parents who raise their children in this way may fear they've failed their kids.

But ultimately, the parent who is failing his children is the one who fails to bring his children up in the Christian faith. Spoiled children who grow up into irresponsible and entitled adults is a shame. But children who grow up without knowing their Savior is a tragedy. Parents who call themselves Christian and yet fail to teach their children about Jesus are truly failing their children in the only area that matters. Ephesians 6:4 instructs, "Fathers, do not provoke your children to anger, but bring them up in the discipline and instruction of the Lord."

There you have it: God's parenting manual. Law and Gospel. Discipline your children with the Law. Show them where they are wrong. And then instruct them about their Savior. God wants parents to pass on the faith to the next generation. "One generation shall commend Your works to another, and shall declare Your mighty acts," Psalm 145:4 says.

Are you passing on your faith to the next generation? Are you teaching your kids about Jesus? If you are, then rest assured that you are not failing them. You may not be a perfect parent, but you are preparing your children for eternity with their Savior.

But perhaps you're reading this with a twinge of guilt. Maybe you've fallen out of the habit of taking your kids to church or praying with them or teaching them Bible stories. Maybe life has gotten so hectic that religion has been put on the back burner. If that's you, don't despair. It's not too late. Prayerfully examine where you need to make some changes, and then ask God for help to make those changes.

Okay, so maybe my kids do eat too much processed food. Maybe I'm not disciplining them well enough. Maybe I don't monitor their screen time as well as I should. But you know what? They are secure in the knowledge of their Savior. They will be with me in heaven one day. And who knows? They might even grow up to be responsible adults in the meantime.

Target Practice

Baptism is a dangerous thing. Think about it. What happens in baptism? A person becomes a child of God. That's a good thing, mind you—a *great* thing. It's a gift beyond comparison. But there's a catch. Someone isn't happy about this gift, and that someone wants to take that gift away. He will stop at nothing to steal that gift right out from under you. That someone is Satan.

I've heard it said that once a person has been baptized it's as if the devil paints a bright red target on their back. That baptized person is now the target of all Satan's attacks. Satan doesn't need to concern himself with unbelievers. He already has them. But he desperately wants to lure Christians away from the one true faith into his kingdom of darkness, so he starts right when a person is baptized and keeps at it relentlessly.

Look at what happened with Jesus. Mark 1:9-11 is the account of Jesus' own baptism, and verses 12 and 13 record the following: "The Spirit immediately drove Him out into the wilderness. And He was in the wilderness forty days, being tempted by Satan. And He was with the wild animals, and the angels were ministering to Him." Even Jesus was tempted immediately following His baptism, and it's a pattern the devil continues to this day. After all, during the baptismal service we do renounce the devil and all his works and all his ways. Them's fighting words, and Satan knows it.

But we aren't left to fight Satan alone, for we have God's Word on our side. Every time Satan tempted Jesus, He responded the same way: "It is written…" Jesus had only to wield the Word of God rightly against Satan, and Satan could not withstand. It's a simple and effective weapon, yet not all who are baptized have this weapon in their arsenals. I can think of a number of families who have had their children baptized, never to be seen in church again. Parents, this is very, very dangerous. The same note of caution that is spoken at weddings could well be spoken of baptism as well—Baptism is not to be entered into inadvisably or lightly. If you baptize your children, you had best make sure you are also doing all you can to train them up in the fear and knowledge of God. Teach them, as the baptismal liturgy exhorts, the Ten Commandments, the Creed, and the Lord's Prayer. Place in their hands the knowledge of Holy Scripture. That's the only defense they have (or need) against the evil foe. Please make sure you're equipping them to withstand the attacks of Satan. Don't let them go unarmed into the fight.

Yes, baptism is a dangerous thing. It opens you to all the attacks of the devil. But the Word of God is strong enough to overpower him. Jesus has overcome Satan for you and for all who are baptized. That's a huge relief, since we just had our newest baby baptized on Sunday. And I wouldn't have it any other way, dangers and all.

What Would Jesus Do?

March 6, 2017

If one is to believe everything one sees about Jesus, one might come away with some very dangerous views about Him. I've heard people make the assertion that Jesus overturned the money changers' tables in the temple to fight economic injustice. I once read a pamphlet that portrayed Jesus as a dualist when He said, "I and the Father…" Some people try to claim that David and Jonathan were gay, so God must approve of that lifestyle. I've even heard that Jesus was a feminist and would have gladly participated in the women's march. And when all else fails, there's always: "Judge not, lest ye be judged," to tell others to mind their own business.

The tactic of twisting God's Word is not a new one. It's been around since the Garden of Eden, when Satan asked Eve, "Did God actually say, 'You shall not eat of any tree in the garden'?" (Genesis 3:1). He's introducing doubt, trying to trick her into questioning God. But he's doing something else at the same time—he's misrepresenting God's Word by adding the word "any." He's making God out to be harsh and unfair.

Not to be outdone, Eve added to God's Word herself: "We may eat of the fruit of the trees in the garden, but God said, 'You shall not eat of the fruit of the tree that is in the midst of the garden, neither shall you touch it, lest you die'" (Genesis 3:2b-3). God never said anything about not touching it, just not eating its fruit. Now Satan has Eve where he wants her. She's confused, so he boldly defies God's Word. "You will not surely die. For God knows that when you eat of it your eyes will be opened, and you will be like God, knowing good and evil" (Genesis 3:4-5).

Satan tantalizes Eve by holding the carrot in front of her that she could be "like God." She can determine for herself what's right and wrong. She can impose her own will upon her life. She doesn't have to follow God's stuffy old rules. She can be free to live as she pleases! Sound familiar? Satan tempts people today in much the same way. Unfortunately, his crafty ways worked on Adam and Eve. They ate the fruit and their eyes were opened, but not in the way Satan had promised. They knew the shame and guilt of sin now. And so do we. So has everyone in the history of the world. With one exception.

Fast forward about 4000 years from Eden, and we find that Satan is still at his same tricks. He hasn't added anything new as he tempts Jesus in the wilderness. He's still tempting people to indulge in instant gratification (filling an empty stomach here), he's still appealing to human pride. He's still twisting God's Word and taking it out of context. But Jesus doesn't fall for the devil's lies, because He knows the Word. Actually, He *is* the Word made flesh.

Even when Satan tries to use Scripture himself, Jesus knows his ulterior motive. On the surface, Satan's use of Psalm 91 might seem very logical. Why yes, God *does* promise that His angels will guard us. "On their hands they will bear you up, lest you strike your foot against a stone" (Psalm 91:12). So Jesus could throw Himself from the pinnacle of the temple as Satan suggests and He'd be just fine, right? Jesus answers that for us. "Again it is written, 'You shall not put the Lord your God to the test'" (Matthew 4:7). Jesus could combat the devil's tactics because He knew the Scriptures inside and out. He knew how to rightly use those Scriptures.

If one intends to quote or represent the Savior of the world, one must be extremely careful while doing so. Downplaying sin by quoting the "judge not" line is not in keeping with Jesus' purpose in coming to the world. Why did Jesus come? He came to die. For sin. That's how serious sin is. We aren't doing anyone any favors by downplaying it or ignoring it. Nor did Jesus ignore it while He walked this earth. Yes, He taught that we are to love our enemies (Matthew 5:44) and forgive our brother without limit (Matthew 18:22). But He also preached seven woes to the Scribes and Pharisees (Matthew 23), calling them "hypocrites," "blind guides," and "whitewashed tombs."

Whoa, Jesus. That's kinda harsh, don't you think? Actually, no, because these so-called religious "experts" were leading people astray by emphasizing the Law over God's grace in the Gospel. Jesus told them, "You shut the kingdom of heaven in people's faces. For you neither enter yourselves nor allow those who would enter to go in" (Matthew 23:13). Jesus was ultimately most concerned about people's spiritual condition.

Jesus didn't come to be a social reformer or radical. He didn't come to fight the injustices or inequalities of this world. He came to win freedom, yes, but not in an earthly sense. He came to win freedom from sin for all people of all times. That includes you and me. By living the perfect life we could never live, by taking the punishment we deserve, by dying and rising again, Jesus won our freedom. Satan no longer has power over those who believe in Jesus. We can point to Jesus and say, "See, my Savior took my sins from me. You have no claim on me anymore."

How are we to apply Jesus' words from 2000 years ago to issues in the twenty-first century? How should we answer those who ask us: *So what* would *Jesus do?* Rather than answering that, let's tweak the question slightly. *What* did *Jesus do?* We can't presume to answer for Him, but we can let Him answer for Himself. In order to do this, you must have a solid knowledge and grasp of what Scripture teaches. You cannot properly reflect Jesus' meaning if you don't truly know the message of the Bible as a whole.

Rule number one in basic biblical interpretation is this: Let Scripture interpret Scripture. In other words, don't just go through and pick and choose random verses to tweak them to fit your purposes. And when others quote Jesus in support of a certain position, look back to the Bible to determine the proper context.

So how can we answer arguments like those in the opening paragraph? As for David and Jonathan, the Bible never says they were gay. They simply had a close friendship that baffles the minds of twenty-first century Americans who equate "loving" someone else of the same gender with homosexuality. As for the money changers in the temple, Jesus was mad that they were defiling His Father's house by making it a marketplace rather than a house of prayer. The claim that Jesus was a dualist? Finish the sentence and you'll see that Jesus was in fact claiming the exact opposite of dualism: "I and the Father *are one*" (John 10:30, emphasis mine). And what of the women's march? Would Jesus have participated, fighting for women's rights? Again, let's look at the Bible. What *did* Jesus do? The only march Jesus took place in was the march to His cross. For you. For me. For all.

Longcuts and Detours

March 7, 2016

Do you ever feel like God is leading you on a detour? Perhaps you think He's taking you on a longer road than necessary, an out-of-the-way route. Rather than a shortcut, maybe it seems like He's actually taking you on a "longcut." And perhaps that's exactly what He's doing.

Consider this verse from Exodus: "When Pharaoh let the people go, God did not lead them on the road through the Philistine country, though that was shorter. For God said, 'If they face war, they might change their minds and return to Egypt'" (Exodus 13:17, NIV).

God took the Israelites the long way around the Philistine country, through the desert road that led toward the Red Sea, and this verse gives us a glimpse into the mind of God. He doesn't want to lead His people the shortest way, because He knows their frailties and weaknesses. He knows their fears. It's actually for their own sake that He leads them the long way. If they face the intimidating Philistines already, they might well be tempted to just give up and go right back to bondage in Egypt. And God didn't want that for them. He'd done too much for them already.

But maybe the Israelites didn't quite see it that way. Maybe some of them wondered why God was leading them toward the very formidable barrier of the Red Sea, rather than the nice road straight through Philistine country. Maybe they grumbled that God was leading them into a trap, or at least that He wasn't taking them the best way. When they realized the Egyptians were pursuing them and that they were trapped by the Red Sea, they cried out to Moses in despair. It was here, at their lowest point, with no possible way out of the situation on their own, that God intervened in a way that could only have come from Him. He parted the Red Sea so they could cross on dry land, then drowned the entire Egyptian army in that same body of water. The Israelites need not fear the Egyptians anymore.

Are you tempted to believe God is taking you on a route or longcut that's more difficult than it needs to be? Take heart. God knows what He's doing, and He's doing it for you. He knows your frailties and fears, and He acts accordingly. He's looking out for your better interests, and perhaps He sees something you don't. If you face something overwhelming, perhaps you'll give up the Christian walk and return to the slavery of sin. And God doesn't want that for you. He's done too much for you already.

Like the Israelites of old, God stepped in to save you. You were trapped, not by the Red Sea and advancing Egyptians, but by the deadly effects of your own sin. You could in no way save yourself. All efforts to do so would be in vain. And it was there, at your lowest point, with no possible way out of the situation on your own, that God intervened in a way that could only have come from Him. He sent His own Son to live a perfect life in your stead, then offered Himself on the cross as the sacrifice for your sins and mine. When He rose, He defeated our final enemy, death. We need not fear sin, Satan, or death anymore.

When it seems God is leading you on a detour or a longcut, remember Israel of old. Trust that God knows what He's doing, and He's doing it with your eternal good in mind.

Did You Hear?

March 13, 2014

Crucifixion was the best thing that could have happened to him. Presumably, the thief on the cross next to Jesus had led a pretty miserable life, resorting to criminal activities that gained for him the death penalty. As he woke up that morning, he was probably looking back upon his life with bitterness and regret, perhaps stewing in anger over how unfair life was and how *he* was really the victim here. What he didn't see coming was an encounter with a man who would alter the course of his eternity.

"Jesus, remember me when You come into Your kingdom," (Luke 23:42) the thief requested a few short hours after being crucified next to Jesus. What he didn't realize was that Jesus *was* coming into His kingdom right then. This was why Jesus had come into the world, to die for the sins of everyone, including this thief.

But how did he know to ask Jesus about His kingdom? How did he know Jesus was a king in the first place? How did he come to saving faith in such a short amount of time?

The answer is a bit surprising. He didn't hear it from Jesus' disciples or other followers, but from Jesus' enemies, albeit unwittingly. When the soldiers mocked Jesus before crucifying Him, they put a scarlet robe on Him, pressed a crown of thorns into His head, put a reed in His right hand, and mocked Him as the "King of the Jews." When they had crucified Him, they nailed the sign above His head, "This is Jesus, the King of the Jews."

The passersby went a step further and quoted Jesus' own prediction as they taunted Him: "You who would destroy the temple and rebuild it in three days, save Yourself! If You are the Son of God, come down from the cross" (Matthew 27:40). The chief priests, elders, and scribes derailed Jesus as well. "He is the King of Israel; let Him come down now from the cross, and we will believe in Him. He trusts in God; let God deliver Him now, if He desires Him. For He said, 'I am the Son of God'" (Matthew 27:42-43).

Even as they mock Jesus, they are spreading the Gospel! By quoting Jesus' words back to Him, they are speaking the life-giving words necessary for the salvation of this criminal. He heard the taunts and read the sign. He observed Jesus' behavior on the cross, so very different from that of the third criminal crucified that day. He realized that Jesus was in fact a king, the Son of God. He believed through the cruel mockery of those watching. It's ironic, really. The chief priests were so upset over Jesus' "blasphemy," as they saw it, that they had Him put to death so people would stop believing in Him. Yet even as He hung upon the cross, He was still bringing others to faith in Him. And what means did He use? The tauntings of His enemies.

Romans 10:17 reminds us that "Faith comes from hearing, and hearing through the word of Christ." The criminal on the cross heard the words of Christ, spoken both by Jesus Himself as well as His enemies who didn't believe in Him. And those words of Christ brought him saving faith. This criminal, rejected by society as unsalvageable, was promised eternal life by Jesus. "Truly, I say to you, today you will be with Me in paradise" (Luke 23:43).

What a beautiful promise! And to such an unworthy man, nonetheless. If the Holy Spirit can even use the mocking and taunting of nonbelievers to work saving faith in a hardened criminal's heart, how much more so can He use our words when we speak the Gospel? Don't be afraid to speak of your faith. Live your faith and speak it at all times and in all places.

You never know who might be listening.

Fragile: Handle With Care

March 16, 2015

Even if you reject radical feminism and are totally okay with the idea that the husband is the head of the household, chances are there's still some small part of you deep down that bristles ever so slightly when you read Peter's words in 1 Peter 3:7: "Likewise, husbands, live with your wives in an understanding way, showing honor to the woman as the weaker vessel, since they are heirs with you of the grace of life, so that your prayers may not be hindered." He has the audacity to call the wife the "weaker" partner! True, many women are often physically weaker than most men, but do we need to point that out? Or does this mean we're weaker emotionally or even spiritually? No matter which way our modern minds read this, it sounds condescending.

And yet...

We have to remember that Peter wrote this under divine inspiration. He's not being sexist or chauvinistic. Quite the opposite, actually. In Jewish homes of that day, many different types of vessels were used. Big sturdy pots were placed at the entrance of each home and contained water for cooking and washing. These vessels withstood much use and abuse. Other vessels were more fragile and were used as vases and containers for valuable jewelry. Because of their beauty and delicacy, they were given places of honor in the home. In 1 Peter 3:7, women are pictured as beautiful, delicate, fragile containers that hold cherished items. Our husbands are required to protect us and give us a place of honor in their hearts and in the home.

Let's look at a more modern-day analogy. I have two Bibles that I use on a regular basis. One is the Bible I received for Confirmation, a Concordia Self-Study Bible. The other is The Lutheran Study Bible, which my husband bought me when it came out more recently. I've had my Confirmation Bible for twenty plus years, and it's seen its share of use. I have notes written sloppily in pen, some of the pages are creased or torn, and I don't cringe if my children open it to find a Bible verse.

But The Lutheran Study Bible, now that's a different story. The pages are much thinner, and I protect that Bible fiercely. It's actually become a joke in our household, because even when my husband uses it I give him strict warning not to mess it up. I only write truly useful notes in the margins, and those only in pencil. I turn the pages slowly and carefully, and I keep it out of reach of my younger children. It isn't meant to take the more vigorous use of a sturdier-paged Bible, and I protect it accordingly. I protect it because I love it, because it is valuable to me.

Peter isn't telling husbands that their wives are weak. He is telling them to step up and be the men God intends them to be. God made men to shield and protect their wives from the abuse of the world. Husbands are to give their wives the honor God intends. And let's not forget the rest of the verse, either: "…they are heirs with you of the grace of life…" Men and women alike are heirs of heaven, on completely equal footing in God's eyes. We are all saved in the same way: through God's wondrous grace. Wives, don't be ashamed of being the "weaker vessel." Rather, thank God that He has placed you in such a position of honor in your household, and much more importantly, that He has made you a member of His household for all eternity.

Thirsty No More

March 19, 2018

It happened with no prior warning. We came home from some out-of-town errands to find the fire hydrant across the street shooting out water. Not long after that, we discovered that our own water had taken on a nasty brown hue, and shortly thereafter the town issued a boil water notice. This put a damper on normal household activities. I didn't want to wash clothes or dishes in water that had dirt in it. There was no way I was going to give the kids a bath in brown water. Drinking it was out of the question. Even after I boiled a pot of water, there was sediment in the bottom of the pot. I resorted to filtering the water, boiling the filtered water, and then filtering it again. Doing this to get enough water for doing dishes by hand (and rinsing them!) was laborious. But what I noticed most was how *thirsty* I was without an unlimited safe water source.

Despite emergency protocol that suggests every family should have a three-day supply of drinking water on hand, I didn't have that. We had the already-filtered water in the fridge, but that went quickly. The second day of the boil water notice, I dashed to the local store and bought six of the last remaining eight bottles on the shelf. I figured that was enough for each of us in the family to have one. But without safe tap water to drink, everyone suddenly seemed parched. On a normal day, we each might drink two glasses, but now it was as if we wanted to guzzle water.

In times of drought (or a boil water notice), water becomes a much more valuable commodity. One realizes just how important it is. We use water to wash clothes, dishes, to take showers, and of course, to stay hydrated. It's an essential part of our daily lives. Yet as critical as water is, there's a different kind of thirst that can never be quenched by all the water on earth.

"As a deer pants for flowing streams, so pants my soul for You, O God. My soul thirsts for God, for the living God. When shall I come and appear before God?" the psalmist asks in Psalm 42:1-2. I don't know about you, but I'm not always that fervent about hearing and receiving God's Word. Yet Jesus shows the Samaritan woman at the well what it means to have the living water He offers. "Everyone who drinks of this [physical] water will be thirsty again, but whoever drinks of the water that I will give him will never be thirsty again. The water that I will give him will become in him a spring of water welling up to eternal life," He tells her in John 4:13-14. *That's* the kind of water I want. And the beautiful thing is that God freely gives it to His children.

The Bible speaks frequently of living water that can quench our spiritual thirst and grant us eternal life. "To the thirsty I will give from the spring of the water of life without payment," Jesus promises in Revelation 21:6. Revelation 7:16-17 declares, "They shall hunger no more, neither thirst anymore…For the Lamb in the midst of the throne will be their shepherd, and He will guide them to springs of living water."

Thankfully, our boil water notice has been lifted. Normal household activities have resumed. I can get a glass of water from the tap again. But only Jesus can quench my spiritual thirst. And the living water that He offers will never run out. So go ahead. Drink deeply.

The Lonely Road

March 20, 2014

There's a fun little website called Despair.com that sells demotivational products, a spoof on those motivational posters you see in office buildings. There's one titled "Loneliness" that has a picture of a solitary tree in a bleak white winter landscape. The caption reads, "If you find yourself struggling with loneliness, you're not alone. And yet you are alone. So very alone."

We chuckle at this, but sometimes it hits too close to home. Loneliness is a real problem. We are made for relationships, so loneliness is contradictory to our natural inclinations. Even Jesus—*especially* Jesus—suffered from loneliness, most particularly when He was hanging on the cross abandoned by God the Father.

One hymn that speaks of this abandonment is "Cross of Jesus, Cross of Sorrow" (*Lutheran Service Book* 428). Stanza 3 says: "O mysterious condescending! O abandonment sublime! Very God Himself is bearing all the sufferings of time!"

Abandonment sublime? That sounds like an oxymoron. Most of us think of *sublime* as something too wonderful for words, like a "sublime dessert." Is that what the hymn writer means? Well, in one sense, yes. Jesus' suffering on the cross, though terrible for Him, resulted in the salvation of the entire world. That fact certainly is too wonderful for words.

But there's another meaning of *sublime,* which is "complete, absolute, utter." Ah, now that makes more sense. God abandoned Jesus completely, absolutely, utterly. Is there a more heart-rending cry than the one Jesus made from the cross? "My God, my God, why have You forsaken Me?" He asks (Mark 15:34). We may have gone through times in our lives that feel as if God is absent, but by faith we know that isn't true. For Jesus it *was* true. God abandoned Him completely on that cross, all alone except for our sins.

What a terrifying picture! Jesus literally suffered hell on that cross for us. What, after all, is hell? It is complete and utter separation from God. We are left alone with our sins to which we stubbornly cling. On the cross, Jesus bore the sins of all mankind. He hung there as the world's worst criminal: the adulterer, the murderer, the thief, the terrorist, the abuser, the liar, the cheater—and He did it alone. His own Father had abandoned Him. Jesus suffered hell on that cross so you need never experience it. He did it for you.

Yet even in the midst of Jesus' piercing cry, there is hope. How does He address His Father? "My God." Even when God had completely abandoned Jesus, still He makes the title personal—*My* God. That's what faith is. When there's nothing left but God's promises, faith clings to those and claims them. Whatever you are experiencing, whatever you have yet to face, claim Jesus' promise that He will be with us to the end of the age. Call upon Him in a personal way—*my* Savior, *my* Lord, *my* God.

Consider also that Jesus is quoting the first verse of Psalm 22, the most poignant prediction in the Bible of Jesus' suffering and death. A common practice of Jesus' day was to quote the first verse of a psalm or other passage of Scripture, with the understanding that in doing so, one was referring to the entire passage. So read all of Psalm 22. You probably know the first half of it pretty well. It's quoted in a lot of Good Friday services.

But look at what happens in verse 19. Suddenly there's a shift, and David starts talking about God's deliverance. *When* God delivers him, he will "tell of [God's] name to [his] brothers" (v 22). "All the ends of the earth shall remember and turn to the Lord, and all the families of the nations shall worship before You" (verse 27). "All the prosperous of the earth eat and worship; before Him shall bow all who go down to the dust" (verse 29, clear reference to heaven). "They shall come and proclaim His righteousness to a people yet unborn, that He has done it" (verse 31).

Do you realize the implications of this? When Jesus quotes the first verse of Psalm 22, He is quoting the entire thing, and look how the psalm ends: with hope and promise. *We* are those "people yet unborn." Jesus knows that His abandonment by His Father will result in salvation for the entire world, that His temporal suffering would mean eternal victory for countless generations. He looked past His current situation and saw eternity. For you.

Jesus was abandoned by God so you need never be. When he "descended into hell," as we confess in the Creed, He didn't do so to suffer the pangs of hell. He'd already suffered that on the cross with His separation from the Father. No, Jesus descended to hell to proclaim His *sublime* victory over Satan and his host. He won eternal life for you in the process. Someday you will live with Him forever, with joy and peace sublime.

Why I Want My Kids to Fight

March 20, 2017

My seventh-grade son has a unique set of friends. A few believe in a generic god out there, some don't believe in God at all, a couple aren't sure what they believe, and then there's my son. He's grown up in the church, attended parochial schools until fifth grade, goes regularly to Sunday School and confirmation class, and hears Bible stories and devotions at home. He has faith in Jesus and isn't afraid to say so, even when all his friends are arguing against him. And argue they do. Religion is a regular topic of discussion at their lunch table. Yet despite the wide variety of views among them, they manage to stay friends even after a lively discussion. And to be honest, I couldn't be happier that he's fighting with his friends in school.

Make no mistake, we Christians are in the midst of a fierce battle. Satan has declared war on those who believe in Jesus. He wants nothing more than to snatch our faith from us, discredit our witness to the world, and keep others from hearing the Good News of the Gospel. And sadly, much of society is falling for his lies. Find a blog about political or societal issues, and you'll see this played out vividly in the comment section. You'll find heated (and often ignorant) accusations hurled on both sides. Society loves to pull the all-powerful "intolerance card" on anyone who disagrees. But of course, Christianity is not to be tolerated because our beliefs are seen as intolerant themselves. It's a toxic and dangerous environment for our children, and they must be properly equipped.

Let's say your child asked to take up boxing. Would you allow him or her to compete without proper protection—boxing gloves, a mouth guard, and head protection? Of course not. Neither should we allow our children to enter the spiritual battle without being protected. Thankfully, it isn't up to us to figure out how to arm ourselves. God has already taken care of that problem.

Ephesians 6:10-18 is the "armor of God" section. Just look at the incredible defense He's given to us: the belt of truth, the breastplate of righteousness, our feet fitted with the gospel of peace, the shield of faith, and the helmet of salvation. That's a pretty thorough defense, covering us from head to toe. We know that we have God's absolute truth on our side, and He protects us through His own righteousness. Whatever flaming darts the enemy may hurl at us, we can extinguish them with the shield of faith, because we know what we wear on our heads—a crown of salvation that Jesus has already won for us. But there's still one more item on the list.

The items above comprise the defensive armor we possess through faith in Christ, but there's one last thing we can't neglect; the one offensive weapon in the list—the "sword of the Spirit, which is the Word of God" (Ephesians 6:17b). This is critical, because it tells us how to "fight."

We aren't to rely on our own wisdom or logic or cleverness. We aren't to turn to popular opinion or what's trending at the moment. We are to use God's Word alone. And what does that mean? We need to know the Scriptures. And we need to make sure our children know them too. We can't properly fight without really knowing what the Bible says.

I can't even count the number of times I've seen the comment, "My Jesus would never…" What follows is usually a feel-good sort of sentiment, the "nice-guy Jesus" defense, leading people to believe that Jesus doesn't really care what you believe or how you live your life. He won't condemn you or judge you, because He loves everyone. This is tricky, because it's a mixture of truth and a lie. So rather than trying to make a clever comeback, point to the Bible and let Jesus speak for Himself. "Actually, Jesus *will* judge everyone on the Last Day, as He says in Matthew 25 when He's separating the sheep and the goats. Those who believe in Him will go to heaven, and those who do not believe in Him will go to hell. That's why it's so important to me that others know about Jesus—so they have the chance to believe in Him and go to heaven one day."

Dear Christians, we possess an incredible gift. We in America still have freedom of worship as well as access to Bibles, devotionals, and other religious materials in print. Some countries do not have these freedoms. Let's not squander the opportunity to study the Bible and worship with other believers on a regular basis. Let's immerse our children in the Scriptures as well. Pose questions and scenarios for them so they can practice defending their faith. Why don't we believe in evolution? Why do we believe that the only way to heaven is Jesus? What does God say about homosexuality? Use current events as a springboard for discussion in your own home. Be honest and open in answering any questions your children have. If you don't know the answer, consult your pastor or a trusted Christian friend. Your kids need to know they can talk to you about religion, even if they have doubts themselves.

As Paul sums up in his section about the armor of God, also be sure to pray at all times. Prayer isn't part of the "armor," per se, but it is a valuable tool nonetheless. Pray that you stand firm in your faith and that your children stand firm in theirs. Pray that God would grant wisdom when called upon to defend the faith.

Someday, in the not-too-distant future, our kids will be the ones blogging and sparring about hot-button topics on social media. Do what you can to equip them for the future, knowing that God will provide the necessary armor. After all, it's a battlefield out there.

To Sue for Pardon

March 21, 2016

Jesus' first word from the cross was, incredibly, a prayer for forgiveness for His enemies. "Father, forgive them, for they know not what they do" (Luke 23:34). Even as they nailed Him to the cross, mocking and jeering at Him, Jesus prayed for their forgiveness. The words of stanza 2 of "Jesus, in Your Dying Woes" explores that as follows:

> *Savior, for our pardon sue*
> *When our sins Your pangs renew.*
> *For we know not what we do:*
> *Hear us, holy Jesus.*
> *(Lutheran Service Book 447)*

The meaning of "sue" in this context is to "appeal formally to a person for something." In this case, of course, Jesus is appealing to God the Father. Synonyms for "sue" include *appeal, petition, ask, solicit, request,* and *seek.* Imagine that—Jesus is petitioning His Father even now for your sake. He requests your forgiveness, He solicits your pardon, He seeks your eternal salvation. When Jesus asked God to forgive "them," He wasn't just praying for the Roman soldiers and His fellow Jews. He prayed for you and me that day as well. We were there with our sins, for our sins put Him there.

Be of good cheer, dear Christian. Even now, Jesus sues for your pardon. Romans 8:34 reminds us that "Christ Jesus…is at the right hand of God, [and] is interceding for us." We read as well in 1 John 2:1, "If anyone does sin, we have an advocate with the Father, Jesus Christ the righteous." Advocate is a legal term, like a defense lawyer. Jesus, our defense lawyer, sues for our pardon before God the heavenly judge.

And what evidence does Jesus present in God's court of justice? Himself. He needs only one piece of evidence—His own perfect life, death, and resurrection. He only needs to show the nail markings in His perfect hands. 1 John 2:2 continues, "He [Jesus] is the propitiation for our sins, and not for ours only, but also for the sins of the whole world." To *propitiate* is to appease, to make satisfaction for something. Jesus appeased the Father's wrath against sin. We deserved the death sentence, but our Savior took that for us. Colossians 2:13-14 assures us that "You, who were dead in your trespasses…God made alive together with him, having forgiven us all our trespasses, by canceling the record of debt that stood against us with its legal demands. This He set aside, nailing it to the cross."

Jesus, our advocate, our defense lawyer, has presented His case before His Father. And in Christ, the verdict is in: Not Guilty. Thank you, Jesus!

Boundaries

March 23, 2015

Our puppy is completely ridiculous. We have a fairly large fenced-in yard that allows her plenty of room to run and play, but what is the one thing to which she's attracted? The gate. There's a little opening between the fence and the gate itself, just big enough for her to squeeze through. Give her a few more months and she won't be able to fit, but for now she can do it, so she does. It's not enough that she has the whole yard—she wants to explore what's beyond that fence. She doesn't understand that we keep her fenced in for her own safety or that she has complete freedom in the yard itself. No, she wants what she can't have. Good thing we aren't that way.

Think back to Adam and Eve in the Garden of Eden. They had everything— that entire paradise was theirs to explore. God gave them only one stipulation. They weren't allowed to eat from the tree in the middle of the garden. So what did they do? Ate from that one tree. Of all the trees and all the fruit in the garden, that one proved irresistible. When they were tempted, they gave in pretty quickly. And every single one of us would have done the same thing.

We aren't any different today. God gives us plenty of freedom but we look with longing "beyond the fence" and wish we didn't have any boundaries. We look at the Ten Commandments as confining and stifling, not realizing that actually God has set them up for our own protection.

The second half of Psalm 19 shows the benefits and goodness of the Law:

The law of the Lord is perfect, reviving the soul. The statutes of the Lord are trustworthy, making wise the simple. The precepts of the Lord are right, giving joy to the heart. The commands of the Lord are radiant, giving light to the eyes. The fear of the Lord is pure, enduring forever. The ordinances of the Lord are sure and altogether righteous. They are more precious than gold, than much pure gold; they are sweeter than honey, than honey from the comb. By them is Your servant warned; in keeping them there is great reward. Who can discern his errors? Forgive my hidden faults. Keep Your servant also from willful sins; may they not rule over me. Then will I be blameless, innocent of great transgression (Psalm 19:7-13, NIV).

Look how David praises the merits of the Law. It's not a cumbersome, restrictive burden on us. Quite the opposite: "In keeping them there is great reward." God's commandments protect us—they warn us against sins so "they may not rule over [us]." God knows that by ourselves we would naturally allow sin to have dominion over us. We would turn to other gods, use His name in vain, neglect church, dishonor those in authority, murder, commit adultery, steal, bear false witness, and covet. He also knows how negatively those actions would affect us, and in His love He wishes to protect us from ourselves. He gives us the Law to protect us and those around us.

Just as my own family keeps our dog in the yard to protect her, so God sets boundaries so we don't wander off and be lost to Him. Lest you doubt this, remember the words of Psalm 16:6: "The boundary lines have fallen for me in pleasant places; surely I have a delightful inheritance" (NIV). Indeed, because God Himself is our inheritance. His boundaries keep us where we need to be—safe in His keeping forever.

Why I Would Never Force My Kids
to go to Church

March 24, 2014

My parents forced me to eat three times a day growing up. No joke. Three times. Every. Single. Day. And it wasn't always stuff I liked, either. Matter of fact, I complained a lot about what my mom made. "Ewww, gross! Sautéed zucchini? Seriously? Mom, you know we hate this stuff!" So as I approached adulthood I made an important decision. Since my parents forced me to eat while I was growing up, I decided I was done with meals. Oh, here and there I'll eat out of obligation. I mean, family traditions like Thanksgiving and Christmas, yeah, I'm there. But daily eating? No way. I'm done.

Set in any other context, excuses people make for not going to church sound completely ridiculous. But set in the context of Christianity, people say these things in all seriousness while others nod sagely in somber agreement.

My son told me a few weeks into school that he didn't like the teacher. He wasn't getting excited enough about learning, and he didn't really feel connected to the other kids in his class, so I told him he never had to go back to school again. Who wants to waste their time going somewhere where they aren't being fulfilled?

We've never forced our daughter to stay off the road when playing. We don't want to restrict her imagination. We allow her the freedom to make her own choices in life.

Okay, Ruth. Come on. That one was just ridiculous. No loving parent would ever say that. That's a safety issue—a matter of life and death. Exactly. And that's just my point.

Church isn't a place you go to get pumped up about life. It isn't entertainment like a movie or concert. It is literally a life and death matter. Eternal life. Just as a loving parent wouldn't allow their child to wander in the road or to quit school, a loving Christian parent also does not give the option to their children about going to church, learning Bible stories at home, and praying together. Do your kids always jump for joy when they hear you say, "Time to get up! Let's get ready for church!" No. They won't. Do they get excited for school every morning? Hardly. But you still make them go. Why? Because you are the parent and you know what's best. Even when they complain, you serve them healthful meals and limit their junk food intake. You set boundaries for their own safety when playing outside. You insist they go to school because you're looking at the long-term picture. And you are right to do those things. How much more so are you responsible for doing all you can to secure their eternal well being?

Yes, kids can be brought up in a loving Christian home and still turn away later. That's on them. But you, parents, have a task of the utmost importance. God has placed these precious children into your homes for such a brief while. You have them with you for perhaps a fifth of their lives. Set a strong foundation while they are under your roof. Take them to church. Make sure they understand that they are sinners and that Jesus is their Savior. They are never too young to learn this. My one-and-a-half-year-old sees a cross and excitedly shouts, "Jesus!"

Don't use the excuse that "they wouldn't understand this." Try them. I don't understand it all myself, but I still believe. And you'd better believe that the Holy Spirit works in their hearts effectively. My children sometimes amaze me with the insights they pick up during devotions or Bible readings. The strength of their faith often humbles me. Once when I was having a terrible day, my oldest asked, "Can I pray with you?" He was nine at the time. He knows there is power in prayer. He perceives that sometimes there's nothing he can say that will make it better, so he'll just go straight to the One who does have that power.

Do my own kids complain about church? Yes. Do they tell me it's boring? Sometimes, yes. They say the same things about school. But church and school are different environments for a reason. School is centered around learning and thus has its own schedule and structure. Church is a hospital for sinners. That would be all of us, mind you. You, me, the drug dealer a few streets away—all of us are sinners in need of a Savior.

So what do we do at church? We confess our sins. Why do we do this at the start? To "wipe our feet" before entering God's house, so to speak. Then we are assured of forgiveness. We hear God's Word. We sing hymns proclaiming what Christ has done for us. We hear sermons where our pastors preach Christ. We don't go to church to hear what we have to do to gain heaven. No, Christ did it all. 100%. We can't do one thing to merit salvation for ourselves. That's why we hear sermons about Jesus and not about us. We take the body and blood of Jesus in Holy Communion for the strengthening of our souls. And we depart refreshed to serve God by serving our families, friends, and neighbors in Christian love.

Parents, don't give in to outside pressures telling you not to force your kids to go to church. Don't give in to them, either, when your kids complain about it. Because at some point an amazing thing happens—that kid who complains about church grows up and takes his or her own kids to church. Going back to my opening analogy, believe it or not, there came a point in my own life where I realized I actually liked sautéed zucchini (although I never would have admitted that to my mother). Keep at it, parents. Just as we need food each day for physical strength and nourishment, so do we need regular worship to refresh and strengthen our souls.

And with that, I need to get started on dinner. Maybe I'll even throw in some sautéed zucchini.

To Brainwash a Child?

March 31, 2014

Apparently I brainwash my kids. Because I teach them about Jesus, I'm forcing my beliefs on them, indoctrinating them so they become mindless puppets, regurgitating back to me what I want them to say. I'm denying them the right to free thinking and the opportunity to choose for themselves what they believe. I use scare tactics like threatening them with hell when they misbehave. It's brainwashing at its worst.

First, let's look at the argument about denying my kids the right to free thinking. I'm going to list different scenarios and I want you to answer for yourself whether each instance is denying a child the beauty of exploration and the gift of choice.

1. A parent who passes on loyalty to a certain sports team, giving their child apparel, pennants, and gear from the team of the parent's choice from a very young age, thus raising their child to be a fan of the same team the parents like.

2. A symphonic violinist who starts his child on violin lessons at the age of five, thus ruling out the possibility of the child exploring woodwind or brass instruments.

3. An Olympic gymnast who signs up her child in gymnastics from the age of three, thus denying the child the chance to explore other options like ice skating.

4. A vegetarian parent who passes on the vegetarian lifestyle to her children, thus denying them the exploration of many types of meat.

Your answers may be different from my own, but here's the bottom line. If you believe that a Christian parent who passes on their beliefs to their children is denying their children the "beauty of choice," then you have to agree that all the examples above are denying their children the beauty of choice as well.

You see, I cannot do anything other than pass on my faith. Living out my faith and passing it on to my children is just what I *do*. It's like speaking English. It just comes naturally. It's my "native tongue," so to speak. Am I denying my kids free choice by speaking English in the house? What if they'd rather speak Italian? Do you see how ridiculous this gets? Just as I speak the English language without a second thought, so do I speak my language of faith, Christianity.

What about the other accusation, that I threaten my kids with talk of hell? My husband and I have never once done this. We've never said, "You know, you're gonna burn in hell for lying to me like that." That's unthinkable. So what *do* we teach them? It's quite simple, actually. It comes down to two main categories.

1. *Law.* In order to have a proper understanding of the second category, one must start with this. Here is where many people bristle, and sadly, if you can't get past the Law, you will never be able to experience the beauty of the Gospel. The Law tells us that we are all sinners. Yes, I said it. You're a sinner, I'm a sinner, my kids are sinners. Does it hurt your pride to hear me say it? It should. No one likes to be told they're wrong, and here's where a lot of people fall away. "I don't need a religion that tells me I'm wrong or makes me feel guilty." But stick with me, because if you stop reading here you miss the best part! When did you teach your kids to lie, hit each other, fight, etc? What's that? You *didn't* teach them these things? That's because we are all sinful. No matter how hard we may try to be "good," we will all fall short. God demands perfection 100% of the time. No one can live up to that. But this isn't the end of the story.

2. *Gospel.* God wasn't content to sit in heaven and watch us ruin ourselves. He sent His only Son, Jesus, to this earth as a human being. Imagine, the God of the universe taking on human flesh! Jesus came down to earth and lived the perfect life we could never live. Then He was crucified for all the sins of everyone in the world, and three days later rose from the dead. His victory over death assures all believers that they will live with Him eternally. Does this make sense to our human minds? Well, no. But the "foolishness of God is wiser than men," as 1 Corinthians 1:25 asserts. God's "foolishness" is the message of the cross, as 1 Corinthians 1:18 points out: "For the word of the cross is folly to those who are perishing, but to us who are being saved it is the power of God."

Friend, I don't know where you are in your beliefs. Perhaps you look at the cross as "folly" and think all Christians to be foolish and ignorant. Perhaps you know the cross to be "the power of God." You fall into one category or the other. As for me and my household, we believe. My children know the message of the cross and believe it as "the power of God." We don't brainwash them to believe this. We simply teach them about their living Savior who was willing to die for them. The Holy Spirit works faith in their hearts. I pray He works in your heart as well.

Water is Thicker Than Blood

March 31, 2014

The sword was piercing her own soul. As Simeon had predicted thirty-three years ago in the temple, Mary now understood what he'd meant as she watched her innocent Son bleeding and dying on the cross. What greater pain for a mother than to see her child hurt when she can do nothing to change it? Yet even as Jesus was dying, He was still caring for others. She'd heard Him ask for forgiveness for those who crucified Him. She'd seen Him promise paradise to the criminal next to Him on the cross. And now He uses precious energy to speak again, this time to see to her own welfare.

> *When Jesus saw His mother and the disciple whom He loved standing nearby, He said to His mother, 'Woman, behold, your son!' Then He said to the disciple, 'Behold, your mother!' And from that hour the disciple took her to his own home.*
> *John 19:26-27*

Women in Jesus' day weren't likely to have jobs outside the home. The daily work of keeping a household running required more work than we in the twenty-first century can comprehend. Multiple times a day women had to lug heavy (probably forty-pound) buckets of water from the well to their homes to use for washing, cleaning, and drinking. The physical duties of running a household were far more demanding than ones we have today. They baked bread from scratch, even down to grinding their own flour. These women were *busy*. There was really no way they could take paying jobs as well. That was the job of their husbands. In Mary and Joseph's case, Joseph was a carpenter. It was a humble profession, one that didn't bring in big bucks, but Joseph was able to provide for his family nonetheless. But tradition has it that Joseph had died somewhere in Jesus' teenage or early adult years, so Mary's earthly care had passed to her eldest son, Jesus. But Jesus was dying.

Now what was Mary to do? Her care should fall to her next son or closest male relative. For Mary, the expected choice would be James or Jude, Jesus' brothers. So why doesn't Jesus leave it at that? Well, you see, neither James nor Jude yet believed in Jesus. They came to saving faith later, after Jesus' resurrection. James came to lead the Jerusalem churches, and historian Josephus tells us he was stoned to death by the Sadducees. Both James and Jude went on to author New Testament books. But at this exact moment, when Jesus was dying on the cross, His brothers were nowhere to be found. Jesus would not entrust His mother's care to those who would not also care for her spiritually. So He changes the order of things and gives Mary's care over to His disciple, John.

While this tender exchange between Jesus, Mary, and John may seem like a sweet gesture on Jesus' part, there's another more important aspect to this. Jesus is setting a precedent. Yes, God places us in earthly families, and hopefully many of us have strong family bonds where we share the gift of saving faith with our loved ones. But not everyone has this advantage. Some families are estranged from one another. Some family members have fallen away from the faith, or never believed in the first place. If that is the case for you, take heart. Jesus is reordering the family. He is showing us that the spiritual family of believers supersedes the blood bonds between families. This is not to diminish the importance of earthly families, but Jesus is expanding the definition of "family." All believers are part of a much larger family, for we are all brothers and sisters in Christ. It is said that "Baptismal water is thicker than blood." The waters of Holy Baptism have united us with the whole church of heaven and earth. Look around you on any given Sunday. Your fellow congregants are your family.

Jesus' words from the cross were not the first time He has reordered the family. Early on in His ministry, when the crowds made it difficult for Jesus even to eat, His family "went out to seize Him, for they were saying, 'He is out of His mind'" (Mark 3:21). When they reached Jesus and He was told that they were there, He replied, "'Who are My mother and My brothers?' And looking about at those who sat around Him, He said, 'Here are My mother and My brothers! For whoever does the will of God, he is My brother and sister and mother'" (Mark 3:33-35). Again, Jesus shows that the family of believers is a more intimate tie even than biological family bonds.

No matter what the makeup of your earthly family might be, know this: Jesus has placed you into a supportive, loving Christian family united not by DNA, but by saving faith through Jesus' blood and the waters of baptism. We share meals together at the communion rail. We recall family history every time we read the Bible and tell the salvation story. We sing together. We support each other and care for fellow family members who are hurting or in need. God is our Father and Jesus Himself is our brother. And we have the rest of eternity to spend with this wonderful family.

Author's Addendum

September 2022

Recently I made a surprising connection that may shed some light on this exchange and render some of the information in the original post inaccurate. When comparing the Gospel accounts of who was at the cross when Jesus was dying, we find that each Gospel writer lists them slightly differently. This makes it difficult to pinpoint with absolute clarity who was there, but let's take a stab at it nonetheless.

In Matthew 27:56, we read, "There were also many women there, looking on from a distance, who had followed Jesus from Galilee, ministering to Him, along whom were Mary Magdalene and Mary the mother of James and Joseph and the mother of the sons of Zebedee." Mark 15:40 lists "Mary Magdalene, and Mary the mother of James the younger and of Joses, and Salome." Comparing the two, it seems a decent possibility that Salome is the mother of the sons of Zebedee. We know from Mark 1:19 that James and John were sons of Zebedee, so that would make Salome their mother. (The early Church held this view, for what that's worth.)

Turning now to John 19:25, the women listed there are "His mother and His mother's sister, Mary the wife of Clopas, and Mary Magdalene." If Mary the wife of Clopas is the same woman as Mary the mother of James and Joseph ("Joses" in Mark), that leaves Salome as "Jesus' mother's sister." If true, that would make James and John cousins of Jesus!

Is that possible? Perhaps. It's logical, based upon the three accounts, although not airtight proof. But it is an interesting possibility nonetheless. If they were indeed related to Jesus, James and John would have had less inhibitions about leaving everything to follow Him. It might explain why Jesus picked the two as part of His inner circle. It makes sense why the two of them along with their mother (who also followed Jesus and ministered to Him) made such a brash request for James and John to sit on Jesus' right and left when He came into His kingdom (Mark 10:35-45). It even gives a possible nuance to the "Sons of Thunder" title (Mark 3:17), perhaps like an old childhood nickname between cousins. And it also gives credence to the account we find in John 19:26-27, of Jesus giving Mary into John's care. If he really was her nephew, that makes a lot of sense.

Ultimately, the Bible doesn't explicitly tell us whether John and Jesus were, in fact, cousins, so we can't say for sure. It does at least give us something to consider. Either way, Jesus loved His disciples and His family members alike, as He loves and cares for each and every one of us!

April

The Secret to Success

April 1, 2019

It's been said that writing is a lonely pursuit, and yet, in the end, it couldn't be done without a lot of team effort. There's a reason most books have a long list of people in the acknowledgments section at the back. Publishing a book is complicated. Writing the manuscript is the easy part. Okay, maybe not *easy*, per se, but enjoyable at least. I love writing the story, arranging the plot like pieces of a puzzle to reveal the finished picture. It's challenging and time-consuming, but I enjoy it. Once that's done, you might think I'm pretty much finished, but alas, this is not the case. Finishing the manuscript is only the first step in a very long process, and can only be accomplished with the help of many others along the way.

Once I reach a point where I'm happy with my manuscript, it's time for multiple rounds of editing. Then there's interior formatting and the book cover to design. There are endorsements and reviews to obtain. It's a good idea to have an up-to-date author website. All these things take time and a certain level of expertise. And I'm honest enough to admit that I don't have the expertise required for some of those things. I need the help of others.

With all these different facets to consider, it's easy to see why writing is a team effort. No author is an island. This can be said of many other areas of life as well, but most notably in the Church. On more than one occasion, the Bible likens the Church to a body with many members. "From Him the whole body, joined and held together by every supporting ligament, grows and builds itself up in love, as each part does its work," Ephesians 4:16 tells us (NIV). Each one of us has a job to do, a gift God has given us to edify the rest of the body. We need one another. Yes, you need fellow Christians, but that also means they need you too.

Perhaps you're tempted to think you don't have anything to offer, or that your talents are less than those of other members. Don't fall for that lie. Some gifts are more visible than others, but that doesn't mean behind-the-scenes workers are less important. My name is on my books as the author, but I couldn't have published them without my editor. I can't write reviews for my own books, so I have to depend on my readers to do so. My circle of acquaintances is limited, so I rely on my friends and my launch team to help publicize my books and tell other people about them. My success as an author depends on other people.

Does not the same hold true in the Church? How often do we see the same members filling multiple roles because there are so few volunteers? People who aren't gifted with teaching are guilted into doing Sunday School because no one else will do it. Some people use the excuse that they don't volunteer their time because no one has asked them. But the work of the Church is one in which all members can and should participate. The pastor can't do it alone. Each member has something to offer. Even homebound members can pray, send cards of encouragement, and support the mission of the Church with their offerings.

There is one important difference between my success as an author and the success of the Church—it doesn't depend on us. God is the one who causes His Church to grow. But He chooses to use us, His children, to be His hands and feet in the world. Whatever your service looks like, it is valuable—teaching, singing, praying, serving on the altar guild, bringing food to members who have experienced loss… The possibilities are endless. And *everyone* can spread the Good News to those around them.

You are part of a vital team effort, my friend. Never doubt that God has given you exactly the right gifts, and He will help you use them to serve Him as you serve others, trusting that He will grant eternal success.

When Doubts Assail

April 2, 2018

What were the disciples thinking? After all they'd seen Jesus do, after all His miracles, after all His teaching, did they *still* not get it? He'd spoken openly to them about His death and resurrection, so why were they surprised when His body wasn't in the tomb? They should have been waiting in anticipation at the tomb on Sunday morning, not locked away in hiding. The sad fact is that the ones who remembered Jesus' promise of resurrection were His enemies—the chief priests and Pharisees. *They* went to Pilate and told him that Jesus had foretold His resurrection. Their motives were completely wrong, mind you. They pleaded with Pilate to post a guard so no one could steal the body. But the fact remains that they, rather than the disciples, were the ones who remembered Jesus' promise. In that sense, the unbelievers put the believers to shame. Yet now Jesus had risen, and that changed everything.

The disciples had just seen their Lord crucified and die a horrible death. Now what? Would they be next? Their actions were driven by fear. They didn't want to be condemned to the same cruel fate as their rabbi had been, so they did what they thought they had to do—they hid. I wonder what they talked about amongst themselves over those three long days? Do you think any of them, in the back of their minds, mused, *You know, He did say He would rise from the dead. Is it possible...?* Did any of them voice the thought aloud? Or were they too scared that they'd misunderstood His meaning or that He wasn't really who He said He was?

But while the disciples were hiding, the chief priests and Pharisees were acting. They weren't afraid to be mocked for listening to Jesus' words. Quite the opposite, actually. They were probably afraid, deep down, that maybe—just maybe—this Jesus actually *could* be the Messiah. What if He *did* rise from the dead, as He'd supposedly raised Lazarus? What would that mean for them? Impossible, yes, but what if His disciples were thinking along the same lines and decided to steal the body and pretend He'd risen? That was much more plausible than a man actually rising from the dead. So not only did they post the guard, they then paid off those guards to spread the lie of Jesus' body being stolen. Their actions were completely wrong, but they were a step ahead of the disciples in taking Jesus at His Word.

What about us? When does fear give way to cowardice? When do we refuse to cling to God's promises for fear of being disappointed? Do we doubt God's Word because He isn't acting according to our own timeframe? Whatever our reasons, there's one thing for certain: the enemy is under no doubt. The enemy, Satan, *knows* God will keep His promises. He knows, because he's already been defeated. He is keenly aware of Christ's imminent return, and that his time is short. So while we're hiding behind our doubts and excuses, Satan is acting. He "prowls around like a roaring lion, seeking someone to devour," as 1 Peter 5:8 reminds us. Those who oppose the Gospel are not scared to speak openly against Christianity, yet we Christians are often timid in our witness to the world, afraid that we'll be mocked or offend someone. So instead we sit quietly, saying nothing, while others mock and offend our faith and the Lord Himself.

Take courage, friends. When Jesus appeared to His disciples, He didn't yell at them for not believing Him. Rather, He gave them His peace, and with it, His power. He breathed on them and gave them the Holy Spirit. He sent those cowering disciples into the world to spread the Good News with boldness and confidence. And they did. Of those disciples in hiding that Easter morning, all but one of them became martyrs for Jesus. They may have doubted Jesus when He died, but no longer. By God's strength, they held firm to their faith even unto death. Why the change? Because Jesus had risen.

And that changed everything.

Drive-Thru Communion

April 6, 2020

Three months ago, the idea of drive-thru communion would have been absurd. Most people would snort and roll their eyes, thinking that this is just one more case of how busy our society has become, always looking for convenience. But since the COVID pandemic, drive-thru communion has become fairly common, people lining up to receive the body and blood of Christ from a masked and gloved pastor. Really, it almost sounds comical, like something you'd see in a bad movie. But in the absence of an actual church service, pastors have had to get creative in ministering to their flocks, and church members have had to rethink the way they worship.

Living in a parsonage has its perks. We had front-row seats to the entire drive-thru communion drama this weekend. My kids were able to spy on the cars lining up and report to me how many were there. We could see my husband (the pastor) and the two elders, all wearing masks and gloves. In fifteen-minute segments, two to four cars lined up for a mini service, complete with confession and absolution, a couple Bible readings, and the Lord's Supper.

I wish you could have seen it. The big picture, that is. The folks in their cars had only a limited view. To them, it was a congregation of less than ten people, sitting in cars with their windows rolled down as their pastor shouted words with proper "social distancing." Perhaps some of them felt like it was a letdown compared to an in-person church service. But in reality, it was one of the most beautiful things I've ever seen. People just kept coming. We have a fairly small dual parish in the country, many of whom are older and didn't want to risk coming out even for this. Yet despite that, there was a great turnout for communion. Just as one set of cars finished, another few cars drove up to take their place. It brought tears to my eyes to see how valuable this was to my fellow brothers and sisters in Christ. They made the effort to come out to partake of the body and blood of their Lord and Savior, even in an unconventional setting.

Like the folks in the individual cars, we can't see the big picture either, even if we're participating in a huge church service with thousands of people present. Our view on this earth is extremely limited. The invisible Church throughout the world is so much bigger than we can imagine, and that *still* isn't a big enough view. When we worship, we sing with the angels and archangels and all the company of heaven. Think about that! The Church includes all believers who have come before us, from Abel to David to Peter to the Church Fathers to your grandparents. We're worshiping with all saints of all times and all places, even when we can't perceive that.

We may not always have the advantage of being surrounded by fellow believers or being able to congregate in our churches. This year, we might think our Easter worship is a letdown. But Christ *is* present with His people nonetheless. He meets us where we are. Even in cars for communion.

Quenched

April 7, 2014

On the surface it seems like such a mundane thing to say, hardly worth recording in Scripture. "I thirst," Jesus says from the cross. Well, yeah. He'd been beaten severely. His back was ripped to shreds; blood was streaming from His head, hands, and feet. He'd lost a lot of bodily fluid, and was therefore dehydrated. So of course He was thirsty. That goes without saying. But Jesus wasn't talking only about His physical thirst. He was thirsting spiritually for our salvation.

"After this, Jesus, knowing that all was now finished, said (to fulfill the Scripture), 'I thirst.' A jar full of sour wine stood there, so they put a sponge full of the sour wine on a hyssop branch and held it to His mouth," John 19:28-29 records. Jesus "knew that all was now finished." What, exactly, was finished? His work on earth. His work of salvation for you was complete. As He hung there upon the cross, He knew His task of coming as the sacrifice for sin was complete. And even in His dying moments, He was still fulfilling prophecy. Specifically, Psalm 69:21, which says, "…for my thirst they gave me sour wine to drink."

I doubt the sour wine quenched Jesus' thirst, because He was thirsting for something else: the "cup of God's wrath," as we read in Isaiah 51:17-23. In this passage, God was calling the Old Testament people of Israel to repentance, pleading with them to turn from their sins. "You who have drunk from the hand of the Lord the cup of His wrath, who have drunk to the dregs the bowl, the cup of staggering…Thus says your Lord, the Lord, your God who pleads the cause of His people: 'Behold, I have taken from your hand the cup of staggering; the bowl of My wrath you shall drink no more'" (Isaiah 51:17, 22).

Jesus drank that cup of wrath. In the garden of Gethsemane when He was wrestling with His Father in prayer, He asked "Father, if You are willing, remove this *cup* from Me. Nevertheless, not My will, but Yours, be done" (Luke 22:42, emphasis mine). He knew exactly what the cup of God's wrath was. Now, hanging on the cross, that's the cup for which He thirsted.

If you've ever been really parched you know that it's all you can think about. Your tongue feels swollen, thick in your mouth. You may get a headache. You can't get your mind off of one thought: "Must. Have. Water." Thoughts of getting that drink consume you until at last you are able to sip that wonderful quenching liquid. That's what consumed Jesus' mind when He was thirsty on the cross. He was parched physically, yes, but more important, He thirsted for God's cup of wrath. Jesus' thirst for you was all He could think about. That occupied His mind entirely. He was suffering in your place, and His thoughts were consumed with your salvation. He knew death was not the end, for in the not-too-distant future stood the empty tomb, declaring His victory over sin and death for all mankind.

He thirsted for you, and through His death and resurrection that thirst has been quenched. He drank the cup of God's wrath to the bitter end so that in return He could offer you His living water.

Running Out of Time

April 8, 2019

I'm running out of time. The closer I get to the launch date for *Faith Alone*, the less ready I am. I'm about to drive my formatter crazy with the last-minute changes I'm making. Why am I *just now* noticing how often I use certain words and phrases in dialogue between characters? And doesn't this need to be hyphenated? Oh, and this word needs to be italicized. And how did we miss that comma through all the rounds of editing? For a "final" proofread, I sure am finding a lot of changes yet to be made. In some ways, I feel like the editing could go on forever.

This is hardly an unusual phenomenon. I was the same way with *Grace Alone* a few years ago. I was still suggesting changes and ways to improve the story when it was being sent off to the printer. And looking back, there are things I would have done differently had I published that book today. It's a good thing I have deadlines. Otherwise, I'd be stuck in a phase of perpetual editing, constantly finding things to tweak. But here's a little secret: my manuscripts will *never* be perfect, and if I wait for a state of perfection, I'll be waiting forever. At some point, an author has to just say, "This manuscript may not be perfect, but it's where I am as a writer right now, and I'm happy with it. Enough excuses already. Let's get this thing published."

Writers aren't the only ones who make excuses. Perhaps you make excuses when it comes to sharing your faith, arguing that you aren't ready yet. *I can't talk to the Jehovah's Witness at my door because I don't know the Bible well enough to back up my beliefs,* you might think. *I want to establish a better friendship with my neighbor before inviting her to church. I don't want to scare her away or get all preachy on her,* you may reason. Or maybe you've convinced yourself that praying for a person's change of heart is enough rather than taking the bold step to witness to them. Perhaps you think it's the pastor's job to deal with conflicts amongst church members, and so turn a blind eye to fighting rather than urge the parties to reconcile. All of these reasons sound entirely logical. But in the end they're just excuses.

The truth is that none of us will reach a point where we feel completely ready and prepared to share the Gospel. Moses wasn't ready either, yet God used him to lead the Israelites out of Egypt. Jonah sure wasn't ready, and even tried to run away from God, but God used his message to bring the cruel Assyrians to repentance. Peter was an uneducated fisherman, not a smooth-talking theologian, but God worked through him to spread the Good News of Jesus to countless people, and even to write two books of the Bible.

You may not think you have anything to offer. You may think you aren't ready. But if you wait until you *are* ready, you'll run out of time. Besides, whatever objections you may raise, God begs to differ. *He* has equipped you with saving faith and has promised to give you the words to say. Mark 13:11 assures us, "When they bring you to trial and deliver you over, do not be anxious beforehand what you are to say, but say whatever is given you in that hour, for it is not you who speak, but the Holy Spirit." I hope you never find yourself being arrested and brought to trial for your faith, but the promise stands: the Holy Spirit will speak through *you*. That's the best possible preparation of all. One might even say it's perfect.

Everything that Hinders

April 9, 2018

I'm going through something of a mid-life crisis right now. Oh, don't worry—I'm not running off to buy a cherry-red convertible. I wouldn't be able to fit all my kids in it anyhow. Nor am I scheduling a facelift quite yet. It's more of what you might call a time of reflection. Not long ago I attended the funeral of a woman who was twice my age. That was sobering. What if half of my life is already over? Am I living to my fullest potential? Then I thought about my kids. One of them only has four years left at home. Am I teaching him the skills he needs to be a responsible adult? Have I instilled strong morals? Have I equipped him to be a faithful witness to a world hostile to the Christian faith? Have *I* been a faithful witness? Has my life been fruitful?

Time is our most precious nonrenewable resource. But even though we know it's limited, it's so easy to waste. It's so very easy to procrastinate because we reason, "There's always tomorrow." And so, too often, we put aside our good intentions for another day. *Tomorrow I'll spend some one-on-one time with my spouse… When the kids are all in school I'll start volunteering… I'll invite my neighbor to church when…* We push things off until a future time, but the longer we push them off, the less chance we'll actually do something about those intentions.

I rather suspect this is what the writer of Hebrews is talking about when he says, "…let us throw off everything that hinders and the sin that so easily entangles, and let us run with perseverance the race marked out for us" (Hebrews 12:1, NIV). Notice that the things that hinder aren't necessarily sinful. "Everything that hinders *and* the sin…" he says. So what is hindering you in your race? Is it fear? discontentment? your job? technology? other commitments? Perhaps you're so busy with all your kids' activities that you don't have the energy to drag them to church on Sundays or maintain your own devotional and prayer life. Perhaps you spend more time on technology than you care to admit, to the detriment of your relationships. Whatever your specific situation, I'm sure you can think of something that is hindering you in your Christian walk.

Lest we get discouraged, read on in Hebrews 12:2: "Let us fix our eyes on Jesus, the author and perfecter of faith, who for the joy set before Him endured the cross, scorning its shame, and sat down at the right hand of the throne of God" (NIV). *You* are His joy. He endured the cross so you could be reconciled to God and could spend eternity in heaven with Him. Oh, the devil tried his hardest to hinder Jesus from fulfilling that mission, but Jesus would not be deterred.

There will always be hindrances in the world. The devil will use anything to distract us from the things that really matter. But our solution is easy—fix our eyes on Jesus. Follow His example. When He was overwhelmed with demands on His time, He withdrew to pray. As busy as He was literally saving the world, Jesus took the time to pray to His Father. If we do likewise, we can trust that God will direct our steps to fulfill *His* purposes in our lives. He will clear our minds of the things that hinder and help us focus on the things that really matter in life. And yes, He will even sustain us through a midlife crisis.

Buried Treasure

April 10, 2014

I had no idea what I was getting into when I had kids. I knew all the answers, of course, and *my* kids would be little angels. I'd never let them eat in the car, they would eat their fruits and vegetables, they would get along with each other, and they would listen right away when disciplined. My rosy vision of life with children was a far cry from reality. All of my expectations above fell short. My kids *do* eat in the car, they don't always eat their fruits and veggies, they fight with each other, and they sure don't listen right away when I have to discipline them. Not only that, but along the way I find myself in situations I never would have imagined before my children were born. These things range from the humorous to the absurd to the poignant. Let me give a few examples of what I mean.

Before I had kids…

- I figured it would be a challenge to get everyone out the door in time for church, but I never would have foreseen going to church in pants because I only shaved one leg after my baby made it past the barricade I erected for her in the bathroom and crawled into the walk-in shower with me.

- I knew I would be cleaning up after them, but it never occurred to me that within the span of five minutes my daughter and I would spill the same bowl of Cheerios three times.

- I guessed someday I'd play make-believe with them, but I never would have dreamed that I would be carrying on a conversation with three paper plate leprechauns named Seamus, Daniel, and Cliff as I made eggs for brunch.

- I figured they would do silly things, but I never imagined one of my children would stand on the street corner begging for money with a handwritten sign that said "We are pore," even as he stood there in a full Sunday suit.

- I knew they would break things, but I never imagined they would stuff rocks down our clean out line, backing up our sewer in the winter when the ground was frozen, requiring the whole thing to be dug out at great cost.

- I was fully prepared to kiss their boo-boos, but I never knew how heart-rending it would be for me when one of them had an emotional scar I wouldn't be able to kiss away.

There's no doubt about it, parenthood changes a person. There are days when bedtime can't come fast enough. There are days when I want to give up. There are days when my kids are cranky and whiny. There are days when *I* am cranky and whiny. It's tough, often grueling work, raising kids, and many of us second-guess ourselves far too often. *Am I doing this right? Should I be doing more with my kids? Less? How many activities should I let them do at one time? I should have handled that differently…* The doubts assail, sometimes overwhelm, us. But just as there are days that seem to overwhelm you, there are also moments that stand out gloriously, among the ordinary (or not-so-ordinary!) moments of everyday motherhood. *God Moments*, I call them, and they often come when I'm least expecting them but most needing them.

Before I had kids…

- I knew I would teach them about Jesus, but nothing prepared me for the emotions I experienced when my baby first pointed to a cross on her own and said, "Jesus!"

- I knew I would sing hymns to them, but I never dreamed my five-year old would be singing along with the CD in the car at the top of her lungs the words of "Holy Spirit, the Dove Sent from Heaven."

- I hoped and prayed that our home would be one where we spoke naturally about our faith, but I couldn't hold back the tears when I overheard my then eight-year-old hold up a baby Jesus figurine from the nativity scene and say to his six-month-old sister, "Do you know who this is? That's your Savior!"

- I knew we would pray together as a family, but I never realized how mature my children would be about their prayers, even asking me on bad days if they could pray for me.

There's a prayer I hear every so often in church that has always intrigued me. It asks God to allow parents to "see in their children the treasures You have buried there." What does that imply? That children's talents and abilities are hidden? That often appears to be true. I don't look at my kids every day and see great potential. When I'm trying desperately to get supper ready and my boys are fighting, my preschooler is whining, and my baby is tugging at my pants to be picked up, quite honestly I'm not thanking God for the treasures in my children.

But those treasures are there. Not just talents they will later develop, like music or art or sports, but attitudes and personalities such as those from my second list above. *God Moments* give us glimpses of those spiritual treasures God has planted in our children through their baptisms. I am often humbled by my children. I learn lessons from them nearly every day. They teach me about forgiveness, love, faith like a child, and so much more.

There's no doubt about it, my children have changed my life, in ways beyond scheduling and eating and playing. They give me a compelling reason to live out my faith. They are observing and picking up on far more than the words I teach them. It's a daunting task, but we don't have to go it alone, parents. Just as our kids need a Savior, so do we. And He is with us every step of the way, forgiving our mistakes, granting us strength and wisdom, and encouraging us through His Word. He does it for our children and He does it for us. We are all forgiven and redeemed children of the same Heavenly Father.

Of course we had no idea what we were getting into before we had kids. But we *do* know that God, the perfect parent, is on our side. Keep your eyes open, because you just never know when your Heavenly Father will allow you a glimpse of the treasures He has buried in your precious children.

Inconceivable

April 13, 2015

How would you feel if you knew you would meet a Nazi in heaven? After all, some of these guys committed unthinkable crimes and implemented programs that caused the murder of millions of human beings. Almost everyone you ask would probably come to the same conclusion—if anyone deserves hell, they certainly do. And yet, like it or not, you will meet a few Nazis in heaven. Inconceivable? Absolutely.

Recently I read a book called *Mission at Nuremberg,* written by Tim Townsend. This book relates the little-known story of LCMS Army Chaplain Henry Gerecke, who was asked to consider a prison ministry position. Rev Gerecke was no stranger to prison ministry. In fact, he had quite a successful prison ministry going in St Louis before he left for chaplaincy during World War II. But this was no ordinary prison. This would require him ministering to the twenty-one high-ranking Nazis who were on trial for crimes against humanity. He would be ministering to hardened men like Hermann Goering, Wilhelm Keitel, and Albert Speer. And he would be sharing the Good News, talking about the Jewish Savior to men who had just tried to annihilate the Jews. Not an ordinary task by any means, and Gerecke had his qualms. It would be like a pastor today being asked to witness to a group of ISIS terrorists. Who would really *want* to do that? After prayerful consideration Gerecke did take the position and ministered to these men during the months of the Nuremberg trials. Believe it or not, a handful of those men came to saving faith in Jesus. Men who had planned the extermination of millions of people repented of their sins and were forgiven by the Creator of the universe. Inconceivable.

That's not the first time God has forgiven people with such a sordid history. Think of the prophet Jonah, who was called by God to preach to Nineveh. Today that doesn't mean a whole lot to us, but it was a frightening enough call for Jonah to try running away. Nineveh became the capital of Assyria around 700 BC, and the Assyrians were the terrorists of their day. They were brutal and merciless in their war tactics, uprooting entire populations of conquered peoples, and torturing and mutilating defeated leaders. It was to these people Jonah was called. I don't blame him for trying to run away! So of course there's the whole exciting episode of him getting swallowed by the fish, but the rest of the book intrigues me far more. Jonah goes to Nineveh and proclaims that their evil deeds and violence are bringing their own doom upon them. Amazingly, the people repent and turn from their ways for the time being, and God relents! He has mercy on them and spares them from certain destruction. He actually forgives those people. Inconceivable.

But that's not the end of the story. How does Jonah react? Does he rejoice that these godless people have turned from their evil ways to believe in the one true God? Not at all. He gets mad at God. So mad, in fact, that he tells God he wants to die! "I knew that You are a gracious God and merciful," he says, "slow to anger and abounding in steadfast love, and relenting from disaster" (Jonah 4:2). He's mad that God is compassionate and forgiving. Inconceivable.

Before you go judging him for his hardheartedness, take a look into your own heart. Would *you* want to minister to those Nazis at the Nuremberg trials? Are you rejoicing that some of them repented and went to heaven? Would you want to see some ISIS terrorists in heaven someday? Would you rejoice to see a serial child molester repent and come to faith? What if it was someone who did an unthinkable crime to you or to someone you love? I'm not at all sure I can answer those questions with a resounding "yes." I'm no better than Jonah, getting mad at God for His mercy. To me, it's just too incomprehensible, too inconceivable, that God could forgive such terrible sins. Someone ought to pay for those sins. Someone should suffer for them.

And thankfully, Someone has.

Jesus died for your sins. It's a refrain we hear again and again, and if we truly believe that, then we have to believe that it's true for *all* people. Jesus didn't just die for "petty" sins. He didn't just hang on the cross for people who go to church every week and try to live a good life. He died for people like that thief next to Him on the cross who only came to faith in his final hours, after living a terrible and godless life. Inconceivable? Yes. But so is the entire salvation story. God becoming man to live a perfect life for us and suffer, die, and rise again for our justification? Absurd. But that's exactly what Jesus did. His death covers the sins of *all* who believe in Him, no matter what those sins might be. He died for you. He died for me. He died for the murderer in prison who has since repented and come to faith. He died for those Ninevites. He died for those Nazis. Absolutely inconceivable. But absolutely true.

Live Like You're Dying

April 14, 2014

My father, a pastor, has been with a number of people who are on their deathbeds. He's even been with people at the moment of death. One particular instance was a fourth-grade boy who had a debilitating disease. As he lay gasping his last few breaths, his parents asked him, "Who loves you?" This dear boy replied, "Jesus." Then his eyes opened wide as he pointed to the corner of the room. No one else saw anything, but my dad is certain that the child saw Jesus or an angel coming to take him home. What a lovely way to face death, in faith and peace, with Jesus in sight and Jesus' name on his lips, following the example of Jesus' own final words.

> *Father, into Your hands I commit My spirit.*
> *Luke 23:46*

As Jesus' death quickly approaches, He is still quoting Scripture, this time from Psalm 31:5. He is committing Himself in calm assurance to the Father's care. We mirror that attitude with a fair amount of frequency in our own lives as Christians. Every time we sing the Nunc Dimittus, we commit ourselves to God's care and ask for His peace, quoting the words of Simeon: "Lord, now You are letting Your servant depart in peace, according to Your word" (Luke 2:29). Childhood nighttime prayers and Luther's evening prayer also commend us into God's hands for safe keeping.

All our lives we make a habit of commending ourselves to God's loving care so that when death comes, we need not fear it. We know we can depart this earthly life with confidence and in peace, for we have been living under God's faithful care all along. In a sense, then, all our lives we are practicing for death.

If you are in Christ, death has no power over you. Yes, we will all die an earthly death, but that is not the end. Jesus commits His spirit to the Father. When your final hour comes you can do the same. Your spirit belongs to the Lord. Because Jesus defeated death for you, death for a Christian is no more frightening than sleeping. So one day, when your own death draws near, commit yourself to your Savior's care and fall asleep in Jesus.

Dirty Socks

April 16, 2018

My socks told the story. The bottoms were more brown than white, with black specks and crumbs peppered generously all over. They were rather disgusting. So I knew it was time to steam mop. I pulled out the mop and worked my way through all the tiled sections of our house, which is everything but the bedrooms. I felt a great sense of accomplishment, but then realized I was still wearing my dirty socks. Well, that wouldn't do. I went to my room and opened my dresser to pull out another pair, and I hesitated. I had a couple pairs of brand-new socks, but did I really want to wear them? Any dirt left would certainly show up on those. Frankly, I didn't want to know if the floors weren't completely clean after all that effort. So I reached instead for a pair I've had for a while. Clean, but slightly discolored on the bottom. It would be better not to know.

Ridiculous, isn't it? But I'd be willing to bet most of us do this same thing in terms of our spiritual housekeeping. We go to church, confess our sins, are assured of God's forgiveness, and breathe in a grateful sigh of relief that God has cleansed us. We are forgiven! How wonderful! But let's not start looking too deeply into the corners of our lives where sin still lurks. It's better not to know about those dirty corners, or at least to ignore them and pretend they don't exist.

In Psalm 139:23-24, David pleads, "Search me, O God, and know my heart! Try me and know my thoughts! And see if there be any grievous way in me, and lead me in the way everlasting!" Whoa, David. Hang on a second. You're *asking* God to examine your heart for sin? I'm not sure I'm ready for that. It's so much easier to know I'm forgiven than to face up to my hidden sins.

Why examine our hearts for sin, anyhow? Is God trying to shame us? Quite the opposite, actually. He wants to save us. James 1:15 warns that "desire when it has conceived gives birth to sin, and sin when it is fully grown brings forth death." God knows that sin—*any* sin—has the ability to lead us down the path of ultimate destruction, and He loves us too much to allow that to happen. Romans 6:16 reminds us that "you are slaves of the one whom you obey, either of sin, which leads to death, or of obedience, which leads to righteousness." I'd much rather be controlled by God's Word than by my pet sins. So I can pray confidently with David that God would search me and know my heart, because I know God's ultimate plan—that He would lead me in the way everlasting. *That's* the path I want to travel.

But I think I'll put on clean socks first.

Tetelestai

April 17, 2014

How does it feel to pay off a bill that's been looming over you? A mortgage, a car, student loans, credit card debt… It's a liberating feeling to officially pay off a debt. If you lived in New Testament times, the Greek word *tetelestai* would have been written on business documents or receipts to indicate that very thing—your bill had been paid in full. And that's the last word Jesus utters from the cross: *Tetelestai!"* The price for sin has been "paid in full."

To understand the implications of His last word from the cross, we need to understand a bit about the grammatical structure of the Greek word itself. *Tetelestai* has a perfect passive indicative structure. English majors may nod in understanding, but let's simplify that for the rest of us. Basically it means that *this was a one-time event with ongoing results.*

Since I rather suspect few of us today are Greek experts, let's break down the English equivalent we have in John 19:30, "It is finished."

It.

What does Jesus mean by "it?" *What* exactly is finished? His work of salvation, the task for which He came to this earth. Jesus is quite clear throughout His earthly ministry about His purpose in taking on human flesh. John 6:38, 40 says, "I have come down from heaven, not to do My own will but the will of Him who sent Me…For this is the will of My Father, that everyone who looks on the Son and believes in Him should have eternal life, and I will raise him up on the last day." Or again, Jesus asserts in John 10:10-11, "I came that they may have life and have it abundantly. I am the good shepherd. The good shepherd lays down His life for the sheep."

Throughout the Gospel accounts, Jesus foretells His suffering and death many times, even though the disciples didn't really get it until after His resurrection. He was adamant all along that He came to suffer and die for us, and on the third day to rise again. So when Jesus said on the cross, "It is finished," He meant that the work of salvation was finished. The sacrifice for sin was complete. Our debt to sin had been paid in full.

Is.

What does this little word mean? It's caused a bit of confusion in recent years, the meaning muddled by politicians who debate the exact meaning. So it's important to remember that the Greek is in the perfect tense, meaning completed. If I say, "It *is* raining," that only means that at the moment it happens to be raining. It doesn't imply that it will be raining tomorrow or the following week or the rest of the year. We know that. But when I say, "I *am* a woman" or "He *is* a man," I'm not indicating a temporary state. I am a woman at this exact moment, but I will be one tomorrow and next year and the rest of my life. That's the perfect tense. So when Jesus says, "It *is* finished," He is declaring that the action has already been completed, and the results are ongoing. Jesus completed the work of redemption, and now we reap the benefits.

Finished.

When I was in college I had to do a senior recital as a requirement for my music major. I practiced and practiced. Then finally came the big day. I performed the recital in front of an audience and then I was done. I was finished. I didn't have to practice those pieces anymore. I didn't have to perform that recital one more time just to be sure it "took" the first time. I was done. I had completed the requirements. So it is with Jesus' sacrifice. It is *finished.* There's nothing more that needs to be done. Jesus leaves no room for the view that "Jesus started it, but I have to finish it in my life by…" No. *He* did *everything* needed for your salvation. You don't have to add one single thing. He meant what He said.

It. Is. Finished.

Jesus' dying word on the cross is in fact a word of life. His death means life for you. *Tetelestai.* Your sin debt has been paid in full. You owe nothing. Jesus' crucifixion was a one-time event with ongoing results. *It is finished* for you now and for all eternity.

The Sun in Darkness Hides

Bonus Post

Imagine yourself at the foot of the cross. Jesus, the Son of God, is dying. He was crucified at the "third hour" (Mark 15:25), which is 9:00 AM. He hung on the cross for about six hours, and Mark 15:33 tells us that "When the sixth hour had come, there was darkness over the whole land until the ninth hour." From noon, when the sun should have been at its peak, until 3:00 PM when Jesus died, there was darkness instead. Luke 23:45 adds an interesting detail: "while the sun's light failed." This wasn't just an overcast sky—there was *darkness over the whole land*. This was a significant event, and creation itself knew it.

While we confess God the Father as the Creator, John 1:1-3 asserts the following: "In the beginning was the Word, and the Word was with God, and the Word was God. He was in the beginning with God. All things were made through Him, and without Him was not any thing made that was made." Jesus is rightly called the Father's agent in creation. And so it is fitting that while Jesus died, the sun hid itself in darkness. It couldn't bear to watch its Creator die.

The failure of the sun to shine was not an accident or a well-timed coincidence like an eclipse. This all took place during the Passover celebration, which occurred during a full moon. An eclipse is impossible during a full moon. This was a deliberate act. Continuing in John 1, we read: "In Him was life, and the life was the light of men. The light shines in the darkness, and the darkness has not overcome it" (vv 4-5).

Jesus, the light of the world shone out in stark contrast to the darkness there at the cross on Good Friday. And guess what? *The darkness did not overcome Him.* No, dear one, all the powers of evil and darkness could not overcome Jesus, for He rose victorious three days later. No matter what darkness seems to prevail in your own life, remember this—Jesus' light is more powerful. His light will always shine through.

An Adoption Story

April 20, 2015

Recently my cousin and her husband adopted a baby. They had been waiting and praying for a child for a long time, as had their family and friends. It was difficult to wait, difficult not knowing when or even if they would have a child of their own. But at last the wait is over, and they have a son. Although he was born to a different mother, he is now legally their child in every way. The adoption papers are complete, and he shares their name and their home from here on out.

Here are a few truths about adoption:

1. *Adoptions are planned.* You hear of unplanned and even unwanted pregnancies, but I've never heard of an unplanned adoption. Adoptive parents choose deliberately to adopt; it doesn't just happen by accident.

2. *Adoption is expensive.* Most adoptions are also rather costly. There are fees to the adoption agency, and if a couple adopts a child from another country, they also have to pay airfare and other expenses to get to that country to take their new child home.

3. *Adoption is a rescue.* Another thing that holds true for most adoptions is that the adopted child has been rescued from a less-than-ideal life. Most children who are given up for adoption are either orphans or are born to mothers who are incapable of raising them for one reason or another. An adopted child may be rescued from a life of poverty, substance abuse, neglect, or life in an orphanage or series of foster homes. They are adopted into homes of loving parents who can provide for them emotionally and materially.

4. *Adoption is legal and binding.* The adopted child becomes the legal child of his or her adoptive parents. Once the papers are complete, the birth mother can't get the child back. He or she has a new name and belongs to new parents. They don't have to fear that the child will be taken away from them.

There's no question about it—adoption is a beautiful thing. This is especially comforting, because you and I are adopted as well. Ephesians 1:5 tells us, "In love [God] predestined us for adoption as sons through Jesus Christ, according to the purpose of His will…" We are adopted by God Himself into His family! And all of those characteristics that I listed above apply to those of us who are adopted Christians.

1. *Adoptions are planned.* Back up a verse to Ephesians 1:4 to see what God's Word tells us about this. "He chose us in Him before the foundation of

the world to be holy and blameless before Him." Think of that! The only perfect parent in the world deliberately chose us as His children even before the world began. Titus 1:2 reiterates that point: "A faith and knowledge resting on the hope of eternal life, which God, who does not lie, promised before the beginning of time" (NIV). We weren't around before the time began, so to whom did God promise this? To the Son! From all eternity, the Triune God has longed for, planned, and worked to establish our salvation. God's work of salvation was no mere accident. He did it purposefully and intentionally.

2. *Adoption is expensive.* It wasn't cheap or convenient for God to adopt us. It cost Jesus His very life. Jesus offered His perfect life as the only acceptable sacrifice when He died on that cross. He suffered God's wrath in our place and rose victoriously from the grave three days later. Like many earthly parents who adopt, God went to great lengths to adopt us as His own. Yes, it was expensive, but it was worth the cost to Him. *You* were worth the cost.

3. *Adoption is a rescue.* We weren't God's children by nature, you see. The brutal truth is that we belonged instead to sin, death, and the devil. But God rescued us from that way of life, which leads only to eternal death. Colossians 1:13 tells us, "He has rescued us from the domain of darkness and transferred us to the kingdom of His beloved Son." What a rescue indeed!

4. *Adoption is legal and binding.* Those of us who are Christians now bear Christ's name, and a new home awaits us in heaven. Sure, the devil will try his hardest to get us back, but he no longer has any claim over us. We are covered in the blood of Jesus, which is more legal and binding than any adoption documents here on earth. We need not fear that the devil can claim us any longer, because our Father won't let that happen. We are His children now.

Whether or not you have been adopted by earthly parents, never forget that you have been adopted by God Himself. He deliberately planned your adoption as His child, He has paid the price for you, He has rescued you from a life of despair and hopelessness, and you are His child now in every way. Your Heavenly Father chose you, and He's not going to let you go.

Meeting Together Apart

April 20, 2020

I sat in my car with my five children, rain steadily pelting the roof, the windows slowly fogging up from our warm air inside. We had only a limited view of the other cars around us in similar situations. My husband was leading a drive-in church service and had partially retreated to the open door of the church to avoid the rain. We could see neither him nor our fellow worshipers on Sunday morning, but we could hear him over a local radio frequency that had a limited range barely reaching the edge of the parking lot. This has become the new normal. Drive-in church.

I admit, it's a letdown. My five-year-old, who was never terribly well behaved in church anyhow, no longer has to sit on my lap during the service, so he slides on and off his seat in the car. My other kids, who are generally very good during church, now take the opportunity to whisper side comments or slouch back in their seats or take off their shoes. Sitting in our car doesn't have the same effect as sitting in a church building with other congregants around us and the organ accompanying us for hymns. Listening over a radio frequency just isn't the same.

Whether you do drive-in church, watch live-stream services on Facebook, listen to the radio, or watch church on TV nowadays, chances are your worship time looks very different than it did six months ago. Certainly, it's a wonderful blessing that these alternate means of worship are available to us, and I'm grateful that technology is being used in productive ways to reach out. But still, it's different.

When we got home from church on Sunday, my husband got a text from an older member of our congregation, who said, "I enjoyed the service this morning! Thank you for being the only one who got wet, as I sat in front of the church on ground that once had a ground water well providing drinking water for horses and mules that were transportation for getting people/children to church/school. And also drinking water for attendees of both church and school. God has brought this church through many changes/crises through its 100+ years existence including many major disease outbreaks—God is good!"

What a beautiful perspective! This dear woman reminded me that things around us are constantly changing, but one thing will never change. "The Word of the Lord remains forever," 1 Peter 1:25 reminds us, quoting from Isaiah 40:8. "Jesus Christ is the same yesterday and today and forever," Hebrews 13:8 assures us. We might struggle to adapt to new ways of worship, but God's Word is not hindered, and more importantly, His Word never changes. The message of the cross and resurrection are always the same.

Over the course of history, God's people have always found innovative ways to meet together. In the early Church, small congregations had to meet in the catacombs in secret to avoid detection by authorities during a time when Christianity was illegal. There are many parts of the world still today where the Church is persecuted, and people meet together at odd times of day and in small groups to avoid detection. There have been periods of history when the Church weathered particularly heinous times, such as Nero's Rome and Nazi Germany. Even during these times—*especially* during these times—Christians still met together whenever possible.

Why do Christians go to such great lengths to meet and worship together? Because God's people are meant to be together. God created us for fellowship with Him and with one another. One day, hopefully sooner than later, we will be able to meet in our church buildings again. But God never promises us this. Indeed, many Christians in the persecuted Church could only dream of such a luxury. What God does promise is that He will be with His Church, working through His Word, to sustain it. Cling to the certainty that He is with you always—even in a fogged-up car in the rain—to the end of the age.

Where Flowed the Water and the Blood

Bonus Post

Crucifixion was a grisly affair. The Romans had invented and perfected this cruel form of capital punishment. Criminals who were hung upon the cross died a painful and slow death. To avoid suffocating, they pushed themselves up with their feet so they could breathe, but that in return caused the nails in the feet to rip through the flesh. It was a cruel cycle. In order to hasten death, the Romans finally broke criminals' legs so they could no longer push themselves up to breathe. Jesus, however, died before they had to break His legs, but these were professionals. They had to make sure this guy was really dead, so they pierced His side.

I'm not a medical expert by any means, but what happens next surprises me. "One of the soldiers pierced [Jesus'] side with a spear, and at once there came out blood and water," we read in John 19:34. Blood, sure, that I understand, but *water?* That's rather bizarre to me. But that goes to show this wasn't just a little poke. This spear plunged deeply into Jesus' side, straight to the pericardium (the sac that surrounds the heart) and the heart itself. Jesus had been beaten badly, was faint with loss of blood and bodily fluids, and was likely going into shock. The sustained rapid heartbeat from this shock also causes fluid to gather in the pericardium. This is called "pericardial effusion." Thus, water and blood both flowed after His side was pierced.

I suppose this oughtn't surprise us. Jesus' earthly ministry was all about water and blood. When did Jesus' ministry begin? At His baptism, with water. When did His earthly ministry end? With His death. In blood. John is deliberate in pointing out the water and blood connection in his Gospel account, but also in 1 John 5:6: "This is He who came by water and blood—Jesus Christ; not by the water only but by the water and the blood."

Jesus' ministry through water and blood didn't end with His death. Even today, the Sacraments revolve around water and blood. We baptize in the name of the Triune God. We eat His body and drink His blood in Holy Communion. We are saved by the water and the blood as we look in faith upon Him whose side was pierced for us.

If It Was Finished on Good Friday, Why Do We Need Easter?

April 21, 2014

Years ago my husband and I took a vacation to Florida. One morning as we were on our way to breakfast we got stopped by this guy who offered us free breakfast and a gift card for listening to a short presentation. Being still rather naïve, we agreed, only to find out it was a sales pitch for a timeshare. And despite what he had said, this was not a short presentation. We were in no position whatsoever to be investing in a timeshare at that point in our lives, but the salesman kept reiterating one point throughout his speech. He said it so often we still joke about it. With a timeshare, he pointed out, you get a deed. When you stay in a hotel, "All you get is a receipt."

All you get is a receipt. So what's wrong with that? I get a receipt every time I go to the store. It's proof that I actually paid for the things I am taking out of the store. If I buy a cartload of stuff and still set off the alarm at the doors of a store, I show my receipt to the worker there to prove I'm not stealing anything. I paid for that stuff. It's mine.

Recall that the Greek word *tetelestai* means "paid in full." It's a transactional word, one that was stamped across bills when they were paid off. Jesus' redeeming work was completely finished on that cross. So why was Easter even needed? Because Easter is the proof that the Father accepted the payment of the Son on the cross, the "receipt," if you will. It's God's guarantee that Jesus' sacrifice was indeed enough.

Let's look at the Old Testament sacrificial system to grasp this a bit better. Jesus' sacrifice took the place of that entire complex system, so it's worth taking a deeper look. The Old Testament people of Israel had numerous types of sacrifices and offerings for different occasions and purposes. It was a lot to keep straight. But the Day of Atonement was a high holy day in their worship year. Once a year, atonement was made for all the sins of the Israelites. Only on this one day of the year could the high priest enter the Most Holy Place. He went in to sprinkle the blood of the sacrifices on the ark of the covenant. This was serious business, because anyone who offered sacrifices in an unworthy or unauthorized way would be put to death. They had to follow God's command exactly if they hoped to live.

So seriously did the Israelites take the Day of Atonement that they tied a rope around the waist of the high priest when he entered the Most Holy Place. If he were to die while inside, they could pull him out so no one else had to go in and risk death themselves. So every year when the high priest emerged from the Most Holy Place alive, that was their "receipt." It was proof that God had accepted the sacrifices and forgiven their sins. Their sins had been paid for, and the high priest walking out alive was their receipt.

Hebrews 9:11-12 makes the connection to Jesus, the ultimate High Priest who offered not a bull or goat for a sin offering, but sacrificed Himself for us. "When Christ came as high priest of the good things that are already here, He went through the greater and more perfect tabernacle that is not man-made… He did not enter by means of the blood of goats and calves; but He entered the Most Holy Place once for all by His own blood, having obtained eternal redemption" (NIV).

As High Priest, Jesus made atonement for the sins of all the people of the world. Like the Old Testament high priests, Jesus entered the very presence of God when He made atonement. He offered the ultimate sacrifice—Himself. And God accepted that sacrifice, because three days later Jesus emerged alive. As the Old Testament believers rejoiced when their high priest came out of the Most Holy Place alive, so we now rejoice that God accepted the sacrifice of Jesus, our High Priest. Easter is our receipt that Jesus' sacrifice was accepted. Our debt to sin has been paid in full by Jesus. We are His. The empty tomb is our proof.

With Easter, all you get is a receipt. And that's all we ever need.

Who Do You Think Jesus Is?

April 23, 2018

Who do you think Jesus is?

The question was addressed to my sixth grader in an email from a friend and classmate. "Mom, what should I write?" he asked me. Half a dozen responses popped into my head, but I bit my tongue. "What do *you* think you should write?" I asked instead. I wanted to see what he would come up with on his own. After all, it's a fairly basic question for a Christian; one that any of us could be asked at any time. So how would you answer?

People have been wondering who Jesus is for about 2000 years. In fact, Jesus Himself asked His disciples that question. In Matthew 16:13-20, they enter the region of Caesarea Philippi. This was an especially pagan area, thought to be the place of a shrine for the Greek god Pan. As they enter this heathen area, Jesus asks the disciples, "Who do people say that the Son of Man is?" (Matthew 16:13). This is a safe question. Easy. The disciples rattle off the answers—John the Baptist, Elijah, Jeremiah or one of the prophets.

But then Jesus aims the question at *them*. "But what about you? Who do you say I am?" (Matthew 16:15, NIV). Suddenly it's become incredibly personal. I wonder how this scene played out in real life. How long did the disciples clear their throats and avert their eyes before Peter spoke up? Or did he boldly answer right away? I know that if someone asks me pointblank who Jesus is, I experience a moment of panic. *What do I say?*

So how about it? Who do *you* say Jesus is? Peter's answer is succinct and serves as a fine creed. "You are the Christ, the Son of the living God" (Matthew 16:16). He clearly proclaims Jesus as the promised Messiah for the world. It's a great response, and Jesus tells him that this was no man-made answer, but had been revealed to him by God in heaven. Peter's faith was a gift from God, and on that confession of faith—that "rock," Christ's church was to be built.

Peter later expounds upon this illustration of the foundation ("rock") of faith in 1 Peter 2:4-10. He asserts that we are "living stones being built up as a spiritual house" (2:4), built upon the cornerstone of Christ Jesus. Two thousand years later, that hasn't changed. We as God's people still hold to the confession that Jesus is the Christ, the Son of the living God. Certainly, we can expound upon that answer if the situation calls for it. But the good news is that it's not something we make up on our own. God has given us the faith to confess Him before others.

Getting back to my son, I watched him as he thought about how to respond to his friend. He goes to a public school, and doesn't have many friends who are Christian. I was amazed that one of his friends had asked about Jesus, and I was dreadfully curious as to how my son would reply. At length, he typed back, "He's God, Savior of the world, all knowing, all powerful, and all merciful." Amen, son. Thank God He has made you part of His house of living stones.

Ministering to Miscarriage

April 24, 2014

"I'm bleeding," I wrote in my journal six years ago. Those two simple words carried with them a world of pain and sadness. I wasn't writing about a cut on my hand. This was a wound that wouldn't heal so quickly or neatly. You see, I was pregnant. Well, I *had* been pregnant. I wasn't sure what to say now that the bleeding had started. This wasn't just a bit of spotting, either. I knew right away what was happening, but I couldn't even bear to write the word: *miscarriage*.

Few things are more personal and more devastating to a woman than to suffer through a miscarriage. It is typical for a woman who has had a miscarriage to feel keenly a sense of failure. After all, it was *her* body that somehow "caused" it. What had she done wrong? Let me first tell you this, dear one: miscarriage is *not* your fault. I know your head knows that, but making the heart believe it is something else entirely. "Yes, but it's my body," you might say. "There must be something wrong with my womb. If only I'd..." And that's a dangerous path to go down, my friend. Trust me, I've been down that path myself. The fact is that there are a lot of early miscarriages for no apparent reason. It's the result of living in a fallen world. The harsh realities of sin are ugly and far-reaching. This is not a punishment for some secret bad thing you've said or done, nor is it an indicator of some failing on your part or your body's part. Because of the Fall, we all have to live daily with the reminder that life here will never be perfect. It makes the promise of heaven that much sweeter to the Christian.

Next, please be assured that you are not alone. I didn't realize until I had my miscarriage how frequent early miscarriages are. When the topic was brought up at one of our MOPS meetings recently, over half of us indicated we had suffered at least one ourselves. It's amazing to know how many women have experienced them. And honestly, the number is probably higher, because for those women who have erratic periods and didn't think to take a pregnancy test, they may well have had a miscarriage without ever knowing they were pregnant. They may have thought it was just a late period. Does it make it easier to know it is so common? No. But it does give the knowledge that you are not alone. There are other women out there who can support you through this.

So how do we deal emotionally with a miscarriage? In my efforts to find comfort I looked for information on the internet about causes, support groups, etc. What I found was quite unhelpful; calloused, even. There seems to be a general sense out there that if you lose a child early on (first trimester), it isn't all that big a deal. "Well," people tend to think, "at least it wasn't when you were eight months along." Physically speaking, yes. But emotionally? A life is a life no matter what stage of pregnancy. That baby had a soul from conception, so those questions of "now what?" arise to trouble the Christian conscience.

Allow me to share some things that helped me deal with my pain. Though it might sound counter-intuitive, don't try to push your pain away. Live through it. It's painful and horrible, but pour out your feelings to God. Don't try to fake pious platitudes of how "God knows best" and "He has His reasons." Yes, those are true, but they aren't helpful in dealing with your raw emotions right now. Be honest with yourself and with God as to how you're feeling, and don't let others tell you how you "should" respond.

Depending on how far along you were and how many people know about it, you may have many or only a few people reach out to you at this time. An article I once read on loss helped me keep things in perspective. The article said that people will say all sorts of things and give all sorts of advice to you, and much of it is unhelpful or even hurtful. Just know that they mean well and are doing their best (even though it may seem otherwise!) to give you comfort. Remember that they care about you and are showing their support, even if what they say falls short.

One important relationship to consider at this point is that with your husband. I actually got a little resentful at my husband because it seemed like he wasn't as upset as I thought he should be, and that made me mad! I wanted him to show he cared, that he was grieving too. He is not by nature an overly demonstrative person, but I wanted him to be in this case. It wasn't until we had a little memorial service and he started to choke up that I knew how much this had hurt him as well. We were finally able to be open with each other, and it was very therapeutic. But it taught me an important lesson as well. Different people handle grief differently. Just because my husband wasn't dealing with it the same way I was didn't make his way wrong or bad. Be honest with each other. Tell your husband what you're feeling and let him tell you how he's coping with it too. At this point, you need to be on each other's side, supporting each other unconditionally.

A miscarriage, as any pregnancy, will change your life in ways that are impossible to measure. I don't say that to sound flippant or overly dramatic, but consider this. If I hadn't miscarried when I did, I certainly would not have gotten pregnant three months later with my now five-year-old. I would have had that baby instead. And likely if I had carried that baby to full term the spacing would have been different between him or her and the next baby, so our youngest as we know her probably wouldn't be here either. And here's where we can't think too much about it. We are human. We cannot presume to give answers from God. Am I "glad" for my miscarriage, knowing that otherwise my two youngest wouldn't be here? I really can't answer that. It's dangerous territory. All I can say is that God is God and He provides for His children even out of a bad situation. Out of grief and loss He gives healing and new life. That is the Gospel. Out of our own spiritual death He granted us eternal life in His Son. We don't understand His ways, and that's a good thing. It keeps us from trusting too much in our own wisdom and points us instead to Him.

I've saved the best for last. The single most helpful thing for me in my healing journey when I miscarried was something my husband told me. As I mentioned, we had our own memorial service for our baby, in which we read Scripture and prayed and cried. My husband gave a little "homily," and he told me that even at that early phase, before the ears were formed on our baby, that child was exposed to and "heard" the Word of God. He or she was present in church with me, listened to the Bible stories we read to our older kids, heard the hymns we sang and the confession of faith in the Apostles' and Nicene Creeds. Although with man this seems impossible, the power of the Word of God is that "faith comes from hearing, and hearing through the word of Christ" (Romans 10:17). That baby heard the all-powerful, ever-living Word of God. The Holy Spirit is not confined to working faith in hearts of babies who are out of the womb. Yes, we grieve and struggle with the question of what happens to the soul that dies before baptism, and ultimately we cannot answer that question with 100% authority, but we entrust the child's soul to the mercy of a gracious God, knowing that the Holy Spirit can work through the Word to bring life and salvation even to those in the womb.

Miscarriage is awful, no doubt about it. Pour out your emotions to God, surround yourself with people who care, and work through the pain in your own way and in your own time. I pray that God grants you the strength and peace that only He can give, dear sister in Christ.

A Time for Silence

April 28, 2014

Most people are uncomfortable with silence. There's something very awkward about it. As an organist, I love the MIDI component in our organ that allows me to pre-record a song and play it when I go up for communion. Before it was installed, I dreaded those silent two minutes like you wouldn't believe. I felt like everyone was staring at me, waiting for me to get back on the organ bench. But with quiet music playing in the background, everything seems better. The same holds true in conversation. We all dread those awkward lapses when no one has anything to say. We try desperately to fill the void with pointless one-liners: "Nice weather, huh?" We just have to say something, *anything* to fill the silence. But sometimes silence is a good thing.

Recently a friend told me devastating news on her end that literally left me speechless. I racked my brain for something to say and came up completely blank. (That's rare for me, by the way. I'm a writer and I'm supposed to have a way with words, so you know things are desperate when even I can't think of a response.) After a while I finally realized something important. Sometimes the most powerful way to communicate is to say nothing at all.

I've been on both the giving and the receiving end of comfort during hard times, and I've learned more by being on the receiving end. When we went through a particularly hard time in our lives a few years ago, people tried to be supportive by encouraging my husband and me. This is a kind thing to do, but a lot of people said things that weren't helpful. I've learned never *ever* to start a phrase with, "Well, at least..." If you're talking to someone who has just received news that their cancer is aggressive and terminal, don't try to make them feel better by saying, "Well, at least you've led a full life so far." When talking to someone whose loved one died unexpectedly, don't say, "Well, at least she's in a better place." None of those responses are helpful. Never try to compare someone's situation with a worse scenario. Even if the things you say may have a nugget of truth in them, grieving people aren't ready to hear them. It only makes them feel worse, as if they should somehow be *thankful* that their situation isn't worse than it is.

Avoid as well pat answers and clichés. When our family was going through that hard time, I can't tell you how many times I heard "This, too, shall pass..." and "God has a plan" and "You just have to trust God in this, Ruth." Again, none of those things are inaccurate, but now is not the time to say them. They aren't helpful because someone who is overwhelmed by their circumstances simply isn't ready to hear them yet. There is a time and place for these phrases, but now is not that time. It made me feel guilty when people said them to me, like my faith was weaker than it should be. And let's be honest, they are usually said (or at least taken) in a slightly condescending way. "Sweetie, I know your life is at its lowest point right now, but this too shall pass. You just need to trust God through it all. He has a plan!" It's salt in a wound. I felt like a kid again, being gently chastised by a parent for my poor response. It simply isn't helpful.

So what *should* you say to someone who is facing something overwhelming? Here's a novel thought—don't say anything. The most powerful response I got when I felt like my world had just been turned upside down was my dear friend who simply hugged me and cried with me. She didn't say a word. She didn't have to. Just her presence and support was enough. Try it. Go to a doctor's appointment with a friend whose diagnosis is grim. Sit with her in the waiting room and hold her hand. Hug your friend who just had a miscarriage and cry with her. Bring a meal to your friend whose loved one died unexpectedly. Let her vent if she needs to while you listen quietly.

The Bible tells us in Ecclesiastes 3:7, "(there is) a time to keep silence, and a time to speak." That can be a difficult thing to discern. But throughout the Bible there are examples of the power of silence. Habakkuk 2:20 says, "The Lord is in His holy temple; let all the earth keep silence before Him." Zephaniah 1:7 says, "Be silent before the Lord God!" and Zechariah 2:13 tells us, "Be silent, all flesh, before the Lord, for He has roused Himself from His holy dwelling."

Even Jesus, who spoke the very words of life, knew when to be silent. At His trial, He remained silent. "Like a sheep that before its shearers is silent, so He opened not His mouth" (Isaiah 53:7). And yes, even in social settings Jesus knew when not to speak. Think about the time He went to Bethany after Lazarus had died. When Mary fell at His feet and told Him in anguish that had He been there, Lazarus would not have died, Jesus was deeply moved, but asked only, "Where have you laid him?" (John 11:34). And when they showed Him the tomb, Jesus wept. He didn't give some great discourse or use that moment to teach a lesson (although He certainly could have). He showed His support and love by standing with Mary and Martha and crying with them.

In a world full of noise, sometimes the most powerful messages are conveyed through silence. Offer your shoulder to cry on instead of offering pious platitudes. It's enough to know that someone is there for you, and that they care enough to be silent.

Signs of Spring

April 28, 2014

It's been a long, hard winter. Most of us in North America experienced a harsher winter than usual, thanks to Arctic blasts that kept temperatures well below normal and gifted us with more snow and ice than we've had in some years. Schools had many cancellations and delays, forcing make-up days that will extend well into June. But even though the winter came at us hard, and we thought it may never end, spring is on its way. Yellow daffodils and purple hyacinths are out in full bloom. Our resident robin who built her nest on our drainpipe just hatched her four eggs. The grass is green instead of brown. The snowy days have given way to rainy ones. Our forsythia bush is starting to get yellow flowers on the end of the branches. Our magnolia tree is starting to bud. There's no mistaking it. Spring is finally coming.

But not all of us are experiencing spring. Some of us have been stuck in a figurative season of winter so long we no longer remember what spring feels like. I've been there for a long time. It's been a long, hard winter, and at this point I'm starting to wonder if spring will ever come.

I know there are those of you who know exactly what I mean when I refer to a "winter" period of life. I imagine there are also people who don't get that analogy because they've never experienced it themselves. Have you ever been hit with devastating news that knocked the breath out of you or even turned the course of your life around? That's winter. And sometimes the best you can hope for is to just survive. Bundle up, hunker down, and live one day at a time. It's hard. Really hard. Winter's icy blasts make it difficult, even painful, to breathe sometimes. Trudging through the deep snow saps your energy. You start to believe that winter will stick around forever. But there's hope. Spring is coming.

In the Church Year we just sojourned through the long, somber season of Lent. We suffered through the harsh realities of the events of Good Friday; events that included suffering and death. You can't get much more "winter" than that. But just as sure as spring buds follow the snows of winter, so Easter follows Lent. Yes, Jesus died on that cross. Yes, it was our fault. Yes, we *should* feel our guilt over that cold reality. But that's not the end of the story.

After death came life. Jesus burst forth from that tomb a mere three days later. To the disciples, those three days must have felt like an eternity, but in retrospect it was really a short time. The empty tomb is our promise of spring, our guarantee that someday we too will live forever in heaven, in eternal spring, so to speak.

But in the meantime, here we are. We *aren't* experiencing eternal spring. Some of us are still in the dreary season of winter. What can we do? *Bundle up, hunker down, and live one day at a time.*

Bundle up. When it's cold out, we wear layers of clothes to keep warm. Do the same in a figurative winter. Only instead of clothes, bundle yourselves with the armor of God, as we read in Ephesians 6. Wear the belt of truth, the breastplate of righteousness, the shoes of the Gospel of peace to help you stand, the shield of faith, the helmet of salvation, and the sword of the Spirit, which is God's Word. Search the Bible for comfort, encouragement, and God's promises. Bundle yourselves with the power and warmth of God's Word so as to withstand whatever storms life throws at you with your faith intact.

Hunker down. Ground yourself in prayer. After discussing the armor of God, Paul exhorts us to "pray at all times in the Spirit, with all prayer and supplication" (Ephesians 6:18). I've found that in my own winter season I've prayed more than ever before. I've found comfort in Scripture in ways I never could have imagined when I was blissfully enjoying the warmth of spring. And even if my exterior circumstances have been less than ideal during my winter season, anything that drives me to my knees and to God's Word cannot be a bad thing.

Live one day at a time. Remember and take Jesus' words to heart: "Do not be anxious about tomorrow, for tomorrow will be anxious for itself. Sufficient for the day is its own trouble" (Matthew 6:34). God gives you strength enough to get you through each day. That strength comes from the armor He provides. Paul tells us to "put on the full armor of God, that when the day of evil comes you may be able to stand your ground, and after you have done everything, to stand" (Ephesians 6:13, NIV). He exhorts us to *stand,* not to *advance.* Because of Jesus, we are *already where we need to be.* Yes, we will face struggles in this earthly life, and the whole purpose of the armor of God is this: God doesn't leave us alone in our struggles here. He gives us this armor to protect us from the devil's assaults so that one day we *will* see the realization of the faith Jesus won for us.

1 Peter 1:3-5 is a beautiful passage that is bursting with signs of spring. "He has given us *new birth* into a *living hope* through the *resurrection of Jesus Christ* from the dead, and into an inheritance that can *never perish, spoil, or fade*—kept *in heaven* for you, who through faith are shielded by God's power until the coming of the *salvation* that is ready to be revealed in the last time" (NIV, italics mine). Peter continues, "In this you greatly rejoice, though now *for a little while* you may have had to suffer grief in all kinds of trials. These have come so that your faith...may be proved genuine and may result in praise, glory, and honor when Jesus Christ is revealed" (1 Peter 1:6-7, NIV). It may not seem like it, but the trials we face on this earth are temporary. Compared with eternity, yes, these trials on earth last only a "little while."

I don't know what your "winter" season is. I don't know if you're already in spring or if you're still stuck with me in winter. Some people's winters are shorter than others. Just like our daffodils bloom before our magnolia tree, so some people enter spring earlier than others. And I can't make any promises that this side of eternity you'll see spring again. You may not, honestly. But regardless, look to the empty tomb. Look to the promises of God in His Word. The signs of spring are there. Yes, dear one, spring is coming.

To the Mom Whose Kids Misbehaved in Church Yesterday

April 29, 2019

I heard your kids yesterday in church. Like, through the entire service. I saw the displeased glances people exchanged and the dirty looks a few people shot your way. I know you were embarrassed and frustrated and probably wish you'd just stayed home. I'm sure you personally didn't get much out of the service. Perhaps you left early to avoid people making comments to you about their behavior afterward. But I wish you'd stayed, because I have something very important to tell you: *Thank you.*

Trust me, I get the challenge of bringing children to church. I'm a single mom in the pews myself. Just because my kids were (mostly) well-behaved yesterday doesn't mean they always are. We've had our share of awful services ourselves, where I've left either fighting tears or seething at my children. I get how hard it is to keep active children quiet and still for that length of time, while trying to teach them what church is all about.

Let me give you a little encouragement: *It won't always be this way.*

I know that's not helpful at this exact moment, with your preschooler and toddler competing to be heard over the organ, but keep the end goal in mind. While my four-year-old still has his moments in church (throwing a tantrum during the sermon because I won't let him go in the kiddie pool in February, say), my teenagers know exactly what to do in church. My ten-year-old brings her Bible and finds the readings on her own so she can follow along. My six-year-old knows the liturgy by heart and is starting to sing the hymns if I point to the words as we go. Your kids won't always be this age, and if you teach them now that church is a priority, they'll catch on (hopefully) sooner than later why we're doing this in the first place.

Come to think of it, why *are* we doing this in the first place? Because Jesus said, "Let the little children come to Me, and do not hinder them, for the kingdom of heaven belongs to such as these." Those words are so important they're recorded three different times in the Bible: Matthew 19:14, Mark 10:14, and Luke 18:16.

The kingdom of heaven belongs to such as these.

Children are a reminder of our status before God. Just as children are completely dependent upon their parents, so are we completely dependent upon God. As children display absolute trust in their parents, so ought we have the same faith in God. Think of a child flinging himself out a tree into his parent's waiting arms. He has no doubt his mommy or daddy will catch him.

The Bible calls believers "children of God," and I've long thought that can be either positive or negative, depending on the situation. Yes, children have absolute trust in their parents and depend upon them for everything, but children can also be…well, children. They fight, they whine, they throw tantrums… In short, they need the discipline of a loving parent to correct them and guide them on the right path of life. Who among us is any different? We may not throw ourselves on the ground kicking and screaming, but we whine about life being unfair, we complain to God, we fight with those around us. We need the correction of a loving God to show us a better way. What a beautiful reminder of life in the family of God, to see and hear children in church!

Years ago, my dad (a pastor) was teaching confirmation class and told them they had to memorize the Apostles' Creed by the following week. They started complaining that it was too long, so my dad brought in my kindergarten brother, who rattled it off in front of them perfectly. One of the students said, "Yeah, well, that's because he's in church every week." Bingo. That's exactly right.

Don't fall for the lie that kids don't get anything out of church. They may not be able to tell you what the sermon was about, but one day they'll surprise you. After my grandmother's funeral some years back, the Gospel reading the next Sunday was the raising of Lazarus, with Jesus' promise, "I am the resurrection and the life" (John 11:25). My three-year-old looked up at me and said in wonder, "Mommy, that's for great-grandma!" I didn't even know he had been listening.

Do you see how powerfully God's Word works in the hearts of children? And *that's* why I bother, week after week, month after month, year after year.

Stick with it, Mom. I know it's frustrating. I'm sorry if you saw a few dirty looks or overheard any snide comments. I've gotten a number of those over the years myself. But please don't let that stop you. You're doing the right thing, bringing your kids to church to hear about their Savior. Thank you for caring more about their spiritual welfare than their current temperaments. Thank you for not allowing them to dictate whether or not you bring them to church. Keep at it. And someday, when your kids find themselves in a similar situation with their own children, pass this letter along to them. God bless you.

Sincerely,

A Fellow Mom

Where is God, Anyhow?

April 30, 2018

It was a confounding problem. It was dinnertime, there were over 5000 hungry people, and they were in a desolate location with little to no food immediately available. So the disciples naturally urged Jesus to send everyone away to fend for themselves. They looked to Him to make things right, and He did. But not at all in the way they were expecting. He told them calmly, "You give them something to eat" (Matthew 14:16).

Um, Jesus? All we have here is five loaves and two fish. That won't even feed the thirteen of us. Still, Jesus meant what He said. He directed everyone to sit down on the grass, blessed the food, and had the disciples distribute it to everyone there. Everyone was fed, and there were twelve baskets of leftovers. Way to go, Jesus! And clearly, yes, He deserves all the glory for the miracle. But there's something we're missing if we stop there—the role the disciples played.

Fast forward 2000 years, and here we are in a world very different from the world in which Jesus walked. Yet some things remain the same. In times of crisis, we still look to God, frantically begging Him to fix things, wondering what He's going to do. This world is a mess. Wars, terrorist attacks, persecution, hunger, and disease are just some of the problems people in the world face on a daily basis. Those of us in America who hold to conservative ideals may wonder at the state of our country. How have we come to a point where abortion is allowed, homosexual "marriage" is legal, and education programs for public schools are incorporating the LGBTQ agenda? Where is God in all this, anyhow? How could He allow it to come to this?

You give them something to eat.

Jesus' response to the disciples is somewhat shocking. He reminds them of their own responsibility in the matter. They brought Him the meager food supply they could find, and Jesus multiplied it. Then they were the ones to distribute that to the people, marveling as they went how the food never ran out. *They* were Jesus' hands and feet. And so it is for us today.

You give them something to eat.

Brothers and sisters, *we* are the ones who are here. We are God's Church on earth, in this specific time and place. Each of us brings his or her own talents and interests and abilities. Jesus blesses us so we may use those talents to further His kingdom. We dare not sit idly on the sidelines, waiting for God to take action. We are here. We can do something. We can speak out against abortion and gay rights and immorality. We can write our representatives. We can volunteer or support pro-life organizations with our monetary donations. We can fight hunger and poverty in our communities. We can be Jesus' hands and feet as the disciples were. And we do so in love, gently pointing others to Jesus, who alone can offer healing and hope.

You give them something to eat.

Nor do we stop with social matters. Remember also Jesus' parting command to His disciples. "Go therefore and make disciples of all nations..." He says in Matthew 28:19. We are also Jesus' hands and feet to spread the Gospel, not just by praying for pastors or sending money to missionaries. Yes, do those things. But look around your own community as well. Who will tell your unchurched neighbor about Jesus? Why not you? *You* are here. You can do something. Go. Tell. Tell them about Jesus, the Living Bread, who alone can satisfy their hunger.

So where is God in this messy world? He is here. He is in His Church, working through His children. Working through *you,* dear brother or sister.

You give them something to eat.

May

A Screwtape Curriculum

May 1, 2017

My Dear Headmaster,

I am flattered and humbled to find that my proposed curriculum has attracted much attention, even so much as to pique the interest of Screwtape himself. I am proud to say that these methods have yielded excellent results in America, and I believe they would prove useful in training up our youth at Underworld University. Allow me to highlight the core classes and summarize each of them briefly for your consideration. I have thousands of success stories to back the effectiveness of these techniques, and I would be happy to appear before the committee to present the ideas personally. Paired with other standard core classes such as Complacency and Entitlement, I assure you, these make a deadly combination that many in the Enemy's clutches cannot resist. So without further ado, here are my recommendations.

1. **Affluence.** In other parts of the world we have tried the opposite of this—poverty. Yet I cannot help but note with a bit of alarm that very often the Enemy's servants are quite willing to live with less. We've even paired physical persecution with poverty, but alas, the strategy has not proven as effective as we'd hoped. The weaker servants of the Enemy fall away, yes, but those firmly in His clutches hold tighter still to His inane promises of how suffering on earth will give way to eternal glory in Paradise. Such poppycock! But they fall for it nonetheless and gladly endure poverty and suffering, even to the point where some of our own defect to the cause. We have seen far too many painful examples of persecutors turning from our side to the Enemy's.

But affluence is another matter entirely. I have found a delightful paradox at play here—the more money a patient has, the less charitable he tends to be. This is especially true of those in the middle-class. Although the American middle-class has more money than most of the rest of the world, many are refreshingly tight-fisted. Remind them that they need to save for vacations, college educations, retirement, and just plain old pleasure. Tantalize them with all the "toys" out there—bigger cars, better homes, summer cottages, new clothes, the latest technology—the list goes on and on. Convince them that they cannot possibly save the world and so there's no need to bother contributing to charity or even worse, the Enemy's Church. I cackle with delight when an Enemy's servant splurges on an outing to the spa or the country club one day and then slips a five-dollar bill into the offering plate the next. Indeed, the mindset is starting to take root that material wealth and possessions are far more to be desired than helping one's neighbor or supporting the wretched Church.

2. **Busyness.** I find that busyness goes hand in hand with affluence. Those patients who can afford it (and those who pretend they can) will keep themselves busy with everything from their toys to their activities. Parents will put their children in every conceivable activity—sports, music, drama, dance, summer camps, and so on. Throw in both parents holding full-time jobs and volunteering for worthy causes, and they'll quickly fray. Yes, even encourage church activities. All the better! They burn out and get resentful that everyone takes them for granted and that their service in the Enemy's cause really isn't worth it. Patients buckle under the stress of jobs, running their children from one thing to the next, volunteering, meetings, cooking, cleaning, socializing, and trying to figure out how to squeeze in family time to "relax." It's quite amusing, in fact. Some even choose to blog about their chaotic lifestyle, ironically adding more to their workload. Hold up one more tantalizing activity in front of them, and their eyes widen—*I must have this, even though I cannot possibly fit in one more commitment.* But patience is critical here. Slowly build up a patient's stress level and eventually they will cave in. Church attendance will slip and sometimes fall into neglect altogether. Private and family devotions and personal prayer are among the first casualties as well. Convince them that if they listen to a semi-religious podcast or radio station during the week that this is good enough to feed their "spiritual" needs. Trust me, many in the Enemy's camp have slipped into complacency and indifference as a direct result of the busyness of their lives.

3. **Technology.** This is a wonderful tool that has been efficiently wielded by many in our cause. With the continued advance of technology and the increasing access patients have to the Internet, it is quite possible to lure them in for hours at a time, shutting others out entirely as the hours fly by. It is not difficult to convince them that technology is imperative to their enjoyment of life. There are so many different ways to use technology to our advantage that it really merits four classes—one for each year of instruction. Start with Movies and TV to dull their sense of morality by constant bombardment of swearing, violence, and promiscuity. Then move on to Social Media, which is a goldmine of opportunity. This flows naturally into Addiction—patients become so obsessed with social media, blogs, gaming, and the like, that they don't realize they are addicted to the glowing screen. I have seen entire families ignore one another while staring at their own technological devices at a so-called family meal. What a glorious sight to behold! And top all that with a class on Vices, and you have a winning combination. Admittedly, this one is a challenge, especially for staunch servants of the Enemy who are instilled with a strong sense of the Enemy's standards. But I can cite for you a number of success stories where even such servants eventually cave in to online temptations. Pornography tops the list. They naïvely believe no harm can come from it, so if a pop-up from a website flashes across their screen enough times, they just might click on it out of curiosity. And then the rest, as we say, is history.

4. **Tolerance.** I've saved the best for last. This strategy has proven wildly effective, even beyond the predictions of some of our seasoned field workers. But it is imperative that this be an upper-level class. Patients can only be effectively indoctrinated once they have bought into the notion that the media is accurately portraying the feelings and beliefs of the majority of the country. They must see that many people are promoting tolerance on social media and that those who disagree are immediately and forcefully condemned. To my great delight, even entire church bodies have wholeheartedly accepted behaviors and lifestyles that are explicitly forbidden in the Enemy's Handbook, all under the guise of "Christian love." Naturally, those who are loyal servants of the Enemy will not be easily persuaded, but they can be made examples to the weaker servants. Slander their reputation and livelihood and so thoroughly chew them up that others are shamed into silence and acceptance. Human beings are incredibly prideful and often even the threat of being mocked is enough to cause them to keep their opinions to themselves. Introduce tolerance slowly enough that they buy one white lie after another, rather than feeding it to them all at once. Their consciences will be silenced ever so slowly, and it becomes that much easier to win the patient to our cause.

As for electives, I see no need to change the course offerings on Resentment, Discontent, and Family Relationships, but I suggest adding Relevancy as well. The Enemy's subjects can be surprisingly eager to throw out His Handbook in favor of topics they consider to be more "relevant" to their daily lives. They claim they tire of hearing the same message every Sunday, namely that of His Incarnation and Passion. This is wonderful news for us, since we know the power that unfortunate episode holds over us. But His servants need not know that. Let them believe there is more value in hearing positive and upbeat sermons about how they can lead better lives on this earth. Basically, keep the focus on themselves and what they can do, rather than on the Enemy and what He has done.

I could go on, but I understand you are busy in considering all your options for next year's curriculum. Thank you for the opportunity to explain my proposal, and please feel free to contact me with any questions or for further clarification.

Your humble servant,

Muddlegrub

Through the Storm

May 4, 2020

The disciples should have known better. Granted, they were in the middle of a fierce storm at sea, and the waves were filling the boat. These men, more than a few of whom were fishermen, were no strangers to sailing, but this storm was beyond their expertise. And somehow, through it all, the one person who could do anything about it was sleeping through it! So they woke Jesus and asked, "Teacher, do You not care that we are perishing?" (Mark 4:38b). You can almost hear the panic in their voices, the accusatory look in their eyes trying to mask the fear. But they should have known better because, you see, Jesus had already made them a promise.

Back up a few verses to Mark 4:35. "On that day, when evening had come, He said to them, 'Let us go across to the other side.'" On the surface of it, there's nothing particularly special about these words. It's a teacher making a suggestion to his followers. But this is Jesus talking, and His Word has power. It *will* do what He says. So Jesus isn't suggesting something. He's promising them what is going to happen. They *are* going to the other side of the lake. But in the midst of the storm, the disciples forgot that promise and focused not on the destination but on the obstacles that were in the way. To their credit, they knew where to turn for help. They prayed to their Savior, and save them He did. But He also chided them for their little faith. "Why are you so afraid? Have you still no faith?" He asks them in Mark 4:40, after stilling the wind and waves with His Word. They'd been around Jesus long enough to see countless miracles, to know His teaching, yet still they doubted when faced with danger. How silly.

But how like us.

It's easy to trust God when things are going well. It's easy to think we're in control of our lives when life is humming along as planned. But then disaster strikes, and we suddenly become like those disciples, pointing an accusatory finger at God and asking if He even cares. What do we do when faced with a serious health diagnosis? What about when we lose a job? Then it's not so easy to trust that God knows what He's doing. "Lord, don't You care that we're almost out of money for groceries?" It's much more difficult to cling to God's promises that He will take care of us when our bank account is perilously low and we have no income to expect in the foreseeable future. It's all too easy to lose sight of the opposite shore when we're going through the storm.

This is when we need to turn to the Scriptures to remind ourselves of God's promises. The disciples had a clear promise for that specific occasion. They *were* going to the other side. We don't have that specific a promise for every occasion. We aren't guaranteed that we won't get terminal cancer or that we won't run out of grocery money or that our rent will always get paid on time. The fact is that we live in a sinful and fallen world, when pain and suffering and death is a reality. But Jesus *does* promise us a far greater destination than crossing a lake—He already has our eternal home prepared.

In John 14:2-3, Jesus promises, "In My Father's house are many rooms. If it were not so, would I have told you that I go to prepare a place for you? And if I go and prepare a place for you, I *will* come again and *will* take you to Myself, that where I am you may be also" (emphasis added). The Greek word used for "rooms" doesn't depict temporary housing, like a hotel room. It literally means "dwelling places," which implies permanence. Jesus has our permanent home prepared. He *will* take us there.

Friend, I don't know what troubles you face today. I don't know what burdens you carry or what storm you're weathering. But Jesus knows, and He promises in His Word that nothing can snatch you away from Him. "I give them eternal life, and they will never perish, and no one will snatch them out of My hand" (John 10:28). The very hands of Jesus that were nailed to the cross for you now hold you safe in His care, in His love, and in His salvation. Don't fear the storm. Jesus *will* bring you safely through it to all eternity.

Politically Correct Christianity

May 5, 2014

Be careful of what you say. In a world of political correctness, that's good advice. It's politically incorrect to say that Jesus is the only way to heaven. Those who dare to make such a claim are labeled "intolerant" and "unloving." If we dare to take a stand on a moral or social issue, we start a firestorm and are called "haters." Hence, many Christians have found it easiest to just say nothing. But let me introduce you to a group of people who weren't concerned about being PC. Let's see what we can learn from their example.

The apostles of the early Church were about as politically incorrect as they come. They talked openly about Jesus everywhere they went. Everywhere. In a Jewish synagogue? Yep. In jail with criminals? Check. In...gasp...political arenas? Oh, yes. It was as natural to them as breathing. They wouldn't have considered *not* witnessing. It's who they were. They didn't get to know people first to "earn" the right to witness to them. They didn't offer exciting programs to entice people into their synagogues. They just spoke of Jesus. All the time. Some listened and believed. And yes, they *did* build relationships with people along their journeys. Some became invaluable supporters and partners in ministry with them. But their bluntness also caused them problems. They were thrown into prison, put on trial, flogged, and persecuted for their bold witness. But still they spoke. This news was too good not to share.

We often look back in awe at the amazing rate of growth in the early Church. It was unprecedented and unparalleled since. After Peter's sermon on Pentecost, 3,000 people were added to their number (Acts 2:41). When Peter and John were speaking in Solomon's portico, 5,000 men believed the word they had spoken (Acts 4:4). They were arrested and given the strict charge not to speak again in the name of Jesus. But what did Peter and John do? They returned to their fellow believers and prayed together for strength and boldness to continue spreading the Gospel. And God answered that prayer. Acts 4:31 says, "When they had prayed, the place in which they were gathered together was shaken, and they were all filled with the Holy Spirit and continued to speak the word of God with boldness."

And the Holy Spirit mightily blessed their witness. Consider these passages: "The Lord added to their number day by day those who were being saved" (Acts 2:47). "More than ever believers were added to the Lord, multitudes of both men and women," we read in Acts 5:14. Acts 6:7 tells us, "The word of God continued to increase, and the number of the disciples multiplied greatly in Jerusalem, and a great many of the priests became obedient to the faith."

Consider how the Holy Spirit could bless our witness today if we shared the Gospel as freely as the apostles did. I imagine that if they lived in our culture today they would still be sharing their faith openly. Talking to the clerk at the store who rings up their groceries, inviting their kid's baseball coach to church, witnessing to their server at a sit-down restaurant, telling the kids on the playground about Jesus… In short, talking about Jesus all the time.

That thought may make you uncomfortable. I know it makes *me* uncomfortable. We've been conditioned to believe that there's a time and a place for witnessing, and those instances I mentioned above simply don't fit the criteria. But why not? When your son's coach calls a practice on a Sunday morning, why not say, "We have church on Sunday mornings. If you'd like to come with us, we'd love to have you." Why not strike up a conversation with your waitress at dinner, or tell the kids at the playground the Bible lesson your kids just learned in Sunday school? The point is that there are opportunities all around us, just as there were for the apostles. The difference is that they took those opportunities while many times, we do not.

But do not lose hope. The same Holy Spirit who worked among the early Church is still at work today, growing His Church. Thank Him for that, and make the words of Peter and John your own: "We cannot but speak of what we have seen and heard" (Acts 4:20).

So go, Christian. Be careful of what you say, indeed, because you never know when God will present an opportunity for you to witness. Pray for boldness when those opportunities come. Remember, the good news of Jesus' saving work is too good not to share.

Lambs Among Wolves

May 7, 2018

It's a familiar enough scene: Jesus is sending out the seventy-two into towns and villages ahead of Him, and His words to them are well known. "The harvest is plentiful, but the laborers are few. Therefore pray earnestly to the Lord of the harvest to send out laborers into His harvest" (Luke 10:2). We know the words well, and we pray that God would do just that—send workers into His Church. What could be more rewarding than working as a laborer in God's field?

But we often stop with that verse and fail to read Jesus' very next words. "Go your way; behold, I am sending you out as lambs in the midst of wolves" (Luke 10:3). Wait, *what?* You *do* know what wolves do to lambs, don't You, Jesus? They eat them. That's not exactly something You ought to put right there in the job description. On second thought, maybe I don't want to be sent into the harvest field after all…

Wolves are predators, plain and simple. The picture of sheep among wolves is not a pretty one. Wolves devour sheep. Sheep cannot defend themselves. And a lamb—a baby sheep—is that much more vulnerable. So why does Jesus make this analogy? Can't He think of something a bit more encouraging? He's very upfront with His followers that they *will* meet with resistance. We will not be embraced by the world. The world is relentless in its attack against Christianity. It always has been. Even Jesus' apostles were not immune to this hostility. Tradition holds that all but John met a martyr's death for the sake of Christ. On the face of it, the situation seems very bleak indeed. We are lambs among wolves and cannot defend ourselves. We can't rely on our own strength or cleverness to evade attack. We are helpless.

But…

On their own, sheep would have little to no chance of survival, which is why they need shepherds to care for them. A shepherd's job is not a glamorous one. Shepherds in ancient times lived nomadic lives, bringing their sheep from one pasture to another when the food supply ran out. They stayed with their flock almost constantly, no matter what the weather. They slept with their flock. They protected their flock. They fought off wild animals who would try to harm the sheep. Without the shepherd, the sheep would most certainly die.

Dear Christians, our Good Shepherd is Jesus. He declares in John 10:11-12,14, "I am the good shepherd. The good shepherd lays down His life for the sheep. He who is a hired hand and not a shepherd, who does not own the sheep, sees the wolf coming and leaves the sheep and flees, and the wolf snatches them and scatters them…I am the good shepherd. I know My own and My own know me."

In Luke 12:32, He assures us, "Fear not, little flock, for it is your Father's good pleasure to give you the kingdom." We, His flock, follow our Good Shepherd, who has already given us the kingdom of heaven, and no spiritual predator can ever take that from us.

Yes, we are as lambs among wolves in this world. The world will stop at nothing to snatch our faith from us. But rest assured. You aren't just any lamb. You are *Jesus'* little lamb, and He is your Good Shepherd forever.

How to Change the World

May 8, 2017

Do you realize that you can change God's mind? Consider the Old Testament prophet Amos. Like many other prophets, he warned God's people that destruction was coming. They would be taken into captivity for their gross idolatry and failure to repent. In Amos 7, God shows Amos two visions of the future. In one, a swarm of locusts completely strips the land of all crops. In the other, a fire consumed the land. After both visions, Amos cried out to the Lord and begged Him not to send such calamity upon Israel. And in both instances, God listened to Amos and relented from sending the disaster. Amos' prayer changed the course of history for his nation.

Amos isn't the only one whose prayer moved God to a different course of action. After the golden calf fiasco in the desert of Sinai, God was going to destroy the entire nation except for Moses, but Moses interceded and God relented (Exodus 32:9-14). Again and again in the Bible we are reminded how powerful prayer is. When Abraham's servant prayed for success in finding a wife for Isaac, Rebekah came out before he was even finished praying (Genesis 24:10-21). Likewise, Daniel 9:23 tells us that as soon as Daniel started to pray, an answer was given.

Clearly, there is power in prayer. But let's be honest—how often do we wield this power? My own prayer life is meager at best, consisting of "popcorn prayers," as we used to call them in college. Little snippets throughout the day—*Lord, please bless Ben during his test today...Lord, please be with Helen who is sick.* I try to pray at night while I'm lying in bed but often get distracted and/or fall asleep before I do any real praying. But if prayer is so powerful, think of how we Christians could change the world just by praying. James 4:2 says, "You do not have because you do not ask." Okay, then, let's ask. But how?

Start with the Lord's Prayer. Since Jesus Himself gave us this example, we can be sure it's a good model to follow. Think about the petitions of this prayer: we hallow God's name and ask that His will be done. We ask Him for our daily bread. We pray that He would forgive us and keep us from temptation and evil. If you're trying to establish a daily praying habit, there's no better place to begin than the Lord's Prayer. Reflect upon the familiar words and let each petition lead you into more specific prayers. *What* sins do you need to confess? What "daily bread" do you need? In what areas do you want to see God's will done in your life, the lives of others, and our nation?

Find a prayer partner. If you're going to train for a race or kick the habit of smoking, it makes a lot of sense to have a "buddy" for support. You're less likely to skip a morning run if you're supposed to meet someone and run together.

You're less likely to reach for a pack of cigarettes if you have someone who's holding you accountable. The same is true of prayer. Maybe you and your spouse can pray together. Perhaps you can find a good friend or a fellow church member. You could even find a long-distance prayer partner. Text each other at a certain time every morning, say, to "check in" or to remind one another to pray. You're more likely to start and continue a habit if you have someone supporting you and holding you accountable.

Keep a prayer journal. This doesn't have to be elaborate. You don't even need to buy anything special. Just keep a list of intercessions and people you're praying for. This helps you to stay focused and also helps you not to forget anyone or anything while you're praying.

Set aside a specific time and/or place. I have a tiny closet office where I write my books. Theoretically, I *could* write anywhere, even the kitchen table. But I feel more professional if I'm in my office. I don't feel like an author when I'm sitting at the kitchen table, because that's where we eat. But when I'm in my office, I'm automatically in the frame of mind that I'm there to write. The same holds true for praying. If you do it while in bed, your mind signals to you that you're there to go to sleep. But kneeling is another matter entirely. It's a posture we use for very few other activities in life. It puts you in the mindset that you're there for a specific reason—to pray. Go ahead and write your prayer time into your schedule too. You're less likely to skip it if it's "officially" scheduled in.

Think of what could happen if all of us prayed consistently. Could we end abortion in our country? Reverse immoral legislation? End Christian persecution in the world? James 5:16 reminds us that "the prayer of a righteous man is powerful and effective" (NIV). The power isn't in us, of course. God is the one who answers prayer in line with His good and perfect will. Daniel 9:18 reminds us that "we do not present our pleas before You because of our righteousness, but because of Your great mercy." *That's* where the power lies. How incredible that God chooses to give that power to us through prayer. So let's pray, fellow Christians.

It's time to change the world.

I'm Just a Mom

May 14, 2018

Being a mother can be a thankless job. Much of what you do goes unnoticed unless it doesn't get done. Your kids will rarely, if ever, thank you. From a toddler throwing a tantrum to a teenager slamming a door in your face, your kids will probably instead give you the distinct impression that you're ruining their lives. A mother's daily tasks are repetitive and mundane. Sure, sometimes we try to glamorize motherhood. We've invented clever terms like "domestic engineer" and "household manager" to describe the mother's role in the home. But at the end of the day, the truth is that every domestic engineer is just a mom.

Just a mom.

Have you ever felt that way? I have. It can be difficult not to compare myself with others who are *doing* something; accomplishing great things in their lives. Think of Queen Esther from the Old Testament, who saved her entire people from annihilation. Or the New Testament apostles who traveled the world of their day to spread the Good News. When Peter preached at Pentecost, 3000 souls were converted in one day! That's a powerful sermon. Consider the many saints and martyrs who followed the apostolic era, men and women who stood strong against false teaching and persecution even unto death.

There are still people today who are accomplishing great things. I have a friend who takes mission trips around the world to distribute Bibles and other Christian literature. Another friend runs an orphanage in Africa. These people are making a difference in countless lives. It's easy to compare oneself with others and get discouraged. While college friends are accomplishing great things, I'm doing the same thing day in and day out, changing diapers, running carpool, making dinner, trying in vain to keep the house clean with children underfoot. It all seems so… uninspiring. Like I said, I'm just a mom.

But hold on a minute. Before you get discouraged, take a look at some other mothers who lived about 2000 years ago, Lois and Eunice. They're mentioned but once in the Bible, as Timothy's mother and grandmother, and to be honest, I can never remember which is which. "I am reminded of your sincere faith," Paul writes in 2 Timothy 1:5, "a faith that dwelt first in your grandmother Lois and your mother Eunice and now, I am sure, dwells in you as well."

That's it. That's all we have to go on for Lois and Eunice. Well, not quite. Fast forward a few chapters to the well-known admonition of 3:14-15. "But as for you, continue in what you have learned and have firmly believed, knowing from whom you learned it and how from childhood you have been acquainted with the sacred writings which are able to make you wise for salvation through faith in Christ Jesus."

From childhood. Who would be teaching Timothy the Christian faith from a young age? Lois and Eunice, of course. And Timothy went on to become a faithful companion of the apostle Paul. He became a pastor and rendered great service among the Gentile churches. Tradition holds that he met a martyr's death. Here is a man who made a difference. But had it not been for Lois and Eunice passing along their faith, he may never have come to know the Lord at all, much less become a pastor and martyr.

Moms, I know it doesn't seem particularly glamorous, raising kids. But raising kids in the fear and knowledge of their Savior is a beautiful work. Not everyone is called to save a nation like Queen Esther or preach a sermon to over 3000 people like Peter. We aren't all called to be missionaries or to work in orphanages or distribute Bibles around the world. God may be calling you to be like Lois and Eunice, little remembered by the world, but making an eternal difference in the lives of your children. In other words, sometimes you're called to be "just" a mom.

And that's just fine.

The Tax Collector Next Door

May 15, 2014

I never gave it much thought before, but I have a few tax collectors for neighbors. The other day I went to a house in my neighborhood to introduce myself to the mother of the kids my children play with. I heard strange music coming from the garage and walked in to find a number of people lounging around, smoking and drinking beer. I told them who I was and who my kids were, and they were all very friendly. One guy introduced himself and his live-in girlfriend. One lady was a divorced mom. One guy had tattoos on his arms. I tried not to breathe in too much of the smoke wafting around, as I imagined my lungs getting black just from being there. Our conversation was pleasant enough, but I was uncomfortable nonetheless. And as I was leaving with an inward sigh of relief, it dawned on me. I was playing the part of the Pharisee, and they were the "tax collectors and sinners."

How many times did the Pharisees turn up their noses at the company Jesus held? They sneered at Him for eating with tax collectors and sinners. They looked down with haughty eyes at the sinful woman who washed Jesus' feet with her tears. They just couldn't wrap their minds around the fact that Jesus came for *all* people. That didn't fit with their idea of a pious Messiah. And it's so easy for us to look back on their pride and shake our heads, but have you ever considered that you just may be a closet Pharisee yourself? It hurts to admit it, but I certainly have a bit of that in me. There are certain lifestyles I look down upon, there are people with whom I'm uncomfortable, and like the Pharisees, I prefer to stick with people who are like me. But while I was walking out of that smoke-filled garage the other day, I realized something. Jesus would have gone to houses just like that.

Jesus sought out people who weren't worthy. That's why He came in the first place. You weren't worthy of His love. Neither was I. None of us were "His type." He humbled Himself and came down to this sin-infested world, lived with sinners, ate with sinners, and died for sinners.

But Jesus specializes in transforming lives. He called a tax collector to be a disciple, and Matthew ended up writing a Gospel account. Pretty impressive transformation. Jesus called Simon the Zealot, a revolutionary militant of the day, who left that radical lifestyle behind as he learned at the Master's feet. Jesus encountered the Samaritan woman at the well, a social outcast in her own society for her lifestyle, as well as an outcast to the Jews due to her heritage. She was transformed by Jesus' message and became an evangelist to her own people, telling them about the Savior. Jesus called Zacchaeus, who turned from his lucrative but dishonest tax collecting practices and gave half of his goods to the poor while pledging to pay back four times the amount he cheated anyone. These were the people for whom He came.

So which one are you: a Pharisee or a tax collector? In Luke 18, Jesus tells us about the Pharisee and the tax collector in the temple. The Pharisee stood there praying out loud and boasting. "God, I thank you that I am not like other men, extortioners, unjust, adulterers, or even like this tax collector. I fast twice a week, I give tithes of all I get" (18:11-12). He was patting himself on the back in full view of everyone.

It's not wrong to thank God for the blessings He has given you. It's not wrong to thank Him for making you a Christian or for a family who instilled in you a solid moral compass. It's the motivation behind that. Are you genuinely thankful to your Savior for calling you as His own? Or are you trying to toot your own horn? Do not measure your righteousness compared to other people. Measure it instead by God's Word. You will always fall short. If you try to exalt yourself by comparing yourself to others, you have completely the wrong motivation. This Pharisee had no intention of really praying in the temple that day. He was only there to show everyone else how pious he was.

But then again, maybe you identify more with the tax collector. He stood at a distance and would not even look to heaven. He beat his breast and pleaded only, "God, be merciful to me, a sinner" (Luke 18:13). That's all any of us can do. And God's mercy is all we need. But perhaps you have a hard time believing that. Maybe you think you're too "bad." Maybe you think God wouldn't want anything to do with you after the terrible choices you've made in life or the destructive behaviors you've chosen. But there's wonderful news. That tax collector in the temple was the one who went away justified that day in God's eyes. Not because his prayer was more sincere, but because he knew that saving action could only come from Jesus.

So whether you're a Pharisee or a tax collector, or even a confusing mix of the two, know this: Jesus came for *you*. He sought you out. It's not wrong to surround yourself with people who are like-minded. We draw strength from those relationships. But don't be afraid to get out of your comfort zone, either. Introduce yourself to your neighbors. Throw a neighborhood barbeque and get to know the people who live near you. Introduce them to Jesus. And you just might meet a few tax collectors along the way.

Highlight Reel

May 15, 2017

What do we know about Adam and Eve? God created Adam from the dust of the ground and formed Eve from Adam's rib. Adam named the animals. Oh, and Adam and Eve were the first ones to sin. That's kind of a big deal. They lived in the Garden of Eden until then, but were barred from it ever after. They had children and one of their sons murdered another. But seriously, Adam lived 930 years, and *that's* all we know of his life? In all that time, *something* important had to happen, right? Or what about Noah? The ark, naturally. And the fact that he got drunk and passed out naked in his tent after getting off the ark. But again, this guy lived 950 years, and we only know two accounts from all that time. How's that for a highlight reel?

Looking at the Bible, we see a lot of this sort of thing. Everyone knows who Adam is. Sunday school kids can tell you about Noah and the ark. But beyond that, the Bible is silent on the rest of their lives, as it is on many other characters from Scripture. Sure, there are notable exceptions—Joseph, Moses, David, and Jesus, for example. But many of the characters come in and out with only a few accounts recorded in God's Word. I wonder how they would feel, knowing that of everything that happened in their lives, *these* are the facts the Holy Spirit chose to record. Do you think Noah would wonder, *Oh, c'mon now. Did you really have to put that part in there about me passing out drunk? Couldn't we have left it at the ark?*

Would you live your life differently if you knew that any and every event could be recorded for future generations? What sort of things would be included? Would you have bold moments of daring, like the three men in the fiery furnace? Or would you have times of doubt and weakness, like Peter denying Jesus three times? If we're honest, most of us have to admit that we'd have far too many moments of weakness and not nearly enough moments of boldness and daring. Our highlight reel wouldn't be anything impressive.

Or would it?

I don't know how you're living your life, or what sort of earthly legacy you'll leave behind. I can't promise the next generation will look back on your life with only good things to say. You're a sinner as am I. But an earthly legacy, as important as that is, pales in comparison to our final verdict before heaven's throne. When our last hour comes and it's time for us to meet our Maker, there's no way we can stand before Him on our own merit. No matter how "good" a person you are, you fall short when measured against God's demands in the Law. Not a single one of us can get into heaven on our own.

But we don't have to. Jesus took our sin upon Himself and gave us His sinlessness. He gives us His "highlight reel," if you will. As 2 Corinthians 5:21 says, "For our sake He made Him to be sin who knew no sin, so that in Him we might become the righteousness of God." Jesus took our sins, our shortcomings, our failings upon Himself and gave us His righteousness. In God's eyes, we are perfect, robed in the white of Jesus' purity. When God looks at His children, He sees Jesus' perfection. And I'll gratefully take that highlight reel any day.

What We Can Learn from the Saddest Passage in the Bible

May 16, 2016

One of the most tragic verses in the Bible is Judges 2:10. "And all that generation were gathered to their fathers. And there arose another generation after them who did not know the Lord or the work that He had done for Israel." What?? How is that even possible? Joshua led the Israelites after the death of Moses, and through Joshua's direction, this band of nomads conquered the Promised Land, defeating strongholds like Jericho simply by marching around the city and blowing trumpets. They had seen God's hand powerfully at work in their lives, and had witnessed what their forefathers only dreamed of—entering the Promised Land of Canaan. But then that generation died and their children grew up, not knowing the Lord. Why? I hate to say it, but it was because of the parents.

This pattern of falling away is not unique, unfortunately. 1 Samuel 2:12 tells us, "Eli's sons were wicked men; they had no regard for the Lord" (NIV). Eli was a priest himself, and apparently a faithful one. He was faithful enough for Hannah to trust him to raise her son Samuel, who then became a faithful judge over Israel, but even Samuel's sons didn't follow suit. 1 Samuel 8:3 tells us, "Yet his sons did not walk in his ways but turned aside after gain. They took bribes and perverted justice."

King Hezekiah, whose reign is recorded in 2 Kings 18-20, "trusted in the Lord, the God of Israel, so that there was none like him among all the kings of Judah after him, nor among those who were before him. For he held fast to the Lord. He did not depart from following Him, but kept the commandments that the Lord commanded Moses" (2 Kings 18:5-6). Yet Hezekiah's son Manasseh "did what was evil in the sight of the Lord, according to the despicable practices of the nations whom the Lord drove out before the people of Israel" (2 Kings 21:2). This guy even sacrificed his own son in the fire! What a contrast from his godly father. Thankfully, he did repent of his sin and turn to the Lord at the end of his life, as 2 Chronicles 33:10-17 shows, but the damage had been done. He had successfully led Judah astray again.

Parents, learn from these grim lessons. You cannot treat your faith casually and expect your children to absorb it by osmosis. I've heard parents make the excuse that their kids "get religion" in a Christian day school, so they don't feel the need to go to church on Sundays. Others may think church and Sunday school are enough, and they don't want to "overwhelm" their kids with Bible stuff, so they talk very little about it at home. Both of these mindsets are dangerous. Kids *need* to hear about the Christian faith *from their parents*. Whatever society may say, parents are still the most influential factor on a child's life, especially at an early age. What you do—or *don't* do—at home will have a huge impact on their own faith walk as they grow up.

Psalm 78:1, 3-6 gives us a glimpse of how God intends the faith to be passed along. "Give ear, O My people, to My teaching; incline your ear to the words of My mouth…[I will tell of] things that we have heard and known, that our fathers have told us. We will not hide them from their children, but tell to the coming generation the glorious deeds of the Lord, and His might, and the wonders that He has done. He established a testimony in Jacob and appointed a law in Israel, which He commanded our forefathers to teach to their children, that the next generation might know them, the children yet unborn, and arise and tell them to their children."

You see, God's design is that children inherit more from their parents than hair and eye color. They are to pass along God's Word to their children as well. As Deuteronomy 6:7 reminds us, we are to "Impress [God's teachings] on your children. Talk about them when you sit at home and when you walk along the road, when you lie down and when you get up" (NIV). In other words, *live* your faith. Make it such a part of your daily life that your kids can't help but grow up to hear about all God has done for them in Jesus.

So parents, pray that with God's help your children will indeed be strong and secure in their faith their entire life through. Teach them Bible stories. Have devotions. Take them to church. Pray with them. Talk with them about Jesus. It's never too early—or too late—to start.

Modern-Day Martyrs

May 22, 2014

Some were beheaded, some were tortured to death, others burned to death, some were crucified, others sentenced to receive eighty lashes. Many of these things were done in public, as an example for all to see of the "dangers" of Christianity. Who were these individuals? The apostles, perhaps? Most of them were martyred for their faith, but the examples I mention above come from an article written on December 9, 2013. These are modern-day martyrs, being killed for their faith in Jesus in our own day and age. The title alone says it all: *Christians are Being Burned Alive, Beheaded, Crucified, Tortured to Death & Imprisoned in Metal Shipping Containers.* According to the author, Michael Snyder, there are 100 million Christians currently facing persecution, and about 100,000 Christians die each year for their faith in Christ. That comes down to about 274 people each day, or about eleven every hour. In the amount of time it will take me to write this article, approximately ten Christians will die somewhere in this world because of their faith.

A number of years ago, I read the book *Tortured for Christ* by Richard Wurmbrand, founder of the organization The Voice of the Martyrs. It is an awful book. And by "awful" I don't mean poorly written. I mean the things he reports are awful beyond words, absolutely sickening to read. He himself suffered under the Communist regime in Romania, and by a sheer miracle survived to tell about it. Doctors have told him since that he should have died. His lungs are scarred from the tuberculosis he suffered in prison, and his body bears the scars of the countless beatings and torture he endured. He realized that his survival was no mere accident, and went on to work tirelessly to bring the plight of the Underground Church to the attention of Christians in free countries. The examples he gives in his book are nauseating and show just how hard the devil is at work in persecuted countries, trying to stop the spread of the Gospel by force. But here's the thing—*it's not working.*

Wumbrand tells of the utter joy of the Underground Church. They considered it a privilege to be persecuted, much as the apostles did when they were beaten (given forty lashes minus one) and "left the presence of the council, rejoicing that they were counted worthy to suffer dishonor for the Name" (Acts 5:41). The beatings didn't stop the apostles from preaching about Jesus, and it doesn't stop the persecuted Church today. Wurmbrand gives countless examples of people who were converted to Christianity, jailors and cruel guards who converted after seeing the firm faith and resolve of those they were persecuting. People may ask why God allows His saints to suffer so. Wurmbrand asserts that the fruitfulness of their witness is answer enough.

The persecuted church is a flourishing church. The devil's plan is backfiring. Instead of scaring people away from following Christ, this persecution actually allows for more of an intensity and urgency in witnessing. Christians are being added daily, despite the fact that they know exactly what will happen to them if they do convert. Their faith amazes and humbles me.

The devil may try to prevent the spread of the Gospel there by force, but the weapons he utilizes here in America are far more insidious and effective. His most effective weapon here is *complacency*. In the persecuted Church, there are no lukewarm Chrstians. They're all in. Not so in America. We have become largely complacent, leading us to be lazy and indifferent in our witness for our Savior. God has given us the great gift of freedom here in America, and our freedoms are being challenged, yes. But while we still have them, take advantage of them. Risk being mocked for your beliefs. That's nothing compared to the physical torture your fellow Christians suffer in persecuted countries. Jesus has promised to be with us. Take Him at His word in Matthew 28:19-20. *Go therefore and make disciples of all nations, baptizing them in the name of the Father and of the Son and of the Holy Spirit, teaching them to observe all that I have commanded you. And behold, I am with you always, to the end of the age.*

He is with them. He is with us. And someday we will all be united before His throne in heaven. But in the meantime, there is much work to be done on this earth. Plant the seed wherever you can, and pray that God will make it grow and bear abundant fruit. So get ready to do some hands-on work in the fields. It's planting time.

One Common Destiny

May 22, 2017

It doesn't matter what you believe as long as you're sincere.

All roads lead to heaven.

People may call God by different names, but we all still worship the same God.

Nice sentiments, aren't they? Why trouble yourself too much about religion, after all? What difference does it really make in the end? If we're all going to heaven, it doesn't matter what we believe or how we live our lives on earth, right? But is that true? Do we all share a common destiny? Actually, in one sense, yes. But it may not be exactly what you have in mind.

The belief that pretty much everyone will end up in heaven is fairly prevalent in our society. It's a comforting thought to our finite minds. Even some prominent religious figures push the idea that we're all going to end up in heaven. The "really" bad people like Hitler won't make it, of course, but normal people who strive to live good lives will be there. And indeed, most major world religions stress good works as the means to attain salvation. You have to earn your way to paradise by living a good life on earth, giving to the poor, praying faithfully, etc. Make sure the good outweighs the bad and you'll be okay.

But please don't be fooled. There is only one way to heaven. There is only one true God. And no matter what you happen to believe right now, one day you *will* acknowledge Jesus as Lord. It's just a question of how you meet Him—as your Savior, or as your judge.

On the Last Day, when Jesus returns, everyone will have no choice but to admit that He alone is God. Philippians 2:10-11 says, "At the name of Jesus every knee should bow, in heaven and on earth and under the earth, and every tongue confess that Jesus Christ is Lord, to the glory of God the Father."

Similarly, Isaiah 45:22-25 tells us, "Turn to Me and be saved, all the ends of the earth! For I am God, and there is no other. By Myself I have sworn; from My mouth has gone out in righteousness a word that shall not return; to Me every knee will bow, every tongue shall swear allegiance. 'Only in the Lord, it shall be said of Me, are righteousness and strength; to Him shall come and be ashamed all who were incensed against Him. In the Lord all the offspring of Israel shall be justified and shall glory.'"

Yet again, Revelation 1:7 repeats the sentiment: "Behold, He is coming with the clouds, and every eye will see Him, even those who pierced Him; and all tribes of the earth will wail on account of Him. Even so. Amen."

When you consider the implications of these verses, it's truly horrifying. If you don't believe in Jesus in this life, you will meet Him instead as your Judge on the Last Day. You will recognize Him as Lord alone. But by then it will be too late. The hymn "Lo! He Comes With Clouds Descending" says it like this:

> *Every eye shall now behold Him*
> *Robed in glorious majesty;*
> *Those who sat at naught and sold Him,*
> *Pierced and nailed Him to the tree,*
> *Deeply wailing, deeply wailing, deeply wailing,*
> *Shall their true Messiah see.*
> *(Lutheran Service Book 336, stanza 2)*

Friends, there is no reason to meet Jesus as your judge. There's no need to be included in those who are "incensed against him." No matter what you have done in your past, Jesus' forgiveness and mercy are there for you. You don't have to earn your way to heaven—Jesus has done that already. His perfect life that you could never live, His sinless suffering and death in your place, and His resurrection to defeat death have earned eternal paradise for you. It's not because of anything you do. It's all because of Jesus. And one day, I know I will be kneeling before Him in heaven, confessing that He is Lord. I pray that you will be there with me.

Blue Skies

May 26, 2015

We've had a bit of rain this month. Okay, a *lot* of rain. We've had some form of rain every day for the past three weeks straight, and the forecast looks like rain for the rest of the month at least. Flash flood warnings are issued on a regular basis. My boys have had rescheduled baseball games canceled. The last time they had an actual game was over two weeks ago. School was dismissed early twice in one week for potential flooding, and this morning we have a two-hour delay. It's been crazy. I've never seen a May quite like this. And with all this rain, it's hard not to get depressed. I feel cooped up, and the skies are usually overcast and gray. Not exactly the weather to keep one's spirits high. But the other day I discovered something that gave me hope.

It was a rare morning because it wasn't raining, so I took the opportunity to take the dog for a much-needed walk. As usual, the skies were overcast, but as I walked I saw an actual shadow. It was faint, true, but it was a shadow nonetheless, the kind that the sun makes on the ground when it's actually shining. So I looked up at the sky and saw it. Blue sky. Just a small patch of it, mind you, but blue sky nonetheless, with just a touch of sun shining through the break in the clouds. The rest of the sky was still overcast, but that little patch of light reminded me that the blue sky is always there, even when we can't see it. It may be covered by clouds and marred by rain, but if you get high enough, it's up there. It never goes away.

I see in that example a metaphor for life. We may have beautiful, sunny periods where life is good and the skies are clear and blue. We bask in the sunshine and feel blessed and know God is watching over us. But life isn't all sunshine. There are also times when we go through periods of rain and overcast skies. We may go through periods in our lives that seem like they will never end. We barely make it through one storm before another hits. It's easy to get depressed and discouraged. Like the sun hiding behind the clouds, we feel like God has left us. We can't see or feel His presence, and we may even start to doubt Him. But He's there.

As much as I'd love to see the sun every day and have its bright light fill my house with a cheerful glow, I know that without periods of rain the crops will die. The earth *needs* rain. God knows this. And it's the same thing in our own lives. Sure, we would love unending periods of happiness and sunshine. But we need trials and hardships to mold us and shape us. Think of the spoiled child who gets everything he or she wants. Not a pleasant person to be around, especially once he or she becomes an adult. Good parents know that they can't give their kids everything, nor should they bail their children out at the first sign of trouble. Their children need to grow and learn from these experiences. But good parents are always there for their children, even when their kids have to bear the consequences of a bad decision. Likewise, God is always there for His children, even when we can't see Him.

Our Heavenly Father knows when to allow gloomy days and trials to afflict us. But there is hope. Even in the midst of overcast skies, you just may catch a glimpse of blue skies underneath, reminding you that the Son is still shining. And someday, *someday*, you will experience the warmth of the Son in heaven, which is described in Revelation 21:11 and 23 as follows: "It shone with the glory of God, and its brilliance was like that of a very precious jewel…The city does not need the sun or the moon to shine on it, for the glory of God gives it light, and the Lamb is its lamp" (NIV).

No matter how gray your skies may be, dear friend, one day you will experience eternal Son-light.

June

On Fire for the Lord

June 1, 2020

Pentecost must have been an amazing sight to behold. Men were quite literally on fire for the Lord, as the Holy Spirit descended upon them in tongues of fire. The apostles began to speak in languages they did not know, so that everyone there could hear the Gospel in his own language. Some mocked the apostles, claiming they were drunk. But many did believe, and after Peter's sermon, Acts 2:41 tells us that "those who received his word were baptized, and there were added that day about three thousand souls." Whoa. *Three thousand people?* And a short while later, after Peter and John healed a lame beggar, John preached again about Jesus, and that day *five* thousand men believed! That's astounding. Suddenly the growth of the Church in our own day can seem very meek in comparison.

While the apostles at Pentecost were on fire for God, sometimes it feels like we struggle to keep a spark lit. It may feel like the Church is just limping along. When was the last time your church received new members? Many churches today struggle with declining church membership as faithful members age and enter their eternal rest, while new families joining becomes increasingly more rare. For some churches, baptism is the only way they receive new members. It's easy to get discouraged. It's easy to think we've lost that passion, that fire for God. It's easy to think that we aren't trying hard enough or doing enough or being relevant enough to the community around us.

That line of thinking is the problem.

Once we start focusing on *our* efforts, *our* zeal, *our* contributions, we somehow imagine that the Church's survival is up to *us*. We take the focus off our Savior and put it on our own efforts. We forget that the Church is *Christ's* Church. He will not forsake it, and He will continue to cause it to grow even when we can't perceive it.

The early Church was a time of amazing growth, true. That's how it is in infancy. Anyone who's ever observed a baby growing knows that they grow at an incredible rate of speed. Every few months babies need a new size of clothes. They more than double their size over the course of that first year. It's an exciting time to watch babies grow and develop, and although the growth curve flattens, they continue to grow and mature throughout childhood and the teenage years. During the first two decades of life, an individual grows from a tiny infant into a full-grown adult. That's something like a 1500% increase in growth over 20% (or less) of a person's lifetime. From there on out, growth is different—less perceptible, and more mental than physical.

So while the Church grew exponentially over the first few decades after Christ's ascension, that growth curve has flattened. We generally don't see 5,000 people added to the Church on any given Sunday. But make no mistake, the Holy Spirit is still very much at work. Every soul who is baptized receives the gift of the Holy Spirit in no less miraculous a way than the apostles on Pentecost. The Holy Spirit creates faith out of nothing and continues to fan that flame as children grow and are nurtured in the faith. Each child who is baptized and raised in a Christian home has the potential to have children of his or her own someday, and the Christian faith is passed along for another generation. The growth is slower—over generations rather than days—but it is still there.

Dear Christian, don't be tempted to think that the Holy Spirit has somehow stopped working. Don't look at the numbers in your congregation and get discouraged. Don't look to yourself to gauge how "on fire" you are for the Lord. Even if you feel like your faith is weak, remember the promise of Isaiah 42:3, that "a faintly burning wick He will not quench." He will keep you in your faith. He will continue to cause the Church to grow. There's no stopping this fire.

Chameleons

June 2, 2014

Not too long ago, a friend of mine posted something intriguing on Facebook. She thanked all her "non-chameleon" friends who were the same no matter what company they held. I found this to be very thought-provoking. I'm sure you can think of a few people who are chameleons. They act one way with a certain group of people, but are completely different with another group. They "change their color" to fit their environment. Now, to a minor extent we all do this. Most of us would be more subdued visiting an elderly relative in a nursing home than we would be at, say, a wedding reception. But that's just two different sides of your personality—the caring, listening side and the fun-loving, have-a-good-time side. You're still being yourself in both situations. But I ask you to consider another facet of your life and ask whether or not you're a chameleon in this aspect—your faith.

Like it or not, most of us would probably have to admit that it's all too easy to be a chameleon when it comes to our Christian faith. After all, we don't want to "offend" people. Church is a safe environment in which to profess our faith. Surrounded by other Christians, we sing loudly and joyfully. There's no fear of others mocking us or rolling their eyes at how "religious" we are.

But once we leave those doors, it's another story. The world is a scary, daunting place. So we often find ourselves mumbling a quick prayer at a restaurant after glancing around to make sure no one is watching, slipping into the vernacular of swearing at our workplace, or skipping over church when others ask us what our weekend plans include. But after a while that takes its toll. If you can't live your faith everywhere, why bother? If you slip into the "neutral" color long enough, you find yourself staying there. It becomes easier to skip the mealtime prayer altogether, and after a while those Sunday morning invitations from co-workers start to look pretty tempting. Be aware of the times in your life when you set aside your Christianity to become a neutral chameleon.

So what can be done? First of all, realize something—*Christianity is not nearly as off-putting to most people as some would have us believe*. On the contrary, I've found that most people are pretty open to talking about religion, even when they don't agree with you. Yes, there are those vocal few who would chase you off their property with a shotgun if you dared to invite them to church, but they truly are a minority.

We had a neighbor once who was a staunch non-believer. He made that very clear. Yet we had more conversations with him about Jesus than I've had with some fellow Christians. We explained to him why we believed in Jesus, and he listened very patiently and responded with his questions and doubts, but it was always incredibly cordial. He never got mad at us for "forcing" our beliefs on him.

In fact, he was often the one who initiated these conversations. To our knowledge, he never did come to saving faith, but that's not for us to know. We Christians don't need to "keep score" and see how many people we can convince. No, that's the work of the Holy Spirit, and all we can do is plant the seed when opportunities arise.

Adults, we can learn something from children. Young kids don't know how to be chameleons yet. They are Christians through and through, no matter where they are. Consider my almost-two-year-old singing "Alleluia! Jesus is Risen!" at the top of her lungs as we walked the aisles of the grocery store the other day. She only knows the opening line, so she sang that over and over again. People may not have understood exactly what she was singing, but "alleluia" and "Jesus" came through pretty clearly.

Or think of my five-year-old carrying around her latest favorite Arch book. The other night at a baseball game for her brother, she asked Grandpa to read the one that recounts John 21, the miraculous catch of fish after Jesus' resurrection. It is blatantly Christian and includes the background of Jesus' death and resurrection. When Grandpa finished reading it to her, he asked, "Did you like that book?" As my daughter happily nodded, the guy next to him said, "Well, I don't know about her, but I sure did!"

Friend, there's no need to be a chameleon when it comes to your faith. Wear those colors boldly and proudly. Chameleons are amazing in their ability to change color. They can be brown, blue, green with vivid red stripes, teal with red spots, bright red, and multi-colored. But the brown ones are boring. They don't catch the eye like the vividly striped or multi-colored ones do. Don't try to blend in and remain unnoticed. The good news of Jesus is far too exciting not to share. Christians *should* be different. People *should* be able to tell that you're a Christian no matter your surroundings. Stand out. Wear your colors proudly. You never know who needs to notice.

Life is Hard and Then You Die

June 4, 2018

Life is hard and then you die.

While the exact origin of the quote may be debatable, it's a sentiment that resonates with many people. When I was a kid, I wanted so badly to be an adult. In my mind, I'd really be free then. Free to do whatever I wanted, whenever I wanted. I could stay up as late as I wanted, eat chocolate whenever I wanted, buy whatever I wanted. I'd get married and have kids and be a perfect mother and a perfect wife with a perfect husband, and we'd all live happily ever after. Basically, I'd have it made.

But then I became an adult and realized that adulthood wasn't all it was cracked up to be. I discovered that I'm not a perfect wife or mom, and neither are my husband or kids perfect. As a child, I never considered things like financial struggles, job loss, relationship difficulties, or the challenges of parenting. Despite my high hopes for adulthood, my adult self knows something my younger self did not.

Life is hard.

All over the world, people suffer from poverty, disease, war, and natural disasters, to name a few. People struggle daily with things like bad marriages, job difficulties, lack of family time, discontentment, or a scary medical diagnosis, and these take their toll mentally. One way or another we realize that we aren't going to get a "happily ever after" here on earth. We will always struggle with *something*, because life is just hard.

Then you die.

Sobering, right? No matter what our struggles look like, everyone on earth shares one common destiny—death. But death isn't actually the end. Heaven awaits those who believe in Jesus. Jesus knows what it is to suffer. He humbled Himself to take on our frail human flesh. He was doubted and scorned for most of His earthly ministry. He whom the angels worship was found guilty of blasphemy and put to death on a crude Roman cross. Add to His physical suffering the fact that on that cross, God laid the guilt of the world's sin upon Him. Jesus suffered hell on the cross, because God abandoned Jesus on the cross, leaving Him utterly alone with the weight of all our sins. Yes, Jesus knows what it means to suffer. He suffered greatly. And then He died.

But death could not hold Him. Three days later, He rose from the dead, triumphing over the grave. His resurrection guarantees our own. Yes, we will all die. But we will also live again.

I don't know what your particular struggles are, but I know you have them, because life is hard. But that's sort of a good thing, actually. We need the reminder that this earth and people in this earth can't fill our deepest need, which is Christ. Only in heaven will we ever be truly satisfied.

Life is hard and then you die. And only then can you truly live happily ever after.

Unchangeable

June 5, 2015

If you were to walk into a seventy-eight degree house, would that be warm or cool? That depends. If it's January in Duluth, Minnesota, walking into seventy-eight degrees would feel ridiculously warm, even hot. But if you're in Houston, Texas, in a steamy heat wave in August, seventy-eight degrees will feel luxuriously cool. So what changed? The inside temperature is the same. How can a constant feel hot in one situation and cool in another? It's because the exterior circumstances have changed. The context colors the constant.

The same holds true for many people's view of God. So often, our view of God is blurred by our current circumstances, which are always changing. Maybe you're going through a period in your life where everything is great. You have a wonderful job, family life is good, you have plenty of money, and you're thinking, *God is blessing me richly. What a wonderful God He is indeed.*

Then again, maybe you're going through a terrible time in your life right now. Maybe a loved one has died unexpectedly, maybe you just got news from the doctor that your illness is terminal, maybe you lost your job and can't afford to pay the mortgage. In those cases, maybe you're thinking, *This is what I get after serving God all these years? Maybe God isn't so great after all. Why would He do this to me?*

The difference in the examples above is the circumstances in one's life. For you see, God's the constant. God doesn't change. He says so Himself quite bluntly in Malachi 3:6: "I the Lord do not change." He's the same God today as He was 6,000 years ago, when He created a world He proclaimed was "good." That world is still in existence today, and despite what some people have done to abuse it, it is still God's creation and it is still good. He created Adam and Eve just as He created you. He is a God who means what He says and takes sin seriously. He warned Adam and Eve not to eat from the tree of the knowledge of good and evil, but when they did, He punished them. God still takes sin seriously, and yes, there are still consequences for our sins.

But there's also hope. Even 6,000 years ago, immediately after punishing Adam and Eve, He promised them a Savior. Genesis 3:15 is the first gospel, the "Protevangel" verse in the Bible. From the very beginning, God promised He would save us. And save us He did.

Fast forward 4,000 years from Adam and Eve. The time was finally right. God kept His promise by sending His only Son, Jesus, to live a perfect life on this earth. Then Jesus took the sins of the world upon His shoulders and died as the sacrifice for everyone else. After Jesus died, He rose three days later to prove once and for all that He has defeated even death for us. Those who believe in Jesus will live in heaven forever with Him. That's the constant. Hebrews 13:8 assures us, "Jesus Christ is the same yesterday and today and forever."

People's life circumstances vary widely, but Jesus' life, death, and resurrection are true all the time; His promises are true for everyone. That's the constant. Eternal life in heaven puts even the worst earthly circumstances in perspective. No matter what I face here on earth, eternal life awaits. And that will never change.

Leaves of Three

June 6, 2016

For as terrible as it got, it had a rather innocuous start. A couple days after contact, I noticed two small bumps on my arm and wondered about them. Over the course of the next few days, more bumps appeared. Then more. Then there were some on my sides. My arms and both sides of my abdomen were covered with blistering sores, and during the dog days of summer I was relegated to wearing long sleeves to cover the gauze that hid the ugly red sores and scabs that lasted the better part of a month. What caused all this discomfort and pain? Poison ivy.

Anyone who's ever had a bad reaction to poison ivy can relate to my experience. And the real kicker is that I didn't even touch the stuff personally. I got it from my nursing baby, who had been held by someone who touched it and got the oils on their clothes. So the oils were transferred onto my baby's clothes and then onto me while I held and nursed her. Thankfully, she didn't break out, but I sure did. And it was ugly. I looked like a leper, like something was eating my flesh away. I thought my arms would be permanently scarred. Even my birthmark on my right arm peeled off as the reaction progressed. There was no possible way my skin would ever return to normal and be healed.

And yet it did.

Today, my arms bear no sign of the poison ivy reaction from three years ago. I have nary a scar from that awful time. Even my birthmark has grown back. It's as if nothing happened at all. It is, quite simply, amazing.

There's a correlation to our spiritual life in this example. Like that poison ivy, sin is tricky. We all know the old adage, "Leaves of three, let it be," but that's easier said than done. Likewise, you "know" better than to mess with sin, yet you do it anyhow. And you may not even realize right away that you've been affected. You may think your little pet sin hasn't caught up to you or that you're safe from the danger it poses. When the first few "bumps" appear, it's not a big deal. But then more and more pop up, and soon enough, you have a big, ugly mess. Sin will do that to you. And it's easy to despair when you realize what a mess you've made of your life. When you truly search your heart and mind and compare it to the absolute perfection God demands in His Law, you can't help but despair, because you fail in so many ways every single day. You have something far more deadly than a bout of poison ivy—you are spiritually sick. There's no possible way you can ever be healed.

And yet you are.

You are cleansed of the guilt of sin not because of something you've done, but because of the perfect sacrifice of God's Son, Jesus. He took all the ugliness of sin upon Himself on the cross, and in exchange gave you His righteousness. As my arms have been completely healed with no scarring, so God has washed you completely. You are spotless. Thanks to Jesus, it's as if nothing happened at all. It is, quite simply, amazing.

When Sunscreen Isn't Enough

June 10, 2019

We should have listened. Here we were, college kids from Michigan, on a choir tour to Florida during spring break, a welcome relief of sun and warmth. Our choir director warned us to be careful in the sun. It was six times more intense that much further south, and we would get a sunburn much more quickly than we would in Michigan. He told us to use plenty of sunscreen, drink lots of water, and stay in the shade when possible. Naturally, most ignored his advice. I mean, come on. You can't very well come back from Florida without a tan. So despite the warnings, many students got some sun on the beach with little or no sunscreen to protect their skin. There were a lot of lobster-red faces for the remainder of that tour.

Living in Texas now, I can attest to the fact that the sun down here is intense. My poor fair-skinned, blond-headed children are no match for the fierce sun. They get irritated with me because I'm constantly reapplying sunscreen and reminding them to drink plenty of fluids. But I know how dangerous the sun can be. Just yesterday we went swimming at a friend's house. With a heat index in the triple digits, the water felt great. Yet despite the fact that I put on sunscreen twice, my shoulders still burned. Sunburn is sneaky that way. You don't notice until it's too late. The damage has already been done. And that's why proper protection is essential *before* you think you're in danger.

Parents, there's a good lesson here, and not just about lathering sunscreen on your kids during the summer. Your children need proper protection to go out into the world, and it's never too early to start. You see, there's a far more dangerous threat in the world than the sun. The devil uses every trick he has to lure us away from the truth and into false belief and sin. But he's sneaky. He doesn't present sin as sin. That would be too easy. He suggests little compromises here and there, slowly leading further and further from the truth. That's why it's important to teach God's Word to your kids while they're young, so they know the Bible and can apply it to their own lives as they grow up. That's why it's also important for you to immerse yourself in His Word day after day.

1 Peter 5:8-9 reminds us, "Be sober-minded; be watchful. Your adversary the devil prowls around like a roaring lion seeking someone to devour. Resist him, firm in your faith..." How is it that we resist him? By God's Word, as Jesus' example during His temptation shows. Be in the Word so you can protect yourself from the devil's schemes.

Yes, you will still fall into temptation no matter how prepared you may be. You will get "burned." But that's when Christ applies the soothing balm of His forgiveness. His Word provides both the protection and the healing you need, a benefit sunscreen can never provide.

As important as sunscreen is, God's Word is far more vital. Apply God's Word daily—if not more often!—for best results. And with that, duty calls. My kids want to go outside. I need to get the sunscreen.

Find Joy in the Ordinary

Bonus Post

Joy is probably not the first emotion one would use to describe something that is ordinary. The word *ordinary* generally has negative connotations. An ordinary person is average, with nothing exceptional to distinguish him or her from others. An ordinary day tends to mean boring, mundane, or dull. Ordinary tasks are more of a burden than a joy. Mothers of young children easily tire of changing diapers, breaking up arguments, cooking, cleaning, and doing laundry. Anything can settle into an ordinary routine: marriage, one's job, even prayer and devotional time. So how can we find joy in the ordinary?

For starters, remember that *joy* is different from *happiness*. The apostle Paul wrote Philippians, the "epistle of joy" while in prison. Peter wrote his epistles to churches that were experiencing severe persecution, and yet the concept of joy is a major theme in his letters. The Greek phrase *agalliaō* (translated as "ye rejoice") is used eleven times in the New Testament, and three of those uses are in the short epistle of 1 Peter (1:6, 1:8, and 4:13). It connotes an exceeding joy, and Peter exhorts the persecuted church to have this joy. Really?

You see, Paul and Peter know something that is sometimes lost in the shuffle of modern-day hectic lives. Peter tells the persecuted believers, "Though you have not now seen Him, you love Him. Though you do not now see Him, you believe in Him and rejoice with joy that is inexpressible and filled with glory, obtaining the outcome of your faith, the salvation of your souls" (1 Peter 1:8-9). Peter was an eyewitness of Jesus' earthly ministry. We are not. Does that diminish our love for or belief in Him? Not at all. Jesus gives us a special beatitude (blessing): "Blessed are those who have not seen and yet have believed" (John 20:29). We believe, and know by faith that we will obtain "the salvation of [our] souls."

Just look at Peter's language in the verse above. He is bubbling over with enthusiasm, barely able to put into words what he desires to express. From a strictly English-speaking perspective, the writing is too repetitive. We "rejoice with joy that is inexpressible"? Tone it down a little, Peter. That's over the top.

And yet it isn't. He's talking about the *salvation of our souls*. He's talking about heaven itself, where we will experience both happiness and joy more than we can even imagine. Talk about an eternal perspective!

Maybe ordinary isn't always boring. Consider the extraordinary things God accomplishes through ordinary means—He created Adam out of dust and Eve out of Adam's rib. Jesus was born of a virgin womb and began life as an infant in an ordinary family. He healed a blind man with mud and saliva. The Holy Spirit creates faith through the waters of baptism, and we receive the very body and blood of Jesus through ordinary bread and wine in the Lord's Supper. Come to think of it, ordinary things can be pretty extraordinary after all.

Life in the Royal Household

June 18, 2018

Americans in general are fascinated with the British monarchy. Everywhere I turn, magazines and tabloids have the latest scoop about the royal wedding, who's fighting with whom, and how the new generation is changing the way things have been done for centuries. I can't imagine how Kate Middleton puts up with the constant paparazzi and being so much in the public eye all the time. Every decision is scrutinized, from what she wears to a wedding to how she and her husband plan to raise their children. She has to be ready at every moment to be photographed, even upon leaving the hospital with a newborn. Very little in her life is truly private. She's being watched all the time. It must be exhausting. Frankly, I'm glad I'm not royalty.

Or am I?

You may not realize it, but in one sense you *are* royalty. All Christians are sons and daughters of the Heavenly King, and therefore, you are a prince or a princess. Strange thought, isn't it? No, you may not have the paparazzi following you around, but people are watching you. Neighbors, friends, and family members want to know if your walk matches your talk. They may notice that you go to church on Sundays, but what about the rest of the week? Do you swear? Lose your temper easily? Drink too much? Gossip? Or is your life different from that of the world?

Paul reminds us that our lives as Christians *should* set us apart. "I therefore, a prisoner for the Lord, urge you to walk in a manner worthy of the calling to which you have been called, with all humility and gentleness, with patience, bearing with one another in love, eager to maintain the unity of the Spirit in the bond of peace" (Ephesians 4:1-3).

That's the kind of life you should live as God's child. The mark of a Christian is a life of humility, gentleness, patience, love, unity, and peace. No, you won't do it perfectly. You're still a sinner, after all. But your sin has been paid for by the blood of Christ. He made you a member of His family, part of His royal household. And to top it all off, one day you will receive the crown of life in heaven.

No doubt about it, you are royalty after all.

How to Scare Kids Away From Church

June 23, 2014

How can we attract the younger generation to our church?

It's a question asked in many churches. But if your church has been searching for new methods to draw people in, you're probably achieving the opposite effect. If you want to make sure your kids won't continue going to church when they're older, there's a surprisingly easy method.

1. Tell them church is fun and exciting and relevant.

2. Dumb it down to reinforce that point.

Adults tend to think that if we only make church and Sunday School more exciting, more appealing, more "cool," then maybe more kids or teens will be drawn in. It's *Sister Act* theology. Use different music and watch them flock in. Play Bible games instead of teaching Bible lessons. Get the latest and most exciting program for Sunday School so they'll be happy to go. Who cares about the content, as long as they're there and having fun, right?

Wrong. Absolutely wrong. What good is it if they're sitting there having fun but learning very little of substance? Consider the "cool" parent who hangs out with her teens, parties with them, even drinks with them, all in an effort to show that they're easy to relate to. While that may seem awesome for a while, at some point, their kids will realize something: Mom or Dad can't be taken seriously. The same holds true for faith. Give kids enough fluff and fun and eventually they'll come to the same conclusion—this whole faith thing is a joke. It can't be taken seriously.

To be sure, you have to do things on an age appropriate level. I'm not going to launch into a lengthy discussion with my five-year-old on the subject of transubstantiation, for example. But at the same time, I'm not going to water down the Bible lessons so much that it's laughable. Sunday School doesn't have to be "God made the world. God made you. Yay, God!" Even a preschooler can be taught the different days of creation. Give them something of substance or you are giving them *a faith they can outgrow.*

Churches have come up with all sorts of silly gimmicks to draw people in, but to what end? Will a twenty-year-old male want to come to church on "Dr. Seuss Sunday"? Will a senior citizen enjoy singing "Splish, Splash, Jonah's Taking a Bath"? Or will they find it childish and look for a more serious church elsewhere? In some cases, that church to which they flee isn't even Christian. England has seen a huge swell of young people joining Islam, because they find a sense of direction there, a seriousness that is sadly lacking in many Christian churches today who are trying to attract new members.

Rather than trying to make church fun and exciting for kids, tap into their amazing ability to mimic you. They don't have the vocabulary to express their faith yet, so give them a chance to develop that vocabulary by expressing it *to* them. Say the Lord's Prayer and the Apostles' Creed and the Confession and the explanations of the Small Catechism so they can hear and repeat that. *Give* them the vocabulary to express, and make sure it's not one they will outgrow, like a childish nursery rhyme.

A good friend of mine recently asked her daughter what she'd like to see changed in Sunday School, and her daughter said she wanted to *study the Bible more*. She knows the typical stories, but now what? She doesn't want little kid lessons that are full of games. She wants to be taken more seriously and take the Bible more seriously too. That's from a ten-year-old, by the way. Don't assume that all kids want is fun and games. Don't think that if we make it exciting and dumb it down, they'll magically flock in. They know there's more to life than that.

Be wary of the mindset that we have to be "cool" when presenting Bible truths. Remember that we are worshiping the *God of the universe*. Don't underscore that amazing fact by trite games and songs and stories. God is a holy God. Isaiah was scared for his life when he was in the presence of God, because he knew that a sinful man could not stand in God's holy presence. Too often we lose sight of that fact. We want our kids and teens to know Jesus as their buddy. We neglect to teach them, however, that He is the Savior of the world, in whose presence every knee will someday bow. If kids are taught only to see Jesus as a buddy, they will most certainly grow out of that faith when reality hits. Who cares if Jesus is a nice guy when calamity strikes?

Teach your children the incredible truth that Jesus, true God, came to earth as a helpless infant. He lived a perfect life in our stead. He took the punishment we deserved and suffered and died for us on the cross. Then He rose from the dead three days later, and even as He ascended into heaven to sit at God's right hand, He promised believers that He would be with them always. Now *that's* an exciting story to retell over and over again. The God of the universe is with *you*. No matter what you face on this earth, Jesus is with you through it. Don't underestimate kids. They'll live up or down to your expectations. Set the bar high for a religious maturity that will carry them throughout their earthly life until they reach eternity.

To Be Hemmed In

June 26, 2014

Psalm 139 is a fairly familiar psalm. From the opening line, "O Lord, You have searched me and known me" (v 1), to the affirmation that life begins at conception in verses 13-16, to the plea at the end for God to "Search me…and know my heart" (v 23), you can probably quote parts of this psalm yourself. But there is one expression in particular that has always made me pause. Verse 5 says, "You hem me in, behind and before." What is that supposed to mean?

At first inspection, it seems to allude to the fact that God is omniscient (all-knowing) and omnipresent (present everywhere). The verses immediately prior to verse 5 talk about God knowing everything about us—our thoughts, our movements, our words. And a few verses later, David picks up the thought that God is present everywhere and we cannot escape Him. Verse 7 says, "Where shall I go from Your Spirit? Or where shall I flee from Your presence?"

But is that truly the sense of verse 5, of God hemming us in? It sounds oppressive, like God is smothering us. Let's continue with the rest of the verse for the full context: "You lay Your hand upon me." In the Bible, God's "hand" is often used as an expression of God's saving power. So if God is placing His saving power upon us, perhaps God "hemming us in" isn't so much God scrutinizing us as God protecting that salvation He gives us.

Skim through the rest of the psalm and you will find much talk of God creating us with His hands—God "knit" us together in our mothers' wombs, He "wove" us together in the depths of the earth, we are fearfully and wonderfully "made." Those are all creative, hands-on actions. So thinking along the lines of knitting and weaving, what is the point of a hem? The hem keeps the garment from fraying and finishes it off. A garment without a hem looks unfinished, sloppy. But with the hem, the garment is protected and finished. It can withstand the wear and tear of normal usage and washing without falling apart.

If God created each of us individually with the care and love of a handmade garment, isn't it comforting to know that He finishes what He started? He doesn't leave us helpless. He protects us. God's Word is the hem that keeps our faith from fraying. We have His all-powerful Word and the armor of God to help us withstand the assaults of this world. And so we can say with confidence the words of Paul in Philippians 1:6, "And I am sure of this, that He who began a good work in you will bring it to completion at the day of Jesus Christ." Thank God for His hem of protection around His chosen ones!

Be Still

Bonus Post

One of the most loved, oft-quoted verses from the Old Testament is Psalm 46:10: "Be still, and know that I am God. I will be exalted among the nations, I will be exalted in the earth!" Most of us—myself included—probably grew up thinking this verse means that we are to wait quietly before God and find peace in the stillness as we reflect on God being God. But does this really fit the tone of the rest of the psalm?

There are a few things to keep in mind when interpreting Scripture. One is to let Scripture interpret Scripture. Another is to look at a verse in its proper context. We have Mary Baker Eddy to thank for the modern-day "nirvana" understanding of Psalm 46:10. The founder of the Christian Church, Scientist movement, Mary Baker Eddy included this on a short list of cherry-picked Bible passages to form their central teaching. Psalm 46:10 is used by Christian Scientists in a very New Age sort of application, as an expression of peace, found in pursuing the father-mother god.

In reality, Psalm 46:10 is a rebuke, not an invitation to "chill out" or "find your own inner peace." Look at what has happened in the previous portion of the psalm. "God is our refuge and strength" (v 1) against things like the earth giving way, mountains falling into the heart of the sea, its waters raging, the mountains trembling (v 2-3). Nations are raging, kingdoms are tottering, the earth is melting (v 6). This is tumultuous, end-times ("eschatological," if you will) imagery. It is reminiscent of Matthew 24:3-14, where Jesus speaks about signs of the end of the age. Notice how Matthew 24:14 ends: "and then the end will come." *What??* Whoa, this suddenly got real. So with the same imagery, we can rightly infer that Psalm 46 is also ultimately a reference to the end times, in addition to all the troubles that occur every day in a fallen world.

So God has "brought [these] desolations upon the earth" (v 8), referring back to the first part of the psalm. This brings us to verse 9, which sounds peaceful and idyllic at first glance. "He makes wars cease to the end of the earth; He breaks the bow and shatters the spear; He burns the chariots with fire." Ahhh. See? God brings peace! Well, yes, but not in the way you might imagine.

Remember, Scripture interprets Scripture. Compare Joel 3:9-10 to Isaiah 2:4 (or Micah 4:3; the two passages are nearly identical). Here the instructions are completely reversed, and the headings of each passage and their surrounding verses help us understand them better. Joel 3:9-10 ("The Lord Judges the Nations") is a call to arms—plowshares are beaten into swords, pruning hooks into spears, all the mighty men are called upon to join the fight. God is summoning His enemies to one last, final confrontation with Him, much as

Revelation 19 portrays. Every enemy is to arm himself with whatever he can, even if that means makeshift weapons like fashioning pruning hooks into spears.

But we already know the outcome of this battle. God, who has already defeated sin, death, and Satan, will completely destroy them at the end of time, which is the description we find in Isaiah 2:4, Micah 4:3, and Psalm 46:9. Once the final battle is finished and God's enemies destroyed forever, there is no need for weapons. God makes the wars cease. The Hebrew word here is *shâbath,* which should look familiar to us. It's the same word as God *resting* on the seventh day of creation—a Sabbath rest. Now wars have stopped and the implements of warfare completely destroyed. In that complete absence and vulnerability (almost nakedness), nations are to "be still" before God.

This brings us at last to Psalm 46:10. Remember, God has just brought desolations upon the earth. He has summoned His enemies for a last climactic battle, which He decisively won, and has now completely destroyed all their possible weapons to use against Him and His Church. So His "Be still" is a stern rebuke, better translated as "Stop!" or "Enough!" It's like a parent stomping his foot and shouting to his fighting children, "That's enough! Stop it!" It's Law, not Gospel.

The Hebrew for "Be still" is *râphâh,* which means to abate, cease, consume, fail, be faint, be feeble, forsake, be idle, leave, let alone, be slack, stay, be still, or weaken. In light of God's power, what other response can His enemies have but to cease their warring, to be weak and faint before the Lord and His might?

Now the earth is to cease its restlessness before God so we can "know" He is God. This is a little weak in English. The Hebrew word is *yâda',* which encompasses far more than head knowledge. I "know" who Donald Trump is, but I "know" my husband in a completely different way. We use the same word in English, but the meanings are entirely different. The Hebrew word *yada* is "to know or be acquainted with by experience" or "to recognize and admit." It's the word used in passages where a husband "knows" his wife and she conceives. Which of these meanings fits into the context of Psalm 46:10? Well, both, depending on whether you're a believer of unbeliever.

By experience, we Christians *know* God is God. We are intimately acquainted with Him. We know His saving power. But the "nations"—meaning the heathen nations, as referenced in Psalm 46:6—among whom He will be exalted will *know* in the sense that they will have no choice but to recognize and admit God is God.

Psalm 46:10 builds upon verse 6. Though the nations may rage (verse 6), God will be exalted and known in all those nations (verse 10). God "utters His voice" in verse 6 and sternly rebukes the nations in verse 10 to "Be still!" The entire psalm ties together beautifully, and ends with the triumphant refrain that the

"Lord of hosts is with us; the God of Jacob is our fortress." Indeed, a mighty fortress is our God!

Life From Death

June 30, 2014

We have an amazing bush in our front yard. I think it may be a holly bush of some type, based on the leaves, but my knowledge of plants is slim at best. At any rate, this bush died over the winter, and once spring came the entire thing was an ugly brown. I didn't know if I was supposed to prune the branches and wait for new growth, or if the bush just couldn't take the brutal winter and was really dead. Once everything else in our yard was starting to bloom again in spring, I finally ventured over to it for a closer look. What I saw shocked me. Green leaves were starting to form, but not as you might expect. Green was actually forming *inside* the brown leaves. Those brown leaves I had supposed were dead were turning green from the inside out. I'd never seen anything like it.

And yet I have.

God specializes in bringing life from death. Each and every one of us was dead in sin. Ephesians 2:1-2a says, "As for you, you were dead in your transgressions and sins, in which you used to live when you followed the ways of this world…" (NIV). The Greek word Paul uses there is "corpse." We could do absolutely nothing for ourselves to merit God's favor or earn our own salvation. As a corpse can do nothing to bring itself back to life, neither could we. Yet God didn't let us remain that way. Ephesians 2:4-5 goes on to say, "But God, being rich in mercy, because of the great love with which He loved us, even when we were dead in our trespasses, made us alive together with Christ—by grace you have been saved…"

God *made us alive* even when we were dead in our sins. Incredible. Like that bush I had given up for dead, we were by all rights lost eternally with no hope. Yet God's great love and mercy breathed new life into us in the waters of Baptism.

When you stop to think about what baptism actually does, it takes your breath away. Consider the words of Romans 6:3-4: "Do you not know that all of us who have been baptized into Christ Jesus were baptized into His death? We were buried therefore with Him by baptism into death, in order that, just as Christ was raised from the dead by the glory of the Father, we too might walk in newness of life." We are literally united with Jesus' death in Baptism. It is as if we, too, died with Him on that cross. But that's not all. We were also raised with Jesus in His resurrection. Life from death.

As we travel through this earthly life, we are sorely tempted to follow the ways of this world. That's why Paul tells us in Romans 6:11 to count ourselves "dead to sin and alive to God." Once we're baptized we don't stop sinning. Yes, we are united with Christ, but there's that tension of the "not yet." While we are on this earth we will face daily temptations, and we don't yet see the ultimate realization of our faith. That's why each and every day we repent and remember our baptisms, drowning over and over again that Old Adam who is a darn good swimmer. "Dead to sin but alive to God." Life from death.

As wonderful as all this is, the best is yet to come, because even your own death at the end of your earthly life is not the end of the story. Jesus didn't stay in that tomb, but rose to life again three days later. Your mortal body will do the same. "If we have been united with Him in a death like His, we shall certainly be united with Him in a resurrection like His," Paul tells us in Romans 6:5. Or again, 1 Thessalonians 4:14 tells us, "For since we believe that Jesus died and rose again, even so, through Jesus, God will bring with Him those who have fallen asleep."

Death is not the end, dear ones. Remember, God specializes in bringing life from death. Those of us who believe in Jesus will live again even after we die. Now *that's* something to look forward to. Life from death.

July

The "Lazy" Days of Summer

July 2, 2018

Whoever coined the phrase "lazy days of summer" obviously didn't have a summer like mine. I could make my own version of "The Twelve Days of Christmas." Between five kids home from school, four summer reading programs, three weddings, two sets of houseguests, and a cross-country vacation just before school starts again, there's nothing lazy about this summer. This past week was particularly chaotic. By Saturday, when we had nothing going on for once, my three-year-old, who never naps, was so exhausted he just fell asleep on the couch. Clearly the busy pace had caught up to him at last. He needed rest.

Rest. It sounds like such a quaint idea in today's society, doesn't it? We seem to pride ourselves on how much we have going on, as though busy-ness is a measure of success. I confess that I fall into that mindset too often myself. When I do get a rare opportunity to be alone, I feel like I have to make the most of that time—folding laundry, vacuuming, steam mopping, etc. I might long for a nap, but seriously, who has time for that?

In days of old, Sundays really were days of rest. In biblical times, there were rules governing how many steps you could walk on the Sabbath without breaking God's command to rest. It was pretty hard core. But even a hundred years ago, people didn't work on Sundays. Farmers didn't plow or harvest, women didn't spend the day in the kitchen, and kids didn't even play outside. Families stayed inside and took naps or read quietly. It sounds so old-fashioned to our always-on-the-move society, but it also sounds very…refreshing.

It just so happens that we could all benefit from periodic rest times, and not just the six hours of sleep we cram in each night. Our bodies weren't made to be working or busy all the time. God designed them for a healthy balance of work and rest, modeling that balance for us when He created the world, working for six days and resting for one.

Nor is this purely an earthly model. Yes, we need physical rest. But in the Bible, "rest" is often used to refer to the peace we have from knowing our sins are forgiven, and even to heaven itself. "Come to Me, all who labor and are heavy laden, and I will give you rest," Jesus promises in Matthew 11:28-29. "Take My yoke upon you, and learn from Me, for I am gentle and lowly in heart, and you will find rest for your souls." He promises that those who are burdened by the weight of their sins will find forgiveness and peace in Him—rest for their souls.

Hebrews 4 gets even more in depth about the "Sabbath rest" for God's people. "So then, there remains a Sabbath rest for the people of God, for whoever has entered God's rest has also rested from his works as God did from His," verses 9-10 tell us. Yes, heaven is the ultimate Sabbath rest. But we also experience the benefits of God's Sabbath rest even now, namely through the Divine Service. There the pastor speaks God's saving Word to us. There we receive the Sacraments of Baptism and Holy Communion. Gathering together with fellow believers is God's gift to us—a brief time to rest from our earthly work while being reminded of the eternal rest that awaits us in heaven.

Unfortunately, that gift can sometimes seem more of a chore than a blessing. If I skip church today, I can catch up on my sleep... I can finally clean out the garage if I don't go to church this morning... I get that challenge. Sitting in church with five kids while my pastor husband is up front is rarely "restful." I don't walk away from church every Sunday feeling refreshed. But every Sunday I hear the beautiful news of the forgiveness of sins Christ won for me on the cross. Every week I am assured that my eternal rest in heaven is won. I don't want to skip out on that just to get a few more chores done around the house.

Okay, so my summer is anything but lazy. On top of that, I'm constantly fighting the battle of wanting to accomplish more in the time I have, even when my body really could use the rest instead. But I know every Sunday is another chance to enjoy God's rest, pointing me to His eternal rest. And come to think of it, maybe I will take that nap today after all.

Taking the Gospel For Granted

July 3, 2017

Familiarity breeds contempt.

So goes the old expression. And we get the basic premise. At first, everything is new and exciting, but over time that excitement fades and one tends to take for granted what once was an amazing blessing. Whether this plays out in a marriage, a job, or even possessions, we can all think of examples. But what happens when you find yourself feeling this way about the Gospel?

It sounds like a terrible thing to say, taking the Gospel for granted, doesn't it? But let's be honest—we all do it at times. We've heard the beautiful news so often that we tend to lose the sense of awe at the incredible message.

Yeah, I know Jesus died for me. Yes, He rose again. Very good. Let's get on with the day.

Church? Oh, shoot. Is it Sunday again already? I think I'll sleep in today. It's been a busy week.

I know I've been there, and I'm sure you have as well. But stop to think of the amazing message of Christianity: Jesus has literally saved your life. And not just your life on this earth, but your eternal life. You were unquestionably guilty, justly deserving punishment, but Jesus took your punishment in your place. It's as if you were on death row and someone else volunteered to die in your place. And because of Jesus' sacrifice, you no longer face hell. You are granted eternal life in heaven. That's absolutely amazing! But I know all this, and still I take it for granted. So what then?

1. Change up (or start) your personal devotions. I don't know about you, but sometimes I feel like I'm in a rut with my devotions. They're sort of like New Year's resolutions—I start off with good intentions, but after a while I burn out. The organized side of my brain loves the idea of reading through the entire Bible over the course of a year or two, but after a number of months I start to get bogged down. Devotions feel more like a chore than a privilege. So why not change things up? Who says I have to do the entire Bible in order? Try the chronological Bible that organizes the text not by individual books, but by the historical order in which the events occurred. Or find a good commentary or Bible study on one individual book so you can finish it in a couple weeks rather than committing to a year-long plan. Try something new, and you might be surprised at what you learn.

2. Immerse yourself in the Law. Admittedly, this sounds like a strange suggestion. Lutherans are all about the Gospel, after all, right? But before a person can be ready to hear the Gospel, he must first understand the full ramifications of the Law. A person who doesn't realize his need for a Savior has no need to hear of Jesus' sacrifice. So when you find yourself glossing over the Gospel, go back to the Law to remind yourself of just how far short you fall when it comes to God's demands. Try reading through one of the major or minor prophets. These men spoke God's Word to ancient Israel, and much of what they said could be spoken to us in America today. Read Jeremiah, for example—"Even the stork in the heavens knows her times…but My people know not the rules of the Lord" (Jeremiah 8:7). I admit, Jeremiah convicts me. Read through the Law, and take time to truly confess your sins to God—a real list, not just "Please forgive me, Lord." Pray through the Ten Commandments and confess specific sins regarding each one. Your heart will be much more appreciative of the Gospel once you know the full extent of the Law.

3. Read some fiction. Another weird recommendation, right? But sometimes (good!) Christian fiction can be a good way to live vicariously through the characters and make the reader look at things in a new and different way. What about a novel set in a society where Bibles are illegal? Is the message of the cross worth the risk of getting caught? Or what about a book where an unbeliever encounters the Gospel for the first time? Well-written fiction captures our emotions and gives us a deeper message to consider for our own lives.

Familiarity doesn't have to breed contempt. Consider the elderly couple whose shared joys and challenges have drawn them closer, and they find their love deeper than it ever was in their earlier years. That's the sort of relationship that is yours with your Savior as you grow more in your knowledge of His Word and His saving acts on your behalf. And that relationship is yours forever.

Life Lessons From a Child

July 7, 2014

Over the weekend, we were able to spend some time with my parents at their house. We had a nice cookout, played games together outside, and enjoyed good conversations. Sounds lovely, doesn't it? And it was, except that one of my children decided to throw a pity party after losing a game of badminton. He accused his adult opponent of cheating, started moping around, and made all sorts of "poor me" comments that got old fast. This is far from the first time such a thing has happened. We reprimanded him on the way home and had a fairly stony ride back. Then we got home and everyone went their own separate ways to get away from each other.

Some time later, I heard a knock on my door. It was my son coming to apologize. Sweet, right? Yet at the same time, as I'm sure many of you other parents out there can understand, also irritating, because I *knew* this wasn't the last time this would happen. It seems like we go through this same silly charade over and over again, and it gets to me after a while. Seriously, you'd think by now he would have learned his lesson, right?

Fast forward a few days to yesterday's church service. We got to the part in confession where there is a time of silence to confess our sins privately. I started reeling off my sins to God, and the confession I made was almost verbatim of the confession I had made the week before, and the week before that, and the week before that...

Okay, I get it, God. I'm no better than my son doing the same things over and over. After more than three decades in this world, you'd think I would have learned my lesson on some of this stuff, right? Yet I return over and over to the same old sins. And each time I come crawling back, God forgives me. No strings attached.

Thank God He isn't like me, an imperfect parent, sighing deeply when a child confesses. "Oh, fine, I forgive you, but I'm getting tired of doing this over and over again. Can't you just grow up and stop this already?" God doesn't do that with us. "If we confess our sins, He is faithful and just to forgive us our sins and to cleanse us from all unrighteousness," we are assured in 1 John 1:9. No fine print. No conditions.

When Peter asks Jesus how many times he should forgive his brother in Matthew 18:21, Jesus tells him either seventy-seven times or seventy times seven (depending on translation). Either way, Jesus isn't setting a limit. He's not saying, "Oh, look—you're at seventy-five times already! Better be careful, because you've almost reached your quota!" Not at all. Rather, He's expanding Peter's rather limited view of forgiveness and telling him that with God there is no limit on forgiveness.

While we are in this world, we will struggle constantly with sin. And trust me, the devil works his hardest on Christians because he desperately wants to turn them away from Christ. So is sin just no big deal? I mean, hey, if God forgives us anyhow, what difference does it make, right? Wrong. "Are we to continue in sin that grace may abound? By no means! How can we who died to sin still live in it?" Paul writes in Romans 6:1-2.

No, we shouldn't get complacent against sin. We should be fighting against it in our own lives, but as Paul laments in Romans 7:19, that's a never-ending process. "For I do not do the good I want, but the evil I do not want is what I keep on doing." Unfortunately, that's how it is as long as we're in this world. It's a constant tension. We won't ever "grow out of" sinning. But don't despair—God doesn't keep score. He doesn't roll His eyes when we confess the same sins over and over again. And so we can say confidently with Paul the words of Romans 7:25: "Thanks be to God, who delivers me through Jesus Christ our Lord!" (NIV).

What wonderful news indeed! No conditions. Just unconditional grace.

Even if He Does Not

July 10, 2014

You know the story well—the three men in a fiery furnace. Shadrach, Meshach, and Abednego didn't bow down to Nebuchadnezzar's gold statue, a "crime" which was punishable by death. So the three were bound and thrown into the furnace, but God saved them by sending "the angel of the Lord" into their midst, so that not one of their hairs was singed. What I really love is the response the three friends gave to the king before they were thrown into the fire. "We do not need to defend ourselves before you in this matter. If we are thrown into the blazing furnace, the God we serve is able to save us from it, and He will rescue us from your hand, O king. But *even if He does not*, we want you to know, O king, that we will not serve your gods or worship the image of gold you have set up" (Daniel 3:16-18, NIV, emphasis mine).

Even if He does not. Think about the full impact of those words. What are Shadrach, Meshach, and Abednego saying? "We know God *can* save us, but even if He doesn't, we won't turn away from Him." That's faith, my friends. Faith trusts God no matter what trials you face. These men were literally facing the prospect of death. I may have faced some tough times in my life, but I've never been threatened with death for my faith in God. These men were thrown into a blazing furnace for their faith, but they did not recant.

As hard as it may be to hear, there are times when it *isn't* God's will to rescue His people from suffering or death. Many of the apostles were martyred for their faith, and that fact stands as a clear testimony and encouragement to believers today who are persecuted for their faith. God doesn't promise that He will swoop in and save us from the trials we face in this life. He doesn't promise us a "happily ever after" on this earth. He doesn't tell us that if we're faithful enough, we will be free from worries. But He does promise to walk through it all with us.

So what is your "fiery furnace"? Perhaps you are experiencing sickness or disease. Maybe you grapple with unemployment or underemployment. Perhaps you're struggling with a bad relationship or divorce. Depression, anxiety, a rebellious child, bad finances—any of these things can seem overwhelming and lead us to despair. We beg God to deliver us and set things right. And He may do just that. In His own time and His own way, for His reasoning, perhaps He will deliver you as He did Job.

But then again, maybe He won't. For His own purposes and reasoning, maybe it's better for you not to be delivered. Maybe someone is watching your situation and will be more impacted by a persevering faith through trial than they would be if you were simply delivered from it all. Maybe you need to be an encouragement to someone in similar circumstances. It's likely that no matter what the reason, you may never even know *why* you need to endure the trials you face.

But there is hope. Even if God chooses not to deliver you from your earthly trials, there is a much greater deliverance in store for you in heaven, and that can never be taken away. James 1:12 reminds us, "Blessed is the man who remains steadfast under trial, for when he has stood the test he will receive the crown of life, which God has promised to those who love Him." That's a promise that *will* be yours in heaven, dear Christian. You can count on it.

Infestation

July 10, 2017

My first clue was the bites around my ankles. Nor could I deny that our dogs seemed to be scratching an awful lot. When I walked across the carpet in my girls' bedrooms one day, I looked at my socks and saw about five little black specks. Upon closer inspection, I realized they were exactly what I was afraid they were. *Fleas.*

Trust me, no one wants a flea infestation. They're hard to get rid of because by the time you realize you have them, they may have already laid eggs, further complicating your problem. A friend of mine once had to stay in a hotel while an exterminator came and "bombed" their house. I didn't want that to happen to us. So I sprang into action. Immediately I vacuumed and carpet cleaned every carpet. I washed sheets and clothes in hot water. I swept and steam mopped the tile flooring in our house. We gave the dogs a flea bath, and we used a flea comb and bought them flea collars and flea spray so we could deal with the problem at the source.

With a flea problem, one really has no choice but to be vigilant, or else it quickly goes from a nuisance to a full-blown infestation. One's hand is sort of forced to deal with the problem quickly. But what if we were as vigilant about rooting out sin in our lives as I am about killing off these fleas? In His Sermon on the Mount, Jesus uses some pretty strong language when talking about sin. He says, "If your right eye causes you to sin, tear it out and throw it away...And if your right hand causes you to sin, cut it off and throw it away. For it is better that you lose one of your members than that your whole body go into hell" (Matthew 5:29-30).

That sounds pretty drastic to me. Obviously, Jesus isn't promoting self-torture here. He's simply showing us how seriously we ought to take sin. And in dealing with sin, as in any other problem, we need to take care of it at its source. In the case of sin, that's the heart. "For out of the heart come evil thoughts, murder, adultery, sexual immorality, theft, false witness, slander. These are what defile a person..." (Matthew 15:19-20a).

James 1:14-15 spells out the process step by step. "But each person is tempted when he is lured and enticed by his own desire. Then desire when it has conceived gives birth to sin, and sin when it is fully grown brings forth death."

Whoa. That's not the kind of ending I want to see. So what's to be done? Stomp out sin at the root. Recognize the warning signs of sin by knowing and studying God's Word. Paul admits in Romans 7:7 that "if it had not been for the law, I would not have known sin. For I would not have known what it is to covet if the law had not said, 'You shall not covet.'" A better knowledge of Scripture makes one aware of what sin is, as opposed to what behavior is pleasing to God.

Of course, despite our best intentions and precautions, we will still sin. But thankfully, Jesus has done what we cannot. "For the law of the Spirit of life has set you free in Christ Jesus from the law of sin and death. For God has done what the law, weakened by the flesh, could not do. By sending His own Son in the likeness of sinful flesh and for sin, He condemned sin in the flesh, in order that the righteous requirement of the law might be fulfilled in us, who walk not according to the flesh but according to the Spirit" (Romans 8:2-4).

I'd much rather walk according to the Spirit than according to the flesh. And chances are, I won't even get black specks on my socks if I do.

The Good Side of Bad

July 14, 2014

My husband knew a guy in college who hadn't sinned for a year. He had found some religious group that showed him how to not sin, apparently, and this guy was completely serious about not sinning anymore. He's not the only Christian who believes this. Even some high-profile religious role models have made similar claims. But where is the focus when you believe you're not sinning anymore? Are your eyes fixed on Jesus, or on your own good works?

I have no qualms about admitting that I'm a sinner. I do it every day, often with great gusto. I don't mean to brag or anything, but if there's something I can do really well, it's sin. I don't even have to think about it most of the time. It comes naturally to me. And if you're being honest, you'd have to say the same thing.

Even the apostle Paul readily admits his own sinfulness. In 1 Timothy 1:15, he says, "Christ Jesus came into the world to save sinners, of whom I am the foremost." He calls himself the worst of sinners, and this he wrote under divine inspiration! So if Paul wasn't able to stop sinning, why should we be so bold as to think that we could overcome sin?

I'm not saying that we should settle into a routine of blatant sinning knowing that we'll be forgiven anyhow. There's a constant tension in the life of a Christian. We know we should stop sinning, but we can't. I *know* I should be patient and loving with my kids, but multiple times a day I lose patience with them nonetheless. It's terribly frustrating, and each night I vow to do better the next day, yet that never seems to happen. This is the Law at work. The Law is supposed to drive us to despair over our sins. It's supposed to show us that there's no way we can ever be right before God on our own accord. There's absolutely nothing we can do to save ourselves. But we can't stop there.

Look back at 1 Timothy 1:15. Jesus came into the world for what reason? "To save sinners." Aaaahhhh. And there's the sweet comfort of the Gospel. If I believed I wasn't sinning anymore, I wouldn't need that Gospel assurance. I could pat myself on the back and tell myself I was a true Christian because I had overcome sin. So if there's a "good" side to being bad, it's that my own sin and unworthiness drive me to the foot of the cross, where the most glorious exchange of all took place. There Jesus took my sin upon His sinless shoulders and gave me instead His righteousness. I can't understand that. Jesus became the most horrible sinner that ever lived as He hung upon that cross. And He did it for you. He did it for me. Don't let yourself get caught up in believing you can ever overcome sin. Only Jesus did that. Instead, when you do sin, turn to Him for His unfathomable forgiveness and mercy. I can't imagine better news.

Sand on the Seashore

July 16, 2018

Last week we went to the beach for a couple days. The kids had a wonderful time splashing in the warm waters of the Gulf of Mexico, jumping into the waves, finding seashells, and of course, playing in the sand. They dug holes, made sandcastles, and had sandball fights. But afterward, the sand was *everywhere*. Despite my best efforts to rinse our bathing suits, shake out our towels, and beat the sand out of the floor mats of the van, we still managed to escape with a fair amount of sand. It was as if a fine layer of sand had settled over everything. When I washed our towels and bathing suits at home, there was so much sand on the bottom of the washing machine afterward that it took two damp paper towels to collect it all. It's still all over the floor of the van. It's probably in our suitcases too, so that when we open them next time we go on a trip it'll be there to remind us of the beach. We just can't get rid of this stuff.

Anyone who has ever been to the beach knows exactly what I'm talking about. Sand is messy and pervasive and seemingly infinite. So maybe that's what God had in mind when He promised Abraham that his offspring would be as numerous as the sand on the sea. Jacob reminds God of this promise in Genesis 32:12: "I will surely do you good, and make your offspring as the sand of the sea, which cannot be numbered for multitude."

We are part of that multitude, for it wasn't just physical offspring to which God was referring. We are Abraham's spiritual descendants, believers in the one true God. Who can count all believers throughout the ages? Only God knows the exact count, but I assure you, it's a huge number.

But there's more to sand than just the vastness of it all. Another one of its qualities is how pervasive it is. If sand from one beach can make a trip of over 200 miles and end up in my washing machine here, how much more are Christians able to be Jesus' witnesses to all nations? The beautiful thing is that you don't need to go anywhere exotic to fulfill the Great Commission. God has dispersed His children all over the world, that all may hear His message of salvation. He has placed you exactly where you need to be to spread His saving Word. You are God's representative in your own family, your own workplace, your own community. You are His witness right where you are.

You don't even need to go to the beach.

Toning Up

July 17, 2017

I used to have toned muscles. Many moons ago when we lived in a bigger city and had two less children, I belonged to a gym, where I split my time between the elliptical and the resistance machines. I went three or four times a week, and with regular use, my muscles got stronger and more toned. But when we moved I didn't have a gym available, and with the addition of another baby, it was too hard to coordinate anyhow. So my muscles lost their nice toned look.

Recently I noticed just how un-toned they are, so I determined to strengthen them again. I found an app that led me through various exercises, and I felt great doing them—wall push ups, overhead presses, triceps dips. Ah, it was good to be working the various muscle groups. But the next day, those same muscles were pretty sore, and I had to admit a harsh truth—I'm not as in shape as I used to be.

If you don't use it, you lose it. So goes the old adage. If you don't practice an instrument, you'll eventually forget how to play it. If you aren't practicing the foreign language you took in high school, you'll forget most of it. If you quit exercising, you'll get flabby triceps. But does the same hold true for faith? That's a tricky question, because on the one hand, faith doesn't depend on us. It's a gift of God, who calls us to faith and keeps us in the saving knowledge of Jesus.

But at the same time, many Christians have been led astray by their own actions (or lack thereof). They are like the seeds in Jesus' parable that fell on rocky ground, where they sprouted quickly but had no root, and therefore fell away in a time of testing. This idea of being *rooted* is interesting. What does a Christian need to be rooted in? God's Word, of course. If we are to withstand the attacks of this world, we need to spend time daily in the Word. Personal Bible study and prayer are important, but so is corporate worship, where we hear God's Word preached to us and receive absolution and Holy Communion for the strengthening of our faith.

If I want to strengthen my arm muscles, I'm going to do a certain number of reps per week. This idea of repetition is important. Unless you repeat the exercises, they'll do you little good. A one-time marathon training session isn't going to help a person over the long haul. That would be nice, but it takes time and a long-term commitment if you want to see lasting results. The same is true of the Christian walk. Think Confirmation here—one or two years of instruction aren't enough to carry a person through his life if he decides to stay away from the church ever after. And yet many people unfortunately do just that.

Consider Paul's words in 2 Timothy 3:14-17. "But as for you, continue in what you have learned and have become convinced of, because you know those from whom you learned it, and how from infancy you have known the holy Scriptures, which are able to make you wise for salvation through faith in Christ Jesus. All Scripture is God-breathed and is useful for teaching, rebuking, correcting and training in righteousness, so that the man of God may be thoroughly equipped for every good work" (NIV).

That's a pretty compelling list of the benefits of being in the Word. Paul exhorts Timothy to *continue* in what he had learned. It's not a one-time deal. You'll never reach a point where you know it all or don't need God's Word to teach, correct, and guide you. There are many out there who would love to lead you astray, even some who call themselves Christian and yet teach things contrary to the Bible. How can you know if someone is correctly preaching and applying God's Word if you aren't immersed in that Word yourself? The Bereans in Acts 17:11 are commended because they "received the Word with all eagerness, examining the Scriptures daily to see if these things [that Paul taught them] were so." Would that the same be said of us!

In Ephesians 6, Paul lists the armor of God, and it's interesting to note that the one offensive weapon is the "sword of the Spirit, which is the Word of God" (v 17). That's how powerful His Word is. We can use it to combat the lies and attacks of the enemy. But again, how can we properly wield that sword if we don't know the Scripture?

So go ahead, pick up that Bible. Spend time in God's Word today. He will strengthen you as He sees fit. And you won't even have sore muscles tomorrow.

The Martha in Me

July 18, 2016

It's better to immerse yourself in God's Word than to spend your time doing menial tasks.

Oftentimes, that's the take-home message in the account of Mary and Martha, found in Luke 10:38-42. And while there's a grain of truth to that, at the same time, you can't take this principle too far. Household chores do need to be done. Your family has to eat. They need clean clothes. The baby has to be changed. You can't just cloister yourself in your room all day to read and pray. Jesus knew this. He wasn't chastising Martha for working. He and His disciples needed to eat too, and Martha was seeing to that need. He was chastising her attitude.

"Martha, Matha, you are anxious and troubled about many things…" Jesus tells her in Luke 10:42). He doesn't tell her she shouldn't be working and serving others. He tells her she shouldn't be anxious and troubled over it. The New Testament for Everyone version (NTE) translates this as "fretting and fussing." I don't know about you, but that hits home. I can fret and fuss like a pro. When I feel like I'm the only one working, I get upset, and I'm not above whining to God about it. *Why am I the only one who does anything around this house?* is unfortunately a tired refrain my kids have heard more than once.

What can you do if you find yourself grousing about your service to others, perhaps feeling like you're taken for granted? Remind yourself who you're serving. Yes, it may be your kids or spouse or coworkers, but it's deeper than that. Colossians 3:23 says, "Whatever you do, work heartily, as for the Lord and not for men." Interestingly, this passage is part of a section addressed to slaves (see v 22). I'm often tempted to think I'm a slave around my household! And yes, slaves serve their masters, but here Paul shows that ultimately, they're serving God. Same is true for you and for me. The service we render to others is ultimately for the Lord.

Jesus affirms this principle in Matthew 25:34-45. To His sheep He says, "I was hungry and you gave Me food, I was thirsty and you gave Me drink, I was a stranger and you welcomed Me, I was naked and you clothed Me, I was sick and you visited Me, I was in prison and you came to Me." When the righteous ask Jesus when they did these things, He says, "As you did it to one of the least of these My brothers, you did it to Me" (v 40).

If God asked you to do laundry for Him, would you do it? If He wanted you to care for young children all day for His sake, would you? Put in that context, the questions sound ridiculous. Yet that's exactly what His children are asked to do. He places us in homes with families who need our service, and sometimes, that service isn't terribly glamorous. Cooking and cleaning and changing diapers aren't exciting, but they need to be done. Remind yourself when you're in the midst of mundane chores that you're not only serving your family—you're serving God.

So Martha and I really do have a lot in common. Industrious, yes, and sometimes a bit miffed when others aren't helping the way we think they should. But the similarities don't stop there. Despite her attitude, Martha had the privilege of preparing food for Jesus Himself. And so, apparently, do I.

Start With the Children

July 20, 2015

I just finished a book about a man who smuggled Bibles into Communist countries to get them to struggling churches and Christians. In some cases, the government had issued "state Bibles," which were watered down and heavily edited to reflect state ideology. In other cases, congregations shared between them one single Bible, or even part of a Bible. They hungered desperately for the Word of God in their own hands. Hard to comprehend for me personally, when I look at my bookshelf and see half a dozen different translations of the Bible. The book was *God's Smuggler,* and the man was named simply "Brother Andrew." His experiences were fascinating to read, and each communist country tried to stamp out Christianity in their own way. But one particular ideology scares me more than the others. It's about the children.

While Brother Andrew was in Yugoslavia in 1945, he was surprised at first to see that churches were allowed to operate openly. He was able to go to these churches and preach whatever he wanted with little to no censure, a real change from other Communist countries he'd visited. But he soon realized what was happening. There wasn't a single person younger than twenty in the church. The schools and the government taught the children that there was no God. The kids were told just to humor the "uneducated" elderly people who believed in God. They were already luring the kids away from Church before they could become strong in their faith.

The tactics are actually very clever. The State replaced government rites for Church traditions—a "Welcoming Service" in place of infant baptism, "Youth Consecration" instead of confirmation, and even free marriage and funeral alternatives, showcasing how truly patriotic one was to his country. The Youth Consecration was especially tempting, since that ceremony took place at an age when conformity and fitting in are extremely important.

Lest we assume this doesn't happen in our own country, think again. Prayer is not allowed in public schools. Kids are taught from a young age not to talk about God or Jesus. Public schools teach evolution as fact from a young grade. As kids get older and enter adolescence, they're taught "safe sex" and given condoms, rather than encouraging the option of abstinence. And of course, kids are already being taught that a "family" can consist of a mom and dad, two moms, or two dads, all being equally acceptable. I've no doubt that as time goes on, the attacks will become more brazen.

What can be done? Beat them at their own game. Start with the children. Know that your children's faith will be under constant scrutiny, and equip them to handle it. Teach them what the Bible says, and be honest about what the world will try to tell them. Give them answers to rebut arguments others may raise against them, and be honest when you tell them that sometimes they may be ridiculed because of their "old fashioned" values and beliefs. But above all, stress that Jesus has already overcome the world. The world may fight against the Church viciously, but in the end, Jesus has already won the victory. This world isn't all there is. Eternity in heaven awaits all those who fight the good fight of the faith.

My own kids may roll their eyes when I pull out the Bible History book, they may whine that they don't want to sit through church or a devotion, but I keep at it because I've already seen God at work in their young hearts. This year my fifth grader had to take a STAAR warm-up science test. One particular question asked, "What created the world?" Then there was a blank for kids to write their own answer. My son, bless his heart, wrote "Jesus." In a public school, that's definitely not the answer they're looking for. So his teacher called him up to her desk and pointed at the question and the answer he had written. Rather than lecturing or scolding him, she simply said, "That's wrong, but good job."

It's never too early. Start with the children.

Who Am I?

July 21, 2014

One of my favorite musicals is *Les Misérables*. The plot is compelling and the music complements the story well. At the very beginning, the main character, Jean Valjean, is released from prison on parole. His jailer, Javert, comes to give him the news and refers to him as "24601," his prisoner number. When Valjean tells him, "My name is Jean Valjean," Javert ignores that and continues to call him "24601."

Later in the story, after Valjean has built an honorable life and is well respected, an innocent man who happens to look like Valjean is captured and thought to be the escaped convict 24601. Valjean sings a poignant song, *Who Am I?*, which highlights his inner struggle of whether or not he should confess who he really is to save the innocent man. As he sings to himself, he keeps asserting his name as Jean Valjean. But when at last he decides to confess to Javert, he ends in a climactic way by identifying himself as Javert sees him: 24601. Throughout the story, Javert sees Valjean as no more than a number, never as a person with a name and a story.

Ah, numbers. We live by them, don't we? When we call about a bill we are asked for our customer number. When we go to the doctor we give our insurance card so they can punch in our number. We need to know our bank account number for access to our account. For legal purposes we have to give our social security number many times, and more often than not, we have to punch in these numbers before we even give our names.

But aren't you more than a number? Does it make you feel nameless to be thought of as a number? Just one in a crowd? Perhaps you've even considered how many people there are in the world and then think in despair, *Why would God care about me and my little problems? He has the entire world to keep in order, and I'm just one insignificant little person.* If you've ever thought that way, you're in good company. David had those same thoughts. Look at what he says in Psalm 8:3-4: "When I look at Your heavens, the work of Your fingers, the moon and the stars, which You have set in place, what is man that You are mindful of him, and the son of man that You care for him?"

When you stop to consider the incredible things God has made, His power is apparent. The mountains, the stars in the sky, the seasons, mighty waterfalls, gorgeous sunsets, towering trees, the depths of the ocean—all of this and more God has created and set in place. What's more, He continues to care for creation. But despite it all, He still cares for us. Personally.

Romans 8:26-27 says, "Likewise, the Spirit helps us in our weakness. For we do not know what to pray for as we ought, but the Spirit Himself intercedes for us with groanings too deep for words…The Spirit intercedes for the saints according to the will of God." Can you imagine that? The Holy Spirit prays for me—*me*, whose own prayers are often halfhearted and selfish. It's true; I don't know what to pray for. My prayers are so limited in their scope it's embarrassing. But the Holy Spirit picks up the slack and brings true intercessions before God on high.

Why would the Holy Spirit bother with our prayers? Most of us won't accomplish great things on this earth. Most of us aren't going to be famous or rich or influential beyond our scope of acquaintances. Relatively few people in this world know our names. Of all the people throughout all the ages who have ever existed, it's easy to feel nameless, just a number in a crowd. But you aren't, dear one. Consider God's words in Isaiah 43:1: "But now thus says the Lord, He who created you, O Jacob, He who formed you, O Israel: 'Fear not, for I have redeemed you; I have called you *by name,* you are Mine'" (emphasis added). Do you see the personal involvement of God? He created and formed you, and He calls you personally *by name*. You aren't just a number to God.

It doesn't stop there. Here's the best part—He doesn't just call you by the name on your birth certificate. He gives you *His* name. When you were baptized, you were baptized into the Triune name of God—the Father, Son and Holy Spirit. You bear Christ's name now—*Christian*. He claims you as His own. What incredible love.

There are numerous examples in the New Testament of God calling us His sons and daughters, adopting us as His own. Ephesians 1:5-6 says, "For He chose us in Him before the creation of the world to be holy and blameless in His sight. In love He predestined us to be adopted as His sons through Jesus Christ." You are chosen by the God of heaven and earth. You are precious in His sight. No matter how insignificant you feel in the vast scheme of things, never forget this amazing truth—God chose you. God knows you by name; You are His.

Out of Our League

July 24, 2014

This past weekend my son had a baseball tournament. It was painful. They were the only local team playing against travel teams. Serious teams that practice during the winter and play in competitions most weekends throughout the summer. Our kids lost every single game. Badly. I think in four games they scored a grand total of five runs, which wasn't even half of what the other teams scored against them in one game. It was obvious from about the second inning of the first game that we were way out of our league. The kids knew there was no way they could possibly win against these other teams, but they kept playing nonetheless. No one quit or walked away or threw their glove down in disgust. I'm sure they were frustrated, but they kept on going. They pulled together as a team and encouraged each other through it all.

Maybe you can relate. Perhaps you've been hired for a job only to realize your coworkers all held PhD's in their area of expertise. Maybe you signed up for a class only to discover that it was way over your head. We can probably all think of earthly examples, but we are all most definitely out of our league when it comes to the spiritual battle waging in the world today. The captain of that team, the devil, is cunning and mean. He will stop at nothing to win. He cheats, lies, and uses whatever other tactics he can to pull out the victory. We're no match for him at all. He's been doing this for 6000 years, and he's gotten really good at it.

Do you ever consider society around you and feel isolated? Do you feel like you're the only one who clings to any semblance of traditional morals? You aren't, of course, but the devil would have you believe that. He wants you to feel out of touch with modern society so he can convince you that the things going on out there aren't really so bad. Take a stand against abortion? Stand up for marriage between a man and a woman? You're judgmental and closed minded, he would have you believe. We see judges making rulings that infringe on our traditional beliefs and religious freedoms, and the devil cunningly convinces us to remain silent. *It's no big deal,* he whispers. *It's not affecting you personally right now, so why bother?* In the spiritual war raging in this world, we are way out of our league, and the consequences are far more serious than a baseball win or loss. We're talking eternal consequences.

There's a reason the devil fights so hard. *He has already lost the game.* He has already been defeated. That happened 2000 years ago when the most unlikely hero of all stepped into this world of sin and death. Jesus, true God, left the majesty and glory that is rightfully His and stepped into the world as one of us. He stood up to the devil and prevailed. The devil's underhanded tactics didn't work on Jesus. But when Jesus hung bruised and bleeding on the cross, the picture of humiliation and defeat, it looked as though the devil had won. He rejoiced in his lair as Jesus' dead body was placed in the cold tomb. He had won!

Or had he? Three days later, Jesus rose victorious from that tomb. Even death could not hold Him. The devil, despite his very best efforts, had lost. *That's* why he tries so hard now. He's still stinging from his loss, and he does all he can to pull us down with him now. Don't let him fool you—you're on the winning team.

In the meantime, what can we do? On our own, it's true, we are no match for the devil and this world. Yes, Jesus has already won the victory for us, but we live in the "now and not yet." We are still here in this world of sin, and although Jesus has earned salvation for us, we have not yet reached heaven.

So now what? Take a lesson from my son's team. Although they consistently lost, they pulled together as a team. They encouraged each other. We need to do the same as Christians on this earth. Pull together and find strength by meeting with fellow Christians. Encourage others in their walks in life. Don't give up or walk off the field. Remember the words of Hebrews 10:24-25: "And let us consider how to stir up one another to love and good works, not neglecting to meet together, as is the habit of some, but encouraging one another, and all the more as you see the Day drawing near."

All true Christians are part of the invisible Church, with members from all times and all places. Moses, David, Peter, John, Paul—they're all on our team. Their words in Scripture still encourage us today. And someday we will gather with them and all other Christians who ever lived in the most glorious victory party ever—heaven. But in the meantime, don't despair. Invite others to join our team. Encourage your teammates. And let's get out there in this world and play some ball.

Predictable

July 24, 2017

I started reading a new book the other day. By the end of the first chapter, I knew who would end up with whom and what seemingly insurmountable obstacle would be overcome in the course of the story. It was completely predictable. And yet I continued reading, and thoroughly enjoyed the book. A number of books and movies are like this. We know pretty much from the get-go what's going to happen. And this knowledge helps us through the conflicts and tensions that arise in the middle of the story. We soldier on, through painful setbacks and embarrassing scenes, knowing that things are going to turn out okay in the end. We trust that the author has the characters' best interests in mind and will bring them to a satisfying conclusion.

It would be nice if real life played out like a book, where all the pieces fall into place exactly the way they should, and you knew for certain that everything would work out in the end. Wouldn't it be nice if you knew you'd suddenly get a huge amount of money to pay for the medical treatment you desperately need? that a strained relationship would be fixed? that you would find the perfect soulmate? But we don't have any such assurances. Things don't always work out the way they would in a book or movie. We don't always get a happy ending. And yet, we do.

Believe it or not, God has a book, and you're one of the characters. "All the days ordained for me were written in Your book before one of them came to be," David says in Psalm 139:16 (NIV). Before you were even born, God knew you would exist, and He knew how long your life on this earth would be.

But He didn't stop there. The insurmountable obstacle in your story is sin. You couldn't fix that, so God solved the problem for you by sending His Son to take the punishment you deserved. Hebrews 12:2a encourages us, "Let us fix our eyes on Jesus, the author and perfecter of our faith…" (NIV). Jesus is the *author* of our faith. He is the one who creates it, and He promises to perfect it, or bring it to completion. Revelation 21:27 gives us a glimpse of that completion in heaven: "Nothing unclean will ever enter it, nor anyone who does what is detestable or false, but only those who are written in the Lamb's book of life."

Dear Christian, *you* are written in that book of life. I can't promise you that your earthly troubles will go away. But I can assure you that your Heavenly Father is with you through those troubles, and you will get your happy ending in heaven, no matter what happens to you here on earth. Trust your Author to see you safely to that happy conclusion. It's completely predictable.

A True Love Story

July 28, 2014

The movie *The Vow* is based on a true story where a wife loses her memory after a car accident and can't even recognize her own husband. Rather than letting her go, the husband works to win back her love. It's an inspiring story, one that makes women swoon to see the husband go to such lengths to win her back. We like this kind of story, because secretly we'd all like to be that valuable in someone's eyes. We'd love to have someone go to all that trouble to win our affections. But the fact is that someone *has* gone to incredible lengths to win you back.

One of my favorite passages in the New Testament is Matthew 13:44-46. We read two parables that are very similar—in one, a man finds a treasure buried in a field and sells all he has in order to buy the field. In the other, a man searches for fine pearls, and when he finds one of great value he, too, sells all he has to buy that pearl. On the surface, these two both imply that the kingdom of God is of such value that we should be willing to give up all we have in order to gain it. That's what the footnote in one of my Bibles tells me, and that's what a lot of Sunday school lessons teach. But that's not what it means at all.

Yes, we *should* be willing to give up all we have to gain eternal life, but that also implies that somehow we can buy or merit salvation, and the Bible is quite clear that we can never do that. And even if we wanted to, none of us could ever truly give up *all* we have to gain eternal life. There's only one Person who can and did do that—Jesus. He gave up His throne in heaven to come down to this broken world. He gave up everything that was rightfully His in heaven to become a man like one of us.

Why? Because *you are that pearl. You* are the treasure in the field. Jesus gave up all He had to come die on this earth because *you* were worth it to Him. He would rather give up everything He had than be separated from you forever. He loves you that much.

Through all the people and generations of the Old Testament, and even the years in exile, God preserved His people and Jesus' family line so that Jesus could be born one day to a poor Jewish couple. He waited through 4,000 years until the timing was exactly right. "When the fullness of time had come, God sent forth His Son, born of woman, born under the law, to redeem those who were under the law, so that we might receive adoption as sons," Galatians 4:4-5 assures us. This was a carefully planned event. Jesus coming into the world when He did was no accident. God carefully planned His entrance into humanity, and He carefully planned your salvation as well.

No matter how you came to faith, it was no accident. Perhaps you were born to a family who has passed on the faith for generations. Maybe you came to faith later in life because of the faithful prayers and witness of a friend. No matter the "how," God planned your salvation from eternity, because when He looks at you He sees a pearl of great worth, a priceless treasure, His joy. And He has been working from all eternity to establish your salvation.

He didn't choose you because of any inherent goodness on your part. We truly have nothing of any worth to offer the Lord of the universe. *He* makes us worthy by giving us His own righteousness. You see, He really did give up everything for you—even His own sinless righteousness. He gave that to you and took instead your sinfulness upon Himself on the cross.

Whenever you doubt your worth or your purpose in this world, remember the words of 1 John 3:1: "How great is the love the Father has lavished on us, that we should be called children of God! And that is what we are!" (NIV). You are God's own child. He has seen to that, and He went to incredible lengths to win you back. Now *that's* a love story. And even better, it's *your* love story. A true love story of a Savior who loved you enough to give up all He had just for you. Thank God for His amazing love!

Far From Home

July 29, 2019

Having returned not long ago from a 4000-mile, three-week family trip, we've seen our fair share of license plates. In our part of rural Texas, we see mainly other Texas plates, with an occasional out-of-state plate from Louisiana or Oklahoma. But in the Northeast, our destination for this trip, seeing another Texas plate was rare. We took an overnight camping trip to Maine while on our trip, and seeing another Texas plate in the campground was really exciting. We felt an instant bond with the other Texas family that had made the long haul north. The further away you are, the more exciting it is to see someone from home.

Home. The word itself can mean a few different things. When you're out shopping and you say you're going "home," it means to the house where you currently live. But there's a deeper meaning too. I personally think of Michigan as my home, even though I now live 1300 miles away. In that sense, *home* is the place where you grew up. Either way, *home* is a place where memories are made, a place where one feels loved and accepted and safe.

Granted, there are some people for whom home is *not* a safe place, and that's heartbreaking. Home is supposed to be a loving, caring, supportive environment, and when one's home does not meet those needs, serious damage can be done to a person. But no matter what your home is like here on earth, you aren't truly *home* yet.

The Bible talks about Christians as strangers in this world. 1 Peter 2:11-12 says, "Dear friends, I urge you, as aliens and strangers in the world, to abstain from sinful desires, which war against your soul. Live such good lives among the pagans that, though they accuse you of doing wrong, they may see your good deeds and glorify God on the day He visits us" (NIV). We are "aliens and strangers." In other words, we're on a long trip through a foreign land, with heaven as our true home.

Hebrews 11 talks about people who lived out their faith in ways the world cannot fathom. Then we read, "These all died in faith, not having received the things promised, but having seen them and greeted them from afar, and having acknowledged that they were strangers and exiles on the earth. For people who speak thus make it clear that they are seeking a homeland. If they had been thinking of that land from which they had gone out, they would have had opportunity to return. But as it is, they desire a better country, that is, a heavenly one. Therefore God is not ashamed to be called their God, for He has prepared for them a city" (Hebrews 11:13-16). Philippians 3:20a reiterates, "But our citizenship is in heaven…" This earth isn't all there is.

On this lifelong trip, people notice us. Like a Hawaii license plate in the Midwest, Christians are *supposed* to stand out from the world around us. As the verse from 1 Peter exhorts, we should live such good lives among nonbelievers that they see our good deeds and glorify God.

Likewise, this comparison means we should seek the company of fellow Christians along our journey. As our family felt a bond with the other Texas family in Maine, so fellow Christians should support one another in this world. In church, we're surrounded by other Christians and draw strength from God's Word and Sacraments together. But when we're out in the world, in the workplace or at school, we probably aren't surrounded by fellow Christians. That's why it's so important to meet together regularly, to remind ourselves that we aren't alone.

Someday we will reach our true home—heaven. But in the meantime, travel wisely. Invite others to journey with you. Support fellow travelers along the way. It may not be an easy journey, but the final destination is absolutely worth it.

What's It All About?

July 31, 2014

The story of Joseph has long intrigued and fascinated me. He was sold into slavery by his jealous brothers who couldn't stand that he was their father's favorite. At the age of seventeen he was taken to Egypt as a slave, and there experienced a lot of ups and downs (Potiphar's wife, prison, etc). This young man had a lot of blows to deal with. He had a few major upheavals that changed the course of his life, yet he didn't abandon his faith. More importantly, God didn't abandon him. And the scene near the end when Joseph finally reveals to his brothers who he is and forgives them—it's a perfect tear-jerker ending. Even Hollywood would be hard pressed to top that. But let's look at an aspect of Joseph's life that may make us uncomfortable.

Psalm 105:16-22 summarizes the story of Joseph, and verse 17 gives a startling revelation. "He [God] had sent a man ahead of them [to Egypt], Joseph, who was sold as a slave." Wait, wait, wait. *What?* You mean to tell me that this evil act on the brothers' part was actually part of God's plan? I'm not sure I'm entirely comfortable with that. Does God really work through evil, through sinning? No, God doesn't work *through* evil. He works *in spite of* it. In other words, God accomplishes His purposes despite what we sinful human beings do to get in His way.

Joseph realizes this by the time his brothers come to him asking for food. As he speaks to them in Genesis 45, he reassures them over and over. "God sent me before you to preserve life" (v 5), "God sent me before you…" (v 7), "So it was not you who sent me here, but God" (v 8).

This is the part that may be difficult to swallow. Sometimes your life isn't about you. I never could have foreseen where my life would take me. Our current situation is a far cry from what I envisioned. In many ways, it looks like defeat from a human perspective. But God doesn't see things from our perspective, and He has a way of working through painful situations to accomplish His purposes. It's a hard pill for my human pride to swallow, but *my life isn't about me.* And neither is yours.

But here's the thing—Jesus' life wasn't about Him either. It was about *you.* He didn't come down to earth to party and be successful and popular. He came to rescue *you.* He lived His entire life perfectly for *you.* He suffered for doing the right thing because *you* did the wrong things. He took the punishment that should have been *yours* upon His sinless shoulders, and He died for *your* transgressions. But that's not the end of the story. He rose from the dead victorious three days later, defeating death for *you.* Because His life was about you, His victory is yours as well. Life here on this earth is hard. It really is. But that's not the end of the story, because eternal life in heaven awaits. *That's* what it's all about.

Expecting a Miracle

July 31, 2017

The disciples should have been expecting it. After all, they'd seen Jesus do it before. But when it came down to it, they still doubted Jesus could fix the problem. Mark 8:1-4 gives the following account:

In those days, when again a great crowd had gathered, and they had nothing to eat, He called His disciples to Him and said to them, "I have compassion on the crowd, because they have been with me now three days and have nothing to eat. And if I send them away hungry to their homes, they will faint on the way. And some of them have come from far away." And His disciples answered Him, "How can one feed these people with bread here in this desolate place?"

Sigh. Just two chapters ago, the disciples witnessed the feeding of the 5,000 with just five loaves and two fish. (Actually, it was a lot more than 5,000, since that number doesn't include women and children.) What's more, there were twelve baskets of leftovers. And now history is repeating itself. Another large crowd, this time 4,000 men plus women and children, again getting hungry after listening to Jesus' teaching. But despite the fact that Jesus had already multiplied loaves and fish for an even larger crowd, the disciples balked at the daunting task of feeding so many people. Did they forget how Jesus had provided for everyone last time? Did they think He wouldn't provide again? Where is their faith?

It's much easier to shake our heads at the lack of faith in others than to acknowledge that same lack of faith in ourselves. We roll our eyes at the Israelites facing the Red Sea with the Egyptians coming behind them, crying out in fear that they should have just died in Egypt. After God clearly showed His power by sending the plagues and by passing over their houses during the final plague, did they think He would let them down now? Did they honestly believe a body of water could stop their God from saving them as He had promised?

Or what about Peter? When Jesus walks on water out to their boat in the middle of a storm, Peter boldly asks Jesus to invite *him* to walk on water also. Jesus complies and tells him to come, but fear gets the better of Peter as he sees the wind and the waves, and he starts to sink. Did he think Jesus would let him drown? Wasn't he in the boat some time earlier when Jesus rebuked the wind and the waves to be still? Does he *still* not realize Jesus has power over creation? So of course Jesus saves him, and then gives Peter a gentle rebuke. "O you of little faith, why did you doubt?" (Matthew 14:31).

The Bible has many examples of such moments of weakness in the life of God's saints, and some seem downright silly. Like those disciples facing the crowd of 4,000 people not so long after the feeding of the 5,000, we might well ask, "Have you already forgotten?" But when we're facing our own crises, then it's not so easy to expect a miracle. It's not so easy to remember what God has done for us in the past. *Yes, I know God has never let us go hungry before, but I don't get paid again until next week and we're already dangerously low on groceries,* you might fret. Or perhaps you've just received the devastating news that your cancer has returned. Maybe a loved one has suffered a stroke and you're concerned that you won't be able to afford proper care. Perhaps the loss of a job has you worried that you won't be able to provide for your family anymore. In the face of such situations, it's not so easy to trust God when the outcome is uncertain, even if we can look back to how He has cared for us in the past.

The fact is that we *don't* know how things will turn out on earth. People do go hungry. There isn't always enough money to pay for necessities. Disease ravages the body. People die from accidents, illness, and tragedy. God doesn't promise every situation will have a happy resolution. But He does promise to be with us in all those situations.

God has proven His love for you in the past by His perfect life and His sinless suffering and death on your behalf. No matter what you must endure on this earth, you can be sure that death will not be the end. Jesus has already performed His most spectacular miracle by rising from the grave to defeat death, and He promises that all who believe in Him will likewise live.

So go ahead. Expect a miracle.

August

Divine Discontent

August 7, 2014

Recently I read a novel called *Upon This Rock* by Frank G Slaughter. It's about the life of Simon Peter, who has long been one of my favorite apostles. One thing that struck me was the use of a peculiar phrase. Three times Slaughter said that Peter had been infused with *divine discontent.*

It's a strange phrase at first blush, but in the context of the story it makes perfect sense. He's not talking about being dissatisfied with what you have or anything related to one's earthly lot in life. This is a spiritual discontent, one that led Peter (in this novel) to expand his horizons for spreading the Gospel. The first time this phrase is used is after Pentecost, when the Church was growing and thriving in Jerusalem, and Jews from all over the world had heard the message and were carrying it back to their own lands. But despite the rapid expansion of the Church, Peter knew there needed to be an even bigger platform from which to tell the news of Jesus' atoning death and resurrection. Thus, he was infected with this "divine discontent."

Later the phrase occurred after Peter had been in Joppa some time, and felt restless, knowing again that feeling of "divine discontent," which this time preceded his dream about the unclean animals and his subsequent trip to Caesarea to visit Cornelius and preach to Gentiles there. It's more of a feeling that he couldn't be content to stay where he was, in a familiar context. He needed to move on and continue spreading the Gospel elsewhere. There were plenty of other people in the world who had yet to hear about Jesus, both Jews and Gentiles. He (and the other Christians) needed to get out there and spread that word everywhere.

Do you ever get "divine discontent"? Are you content with the ways you are sharing the Good News of Jesus? Have you become complacent about telling others about the Savior? Satan works hard to infect Christians instead with a sense of complacency. *Hey, I'm doing what I can. I don't want to force Jesus down anyone's throat. I'll just live a good life and let others see my actions, since actions speak louder than words, right?*

We've been duped into thinking that we shouldn't offend people by sharing our faith. But the Law *does* offend. That's its whole purpose. We're supposed to see in the Law the complete hopelessness of our situation; the fact that we can never hope to free ourselves from our sinful condition. That offends people. We don't like to admit that we're helpless in anything.

Here's where the beautiful news of the Gospel assures us that Jesus has taken our punishment upon Himself. He offers the free gift of eternal life to all who believe in Him. Will everyone jump for joy when you tell them this message? No. Some will reject it. That's not on you. Spread the Word regardless, like the sower whose seed falls on fertile and hostile soil alike. Yes, the message of the cross is "a stumbling block to Jews and folly to Gentiles, but to those who are called…Christ the power of God and the wisdom of God" (1 Corinthians 1:23-24).

But isn't it "unloving" to claim that Jesus is the only way to heaven? Are we intolerant? Not at all. Quite the opposite, in fact. If you saw a friend destroying his life by abusing drugs or alcohol, is it loving to ignore that and let him continue on the path of destruction? Of course not. Although it may be hard, the loving thing to do is to correct him and get him the help he needs. Likewise, if you see your fellow man on the path of eternal destruction, following a false god blindly, the most loving thing you can do is to point him instead to the One who alone gives eternal life. It is unloving to ignore his need and let him continue in his false beliefs that can only lead to eternal separation from the true God.

So Christian, *go*. Don't fight the feeling of "divine discontent." That's the Holy Spirit working on you, urging you to get out there and spread the Word of life in a world that desperately needs it. I admit that I don't always have that discontent. Oh, I'll get spurts of it here and there when I really stop to consider all the people who need to hear about Jesus, but by and large, I've become quite good at being complacent about sharing my faith. But I've found a curious thing to be true. The more you share the Gospel message, the more your eyes are opened to the true need to share it, and the more discontent you are. Don't ignore those urgings, but thank God for such divine discontent.

God's First Words

August 12, 2019

First words are a milestone. Parents encourage their babies to make meaningful sounds when they start babbling, coaxing them to say "Mama" or "Dada." When the baby finally does say his or her first word, proud parents share the news and brag to their friends about how smart their child is, perhaps even teasing each other about which parent got the honor of being named first. It makes me wonder what Jesus' first word was. The Bible doesn't see fit to tell us, but it is interesting to read God's first recorded words in Scripture.

In Hebrew narrative, first words are very important. A character's first words help us understand that person better, as those words give insight into his character. So it is interesting to see that the first character in the Bible to speak is none other than God Himself, and His first words in the narrative of Genesis are indicative of His character: "Let there be light" (Genesis 1:3).

The account of creation is one of the more well-known stories in the Bible. It seems like every Sunday School curriculum, every VBS program, and every children's Bible story book begins with creation. After a while, people may be tempted to glaze over it and think, *Yeah, yeah, I know all this. God created the world. Let's move on already.* But take a moment to think about God's first recorded words about light.

Anyone who knows the Bible knows that there are many references to light in Scripture, and not just physical light. Yes, God was creating light and darkness, day and night, that first day of creation, but there's a deeper level here. The Bible often contrasts light and darkness, referring to faith and spiritual blindness. The book of John, in particular, highlights this theme. In fact, the beginning of John refers back to creation, parroting the first words of Genesis, "In the beginning…" We learn from John 1 that "all things were made through [Jesus], and without Him was not any thing made that was made. In him was life, and the life was the light of men. The light shines in the darkness, and the darkness has not overcome it" (John 1:3-5).

What is this "light" of which John speaks? Jesus, of course. Later in the Gospel of John, Jesus states, "I am the light of the world. Whoever follows Me will not walk in darkness, but will have the light of life" (8:12). Jesus *is* the light who was with God from the beginning, who came into the world as a man, and who will be our light into eternity. As the Bible begins with light, it also ends with light. In speaking of the New Jerusalem (heaven) John writes, "Night will be no more. They will need no light of lamp or sun, for the Lord God will be their light, and they will reign forever and ever" (Revelation 22:5, see also Revelation 21:22-25).

Yes, God's first words are indicative of His character, for He brings light into a world of spiritual darkness. He brings us to faith in Jesus, the light of the world, and He will keep us in His light forever. Indeed, "Let there be light."

Surviving in a Hostile Environment

August 14, 2017

I'm only half-joking when I say that I live in a hostile environment. As a Michigan transplant to Texas, I'm not used to the climate. It's much hotter here, and the sun is a lot more intense. Some days I can't get enough water. When the heat index is over 100 and the air conditioner runs constantly to keep it at eighty, even being inside is dehydrating, and I drink water all day long. Summertime is downright miserable. My poor blond-haired children are no match for the sun, so I need to be extra vigilant about protecting them, lest they burn or get dehydrated.

When you live in a place with excessive heat, you plan accordingly by limiting exposure to the sun, protecting your skin, and staying hydrated. I limit the amount of time my kids can play outside in the summer. If we go swimming or to the beach, we lather up with sunscreen and reapply it multiple times. I have long-sleeved swimsuits with shorts for my youngest kids who burn more easily. They wear hats to protect their faces and keep the sun out of their eyes. And we all drink plenty of water. We need to do these things for our own protection.

If you're a Christian, you are also in a hostile environment, no matter your earthly address. Jesus tells His disciples, "If you were of the world, the world would love you as its own; but because you are not of the world, but I chose you out of the world, therefore the world hates you" (John 15:19). This is painfully obvious when Christians are ridiculed and insulted for being "narrow-minded" on things like the LGBTQ agenda. When it comes to life issues, we are not "pro-life," but "anti-abortion" or "anti-women's rights." Those who dare to take a stand for truth are belittled or defamed, causing many to choose silence or compromise instead.

So how can you protect yourself? Limit exposure, protect yourself, and drink up. Limit your exposure to dangerous influences like movies or TV shows with bad morals, questionable websites, and unwholesome books. "Put on the full armor of God, that you may be able to stand against the schemes of the devil," as Paul advises in Ephesians 6:11. Drink deeply of the living water. Jesus says in John 7:37-38, "If anyone thirsts, let him come to Me and drink. Whoever believes in Me, as the Scripture has said, 'Out of his heart will flow rivers of living water.'"

In addition, surround yourself with like-minded Christians both in and out of church services on Sunday mornings. The writer of Hebrews reminds us, "And let us consider how to stir one another to love and good works, not neglecting to meet together, as is the habit of some, but encouraging one another, and all the more as you see the Day drawing near" (Hebrews 10:24-25). Just as I need to remind my kids to reapply sunscreen or drink water, so believers encourage each other to give up sinful habits, to keep the faith, and to study the Scriptures.

Yes, you do live in a hostile environment in this world, but it won't always be that way. Revelation draws a beautiful picture of heaven, the "new Jerusalem." Revelation 21:23 tells us that heaven "has no need of sun or moon to shine on it, for the glory of God gives it light, and its lamp is the Lamb." A few verses later in 22:1, we read about "the river of the water of life, bright as crystal, flowing from the throne of God and of the Lamb." That's what we get to look forward to—an environment that's absolutely perfect.

Perfect Preparation

August 18, 2014

When I was in high school, there was an eight-way tie for valedictorian. Rather than each of us making a lengthy speech, we worked together to make one speech split up into eight sections. Each of us had a different topic to address in three to four minutes. But there was one quote that tied everything together. We all referenced a quote attributed to Corrie ten Boom: "Every experience God gives us, and every person He puts in our lives, is the perfect preparation for the future that only He can see."

Corrie ten Boom was in a Nazi concentration camp for some time. Her family died there. And yet, years later, she was able to say that all of her life experiences were preparing her for a future only God could see. She went on to be a powerful speaker who spoke of forgiveness and God's love. Many people heard the Gospel message through her. She perceived that God was using those horrible experiences of her youth to prepare her for greater things as she got older. I doubt she would have chosen to see her life lived out that way, but God used even those terrible experiences to bring hope to others who were hurting.

Most of us will probably never be in a concentration camp or speak to large audiences about our experiences like Corrie ten Boom did, but God is working through our lives nonetheless. Romans 8:28 reminds us, "And we know that for those who love God all things work together for good, for those who are called according to His purpose."

All things work together for good? I can think of a few things that sure don't look like they're working out for my "good." In my college days, I naïvely thought this passage meant I would have smooth sailing in life. I underlined it and put a cute smiley face next to it. But that's not at all what this passage is implying. One of the basic maxims of biblical interpretation is to let Scripture interpret Scripture. Jesus says in John 16:33, "I have said these things to you, that in Me you may have peace. In the world you will have tribulation. But take heart; I have overcome the world."

Jesus never promises that everything in life will be good. He tells us instead to expect trouble in this world. But He has overcome the world. He has defeated our worst enemies for us already. Sin, death, and the devil have already been overcome. They cannot harm us eternally.

So let's return to Romans. Another principle of biblical interpretation is to take a passage in context. You can't just pull one verse out at random and make it mean what you want it to mean. Read on in Romans 8. Paul asserts that despite "tribulation, or distress, or persecution, or famine, or nakedness, or danger, or sword," we are "more than conquerors through Him who loved us. For I am sure that…[nothing] in all creation, will be able to separate us from the love of God that is in Christ Jesus our Lord" (Romans 8:37-39).

You see, *that's* the "good" God promises us—the unending love of Christ. He's talking about our eternal good. We may have a really crummy life this side of eternity, like the poor beggar Lazarus from the story of the rich man and Lazarus, but no temporal circumstances can snatch away the eternal victory Jesus won for us.

God is working in *all* things toward your eternal good. Yes, "every experience God gives you and every person He puts in your life is the perfect preparation for the future that only He can see." That can apply to circumstances on this earth, but far more importantly, God is preparing you for a future that only He can see—a future in heaven with Him forever.

Commending Dishonesty

August 21, 2014

I've always wondered about the parable of the shrewd (or "dishonest," depending on translation) manager from Luke 16:1-9. That sentence at the end is so bizarre: "I tell you, use worldly wealth to gain friends for yourselves, so that when it is gone, you will be welcomed into eternal dwellings." That doesn't sound like something Jesus would say, especially as a summary of the parable. And unlike some of His other parables, Jesus doesn't take His disciples aside and explain things to them privately afterward. We're sort of just left to figure it out on our own.

The key to understanding this parable is to realize that it's not about the manager at all (title notwithstanding). It's about the master. The manager is wasting (literally "squandering") his master's wealth, and his master knows it. Luke uses the same word here as he does in the parable immediately preceding this one, the parable of the prodigal son. In fact, these two parables are very closely related. Both the prodigal son and the dishonest manager are "squandering" wealth that is not their own. Both face a crisis—the prodigal son is forced to feed pigs and eat their food, the dishonest manager is fired and sees no viable options to escape from his dilemma. Both the prodigal son and the dishonest manager come to the same conclusion: their only option is to throw themselves to the mercy of their benefactor—the father of the prodigal son and the master of the dishonest manager.

Both parables are also based on the assumption that the authority figure in each is honorable and merciful. The prodigal son's father does not receive him back as a slave, but as a son, which was far more than he deserved based upon his actions. And rather than throwing the manager in jail immediately, which was the master's right, he allowed his wasteful servant time to prepare for his termination. During this time, the manager realized that his only solution was to bank on the mercy of the master. The readiness of the debtors to accept the lessening of their accounts without question shows that they, likewise, believed the master to be merciful.

When the master finds out what the manager had done, he has a choice. Yes, the manager was acting on his own accord in lessening the accounts. No, that money was not his own, nor was it his decision to make. But what is the master to do? If he reverses the decision, he looks bad. The debtors will realize that he is, in fact, not merciful after all. But if he lets the decision stand, his renters are more indebted and committed to him. The manager has benefited not only himself, but the master as well, by further securing the goodwill and love of the debtors.

Can you see in the manager a picture of yourself? Which of us has not squandered what our Master has given us? The gifts, talents, time, and possessions God has entrusted to us are far too often wasted on frivolous things. When called to give an account, we would have to be honest and admit that we have squandered our Master's gifts. And how can we justify ourselves to our Master? We have no case against Him, no defense to make for ourselves. We can't argue the righteous decision that we are unworthy servants. Humanly speaking, there is no way out for us. We can't make it up to our Master or find a satisfactory way out when we look to ourselves. It is only when we throw ourselves completely at the mercy of our Master that we find a solution—not in ourselves, mind you, but in the Master.

Back to that pesky statement in verse 9, where Jesus tells us to make friends for ourselves with worldly wealth in order to be welcomed into eternal dwellings. We know from 16:1 that Jesus is speaking to His disciples at this point. We learn later in 16:14 that the Pharisees were listening as well, but since Jesus is speaking this parable mainly to His disciples, the comments after the parable are largely catechetical. Jesus is setting an example of how to make proper use of worldly possessions. As the master of the parable was known as a merciful man, his manager imitates that mercy in dealing with the debtors.

In other words, use your earthly possessions for the benefit of others, mirroring the mercy of the Lord, who has shown you infinite mercy in forgiving your debt of sin. Our faith compels us to show mercy to others as God has shown mercy to us. Our earthly possessions won't be of any use to use once we die. Instead, while we live, we should use those possessions wisely and for the benefit of others.

Go back and read the parable again, focusing on the mercy of the Master rather than any dishonesty on the part of the manager. Indeed, God is that Master who has forgiven us our debts. Go ahead and stake everything on the mercy of your Master, even your eternal well-being. You will not be disappointed.

Demons Who Confess Christ

August 21, 2017

I don't know about you, but I've never met anyone suffering from demon possession. Yet a quick reading of the Gospel accounts of Matthew, Mark, or Luke will show you numerous instances of Jesus driving out demons. It seems to have been a common ailment back then. But even more intriguing is this fact: the demons know who Jesus is, and they confess Him as the Son of God.

Mark 3:11-12 tells us that "Whenever the unclean spirits saw Him, they fell down before Him and cried out, 'You are the Son of God!' And He strictly ordered them not to make Him known." Hmm. Interesting. The evil spirits actually acknowledge Jesus as the Son of God. They recognize what the disciples don't realize until much later. The demons don't believe in Jesus in faith, mind you, but in fear. Elsewhere in the Gospel accounts, demons refer to Jesus as "the Holy One of God" (Mark 1:24, Luke 4:34) and "Jesus, Son of the Most High God" (Luke 8:28). They knew exactly who they were dealing with, and they knew His power. They often begged Jesus not to send them to the abyss or not to torture them, because already they knew He was stronger than they. They couldn't help but confess Jesus when in His presence.

What follows is particularly intriguing. "[Jesus] strictly ordered them not to make Him known." Why? Jesus does this a number of times with other miracles, warning people not to tell who He was. He didn't want people to spread the wrong message. He wasn't on earth just to wow people with miraculous healings. He was on earth to deliver people, not from physical ailments, but from spiritual death. He didn't want people to recognize Him only as a miracle man.

But why the warning to the demons? They certainly weren't going around singing His praises as a divine healer. They were calling Him the Son of God. Didn't He want people to know this truth? Yes. But He didn't want defeated demons to be His tool for spreading that news.

Read through Mark 5:1-20, the account of the man possessed by a host of demons who called themselves "Legion." They asked Jesus to send them into a herd of pigs, and He did so. The man whom Jesus healed begged to go with Jesus, but Jesus did not grant that request. Instead, He told him, "Go home to your friends and tell them how much the Lord has done for you, and how He has had mercy on you" (Mark 5:19). This man, who had once been demon-possessed, now sat in his right mind, telling everyone what Jesus had done for him. Pretty powerful testimony. And here we see Jesus' intention for how to spread the Good News. He wants those who have been delivered by Him to confess Him to the world. Dear Christians, that's us!

Perhaps you're thinking that your "deliverance" story isn't all that impressive. Maybe you've grown up in a Christian home and been a Christian all your life. Nothing exciting. And yet, it is. *All* Christians have been delivered from bondage to the demonic realm. Colossians 1:13-14 says, "He has delivered us from the domain of darkness and transferred us to the kingdom of His beloved Son, in whom we have redemption, the forgiveness of sins." Jesus *died* for you and rose for you. I'd say that's pretty exciting! Don't be afraid to share that amazing story. You're exactly the tool God has chosen to confess His name.

When You've Been Hurt by the Church

August 24, 2015

I don't go to church anymore because someone offended me five years ago. I can't sit there and pretend nothing happened while she's right across the aisle. There's no way I'd ever go back there.

I've heard excuses like that a number of times, and quite often, it boils down to something rather petty, too—a fight over carpet color, a comment taken the wrong way, someone who was offended for not getting a thank you note... But none of these issues are insurmountable. They might cause hard feelings at the time, but they cannot be used to justify leaving the church entirely. And I find a strange thing at work here—very often, the people who have been hurt the most, those who have the greatest cause to leave, are the ones who stick with it through their pain. They know something important. It's not Christ who is failing you, it's His people.

There's no such thing as a perfect church. We are the people of God, yes, but we are still *people*—sinful, stubborn, even stupid at times. We say things in the heat of the moment, we do unwise things, we offend each other. But when those things happen, as they will, who is to blame? We are, not God. Just because a fellow member does something mean spirited, that doesn't discredit God's saving work on our behalf.

Think about your family. You fight with them too, don't you? You make each other mad, you insult each other at times, and you disagree with one another. But you're still a family. You learn to forgive each other and carry on. That's how it should be with the family of believers. We may disagree at times, and honestly, yeah, there are some people we may not even get along with, but we are still a family.

The tricky thing about "church" is that there is a difference between the (lowercase) church and the (uppercase) Church. Every church has its own unique blend of personalities, and some churches almost seem to *want* to be mean. But the Church of God is the invisible Church, made up of all true believers. Even if you're at a church that is unwelcoming or has hurt you, the true Church of God is still there for you. *God* is still there for you.

I know pastors and other church workers who have been removed from their positions in very hurtful ways. I know churches where the members are divided over a pastor who has been removed. I know people who have been informed that the position they held at their church is being given to someone else with no explanation. Undoubtedly, these people have been hurt. Their families have been hurt with them. Their children see the pain caused by fellow "Christians" and wonder what to make of it. Families are hurt and confused and scared together.

If you've been seriously hurt by someone in your church, I am truly sorry. I've been there myself. It's painful and confusing and hard to explain to your children what really happened. But don't turn your back on your faith because of it. There are other congregations. Sometimes it's best to find a new church home where fellow members accept and embrace you as you seek healing and comfort. Find a faithful congregation that points to Christ and His saving work for sinners.

If, on the other hand, you've been offended by someone over something fairly minor, set an example of reconciliation instead of holding a grudge. I have also witnessed forgiveness at work between members who have been fighting, and it is a beautiful thing. Forgiveness always is.

Unfortunately, this side of heaven, we will never find a church without problems. But remember that God's Church lasts into eternity. The failings and shortcomings of sinful humans point us all the more to Christ, who alone can never fail us.

The Measure of Success

August 25, 2014

What does success look like to you? A great career? A confident, eloquent person? Fame? Fortune? Most of us, whether we like to admit it or not, probably associate success with wealth. After all, we've been programmed to believe that "He who dies with the most toys, wins." After all, would you consider someone a success who goes about in sheepskins and goatskins, destitute, persecuted, and mistreated, wandering in deserts and mountains, in caves and in holes in the ground? Does that sound like *any* definition of success? Certainly not.

But actually, yes.

That theoretical scenario actually comes from the end of Hebrews 11, the great "Heroes of Faith" chapter. The writer lists a number of Old Testament characters, but he runs out of room to keep naming them and has to be content to summarize the rest. Some of these were indeed victorious on this earth—these saints "who through faith conquered kingdoms, enforced justice, obtained promises, stopped the mouths of lions, quenched the power of fire, escaped the edge of the sword, were made strong out of weakness, became mighty in war, put foreign armies to flight. Women received back their dead by resurrection" (Hebrews 11:33-35a).

Now *that* sounds like success there, doesn't it? We can see Daniel in there shutting the mouths of lions, and his three friends in the fiery furnace quenching the fury of the flames. Hey, sign me up for that kind of life! If that's what it means to live by faith, I'm in!

But that's only half of the story. The writer continues, "Some were tortured, refusing to accept release, so that they might rise again to a better life. Others suffered mocking and flogging, and even chains and imprisonment. They were stoned, they were sawn in two, they were killed with the sword. They went about in skins of sheep and goats, destitute, afflicted, mistreated… wandering about in deserts and mountains, and in dens and caves of the earth" (Hebrews 11:35b-38).

Okay, hold on. Maybe I don't want to sign on to this faith thing after all. That doesn't sound at all appealing. Jeremiah the prophet was flogged, Zechariah was stoned to death, and tradition holds that Isaiah was sawed in two. *This* is the thanks they get for their service as the Lord's prophets? I'll pass.

Ah, but that's *still* not the end of the story. See those three little dots in my quotation of Hebrews 11:35-38? I skipped a short little side note there. It says, "of whom the world was not worthy." These prophets, who to human reason looked like complete failures in the world, were in fact the exact opposite. The world wasn't even worthy of them. Their measure of success wasn't in how popular they were or how much money they had. Their only measure of success was that they remained faithful to God and the message He gave them to proclaim. And in return look what they received: "These were all commended for their faith, yet none of them received what had been promised. God had planned something better for us so that only together with us would they be made perfect" (Hebrews 11:39-40, NIV).

Both the victorious and the suffering saints were commended for their faith. No matter what end they met on this earth, all received eternity with the Lord. When it says that "none of them received what had been promised," that means that none of them saw the fulfillment of the prophecies about the coming Messiah. Jesus was yet to come, but they believed in Him nonetheless. And when it says that "God had planned something better for us," that isn't inferring that we somehow get a better reward in heaven. It means that their faith was based on so much less than ours. They only believed the promises of the Messiah, but we have seen those promises fulfilled in Jesus. We know the end of the story. We know about Jesus' perfect life, suffering, death, and resurrection. But without those Old Testament saints to point to Jesus, we wouldn't completely understand the purpose of His coming either. We need both the witness of Old Testament and New Testament saints for our faith to "be made perfect."

So what about you? Will you be like Daniel in the lions' den, showing mighty examples of God's power to save? Or will you be more like the prophets who suffered for their faith? Maybe you'll be somewhere in the middle of those extremes. But no matter what your earthly outcome, remember this—you *are* a success in God's eyes, not because you've earned His favor, but because He has already made you a success through Jesus' victory over sin and death. His success is yours, and you will reap the benefits eternally.

A More Effective Workout Routine

August 26, 2019

Apparently I've been exercising all wrong. According to my teenage son, who fancies himself an expert on fitness, there are three phases of strength training one ought to do in order to maximize the benefits. Silly me, I'd just been following the number of reps and sets suggested in my program, gradually increasing the amount of weight for each exercise.

But my son set me straight. One ought to rotate *strength*, *hypertrophy*, and *endurance* workouts for the best results. With a strength workout, you add as much weight as possible, enough that you can only lift 2-6 reps for each set. Hypertrophy is the "normal" workout, where you do 8-12 reps with a challenging but doable weight. And endurance is a slightly less challenging weight so you can do 15-20 reps per set. All three of these work together for the best results.

Armed with this knowledge, I set out to start my rotation of "strength" workouts, adding extra weight. I was a bit afraid of this one, but the results surprised me. What I thought would be difficult or even impossible really wasn't all that hard. In some cases, I added nearly double the normal weight in order to achieve an acceptably challenging level. And while I could feel the burn during the workout, I wasn't overly sore the next day. So why wasn't I adding more weight to my normal exercising routine? Rather than progressing, I'd been stagnating, but I could handle more weight than I thought I could.

This revelation made me wonder where else in my life I was stagnating. As humans, our natural tendency is to stick with the path of least resistance. But that doesn't result in growth and can often lead to discontentment when we feel like we're stuck in a rut. This is especially true of spiritual growth. Think of the writer of Hebrews, admonishing his readers that they need milk and not solid food (Hebrews 5:11-14). They weren't flexing their "spiritual muscles," and were content to remain at the entry level of knowledge, needing to be reminded again and again of the basic principles of faith.

What might this look like in your life if you were to flex your spiritual muscles? Which areas of your life could use "more weight"? Perhaps God is leading you to be more generous in your giving. Let's be honest—most of us could easily give more money. Many congregations struggle to meet budget goals because so few members actually tithe. If you already tithe, think beyond your church too! Consider adding an additional monthly financial commitment to a Gospel organization, a missionary, or a humanitarian effort.

Or what about time? Everyone is so busy in our society, but how much of that is really necessary? Examine your life and see if God is encouraging you to cut back on some activities to make room for others. Or maybe you just need better time management to be more effective in your daily tasks so you can allow time for volunteering elsewhere.

Then again, perhaps you need more weight in your devotional life. It's easy to get stuck in a rut, reading a quick devotion here and there without much depth to it. But go ahead and stretch yourself. Find a good Bible study to work through in addition to your devotional reading. Listen to a solid Christian radio program or podcast throughout your day. Add some variety to your daily devotions so you're getting some "solid spiritual food," as our reading from Hebrews encourages.

Go ahead. Flex those muscles. Yes, it might burn a bit at the beginning, but my guess is that you could add more weight than you think. After all, *God* is your strength. No actual weight lifting required.

Deathbed Requests

August 27, 2018

It plays out like a scene from *The Godfather.* The aged king is passing along final instructions to the son who is to succeed him. He starts off admonishing him to be God-fearing and of noble character. But then he gets personal. He tells his son to "deal wisely" with two men who had wronged him. It doesn't take much reading between the lines to know what the king means. "Do not let his gray head go down to the grave in peace," the king says of both men. In other words, *kill these guys.* These are his final words. Cue the climactic music and get one last close-up of the characters in this scene, who are none other than King David and his son Solomon.

If you aren't familiar with David's last words, look at 1 Kings 2:1-12 to refresh your memory. He tells Solomon, "Be strong, and show yourself a man, and keep the charge of the Lord your God, walking in His ways and keeping His statues, His commandments, His rules, and His testimonies, as it is written in the Law of Moses" (v 2-3). Excellent advice, David. Well spoken.

But in the next breath he tells Solomon to kill Joab, who had wrongfully killed Abner (2 Samuel 3:22-39) and Amasa (2 Samuel 20:8-10) in a time of peace. Shortly thereafter, David brings up Shimei, who had cursed him with "a grievous curse" when David had to flee Jerusalem to escape Absalom (2 Samuel 16:5-14). David had sworn to Shimei that he wouldn't put him to death (2 Samuel 19:23), but now he instructs Solomon to deal with him instead. Hmm.

From a human standpoint, David's instructions may seem justified. We like the sense of closure. These guys will get what they deserve. One might even argue that his instructions regarding Joab could be reconciled with the law of Moses, removing bloodguilt from the land (e.g. Numbers 35:31). Justified or not, it can't be denied that his deathbed instructions included murder. And Solomon carried out those requests. (See 1 Kings 2:28-46 for the full story.)

Now contrast David's last request with that of his greatest descendant: Jesus. While hanging on the cross, this King pleaded, "Father, forgive them, for they know not what they do" (Luke 23:34). He asked God to *forgive* the very men who were murdering Him. If anyone was justified in seeking vengeance on His enemies, it was Jesus. He was innocent of all charges brought against Him. Those who crucified Him were shedding innocent blood. Jesus had every right to seek "a life for a life." But He didn't. While David sought the death of his enemies, Jesus sought the life of His. And that's *really* good news for us, because we were His enemies as well.

"For if while we were enemies we were reconciled to God by the death of His Son, much more, now that we are reconciled, shall we be saved by His life," Romans 5:10 says. In Colossians 1:21-22, we read, "And you, who once were alienated and hostile in mind, doing evil deeds, He has now reconciled in His body of flesh by His death, in order to present you holy and blameless and above reproach before Him." *Enemies. Hostile. Evil.* Yet despite our unquestionable guilt, Jesus has *reconciled* us to Himself. He has made us right with God.

As Solomon honored David's dying request, so did God honor Jesus'. He forgave us our sins. We are declared innocent and made members of His family. Now, *that's* a true "God Father."

Defining Moments

August 28, 2014

There are defining moments in everyone's life. Perhaps you look back over your life thus far and see an important decision that shaped the course of your future. Maybe it was an event, like a stroke or accident that left you or a loved one incapacitated and altered the course of the rest of your life. Some defining moments are good. Many would point to Martin Luther King, Jr's famous "I have a dream" speech as a moment that defined not only his life, but much of the civil rights movement. But other defining moments are far less illustrious.

One of the most comforting things about the Bible is that the people depicted in it are so…well, *human*. The Bible doesn't whitewash their sins and mistakes. Sometimes it almost seems that the writers go out of the way to point out flaws in the main characters in order to make the sinlessness of Jesus stand in sharp contrast. Consider some of the heroes of faith—giants, if you will. People like Abraham, Moses, Aaron, David, Elijah, Matthew, Peter, and Paul. Each of them had some serious shortcomings in their lives, things that today would be the end of their pristine reputations, things that would define them in the eyes of the world.

- Abraham tried to "help" God by his affair with Hagar, hoping to produce the promised offspring through her rather than through his own wife, Sarah.

- Judah, through whose family line would be born the Messiah, fell victim to Tamar's prostitute charade and had a fling with her that resulted in her pregnancy with twins.

- Moses initially fled Egypt because he killed a man and was found out. He spent the next forty years in the desert until he was called from the burning bush.

- Aaron, the first high priest, stumbled badly when he made a golden calf for the Israelites to worship when Moses was so long in coming down Mount Sinai.

- David committed adultery and murder in the whole sordid Bathsheba affair.

- Elijah, after seeing the Lord's bold display of power on Mount Carmel with the prophets of Baal, fled for his life after Queen Jezebel threatened him, ran into the desert and sat down under a broom tree and pleaded for God to end his life.

- Matthew was a tax collector, one whom his own people considered a traitor. No one would have given him a chance, but Jesus called him from that lifestyle and made him a disciple, one who went on to write a gospel account that we still read today.

- Peter rebuked Jesus when He predicted His own death, and later after vowing to die with Jesus, he denied even knowing Him three times.

- Paul, one of the greatest missionaries of all time, who wrote nearly half of the books in our New Testament, had been a zealous persecutor of the early Christian church. He approved of Stephen's death by stoning, and was on his way to Damascus to bring back Christians as prisoners to Jerusalem.

Just look at that laundry list of sins and failures. These are the great saints of old, and look at the impressive number of sins they have between them—adultery, murder, idol worship, cheating, doubting God, denying the Lord, and persecuting God's people. These aren't just your little "petty" sins like gossip or white lies. These are big sins, ones that today would hit the headlines. Imagine what would happen if a powerful religious leader were to be found worshiping a golden idol. Think about what would happen if a state leader was found to be having an affair and then hired a hitman to take out the pesky husband in the situation. What would church members say if a prominent and respected male in the church had sired twins for his daughter-in-law? Or what if an ISIS member who was rounding up and crucifying Christians in Syria suddenly had a "conversion" moment and wanted to join the Christian church?

In a world where bad news and gossip spreads almost instantly around social media, these people wouldn't stand a chance today. Just think of the splash this stuff could make on the front page of the tabloids—"Tamar confirms, 'It's Twins!' Exclusive interview inside…" or "Who's the Daddy? Tamar tells all!" There's no doubt about it, all of those things listed above could very easily have become defining moments for those individuals. But they weren't.

What, then, defined these saints of old? God's abundant and lavish grace. He didn't cast them away because of their sins, however serious those sins may have been. All of those people believed by grace in God's promise of forgiveness and salvation through His Son. Keep in mind God's promise in Jeremiah 31:34: "For I will forgive their iniquity, and I will remember their sin no more." The world may not forget the wrongs you have committed, but God does. Those wrongs don't define you in God's eyes. No matter what you have done, God's grace is for you.

What is there in your past of which you are ashamed? An illegitimate pregnancy? an abortion? a stint with drugs or alcohol? an affair? stealing? For those who believe in Christ, even those things need not define you. Yes, there are earthly consequences for such choices, but eternally there need not be, for Christ has already paid that penalty for you. Even if your earthly choices have become a defining moment in the eyes of the world, in God's eyes something else defines you. His grace. You are *His* child, and ultimately, that's all that matters.

Preparing for Harvey

August 28, 2017

I was completely unprepared for Hurricane Harvey. Granted, we don't live in the immediate danger zone, but being only a few hours from Houston, we knew we'd be getting heavy and persistent rains. The country roads in our area get washed out or flooded during heavy rain, making them impassable. Kids basked in the novelty of having their first day of school canceled. Flash flood warnings popped up all over. Towns not too far from us had forced evacuations due to rivers flooding. In the face of such inclement weather, certain preparations are advised. Stock up on food and make sure you have plenty of potable water on hand. Excellent advice. And I didn't do any of it.

Our grocery supply was perilously low. I had next to nothing in the fruit bowl, three slices of bread left, little peanut butter, a nearly empty freezer, and an alarmingly low supply of coffee. I mean, bread I can make from scratch, but coffee? I had no bottled water, so on the first day of the storm I found myself filtering water and storing it in empty milk jugs just in case. We have a gas stove, so I was fairly certain that if the electricity went out I'd still be able to cook, but the more immediate concern was *what* I would cook. Other than a package of chicken, I had no meat in the freezer. I simply didn't plan ahead. I was like the foolish bridesmaids in Jesus' parable, the ones who didn't have enough oil in their lamps.

Whether it's a predicted blizzard in the north, a tornado warning, or a hurricane on a coast, people prepare for inclement weather much the same way. It's not uncommon for grocery stores to run out of milk and bread because people raid the store and buy even more than they probably need for the few days of bad weather. Those who wait until the last minute (ahem) often find only empty shelves at the store. Why all the fuss? Because people like to be prepared. We like the peace of mind that comes with a good plan. And yet, many people fail to plan ahead for the most important event of all—the day they stand before God.

Let's look more closely at the parable of the wise and foolish virgins in Matthew 25:1-13. Jesus gives us faith (the oil), but those who continually neglect it will fall away by their own fault. Those who choose to distance themselves from the Church, who decide not to read the Bible, who put off nurturing their faith until they're older, who value other things or activities more than their faith, are in grave danger of being unprepared when Jesus returns. It's far more dangerous to be unprepared for Christ's return than it is to be unprepared for a hurricane. And unlike Harvey, there will be no warning when Jesus comes. Meteorologists were able to warn people in advance about the approaching hurricane so people could evacuate and take proper precautions. But speaking of His return, Jesus says, "Watch therefore, for you know neither the day nor the hour" (Matthew 25:13).

I don't know when the rain will end or when I'll get to a well-stocked store. We may lose power. I may run out of coffee. But we'll survive. Eventually the sun will shine again and the waters will recede. And in the meantime, I take comfort in the fact that I know the One who controls the wind and the waves. And ultimately, that's the only preparation I need.

When Fighting is a Good Thing

As a mother of five, I see my fair share of fighting. It seems like some days all I am is a referee, mediating one fight after another. And it gets old pretty fast. Most parents can probably agree with me on this point. In general, fighting is looked upon as a bad thing. Kids are encouraged not to fight, especially with their fists. We try to teach our kids to work things out by talking through their differences rather than fighting. But sometimes fighting can be a good thing.

Anyone who's familiar with the Bible has to concede that it contains many references to fighting. God's people fight the pagan nations around them, but God Himself fights as well. When David inquires of God whether or not he should attack the Philistines, God tells him, "When you hear the sound of marching in the tops of the balsam trees, then go out to battle, for God has gone out before you to strike the army of the Philistines" (1 Chronicles 14:15). *God* is actually going to fight for Israel! But that's neither the first nor the last time He does this.

When the Israelites leave Egypt after the plagues, the Egyptian army comes after them and appears to corner them at the Red Sea. But God tells His people not to fear. "The Lord will fight for you, and you have only to be silent" (Exodus 14:14). His people didn't need to do anything at all—the battle was God's alone. Later, in Deuteronomy, Moses reminds the people of all God has done for them. He tells them before they enter the Promised Land, "The Lord your God who goes before you will Himself fight for you…" (Deut 1:30). After the exile, Nehemiah encourages the Israelites, "In the place where you hear the sound of the trumpet, rally to us there. Our God will fight for us" (Nehemiah 4:20).

God's people didn't win all these wars because in and of themselves they were so powerful. Many times their enemies vastly outnumbered them and were more powerful than they. But those powerful armies were no match for the true God. He gave His people the victory over their enemies. And He's done the same thing for you.

Most of us will probably never face an actual army in our lives. But we still face deadly enemies who seek to defeat us. Our "deadly three" are sin, Satan, and death. And they are relentless. Satan is compared to a roaring lion seeking someone to devour in 1 Peter 5:8. That's pretty daunting. But don't despair. Jesus already fought him for you and won. The hymn "A Mighty Fortress" puts it like this: "This world's prince may still scowl fierce as he will, He can harm us none. He's judged; the deed is done; One little word can fell him" (*Lutheran Service Book* 656, stanza 3). And what is that "little word?" Jesus.

The same God who fought for His people in the Old Testament has fought for you and now gives you strength as you "fight the good fight of the faith," as we read in 1 Timothy 6:12. He gives you the armor of God. You *will* be victorious, because the fight has already been won. You have in store for you a "crown of righteousness" (2 Timothy 4:8) in heaven because of Jesus' victory. I've never been so grateful for fighting.

Church Isn't Church Isn't Church

August 31, 2015

I had to buy a car to make a cross country trip. The salesman was trying to get me to buy a fancy new car with all these bells and whistles—side airbags, traction control, good safety ratings, and of course the extended warranty. I say, forget all that. A car is a car, after all. I just need a set of wheels. So I went to the used car lot instead and bought a beat up thing for a lot less money. I mean, the gas mileage is terrible, and the oil apparently leaks, but it runs, right?

I used to try to eat well, but it's just too much effort. Making food from scratch is too time consuming, and I just don't want to do it anymore. So now I live on frozen pizza, fast food, and convenience store snacks. After all, food is food. I'm getting the calories I need.

I'm just glad she's going to church. I don't care where she goes as long as she's going. Church is church, you know.

Ridiculous scenarios, aren't they? Yet I've heard the last one about church more times than I care to admit. The underlying theme is that as long as someone is going to church, it really doesn't matter what's being preached and taught there. "Church is church," people figure. "All churches are created equal." But are they? I hate to break it to you, but that's not true. There are many churches out there that are teaching false doctrine or at best weak doctrine. I wouldn't entrust my soul to such a church.

Check out a listing of churches in your town and you'll find any number of entries. In our small town of 1177, we have nine churches: Lutheran, Baptist, Methodist, Catholic, Church of Christ, and two generically-named "Christian" churches, plus one called "The Gathering Place," and one called "The Lighthouse." I don't even know what those last two are. But if I were to go to each of those churches over the course of nine weeks, I guarantee I would have very different experiences. Worshiping at a Catholic church would be very different than getting together at The Lighthouse.

Many people can probably agree that the "church is church" sentiment only holds true for Christian churches. Most Christian parents wouldn't say of a college daughter, "She's going to a Buddhist temple, but hey, I'm just glad she's going to church at all." There's a fundamental difference between Buddhism and Christianity. The two are not compatible. But why stop there? Not all Christian denominations are equally sound. Even within a denomination, churches can vary widely. One can find anything from a "high church, incense burning, women wearing head covering" congregation to a "praise band, auditorium, pastors wearing jeans and T-shirts" kind of place, and everything in between. Clearly church isn't church isn't church.

To those who hold to this "church is church" belief, I ask you this: Would you agree with any of the other opening statements? I mean, hey, a car is a car, right? And food is food. What's the big deal? The obvious difference is quality. You wouldn't settle for an old clunker when your safety could be compromised. And most people wouldn't settle for a diet of grease and empty calories when they could be eating food that's good for them. So if that's true for cars and food, why shouldn't it be true for churches as well? Why wouldn't you want a "quality" church?

Then how exactly do you define "quality" in this case? Litmus test—does the church teach what the Bible teaches? Many churches compromise their beliefs in order not to offend anyone. Stay away from such churches. If they can't preach the Law properly, neither can they properly administer the Gospel. Some churches stress a giddy emotional high as proof that your faith is real. How does that minister to the woman sitting there devastated that her husband just left her for another woman? No, these churches are not the real deal.

A church should rightly teach the Word of God and administer the Sacraments. It should be equally applicable to all members—young and old, male and female, those hurting and those experiencing joyful times, the sick and the healthy alike. Impossible? Not at all. Because no matter what earthly situation you find yourself, you have one thing in common with every other human being on this earth—you are a sinner.

It's an ugly truth, but it's necessary. And churches that tell you otherwise aren't doing you any favors. You are a sinner who can never be good enough for heaven. That's why Jesus lived a perfect life for you and took your punishment on the cross. He did it in your place. Jesus is the only way to heaven. Make sure your church teaches that.

No, church isn't church isn't church. Don't settle for a wishy washy church when you're dealing with your eternity. Find a solid, faithful church that preaches Christ crucified for us sinners. That's the kind of church you need. Even if you do drive a jalopy to get there.

September

Bearing the Cross

September 4, 2014

My hair has always been unruly. I can't keep it under control for anything. I guess that's my cross to bear...

I'd love to be able to have a deep, meaningful conversation with my husband, but he's so private I can barely get a word out of him. Must be my cross to bear...

Have you heard statements like these? "Bearing one's cross" has come to mean putting up with something that's irritating or annoying. But what does it really mean? Let's look to the original source of the phrase to determine that.

After Jesus predicts His own death, Peter adamantly denies that such a thing should occur. Jesus rebukes him, then turns to the rest of the disciples and tells them, "If anyone would come after Me, let him deny himself and take up his cross daily and follow Me" (Luke 9:23). I'm pretty sure Jesus isn't talking about unruly hair or a spouse who stonewalls you. This is far more serious. The key word is "daily." Jesus is referring to an ongoing process in a believer's life.

To "bear the cross" is to live in the tension of the now and not yet, to live in the world and not of it. We have the assurance of eternal life with Jesus, but we aren't there yet. We are on this sinful earth being constantly bombarded by ridicule and contempt from the world. Think of the Christians who are being persecuted for their faith. That is indeed their cross to bear.

For those of us who don't face physical persecution, our cross is of a different nature. We live in a society where pretty much anything is tolerated. We see homosexual "marriage" being accepted and even applauded, and those who oppose it are intolerant. Abortion is an issue of "women's health," and we are boorish and old-fashioned if we oppose a woman's "rights." We are hopelessly naïve to believe that Jesus is the only way to heaven, and we are accused of brainwashing our kids if we dare to teach them such an outlandish notion. Christians who stand on the Word of God are indeed opening themselves up to scorn and contempt from the world.

Yet another facet of bearing the cross is that we Christians struggle against our own sinful nature, and all too often, lose the battle. We want to do the right thing, but our sinful nature is impossible to subdue. This is the constant struggle of the life of a Christian, the daily bearing of the cross.

No, your "cross" isn't something petty like bad hair. To bear the cross is to constantly face temptations within and contempt from the world without. But we aren't in this alone. Jesus has already borne His cross for our gain. He faced temptations and ridicule and withstood them all. He even faced physical death on the cross. But it didn't defeat Him. And because of His victory, neither can your cross defeat you. It won't be easy, and you'll be tempted to put down that cross again and again in favor of an easier earthly life. But Jesus promises that "whoever loses his life for My sake will save it." So take up that cross, dear Christian. Trust Him. It's worth it.

Dare to Be Different

September 8, 2014

I don't envy the prophet Jeremiah. This poor guy was called to proclaim the Law in all its fury to the wayward people of Israel. He had to give news of the exile to a nation who largely scorned or ignored him. He may have been called "the iron prophet," but he also earned the nickname "the weeping prophet." Jeremiah really did have a tough assignment. So it isn't surprising that at times he broke down and questioned God.

Look with me at Jeremiah 15:15-21. The first few verses are Jeremiah's complaint. He basically says, "C'mon, God. I'm doing Your work here, but look at the thanks I get. My pain is unending and You seem far away. Where are You?" He throws some pretty poignant questions at God, and I can't say I blame him. He didn't have a popular ministry, nor were people flocking to him to repent from their ways. Most of the time his message fell on deaf ears or got him into trouble with the king. His questions are very human, a normal response to why "bad things happen to good people." But God's response is intriguing to me.

God calls Jeremiah back to the task at hand and tells him he is still His messenger. Then God says, "Let this people turn to you, but you must not turn to them" (Jeremiah 15:19, NIV). Think about the other "prophets" in Jeremiah's time. "From the least to the greatest, all are greedy for gain; prophets and priests alike, all practice deceit. They dress the wound of My people as though it were not serious. 'Peace, peace,' they say, when there is no peace. Are they ashamed of their loathsome conduct? No, they have no shame at all…" Jeremiah 8:10b-12a reveals.

Those words could have been uttered by God to our very own nation today. There is no end to "religious leaders" who preach a message of good works, positive thoughts, and prosperity, when in actuality God's Word teaches something quite different. It was the same in Jeremiah's time, and it would have been so very easy for Jeremiah to give in and tell the people what they wanted to hear. But that wasn't why God called him. And neither is that why He calls you.

In a world of so many false beliefs, it would be easy for Christians to compromise their beliefs in an effort to "keep the peace." Many Christian bodies have done just that. *Homosexuality? We accept you as you are. We won't judge.* Many Christians don't want to speak out against sins for fear they'll be labeled "intolerant" or "unloving," so they keep silent. But what's really happening when we compromise with the culture? Before you know it, we've become indistinguishable from the world around us. We dare not become the voice of the false prophets of Jeremiah's day, saying only what people want to hear. We have been called to something higher.

Speaking the Law has never been easy. Just ask Jeremiah. Ask any of the prophets of old. I can't say any of them had an easy life. But they had a serious mission. God has some deep words for Ezekiel in Ezekiel 3:17-19. He tells him that if he warns a wicked man to turn from his ways, and he doesn't repent, that wicked man will perish for his sins. But if Ezekiel *doesn't* warn a wicked man to turn, that man will still perish, but Ezekiel will be held accountable for his blood. Ouch. How many times do we see others living in blatant sin, yet refuse to speak out to them? How often do we see others ruining their lives by following a worthless religion, yet we don't take the time to share the news of Christianity with them? We might be afraid to be different, or we may be scared to stand out in such a bold way, but stand out we must.

Why do people need the Law? Because without it, people don't see the need for a Savior. If "all roads lead to heaven," why is Christianity any different from any other religion? People *must* be brought to despair over their sins before they can receive the beautiful message of the Gospel. Some people, like most of the Israelites in Jeremiah's day, are so hard-hearted that they are never ready to hear the Gospel. They can't get past the Law. But for those who despair over their sin and realize that they can't save themselves, the healing message of the Gospel can work its saving power in full force.

That Gospel, that Good News, is unique to Christianity. Every other religion teaches that if you're "good enough" you can earn heaven. Dare to be different. Dare to stand upon God's Word. Dare to preach the Law, and then dare to preach the Gospel. That message can change lives for all eternity.

Jesus in the Old Testament

September 10, 2018

I came from a no-name town. My ministry began at the Jordan River. I performed many miracles, which include healing a leper, multiplying food to feed a crowd, and raising someone from the dead.

Who am I?

When I pose this riddle to the students in my Midweek School class, they all give the safe answer: Jesus. Jesus came from Nazareth, a no-name town in His day. His earthly ministry began at the Jordan River when He was baptized by John, and He performed all those miracles listed above. But my students are usually surprised to learn that Jesus wasn't the first biblical figure to fit the description. To find the answer we need to look back nearly 900 years before Jesus was born.

Let's go back to the days of the split Kingdom of Israel in the Old Testament. King Solomon's son Rehoboam had been foolish and caused the Northern tribes to revolt. So from then on, the northern kingdom was known as "Israel" while the southern kingdom was "Judah." There was a lot of idolatry going on in both kingdoms, and God sent prophets to His people to preach repentance. One such prophet was none other than Elisha.

Elisha had an amazing ministry marked with many miracles. Unfortunately, he tends to get overshadowed a bit by his predecessor, Elijah. Many people know the story of Elijah getting fed by ravens, the showdown with the prophets of Baal, God coming to him in the "still small voice," and his dramatic exit from this world in a whirlwind amidst the horses and chariots of fire. That's exciting stuff. But what about Elisha, who received a "double portion" of Elijah's spirit? Most people might recall the story of Elisha cleansing Naaman the leper, but he also performed many other miracles, some very similar to those Jesus later performed.

Elisha first appears in the Bible in 1 Kings 19:16, when God tells Elijah to anoint Elisha from Abel-Meholah as his successor, and Elijah proceeds to do just that. I'm no expert on biblical geography, but I can't recall any other mention of Abel-Meholah in the Bible. Definitely not a well-known town. And although Elisha then became Elijah's assistant, his public ministry didn't begin until after Elijah was taken up into heaven by the Jordan River (2 Kings 2:1-14). In fact, his first miracle was parting the Jordan River (v 14) to cross back, just as Elijah had parted it on the way over (v 8). During his ministry, he performed other miracles, including healing Naaman's leprosy (2 Kings 5:1-14), multiplying twenty barley loaves to feed a hundred prophets and still have leftovers (2 Kings 4:42-44), and raising the Shunammite's son from the dead (2 Kings 4:18-37). All miracles that Jesus would later perform—cleansing lepers, multiplying loaves to feed a crowd, and raising people from the dead. It's clear that God's power was at work in Elisha's ministry.

When I ask my students where Jesus is in the Old Testament, they usually reply, "He isn't born yet. He only shows up in the New Testament." But that's not true either. Jesus is present from the very beginning, from the account of creation all through the Old Testament. He's first promised to Adam and Eve in Genesis 3:15, where God says to the serpent, "I will put enmity between you and the woman, and between your offspring and her offspring; He will bruise your head, and you shall bruise His heel." He's promised and prophesied many other times throughout the Old Testament, most notably in the books of Isaiah, Psalms, Malachi, Micah, Exodus, Zechariah… You get the picture. He's all over.

Beyond that, there are many people in the Old Testament who are "types" of Christ; people who foreshadow the work of the coming Messiah: well-known people like Noah, Isaac, Joseph, Moses, Joshua, David, and Jonah, as well as lesser-known characters like Melchizedek. The miracles performed by prophets such as Elijah and Elisha call to mind the later miracles of Jesus. Take the time to brush up on your Old Testament reading and see for yourself how rich it is with the good news of Jesus. Jesus opened the Scriptures to the Emmaus disciples by examining the Old Testament. "And beginning with Moses and all the Prophets, He interpreted to them in all the Scriptures the things concerning Himself" (Luke 24:27).

So where is Jesus in the Old Testament? In short, He's everywhere.

Hungry Babies

September 14, 2015

Babies are not discreet. When they're hungry, they let you know. It doesn't matter where you are or who is watching. They'll search for the source of milk no matter what. I was holding my infant in church last week and he opened his mouth and started rooting around, bouncing his head off my chest in an attempt to be fed. It was obvious to anyone watching what he was trying to do. Though slightly embarrassing for me, his actions displayed a simple trust that gives us a model of how we should act as well.

When was the last time you read your Bible? I mean, really read it? Not just a quick verse look up. I don't know about you, but regular study is something I struggle with. There are so many other things to do, and devotional time is often very difficult to come by. But the Bible itself tells us that we should long for God's Word, just as my baby longs for milk. 1 Peter 2:2-3 tells us, "Like newborn infants, long for the pure spiritual milk, that by it you may grow up into salvation—if indeed you have tasted that the Lord is good."

You see, babies know and trust that the milk they want will be there when they need it. When they get hungry, they look for the milk that has sustained them before. They know it will satisfy their hunger. How much more will God's Word satisfy our hunger and sustain our souls? So often we starve ourselves spiritually, putting off Bible study or devotions or church attendance. Yet God longs to feed and nourish us in His Word.

Peter isn't the only inspired writer to speak of the longing a believer should feel. King David says in Psalm 63:1, "O God, You are my God; earnestly I seek You; my soul thirsts for You; my flesh faints for You, as in a dry and weary land where there is no water." He wrote this when he was in the wilderness of Judah, by the way, so he knew a thing or two about being thirsty in a dry land. That's how much he desired God.

So go ahead. Crave the pure spiritual milk as found in the Bible. Thirst for God and His Word. Search the Scriptures. Don't be discreet about it. Don't worry about who may be watching. God will satisfy your hunger. You can count on it.

A One-Track Mind

September 15, 2014

My son has a one-track mind. When he focuses on something, he cannot get it out of his head until it's resolved. Each weekend he seems to have something else on which to dwell. Sometimes it's a certain book or movie he just *has* to have from the library. Sometimes it's something he desperately wants to order online. This past weekend suddenly a new bike (which he needed, admittedly) was of utmost importance, and he didn't want to wait. He wanted it *now*. He won't rest until whatever he's been focusing on has come to a proper conclusion in his own mind. He harps on the subject at hand over and over, which gets very wearisome after a while. In time I have hopes that this can become a favorable trait and work for his good. He just can't give up or forget whatever it is that's on his mind. It's that important to him.

My son isn't the only one who has ever had a one-track mind. Paul had a one-track mind too. Look at his request in Ephesians 6:19-20: "Pray also for me, that whenever I open my mouth, words may be given me so that I will fearlessly make known the mystery of the gospel, for which I am an ambassador in chains. Pray that I may declare it fearlessly, as I should" (NIV).

That's dedication for you. This isn't a vague request of, "Pray for a chance to share the Gospel with someone someday." Paul wants to be proclaiming the Gospel "whenever [he] open[s] [his] mouth." Paul is not halfheartedly Christian. This thought of spreading the Gospel consumes him. He can't help but speak about Jesus to everyone he possibly can, whether they believe it or not. In Romans 10:1, Paul says, "Brothers, my heart's desire and prayer to God for them [the Israelites] is that they may be saved." This is his *life*. He thinks about it, prays about it, writes about it, and talks about it. He can't give up or forget that burning desire within him to tell others about Jesus. It's that important to him.

Jesus had a one-track mind as well. Throughout His earthly ministry, the devil tried to pull Him away from His task of redeeming the world, but Jesus resisted him. Religious leaders tried to trap Jesus with silly questions. Jesus wasn't deterred. He didn't spend His time arguing with them. He was out preaching, healing, and performing miracles around the entire region so everyone would hear about Him. And when it came time to get on with His suffering and death, Jesus didn't bail out. On the contrary, Luke 9:51 tells us that "As the time approached for Him to be taken up to heaven, Jesus resolutely set out for Jerusalem" (NIV). The ESV says that Jesus "set His face to go up to Jerusalem." Both versions emphasize that Jesus was completely resolved to get to Jerusalem.

What was in Jerusalem? What was so consuming His thoughts that He just *had* to get there? The cross. His entire purpose in coming was to be the perfect sacrifice for your sins and mine. Jesus had a one-track mind for sure. Dear one, *you* were the one on His mind. *You* were the reason He suffered and died. He loves you so much that He would rather suffer humiliation, pain, and even death rather than be separated from you eternally. Even on the cross, people jeered at Him and taunted Him to come down and prove Himself. He would not be sidetracked. He *did* prove Himself, not by coming down with a show of might, but by dying in what seemed to be utter defeat. Then three days later, He rose victorious from the grave, showing His power over even death. And that's why Paul had a one-track mind as well. That good news was just too amazing to keep to himself.

What is it that consumes your thoughts? Make Paul's prayer your own. Ultimately that's the only thing that matters—knowing Jesus as your Savior. So don't be afraid to speak out and tell others the wonderful news. Jesus had a one-track mind for *you*. You are that important to Him. That's too wonderful not to share.

Lost in the Fog

September 17, 2018

Driving in heavy fog is very unsettling. Yesterday morning I had to drive to church in such conditions, and although it's a road I've taken dozens of times before, everything looked different in the fog. Each turn seemed unfamiliar, large trees weren't visible until we were practically next to them, and cars coming from the opposite direction didn't emerge from the fog until they were pretty close to us, which was startling and a bit scary. I was on edge the entire time, not knowing if a deer would suddenly leap out in front of me or a car would pull out without being able to see me coming. I felt disoriented, but I was not lost. I may not have been able to see a hundred yards ahead of me, but I knew I was on the right road, and I knew that road was going to get me to my destination.

Being on the right road is important. Anyone who's ever missed a turn or taken the wrong road can tell you that. On our honeymoon, back before the days of iPhones and Google maps, we took a wrong turn on our way to Gatlinburg, TN, and ended up in North Carolina. North Carolina is a lovely place, but it's not where we intended to go. We were on the wrong path.

The Bible speaks often of being on the right path, but it's not giving advice on getting to Gatlinburg. It's talking about a much more important path—the way of salvation. Jesus tells His followers in Matthew 7:13-14, "Enter by the narrow gate. For the gate is wide and the way is easy that leads to destruction, and those who enter by it are many. For the gate is narrow and the way is hard that leads to life, and those who find it are few."

In other words, there are a great many people who are lost out there, wandering in the fog or driving down the wrong road. They may not even know they're lost in the first place. Or they might think they're on the right path even when they aren't. But just because you think you're going the right way doesn't necessarily mean you are. We believed we were on the right road to Gatlinburg all those years ago, but that didn't change the fact that we crossed into North Carolina. And the stakes are so much higher when it comes to the way of life Jesus speaks of. We aren't just talking about a detour; we're talking about eternity.

Thankfully, God doesn't leave us to find the way on our own. Psalm 16:11 says, "You make known to me the path of life; in Your presence there is fullness of joy; at Your right hand are pleasures forevermore." And in the well-known words of Psalm 23:3, we are assured, "He leads me in paths of righteousness for His name's sake." God not only points us in the right direction, He leads us on our way. Specifically, what is that way? Jesus.

In John 14:6, Jesus clearly tells His disciples, "I am the way, and the truth, and the life. No one comes to the Father except through Me." Don't fall for the world's lies that there are many ways to heaven, or that it doesn't matter what you believe as long as you're sincere. Stay on the narrow path, fixing your eyes on Jesus. The way may be difficult. At times you may feel like you're driving in fog, unable to see everything clearly, coming upon obstacles suddenly and without warning. But remember that Jesus is with you every moment of the journey. You're on the right road, and it will get you safely to your eternal destination.

Playing Second Fiddle

September 18, 2017

Recently my son joined the high school marching band even though he's only in the eighth grade. In one sense, this is a promotion. He's moving up from the middle school band to the high school band. But in another sense, he's moving down. He went from being first-chair trumpet in middle school to playing secondary parts with the high school, and that's an adjustment. He's used to playing the melody. The harmony for "Phantom of the Opera" doesn't sound nearly as glamorous as the melody. My son is learning what it's like to play second fiddle…er, trumpet.

Ask anyone who has ever been consigned to sing the alto or tenor part for hymns, and they'll tell you it's usually pretty dull. Alto and tenor lines are functional, though hardly beautiful. But couple that with the soprano and bass lines, and you have something much more exciting. You have *music*. We can't all sing melody, after all. If the organist were to get on the bench on Sunday morning and play only the melody line, we'd assume he or she hadn't practiced. "Johnny One-Note" isn't the best way to play a hymn. Those other voices may not sound terrific on their own, but together they make up a beautiful composition.

Do you ever feel like you're playing second fiddle, always behind the scenes rather than in the limelight? Sometimes it takes *more* grit to play a secondary role than a starring one. In some choirs, people who can't read music are automatically slotted as sopranos, whether their vocal range supports that or not. Why? Because the melody is usually the easiest to sing. It's recognizable and familiar. But to sing alto or tenor—ah, now that takes a bit more effort. One has to read the music and find one's notes against the backdrop of the more familiar melody. It's challenging. And although most people won't come up to an alto after a performance to congratulate her on how well she sang, you can guarantee that if the altos didn't sing, people would notice. The altos aren't the stars, but without them the performance wouldn't be complete.

As in a band or choir, so it is in life. Remember St. Paul's analogy to the body? The body is made up of many parts, each doing its job. Some seem less glamorous than others, but are no less important. "The parts of the body that seem to be weaker are indispensable, and on those parts of the body that we think less honorable we bestow the greater honor, and our unpresentable are treated with greater modesty, which our more presentable parts do not require. But God has so composed the body, giving greater honor to the parts that lacked it, that there may be no division in the body, but that the members may have the same care for one another…Now you are the body of Christ, and individually members of it" (1 Corinthians 12:22-25, 27).

Paul goes on to list some spiritual gifts in the Church—apostles, prophets, teachers, miracle workers, healers, helpers, administrators, and the gift of tongues. Although some of those gifts only applied to the apostolic era, the application is the same today: God gives each of us gifts, and *all* of them are needed in the church. I love that "helpers" made Paul's list. On the surface, that doesn't sound very flashy or impressive. Yet who among us doesn't appreciate the gal at church who makes meals for new moms or offers babysitting services for free? Who doesn't appreciate the handyman who's always willing to stop by and help when the washing machine conks out? We may not even notice the many areas where church members use their gifts of service. We might not admire the clean paraments on the altar, but if the Altar Guild forgot to change the Advent paraments to white for Christmas, we'd take note. We may not appreciate the fact that someone has to climb a huge ladder to reach the lights in the sanctuary, but we'd notice if a few light bulbs burned out. The fella who changes light bulbs won't get as much attention as the pastor in the front, but he's doing his part to keep the church running smoothly, and his service is also a gift to the congregation.

No matter what your role, remember this important truth from 1 Corinthians 12:18: "But in fact God has arranged the parts in the body, every one of them, *just as He wanted them to be*" (NIV, emphasis mine). God has placed *you* exactly where He wants you in the body, so be proud of the part He's assigned you. Even if you're playing second trumpet.

Surface Cleaning

September 22, 2014

Last week I unearthed a surface or two that I haven't seen since…well, maybe since we moved here. And I have to admit, that empty surface looks really nice. But I know it won't stay that way for long, because in our household we cannot keep a surface clean. Any cleared-off surface area attracts clutter automatically. Whenever we wish to have a family brunch at the dining room table, we have to clear it off before we can eat. By dinnertime, it's right back to being cluttered. Kitchen counters, dressers, even the washing machine. No surface is safe. Kids' homework, books, keys, coats, papers, crayons, Legos, you name it. There's something irresistible about a clean surface. It's just waiting to get cluttered again.

The Bible talks about this "empty space waiting to be filled" phenomenon as well. Look at Jesus' warning in Matthew 12:43-45. Granted, He's talking about evil spirits, but stick with me here. "When an evil spirit comes out of a man, it goes through arid places seeking rest and does not find it. Then it says, 'I will return to the house I left.' When it arrives, it finds the house unoccupied, swept clean and put in order. Then it goes and takes with it seven other spirits more wicked than itself, and they go in and live there. And the final condition of that man is worse than the first. That is how it will be with this wicked generation" (NIV).

I doubt you've dealt with demon possession, but the comparison Jesus makes at the end of this parable merits another look, "That is how it will be with this wicked generation." What does He mean by that? Many of the people in Jesus' day rejected Him and His message. Things haven't changed much since then in that regard. A person can be a "good" person, moral, upright, and law-abiding, without being a Christian. They can give to charity, volunteer at homeless shelters, and so on. But someone whose heart has been "swept clean and put in order" is in a precarious position indeed. A heart that is "neutral" is just like those tempting cleared-off surfaces in my house, just waiting for clutter to come and regain control.

Lest you think this only applies to non-believers, look with me at 2 Peter 2. This whole chapter deals with false teachers and warns God's people against them, for their message leads only to destruction. Peter says in verses 20-22, "If they have escaped the corruption of this world by knowing our Lord and Savior Jesus Christ and are again entangled in it and overcome, they are worse off at the end than they were at the beginning. It would have been better for them not to have known the way of righteousness, than to have known it and then to turn their backs on the sacred command that was passed on to them. Of them the proverbs are true: 'A dog returns to its vomit,' and, 'A sow that is washed goes back to her wallowing in the mud'" (NIV).

We just can't help ourselves. Our sinful nature runs so deep that we're just like that dog or that sow, returning to the disgusting filth. Don't think that once you're a Christian, you can never fall away. This passage shows otherwise, and is a solemn warning against willfully returning to our sinfulness. Don't think your little pet sin is "okay" because you're forgiven anyhow. Grace is not an excuse to sin freely. Sin is that clutter that threatens to overtake each and every one of us.

There are certain sins I really don't *want* to get rid of, and I confess them every week at church but then go right back to them. Like the clean surface at my house, it begins innocently enough. A few papers here, a few Legos there. But before you know it, that surface is overtaken by so much clutter you can't see the counter at all. If you claim to be Christian yet have too much clutter, people won't be able to see underneath all that clutter to the clean surface underneath. We have to get rid of the clutter so our forgiven, clean nature can shine through.

Thankfully, it's not up to us to do it alone. God gives us something to fill the void, "cleaning agents" to fight the clutter—His Spirit, His Word, and His Sacraments strengthen us and combat the sin that would otherwise overtake us. Don't think you can do this on your own. God freely offers to help, and gathering together for mutual support and encouragement with fellow believers is crucial. Don't imagine you can neglect worship and be okay. Where else do you have access to the Sacraments and to so many fellow believers gathered around God's Word? Only God can remove the clutter of sin in your life, and only with His strength can you keep clearing those spaces when they start to gather clutter again. And with that, please excuse me. I've got a few more surfaces to declutter.

Perfect Timing

September 24, 2018

Timing is everything in music. No one wants to be the one who miscounts the measures of rest and comes in at the wrong time. Take the iconic ending of G.F. Handel's "Hallelujah Chorus," for example. The music is climaxing with the singers repeating, "Forever and ever! Hallelujah! Hallelujah! Hallelujah! Hallelujah!" (Dramatic pause) "Hal-le-lu-jah!" It's that rest right before the last "Hallelujah" that makes the ending. If the singers ignored that final rest or sang one too many "hallelujahs," it would ruin it. Like I said, timing is everything.

As in music, so it is in life. Timing is everything. But the catch is that our timing may not be what God has in mind. Recall with me the story of Joseph in the Old Testament. His jealous brothers sell him into slavery, and he performs his duties faithfully but gets thrown into prison when Potiphar's wife lies about him. But even in prison, he finds favor with the jailer and ends up in a position of authority there. Then he correctly interprets the dreams of the cupbearer and baker, and he sees a possible "get out of jail free" card to play. He urges the cupbearer, who is restored to his position with Pharaoh, to speak of him to Pharaoh so he will be released. By human standards, this is a great plan. Joseph is using the abilities God has given him to get himself out of a bad situation. Smart, right?

Only it doesn't work. Genesis 40:23-41:1 makes the transition for us. "Yet the chief cupbearer did not remember Joseph, but forgot him. After two whole years…" Imagine poor Joseph's disappointment when he realized the cupbearer wasn't going to commend him to Pharaoh after all. He was stuck in this prison. For two more years. You see, it wasn't God's timing. God had a much greater plan in store. Had the cupbearer put in a good word to Pharaoh and had Joseph released from prison, he would have come out as a virtual nobody, completely unknown in Egyptian society, and likely gone back to menial work as a household servant. God's plan was so much more dramatic. Instead, Joseph waited two years until Pharaoh had dreams that troubled him, and then correctly interpreted the dreams, saved Egypt from a dreadful famine, and was placed over everything in Egypt save Pharaoh himself. Definitely a better plan than Joseph's short-sighted one. But timing was everything. Specifically, God's timing.

I've been in Joseph's position before. Well, okay, not really. I mean, I've never been in prison unjustly after being sold into slavery by my brothers, thank goodness. But I've been in situations I thought were unfair or at least not ideal. I've tried to "help" God along by putting my own plan into action, only to be disappointed when the results weren't what I'd hoped they would be. I've tried to rush God's timing. And not surprisingly, that hasn't worked.

Discerning God's timing is awfully hard. There are times when yes, we should act. God gives us abilities and intelligent minds that we are to use to serve our fellow man. If we see an injustice we know we can fix, we shouldn't stand by idly, waiting for a neon sign from God before we do something. There's a time for waiting and praying, and there's a time for action. So how can we tell the difference between the two? Let's look to Nehemiah for an example.

Nehemiah was another cupbearer, but he served King Artaxerxes in Persia many years after Joseph lived, during the period of the exile. King Cyrus had allowed some Jews to return to Jerusalem, as recounted in the book of Ezra. But even though they had been allowed to return to their homeland, it wasn't exactly a walk in the park for them. Jerusalem was in great disrepair, and Nehemiah heard the report that the walls of Jerusalem were broken down and its gates destroyed by fire. The people there were in "great trouble and shame" (Nehemiah 1:3). Nehemiah had a good position in Persia, but he knew he could—and should— help in Jerusalem.

At this point in the story, I would likely have jumped right into action. Okay, so they need help in Jerusalem? Great! I'll ask the king tomorrow if I can go. I'll start packing tonight. Clearly this is from God, right? But look what Nehemiah does instead. "As soon as I heard these words I sat down and wept and mourned for days, and I continued fasting and praying before the God of heaven," Nehemiah 1:4 reports. Wait, what? He just...prayed? (It's a great prayer, by the way. Check it out in Nehemiah 1:5-11). Yes, he prayed. And waited. He had to be sure he was acting on God's timing and not his own.

Chapter 2 opens with Nehemiah still serving Artaxerxes, in the month of Nisan. He'd originally heard about the trouble in Jerusalem in the month of Chislev. Translation: three months have passed before he gets a good opportunity to ask the king for permission to leave and go back to Jerusalem. He's had plenty of time to pray and plan. When the king asks him how long he'll be gone, Nehemiah has an answer ready. Not only this, but he also has the prescience to ask the king for letters for safe passage on the journey. Those three months of waiting have allowed him the opportunity to think through the logistics and get a clearer picture of what his plan needs to be. And now that the timing is right, he's ready to act.

Whatever your situation, pray for God's discernment to tell whether you need to wait on Him or whether it's time to act. Take time to reflect and pray before jumping straight into a course of action. God knows the big picture, and He will grant you the wisdom you seek. Yes, timing is everything, and God's timing is always perfect.

Unbelievable

September 25, 2014

One of the things I love about Jesus' parables is how unbelievable some of them are. He throws in so many unexpected twists and characters that there's no possible way some of those parables could ever actually happen. A man who sells all he has to get one pearl? Sure. The story of the workers in the vineyard, where the owner pays the guys who worked one hour the same thing he paid the guys who worked twelve hours? Never going to happen in the real world. Imagine pitching, say, "The Parable of the Unforgiving Servant" as a TV show idea. *Um, yeah, we can't use this. Sorry, but it's just too far-fetched. This guy's debt is unrealistic, and there's no way the king would just cancel it all because he asked him to. And then for him to be such a jerk to his fellow worker regarding his small debt is completely ridiculous. Give us something people can believe.* But here's the thing—this story *has* happened. And you're one of the main characters.

In case you can't recall all the details of this particular parable, check out Matthew 18:23-35. This servant owes the king a fantastic sum. 10,000 talents was insanely high. One single talent was the equivalent of "about twenty years' wages for a laborer," according to the footnote in my ESV text. Okay, so let's translate this into modern terms. Let's work with a fairly low sum for a blue collar worker in America today. Let's just start with a modest $30,000 a year. A "talent," therefore, would be $30,000 x 20, which is $600,000. Now, this guy owed 10,000 talents, so 600,000 x 10,000 = 6,000,000,000. That's six billion dollars, and that's even using a low salary from the start. That's just crazy. How he got the debt we'll never know, but there was obviously no way he could ever pay that back. So he begs the king to have mercy on him until he pays it back. Amazingly, the king doesn't just give him an extension—he cancels the *entire thing!* That $6 billion debt is just erased, no questions asked. Incredible!

What happens next is equally incredible. This newly debt-freed servant goes out and sees a fellow servant who owes him money. One hundred denarii, to be exact. Again, let's translate that into modern terms. The ESV note says a denarius was a day's wage for a laborer. So assuming a minimum wage of $10 an hour, and an eight-hour workday, that comes to $80. $80 x 100 = $8,000. Now, honestly, that's a fairly significant sum as well. I mean, if someone owed me that much, yeah, I'd see to it that they paid me back. But compared to the six billion dollars the first guy originally owed, this is nothing. It's nearly 1,000 times less. But the first servant hasn't learned much from the mercy of the king. Instead of giving his coworker a break, he has the guy thrown into jail until he pays everything back, which the king isn't thrilled about. In fact, the king throws that first guy into jail himself, this time to be tortured. His second condition is worse than the first would have been, and all because he was unforgiving to his other servant.

This parable has both Law and Gospel in it, so let's look at the Gospel first. The king, of course, is God, and you are the servant who had an impossible debt to pay. We had the debt of sin. Every single person on this earth has that debt, and there's no possible way any of us could ever repay it. Not in a billion years. God demands absolute perfection, and even the tiniest sin separates us from Him. But because of His love and mercy, He didn't give us what we deserved. We should rightfully have been sent to jail (aka, hell) until we could pay back our debt, which we could never do. But amazingly, He canceled our debt because of Jesus' work on our behalf. That unpayable debt is completely erased. We owe nothing. Unbelievable!

Now for the Law. All too often, we go out and act just like that unforgiving servant. We find a fellow believer who has wronged us and we hold it against them with a grudge in our hearts. We remind them of their transgression over and over, we gossip about it to others, we may even stop going to church because of an offense. In short, we refuse to have mercy. Even after being forgiven an enormous debt ourselves, we can't seem to extend that same mercy to others. Granted, some people may hurt you badly. Like I mentioned above, that $8,000 was nothing to sneeze at. It's a significant sum. There will be people on this earth who wrong you greatly, causing much damage to you personally, financially, or emotionally. As sinful humans, we want to hold on to that hurt and remind them of it whenever we can. We want others to know how they've made us suffer.

But that's not the way of God. Our sins put Jesus on that cross. It was because of *you* that He suffered and died. But He did it gladly. He doesn't hold any grudges. He did it freely, out of love. We didn't even ask Him first. It was "while we were still sinners [that] Christ died for us" (Romans 5:8). It wasn't because we were sorry enough or worthy enough. That would never happen. He forgave freely so your debt could be erased forever. Unbelievable.

Learn from that unforgiving servant. There *will* be people on this earth who sin against you. It's a harsh reality of life. But remember that God has first forgiven you an enormous debt. With His help, you can be an instrument of forgiveness and mercy in this world, telling others of the generosity of your heavenly King. Believe it, because it's all true.

My Way

September 25, 2017

The three most common words in our household are currently, "I do it!" This phrase is often spoken in an urgent, indignant tone by my two-year-old, who thinks he can do everything. From strapping himself into his car seat to feeding the dogs to pouring milk into his cup, my toddler erroneously assumes he is competent enough to handle every task that comes his way. He gets mad at me if I do something he thinks he can do. He will shut the door to the dryer in protest just so he can be the one to open it again. It's cute and irritating all at the same time, because clearly there are things he has no business trying to do. He thinks he can do anything, but he's wrong. But he's not the only one to think this way.

Frank Sinatra may have popularized the song "My Way," but the sentiment is far from unique. The thought of doing things one's own way appeals to something deep in the core of a human being. *I am capable! I am strong! Look what I have done!* one thinks with pride. Toddlers and adults alike hate to be told what to do. We'd much rather do things our own way, thank you very much. It's especially abrasive to think there's a higher power out there, setting rules and boundaries for us. Through the ages, people have rebelled against this notion, and the Bible is proof of that. There are numerous biblical examples of people taking matters into their own hands, thinking they could solve their own problems or make decisions apart from God. Adam and Eve thought they knew better than God when they decided to take a bite of that fruit. Cain thought he would get rid of his guilt by getting rid of his brother. Sarah thought she'd help God by asking Abraham to bear a child with Hagar. Joseph's brothers devised their own plan to deal with the sibling rivalry and parental favoritism in their family. David thought he could fix his dilemma with Bathsheba by his own cunning. By doing things "my way," these people royally messed up their lives.

What are you struggling with in your life? What problem are you trying to fix on your own? Where are you desperately trying to do things your own way, rather than God's way? Are there commandments you think you can redefine to accommodate a pet sin or cover up another sin, as did David? Are you impatient for God to act and looking to "help" Him out, as Sarah did? Be very careful, for Proverbs 14:12 warns us, "There is a way that seems right to a man, but its end is the way to death." Yikes. That certainly doesn't mince words. Rather than taking matters into our own hands, Deuteronomy 8:6 advises us, "You shall keep the commandments of the Lord your God by walking in *His ways* and by fearing Him" (emphasis added). These verses acknowledge that God's way is the best and only way. Just as my two-year-old cannot understand why I won't let him cross the road without holding my hand, so we may not understand our omnipotent God's rules sometimes. We may think He's trying to unfairly restrict us, when in actuality, He's trying to keep us safe.

Isaiah 55:8-9 tells us, "My thoughts are not your thoughts, neither are your ways My ways, declares the Lord. For as the heavens are higher than the earth, so are My ways higher than your ways and My thoughts than your thoughts." God's ways are so, *so* much better, and Jesus is proof of that. On our own, we never could have come up with God's way of salvation. While we were sewing together fig leaves, God was already setting in motion His plan to send His Son to die for our sins. He was already promising Jesus, *the* Way. "There is salvation in no one else, for there is no other name under heaven given among men by which we must be saved," Acts 4:12 reminds us. The meaning is clear. There's no room for "my way" in this. We may feebly protest, "I do it!" But God gently answers, "No, My child, I already did it. And I did it My way."

The Depths of Despair

Bonus Post

Psalm 13 is one of the most brutally honest expressions of the tension between despair and hope in the life of a believer. For those who battle hopelessness, the seeming paradox between the beginning of the psalm and the end makes sense. They "get" it because they live it. David's prayer—his raw, emotionally charged prayer—becomes their own. They can use these words, which were written under divine inspiration just like every other verse in the Bible, to express to God their own jumble of emotions.

The first two verses lay it all out there: "How long, O Lord? Will You forget me forever? How long will You hide Your face from me? How long must I take counsel in my soul and have sorrow in my heart all the day? How long shall my enemy be exalted over me?" (Psalm 13:1-2).

Wow, David. Those pointed questions seem almost irreverent, unholy, faithless. You're in effect asking, "Hey, God, are You even listening? Are You ever going to answer me?" Brother or sister in Christ, can you relate? Have you ever felt that way? It's only natural. David is hailed in Scripture as "a man after [God's] own heart" (1 Samuel 13:14), and yet look at him here.

Think about David's life for a moment. He went through a lot of down times himself. Some were admittedly brought about by his own sin (hello, Bathsheba!), but think of all those years he spent on the run from Saul, hiding as a fugitive. Can't you just hear him in a deserted cave, crying desperately to God the words of those two verses above? "God, You promised me I would be king, and yet here I sit like a criminal, hunted down, a wanted man. What's going on?" Yes, David experienced sheer despair. He had his doubts. And here's the thing: it's okay!

You know as well as I that when you're going through that kind of despair, people will chide you to have faith. That doesn't help. It just adds to the feelings of guilt and shame. "I should be more faithful," you think to yourself. "What's wrong with me?" Nothing, fellow Christian. Own up to those feelings. Tell God. He already knows them anyhow. Be honest with Him and with yourself. Take the time to read out loud David's agonizing pleas, and then express to God your own doubts. "God, I feel like this too. I wonder if You care. I don't know if You will ever deliver me." Tell Him when you're mad at Him. Tell Him when you doubt His love. Yell at Him. Cry if you need to. It's liberating.

Moving on in Psalm 13, we read, "Consider and answer me, O Lord my God; light up my eyes, lest I sleep the sleep of death, lest my enemy say, 'I have prevailed over him,' lest my foes rejoice because I am shaken" (vv 3-4).

Here's the "why" of the questions raised in the first two verses. What difference does it make if God answers us or not? Why should we care? David supplies us with two answers. First, without God giving light to our eyes, we will sleep in death. Physical death as well as eternal death. Those who struggle with terminal illness realize poignantly that each day, each breath is a gift from God. It's true for all of us, of course, but we don't always think about it quite that way.

The second reason is that David not only foresees death without God's intervention, he sees the triumph of his foes. Imagine if Saul had captured and killed David. Can't you just hear Saul's arrogant boasts? "Ha! So *that* was the mighty David? He had the audacity to claim God told him he would be king! So much for David's so-called God!" And this boast is so much more deadly than a personal dig, for it defies the living God. Do you have those kinds of enemies? Are there people who would rejoice in your downfall? We all have at least one bitter adversary: the devil, who is *very* invested in your final outcome. He would like nothing more than for you to give up. And he tries his darndest to speak those gloating words over you every day, to make you believe you have already lost the fight. You haven't, my friend. Specifically, *God* hasn't. Jesus already defeated Satan for you. Do not listen to the devil when he tempts you to think otherwise.

The psalm concludes: "But I have trusted in Your steadfast love; my heart shall rejoice in Your salvation. I will sing to the Lord, because He has dealt bountifully with me" (Psalm 13:5-6).

Um, David? Weren't you the one who, only a few verses ago, wrestled with whether or not God even cared? That's quite a turnaround. And here's where this doesn't make sense to those who have never felt the raw pain of the first two verses. It's such a seeming paradox, but those who are experiencing that pain get it. They know what it is to have both despair and hope. They can see how, yes, God has sustained them faithfully through it all, working in unexpected ways.

Had I never experienced the "Job" years in my life, I would never have started writing. And as I look back over that period, I can see specific examples of how God provided. He raised up for me friends I never knew I had, gave me devotional insights that strengthened me, taught me empathy (often the hard way!), and so much more. Yes, with David I can say that I rejoice in the Lord, for He has been good to me.

Maybe you aren't there yet. Maybe you can't honestly say that God is good. That's okay too. David first had to work through bitter despair. He struggled with God in prayer. You need to do the same. It is as vital a step in healing as is the admission that God is good. Follow David's model in your own life. Work through the junk first. And here's the best part—this isn't about you, dear brother or sister. This is about our Lord. You don't have to be "holy enough" or take the "glass is half full" mentality. You don't have to pull yourself up by your own bootstraps. God will give you His peace in His timing. Yes, God *is* good, but you can't force that or guilt yourself into that belief. As with every good and perfect gift, His peace comes from above.

So when you're struggling with despair, make David's prayer your own. It's like having an argument with a loved one. Confronting them and getting your feelings out in the open can be incredibly painful and usually produces tears at some point. Yet oftentimes such an honest discussion gives peace afterward simply because you're finally being honest with one another. If that is true of human relationships that are imperfect, how much more so with a perfect God. Be honest with Him. Pray Psalm 13 as often as you need to. And know this: at the end—even if that means your eternal end in heaven—you *will* be able to say with David in confidence, "I have trusted in Your steadfast love; my heart shall rejoice in Your salvation. I will sing to the Lord, because He has dealt bountifully with me" (Psalm 13:5-6).

October

Fender Benders

October 1, 2014

It was not a good morning. At. All. I had accomplished the crazy morning dash of getting the kids ready for school and out the door on time, but as I pulled into the empty parking lot I realized we were on a two-hour fog delay. At least, that's what I assume. We didn't have fog by our house, and since this was before the days of text notifications for delays and cancellations, parents were left to their own discretion to check the radio or TV for delays. I, obviously, hadn't deemed it necessary to check, so here we were sitting at school fully ready for the day two hours early. But the day was about to get worse.

Grumbling about how we could have all slept in, I debated my next move. I really didn't want to return home just to come back shortly thereafter, so I figured I'd take the kids with me on a few errands. Since we were already at school, I decided to go to the drugstore closest to school, rather than the one I usually frequented near our house. The one near school was a bit more dumpy, it was harder to access from the main road, and the store layout was completely different. I was disoriented and flustered, and it turns out that the product I was looking for wasn't even in stock there. Lovely. Waste of time, and with the kids pulling at me whining for candy, my mood was getting darker by the minute. I stomped out to the van, buckled everyone in, and started to back out when it happened. *Crunch.* I backed into another car.

If my day had been lousy already, this was quickly spiraling out of control. I sheepishly pulled back into my parking spot and slunk out to inspect the damage. My van had nothing at all. Not a scratch. But when I walked over to the other car, a junky little thing, I could see right away the dent in the back fender. *Oh, great!* Now I was really fuming. *If we hadn't had this stupid delay, I wouldn't even be here in the first place and none of this would have ever happened!* My thoughts were filled with filing claims and rising car insurance rates, even as my kids restlessly pestered me to leave. I sat there for five minutes to see if the car owner would emerge, then I started to write a note to leave on his windshield with my name and number. But just as I finished the note, he came out and headed for his car. It was the moment of truth.

I got out of my vehicle and walked over to him and confessed my guilt. I pointed out the dent and waited for him to yell at me or chastise me for being so careless. Instead he looked at the dent casually and said, "Oh, that's been there for years. It's not your fault at all." I hugged the guy on the spot, thanked him for his honesty, and fairly danced to the car, my entire outlook for the day completely turned around. None of the things that had so irritated me that morning had changed, but they all seemed petty now compared to what *could* have happened. I had been caught red-handed and yet was let off the hook with no consequences whatsoever. Maybe it was going to be a good day after all.

On a much grander scale, the same thing has happened to every single one of us. You were caught red-handed in the guilt of sin. And it was undeniably your fault. You couldn't blame it on a pre-existing dent like in my example above. No, you were completely, totally, 100% guilty, with no way out. You had no excuse. All you could do was admit your guilt and wait for the consequences. But amazingly, there weren't any. God looked at your sin and said, "Oh, that's already been taken care of, My child. Your debt has been paid. You're forgiven." Jesus took your punishment and paid the penalty for sin in your place. You didn't deserve it, but He did it out of love for you. Does that take away the day-to-day irritations and hardships we face in life? No. But when we compare those things to the price He has already paid, all else pales in comparison. Your biggest debt has been erased. You're free. It will be a good day after all.

In the Presence of the King

October 1, 2018

This was a matter of life and death. The rule in the royal court was that anyone who approached the king without being summoned was to be put to death. There was one exception. If the king held out his scepter, the person who dared approach him uninvited would live. Queen Esther knew this rule applied even to her, and when she agreed to plead with the king on behalf of the Jews, she knew she could be walking to her own death. Mordecai had tricked King Ahasuerus into signing a death edict for the Jewish people, and Esther knew it was up to her to save them, provided she didn't get killed first. But she didn't just run to the throne room. She told Mordecai to gather as many Jews as he could and fast and pray for her for three days before she would dare to approach the king. This was too serious a matter to attempt without proper preparation.

This wasn't the first time Esther had prepared to be in the presence of the king. Why, back in the second chapter of Esther, she had undergone a *twelve month* period of preparation as part of the king's harem before she was allowed in the presence of the king. That included six months with oil and myrrh and six months with spices and ointments, as Esther 2:12 tells us. This was no small task.

Even Nehemiah, who was cupbearer to King Artaxerxes and therefore with him on a daily basis, didn't get too casual with Artaxerxes. When he felt the call to go back to Jerusalem to help rebuild the walls, he prayed and waited until the king opened an opportunity for him to make his request—three months later. And Daniel, King Nebuchadnezzar's advisor, asked his three friends to join him in prayer before approaching the king to not only interpret the king's dream, but also to tell the king what that dream was! All these individuals realized that approaching the king was serious business, not something to be taken lightly or irreverently.

We have the privilege of being in the presence of the King of heaven and earth on a daily basis. This is a more serious matter than many people make it out to be. Just as Esther, Nehemiah, and Daniel prepared for their time with the king, so ought we prepare our hearts and minds to be in God's presence. He is holy. We are sinful. And as such, that's a problem we need to address right away. I heard some years ago that going to church is entering God's house, and we cannot enter without proper attire. That's why we do confession and absolution at the beginning of the service. It's us wiping the dirt off our feet before we come in, and putting on the white robe Christ won for us. I love that analogy. Sin cannot stand in the presence of our holy God. To be properly prepared, we must confess our sins and put on Christ's righteousness so we are acceptable in the sight of the King.

Thankfully, we don't have to wait a year to come before our King as Esther did. Nor do we have to wait three months as Nehemiah did. We don't even need a three-day fast like Esther arranged for her people. But do approach God's throne with proper reverence. Wipe your feet and put on Christ's royal robe. Remember, you're in the presence of the King.

Life on the Plain

October 5, 2015

Last weekend I was blessed to attend a pastors' wives retreat. It was refreshing and uplifting. I was able to meet other pastor's wives and swap stories with them. I stayed up late with new friends, sipping wine and eating chocolate. I had free time to walk, write, and relax. I went kayaking. Our group of ladies had wonderful sessions together. We sang together. We did devotions together. We learned different methods of doing personal Bible study. It was a wonderful weekend. And then I came home.

I'm not gonna lie to you. The homecoming was rough. The day after I came home my three-year-old was exceedingly whiny, my sixth grader needed help with homework that confused even me, and one of my children had a major meltdown, followed quickly by an equally major meltdown on my own part. Even my Bible study time was interrupted by my son dropping (and breaking) a bowl of ice cream in the living room, plus a fight between my two oldest children. I had been so excited to come back and put into practice all these wonderful Bible study techniques I had learned, and the first day back was simply awful. *Welcome home.*

The problem with mountain top experiences is that at some point you have to come back down, and sometimes there's a valley awaiting you. It's a hard fall. But eventually the mountain and valley equal out, and you're left with life as usual—life "on the plain." Yes, you'll have peaks and valleys in your life, but usually you'll find yourself simply on the plain. Nothing tragic, but nothing phenomenal either. Compared to a mountaintop experience, life on the plain is pretty dull.

What can we do when we're stuck in the monotony of the plain? Look to the Mount of Transfiguration. Peter, James, and John got to see Jesus transfigured into His glorified state before their very eyes. That in and of itself is mind-blowing, but then suddenly Moses and Elijah appeared with Him. Talk about a mountaintop experience! But they couldn't stay there. Eventually Moses and Elijah left, and Jesus returned to His normal earthly appearance. They had to leave the mountain and come back to the bitter reality Jesus had revealed to them—that He was going to suffer and die. Not a compelling motivation to come back to life as usual.

But wait—there's something important here that's easy to miss. Matthew 17:9 tells us, "As they were coming down the mountain, Jesus commanded them…" The disciples weren't alone. Jesus was with them. He didn't give them an amazing mountaintop experience only to send them off on their own. He personally accompanied them back down. Stanza 5 of the hymn "Tis Good, Lord, to Be Here" (*Lutheran Service Book* 414) puts it like this:

'Tis good, Lord, to be here!
Yet we may not remain;
But since Thou bidst us leave the mount,
Come with us to the plain.

You aren't alone. Jesus is with you through it all. He is, after all, Immanuel—"God with us." He is with us on the mountaintop, He is with us in the valley, and yes, He is with us on the plain.

Unexpected Answers

October 6, 2014

Some time ago, my son mentioned an acquaintance who had a sarcastic sense of humor. This person used sarcasm to be funny, but my son perceived that it was often cutting, as is the nature of sarcasm. We started praying for that individual, that God would lead them to see that sarcasm was not the best way to communicate. We prayed about this together for a while until my son informed me one day that this acquaintance had actually apologized for the sarcasm. Sadly, I was stunned. I honestly hadn't expected that at all. Although we had been praying about it regularly, I really hadn't expected a response quite like that. It was as if I was surprised that God had answered our prayer.

Be honest; have you had an experience like that? Perhaps God answered a prayer right away and it surprised you. Maybe He granted a request you thought He wouldn't. Or maybe you're just too much of a "realist" to believe that God would answer prayer. Maybe you pray without believing God will answer. How often we come before God with our petitions, inwardly thinking, *There's no way He's going to answer this.* Perhaps a loved one has cancer and you know the medical statistics. You pray that God would heal your loved one, but secretly you know that request won't be granted. You go through the motions and start the prayer chain and everything, but you know there's no way God will really answer. But is that really true?

Look at Jesus' words in Matthew 7:7-11. He promises that if we ask, it will be given to us. He even compares prayer to sinful parents granting good things to their children. "If you then, who are evil, know how to give good gifts to your children, how much more will your Father who is in heaven give good things to those who ask Him!" Does this mean that God will give us everything we ask? No. Just as a loving parent uses discretion in granting their child's requests, so our perfect Heavenly Father knows what is best for us, and sometimes the answer has to be "no." If your seven-year-old asks you for an iPhone and a gaming system and a DVD player in his room with a bunch of PG-13 and R-rated movies, will you grant his request? I certainly hope not. You have a better perspective and know what is best for him in the long run. In the same way, God sees things from His heavenly perspective and knows what is best for us and for those around us. Sometimes, He will answer a simple "yes," like in my opening example. But often, He will answer it differently than we might think.

Let's look at another example: Jesus' prayer in the Garden of Gethsemane. Jesus knew exactly what faced Him. He had the weight of the entire world's sin laid squarely upon His shoulders. He knew the suffering and physical agony He would face, and He knew that He would have to experience even the abandonment of His Father on that cross. It's a weight none of us will ever know. But in Gethsemane, Jesus prayed fervently to His Father. Hebrews 5:7 tells us this: "In the days of His flesh, Jesus offered up prayers and supplications, with loud cries and tears, to Him who was able to save Him from death, and He was heard because of His reverence."

Now here was a fervent prayer. I've cried before while praying, but never like that. Jesus was groaning and crying loudly, physically moved during this prayer session. And we know from the Gospels that His prayer was, "Father, if You are willing, remove this cup from Me. Nevertheless, not My will, but Yours, be done" (Luke 22:42). Now, did God grant His request? Did God remove that cup from Jesus? No, He didn't. Because God knew that only Jesus could save us all from sin and death. If Jesus didn't die as the sinless Lamb of God, we would all be lost forever. God was looking not to Jesus' personal comfort, but to the good of the entire world.

On the other hand, God *did* answer Jesus' prayer. Look what happened immediately after He prayed. Luke 22:43 continues, "And there appeared to Him an angel from heaven, strengthening Him." God wasn't going to remove the cup of suffering from Jesus, but He did ready Him and strengthen Him for the task at hand. And look again at the words of the Hebrews passage above—"to Him who was able to save Him from death." God *was* able to save Jesus from death, and in fact did so through the resurrection. Death did not have the final victory here. Jesus' resurrection assured us of our own new life with Him. Death has no power over us anymore. Now *that's* an answer to prayer!

So pray with confidence, dear one. Present your petitions to God, who knows what is best. Pray that His will be done. It's hard to do, I know. There are some instances even now in my own life where I honestly don't think I *want* God's will to be done if it doesn't match my own selfish desires. But He answers all prayers in ways better than we can ever imagine. Just ask, with the words of Ephesians 3:20-21 in your heart. "Now to Him who is able to do far more abundantly than all that we ask or think, according to the power at work within us, to Him be glory in the church and in Christ Jesus throughout all generations, forever and ever. Amen."

Mustard Seeds

October 7, 2019

When I was a girl, I had a bracelet with a mustard seed in it. The mustard seed was enclosed within a clear ball, like a marble. The seed itself was tiny, a visual reminder of Jesus' mention of the mustard seed. Indeed, the mustard seed has become symbolic of faith. Many times we think of Jesus' words in Matthew 17:20, where He says, "'Truly, I say to you, if you have faith like a grain of mustard seed, you will say to this mountain, "Move from here to there," and it will move, and nothing will be impossible for you.'" Oftentimes the implied question is this: do *you* have that kind of faith?

But there's another mustard seed reference in the Gospels. Matthew, Mark, and Luke all record the parable of the mustard seed, which has a completely different nuance. Instead of likening one's faith to a mustard seed, this time Jesus is talking about the kingdom of heaven, a far broader scope that places the action solely upon Him.

> *He put another parable before them, saying, "The kingdom of heaven is like a grain of mustard seed that a man took and sowed in his field. It is the smallest of all seeds, but when it has grown it is larger than all the garden plants and becomes a tree, so that the birds of the air come and make nests in its branches."*
> *Matthew 13:31-32*

I don't know about you, but I'm not terribly familiar with a mustard plant. I have mustard seeds in my pantry thanks to a spice collection I bought some time ago, so I know how small the seeds are (1-2 mm), but that's about where my knowledge ends. A bit of background info is helpful to understand Jesus' parable.

- Mustard seeds need no cultivating and are characterized by rapid germination. A mustard seed planted one day could start growing the very next day.

- Few plants grow so large in one season as a mustard. A mustard plant is still an herb, but its stem would grow dry and wood-like, making it look like a tree. Holy Land trees generally don't grow very tall, so the mustard plant would likely only reach a height of 5-10 feet.

These facts help us keep in mind the focus of this parable. By choosing a mustard seed, which grows a lot in a little amount of time and needs no cultivation, Jesus is showing us that *He* makes the kingdom of heaven grow. From a seemingly small beginning—one man and His twelve followers—Christianity spread like wildfire throughout the world, even despite persecution and man's attempts to stop the growth.

This growth continues still today. Look in your own life. What seemingly small beginnings have been planted? What about your family? My parents, for example, had a seemingly small beginning: two people getting married. But they had three children and raised us in the faith. Each of us married fellow Christians and had kids of our own, who are also being raised in the faith. In the span of two generations, they've grown from two people to nineteen (and possibly counting). In another generation, that number will multiply even more, perhaps doubling or tripling (or more!) the number in a single generation.

Sometimes we fall into the trap of thinking that we have to do great things to make an impact in the kingdom of heaven, but this parable shows us otherwise. We can't make seeds grow. Yes, we can provide ideal conditions for our garden plants: good soil, appropriate sunlight, and water. But we can't make a seed grow. In the same way, we can't make the kingdom of God grow. We can provide ideal conditions for that faith to grow: devotions, Bible study, regular worship, bringing up children in the faith, and sharing our faith with others. But the results aren't up to us; they're up to God. Paul reminds us in 1 Corinthians 3:6: "I planted the seed, Apollos watered it, but God made it grow" (NIV).

So yes, share your faith, by all means. Nurture the seed that has been planted. And rest assured that God, in His own mysterious way, will make the seed grow and flourish. Maybe even into a mustard tree.

A Perfect Rescue

October 8, 2018

It was the perfect rescue story. We found a stray cat nearby, looking dirty, hungry, scared, and overall pretty pathetic. We didn't want to commit to another indoor cat, but we figured she could be an outdoor cat if she so chose. So we took her home, fed her, brushed the burrs out of her fur, and the kids gave her lots of love. They made a little bed for her inside a box, and she curled up in it rather cozily to spend the night. The next morning we couldn't find her right away, so the kids went looking for her. They found her in a hole the dogs had dug in the backyard. This hole goes underneath the patio, and the dogs slide under there to stay cool in the hot Texas sun. We tried coaxing the cat out, to no avail. We bribed her with food. Nothing. So my oldest son volunteered to slither down as far as he could to reach her. I had visions of him pulling her to safety while she purred gratefully, glad to have been rescued. Only it didn't work out that way at all.

The cat resisted our attempts at rescue, and we were running out of time and ideas. The dogs had been in their kennel all night, and needed to get out. So we had the bright idea to let them out, thinking they'd scare her out of the hole. That was a mistake. Our bigger dog cornered her in that dark hole, and all we could hear was growling and hissing. At length, the cat managed somehow to slide around the dog and run out, but the dog was fast too. He pounced on her and what ensued was a dog/cat fight I hope never to witness again. The dog had the cat pinned on her back as he snarled and bared his teeth and tried to bite her, all while she was hissing and taking swipes at him with her claws. I managed to grab the dog and allow the cat to escape, but she only ran to the other end of the yard, so the dog wriggled out of my grasp and caught her again. After a struggle, I grabbed the dog again, and my oldest son wrestled the cat out of its grasp and literally threw it over the fence to safety at last.

The thing is that the cat brought it upon herself. Had she stayed in the safety of the box we provided for her, she never would have encountered the dog. Had she taken the first opportunity to run away from the dog, she wouldn't have been attacked by it again. We rescued her, but she insisted on facing her opponent on her own. Clearly, this cat isn't very smart.

Yet we have a lot in common with that cat. We were lost, and God found us. He brought us into His family and fed us, washed us, and loved us. He stooped to our level, coming down to this earth to "get dirty" so He could rescue us. Jesus knew we couldn't get to Him, so He came to us. Yet how often, even after such a beautiful rescue, do we still insist upon going our own way or handling our problems by ourselves? How often do we think we can face the enemy with our own power? How often do we dare to presume that we don't need church or the

Lord's Supper or Bible study or prayer? Yet these are the very means God gives us to strengthen us with *His* power. Ephesians 6:10 tells us to "be strong *in the Lord* and in the strength of *His* might." Paul goes on to list the weapons at our disposal—the armor of God. Of course we aren't strong enough to face the devil on our own. We don't have to. Jesus has already defeated him for us.

Our stray cat continues to get into trouble. The same day of the episode with the dog, she got herself stuck in a tree and needed rescue again. She's run off multiple times, risking a run-in with the feral cats in the neighborhood. But my kids aren't giving up on her. Even though the cat hasn't shown them any love or gratitude, they love her and seek her out every time she runs off. God does the same for us. Like the shepherd seeking for the one lost sheep, like the woman looking for her one lost coin, and like the father, anxious to welcome back his prodigal son, so God searches us out when we wander, His love for us never wavering.

It's a perfect rescue story.

It's *your* rescue story.

Prowling Lions

October 9, 2014

Have you ever come face to face with a hungry lion? Unless you lead a thrilling life of daring safari adventures, my bet is the answer is no. The only place I've ever seen a lion is in a zoo, from the safety of the thick restraining glass. Even when the lion dares to walk right next to the glass on the other side, I know I'm safe. He poses me no threat at all. But there's another lion I do face on a daily basis, one who is much more dangerous than the lion I see in the zoo. This lion is constantly prowling around, looking for his next prey. I don't know where he'll show up or what tricks he'll use, but I know I'm never safe from him.

By now you've probably realized that this lion of whom I speak is actually the devil. We read in 1 Peter 5:8, "Be sober-minded; be watchful. Your adversary the devil prowls around like a roaring lion, seeking someone to devour." Now that's a chilling thought. And remember that the Bible often refers to Christians as "sheep" and to Christ as our "Good Shepherd." So let's think about this. How do sheep keep safe from prowling enemies outside the fold? They stick with the flock and follow the shepherd.

If we hope to protect ourselves from the worst enemy of all, Satan, we absolutely *have* to stay with the flock and follow our Shepherd. If there were no wolves or lions or predators out there, sheep could resist the shepherd and wander off with no real fear of consequences. Likewise, if Satan weren't lurking about, we could resist our Shepherd and wander away from the fold. No big deal. But you see, Satan *is* real. Very real. And as an actual lion looks first for the weak, the lame, the vulnerable sheep, so Satan preys on weakness. Those who have already distanced themselves from the fellowship of believers are in an incredibly vulnerable position, wide open to attacks from Satan. Without the rest of the flock to surround him and protect him and point him to the Shepherd, such a wandering sheep is an easy target for the devil's tactics to draw him away. But no Christian is ever truly safe.

You see, the devil *knows* he has the rest of the world. He doesn't bother too hard to entice away non-Christians, because they're already in his lair. He's still smarting from his defeat when Jesus rose from the dead, so he focuses his attention on drawing Christians away from their Shepherd so he can devour them.

Do you ever notice how your kids seem to be on their worst behavior in church or during devotions? Ever notice how easy it is to let your own mind wander during a sermon at church, or even to nod off? The devil works his hardest when the Word is being proclaimed. He's there in our midst, whispering and enticing us away, promising us he has something better, more exciting, more popular, whatever. And he knows your weaknesses. If you're easily tempted to gossip, say, he'll give you plenty of opportunities for that. If you struggle with an addiction, he'll see to it that you have access to whatever it is that seeks to control you. He plays upon your weaknesses. He's really good at what he does, because he's been doing it for years. He even tries to lull you into a sense of complacency or indifference. *It doesn't really matter what you believe, as long as you believe it with all your heart… You don't need to tell others about Jesus. After all, you don't want to offend anyone. Keep your beliefs to yourself…* And if we hear these lies enough, we just might believe them ourselves. On our own, we will fall for his lies every time.

But we aren't in this alone. We have a Good Shepherd, one who has already laid down His life for us, His sheep. He faced the attacks of Satan and resisted them, which we could never have done. Then He allowed Himself to be killed in our place. We should by all rights have been devoured, but our Shepherd loved us too much for that to happen. He died in our stead, and rose to defeat that evil lion, the devil. Oh, he still prowls about, and he is dangerous and powerful indeed, but your Shepherd is more powerful. Stick with Him. You are Jesus' little lamb. He will keep you safe in His arms until He carries you to your eternal home in heaven.

No Big Deal

October 9, 2017

I did the dishes in my kitchen sink yesterday. I know, big deal, right? But it *was* a big deal. We had been without a kitchen faucet for four and a half days, due to a comedy of errors. I'd never realized how much I used the kitchen sink until I was without one. Washing hands, rinsing fruits and veggies, filling a pot of water, cleaning off plates before loading them in the dishwasher—simple tasks I take for granted suddenly weren't so simple, and it wasn't until I didn't have the luxury of a kitchen sink that I realized how blessed I was to have a working faucet.

There are a number of things we take for granted or don't realize their value until we lose them. Perhaps you've experienced this when your air conditioner gives out in the middle of a heat wave, or when you lose electricity due to a storm. If you've ever had to make do without a vehicle, you quickly realize how convenient it is to have a car in good working condition. When my son broke his leg two years ago, we realized we'd rarely stopped to thank God for the use of our arms and legs before, but you can bet when he was able to walk again, we were all praising God! Sometimes we don't realize our blessings until we have to do without them.

Are we like this with our faith? All too often, yes. Most people in America can't even fathom what it would be like not to have freedom of religion. I can walk across the street and talk to my neighbor about Jesus in broad daylight without having to worry that she'll report me to the government. I can walk into church on Sunday without fear of being arrested. As a result, this incredible blessing loses some of its incredible-ness. We can easily become apathetic or think of church as no big deal. We can even see it as a burden—just one more thing to squeeze into our busy schedules. Persecuted Christians in other parts of the world would love to have the freedoms we have to worship publicly. They would be shocked and saddened at our apathy.

Many life-long Christians who have never known anything else can sometimes lose sight of the powerful impact of the Gospel. We've heard it so many times that we sort of become dulled to it. We need to step back and recall exactly what the message of the Gospel is. What would it be like for someone who has never known this message to hear it for the first time? Often, people who have converted from other religions to Christianity are more zealous to spread the Gospel because they know how freeing it is to hear the beautiful message of forgiveness through Jesus after toiling under the burden of a false religion and its impossible demands.

Imagine what it would be like to be uncertain of your salvation. If your eternal destiny was up to you and how well you lived your life, you could never know for sure where you stood in the balance. How many good works negate a bad one? How can you keep track of your tally? How will you ever know if you've done enough? But the Good News tells us that none of that matters. We can't live a good enough life no matter what. We don't have to. Jesus did what we could not. His perfect life and sinless death in our stead gave us the gift of eternal life with Him! When you stop to really think about that, it's mind-blowing. God became man to save us. That's a message that's too good to keep to ourselves. So go ahead and share it with someone today. Because it's a very big deal indeed.

McDonald's Evangelism

October 15, 2018

I was sitting in McDonald's with an hour to get some work done. I had my large coffee, my iPad was open and ready, and my Bible sat next to me on the table. I relished the opportunity to be alone and work without distractions. Only...wait. That guy over there. He's looking at me. He looks like he wants something. Shoot. Look down, Ruth. Act busy. You shouldn't have made eye contact. Drat. Now he's coming over, limping slightly as he walks. It's cold and rainy outside, and he has an umbrella he's sort of using as a cane. Okay. Sigh. He's at my table. *Here we go.*

"Yes, sir? Can I help you?" I ask, trying to be polite.

His voice is accented. "Yes, ma'am," he answers. "I'm trying to get to Houston. My daughter is having surgery. She's a cancer doctor, but now she has cancer herself. Stage Three bone cancer. I want to be there for her 10:30 surgery, but I can't figure out the way."

Oh. This isn't the way I saw this conversation going. Immediately I am ashamed of my selfishness. This gentleman obviously has more important concerns than my alone time. He hands me his phone and asks if I can find the address on Google maps. Sure, I can do that. Or can I? His phone is a different brand, and even after I connect to the free WiFi, his maps aren't working. I find the exact address on my own phone, then plug it into his app, to no avail. "No results found." This isn't going well. The guy was telling the truth. He really can't get directions.

I decide to go old-fashioned. I pull up the directions on my phone and write them down on a scrap piece of paper. It's not hard, and he's been there before. As I get within a few miles of the hospital, he's nodding his head. He'll recognize his surroundings once he gets to that point.

All this time we've been chatting, making small talk. We exchange names. He asks if I have kids. He tells me he's from Persia. I learn he's handicapped and shouldn't really be driving, but he desperately wants to be there for his daughter. He sees my Bible and asks if I'm a Christian. I affirm this, and he tells me he's Baha'i. I make a mental note to look it up when he's gone.

I finally get the directions written down, and on a whim I ask him if I can pray with him. This is new for me. I never do stuff like this. I mean, I've always thought it would be neat, but I've never had the guts to do it right then and there. If anything, I'd normally just assure him I'll be praying for him. But the Holy Spirit is tugging on my heart and I really can't ignore it. So despite the fact that here we are, smack dab in the middle of McDonald's in the midst of their breakfast crowd,

I take his hand and pray for him, for his daughter, for the surgeons, and that they will know the peace of Jesus.

When I'm done, he asks if he can say a prayer also. I really can't say no, so he prays something that sounds sort of like a mixture between a psalm and the prayer of St Francis ("Lord, make me an instrument of Your peace..."), though I note there's no mention of Jesus. We're still holding hands when he finishes, and he tells me the Baha'i religion respects all other religions and beliefs and works for peace and love among all people. I tell him, "I already have peace in Jesus. I pray you can have this peace too."

It's not the best witness I could have given. Looking back, I see so many things I could have or should have said. I didn't give a clear testimony of *why* I have peace in Jesus. I said nothing about His atoning work for my sins on the cross. But I prayed in Jesus' name with and for a non-Christian; something I've never done before. And I will continue to pray for him. Perhaps you too, dear reader, would say a quick prayer for him and for his daughter, not only for her health but that they would both come to know Jesus as their Savior.

1 Peter 3:15 tells us to "always be prepared to give an answer to everyone who asks you to give the reason for the hope that you have. But do this with gentleness and respect" (NIV). Pray that God opens your eyes to the opportunities He sends you to speak of His Son to others, and that He gives you courage to take those opportunities when they come. Because you just never know when you'll be called upon to be a witness to someone else.

Maybe even in the middle of McDonald's.

Replacement Tools

October 17, 2016

It was not a good start to the week. My baby had been fussy all weekend long, waking multiple times during the night. I was exhausted from lack of sleep, and his crankiness during the day was not fun to deal with under such circumstances. Then on Sunday evening, my fifth grader started complaining that his ear hurt. That night was his turn to be up multiple times, crying because of pain in his ear. Come Monday morning, I loaded them up and hauled them off to the doctor, to find that both had rip-roaring ear infections, and that my ten-year-old's eardrum had actually burst. My four-year-old had fluid in her ears but it wasn't infected, but that evening she started complaining that she had "crumbs" in her ear. Off to the doctor we went again the next morning. No, she didn't have an ear infection. She had strep. Lovely. With three sick kids, a house full of germs, and myself going on zombie hormones to begin with, it was shaping up to be a pretty awful week.

The irony of the situation is that barely a week before I'd been at a restful and relaxing pastors' wives retreat. Our speaker had introduced to us the concept of God's "replacement tools," godly attitudes to replace our old mindsets. Our theme verse for the weekend was Romans 12:12, "Rejoice in hope, be patient in tribulation, be constant in prayer." But the verses surrounding that verse are chock full of other nuggets of wisdom. Read through Romans 12:9-21 and you'll see what I mean. At the retreat, we read through these verses and made lists of God-given tools to replace the attitudes of the world. Instead of hate, choose love. Instead of despair, hope. Rather than curse others, pray a blessing upon them. Pick humility over pride. The list goes on and on. Sounds great, doesn't it? But in and of ourselves, we aren't going to automatically reach for the replacement tools. It's far too much "fun" to wallow in self-pity or bear a grudge or play the part of suffering martyr. Our sinful human nature wants to hold onto these things for some reason. Yes, God offers alternatives to our sinful inclinations, but only HE can give us the power and desire to actually use those alternatives.

What in your life needs replacing right now? Are you nursing a grudge against someone? Are you complacent in your prayer or devotional life? Greedy with your time or your money? Do you tend to fall into despair? Are your thoughts impure? Have you gotten pretty good at, ahem, complaining? Maybe your list looks different from mine, but we have one thing in common. No matter what our sinful behaviors, God offers a replacement tool. But He offers something else as well. Forgiveness. Even if we're serious about replacing old attitudes and praying for God's strength to do so, we won't succeed every time. We will still revert to our old choices and mindsets. And God offers forgiveness through His Son, Jesus, each and every time.

So what, exactly, does this replacement thing look like in real life? I'm glad you asked. Let's go back to my earlier example. Yes, my baby had an awful weekend for sleep, but I can be thankful he's usually a great sleeper. Two of my children had terrible ear infections, but I was able to get a doctor's appointment at 9:15 on a Monday morning with no advance notice. I'd say that's pretty incredible. And despite waiting nearly an hour for the antibiotics at the pharmacy, I am exceedingly thankful that we have medicine so readily available and at a reasonable enough cost. The next day, I was able to get another morning appointment for my daughter and more antibiotics, and by that Wednesday, everyone was back in school already. I'm thankful for disinfecting wipes to kill germs, washing machines to clean sheets and pillows, and the chance to scrub down the bathrooms in an effort to get rid of germs in the house. I'm grateful neither of my other two children got sick at all, despite the fact that my seven-year-old shares a room with her four-year-old sister, and that strep is terribly contagious. And I'm glad that neither my husband nor I caught anything, either. Come to think of it, it really wasn't such a terrible start to the week after all. Quite the opposite, actually. It was a reminder of how incredibly blessed I am.

Yes, God is Unfair

October 20, 2014

If there was such a thing as the "fairness police," my children would be prime candidates for a place on the force. Every real and perceived injustice in this house is met with protests of, "It's not fair!" They see to it that I am well aware of any inconsistencies in my parenting. "Hey, when I did that, you made me copy the Fourth Commandment! How come he doesn't have to do that? No fair!" Any parent of multiple children knows exactly what I'm talking about. Kids seem to constantly have their radars on, looking for unfairness. But they're not entirely wrong. I *am* "unfair" in that I *don't* treat my kids all the same.

I don't treat my children differently because I love one more than another. It's because they are different ages, have different levels of maturity, and each has his or her own unique personality. When my two-year-old proudly comes out of the bathroom and announces that she went potty all by herself, you'd better believe I'll be dancing around and giving her high fives. Would I do the same thing for my ten-year-old? Hardly. Or consider the games I play with my kids. My five-year-old loves the Clifford board game she got for her birthday, but I wouldn't play that with my older boys. I talk differently to my two-year-old than I do to my older kids. I discipline them differently, based upon their ages. They have different chores around the house. As they get older, they are given more responsibility. But at the same time, they also gain more independence. My boys have a fair amount of freedom in where they can go on their bikes and how long they can be outside on their own. Would I let my toddler roam the neighborhood for an hour alone? Definitely not. With age comes more responsibility as well as freedom, and wise parents dole these things out accordingly. As our kids get older, we treat them differently.

Personality determines how we treat kids as well. The stronger form of discipline necessary for a strong-willed child will crush the spirit of an overly sensitive child. On the flip side, a sensitive child might only need a parent to say, "That's not a good choice, honey," and the tears will well up because she knows she's disappointed her parents. But a strong-willed child would shrug off such a meek statement and it would make no difference at all. Children have to be treated differently, but the goal is the same—parents do the best they can to ensure that their children grow up to be responsible and caring individuals who can function well in society. We're shaping them for a future they can't even imagine, and not just for their own sake, but for the sake of those with whom they will come into contact—future spouses, employers, etc.

So if we as adults can understand this concept, why do we expect God to treat His children all the same? If my ten-year-old were to say to me, "It's not fair that you give her an M & M every time she goes to the bathroom. Why don't I get one?" I would roll my eyes. But don't we often do the same thing to God? *How come Jim has such a great career with a great salary while I'm struggling to make ends meet in a job I hate? It's not fair!* Sadly, we adults are not immune to the comparison game.

Consider an analogy that Paul uses quite a bit—the body. He compares the body of Christ to a physical body multiple times throughout his letters. In Romans 12:4-8 and 1 Corinthians 12:12-31, he makes this analogy for spiritual gifts, showing that all different kinds are needed, just as many parts are necessary for the function of a physical body. Already, we can see that God treats us differently. God doesn't give us all the same abilities and gifts. How boring would that be? Paul makes the analogy of a foot complaining that it is not a hand, or an ear complaining that it is not an eye. Even if your place in the body seems less glamorous than another, your part is needed and valued. Think about your feet. Chances are, they take a lot of wear and tear. They may have blisters or calluses. They can't do dexterous things like your hands can—playing the piano, painting pictures, typing a blog. To all appearances, they're kind of...well, plain. Functional. They're made to take more abuse than most other parts of the body, but they play a vital role. Without them, we'd have an awfully hard time getting around.

God has placed you where you are and given you specific talents and abilities for a reason. When you compare yourself to others, you might be tempted to believe that God has given you fewer gifts, a harder lot in life, etc. But God works through His people in different ways. Yes, He treats us differently, because this world is made up of different people in different walks of life with different personalities and different hardships and talents and weaknesses. Yet somehow God orchestrates all of that to work for His purposes. He's readying all believers for a future we can't even imagine, and in the meantime He's shaping us and using us to reach those around us. Sometimes that means an "easy" life, and other times that requires one of great hardship. Accept your place in the body and don't worry about whether or not God is "unfair" in His treatment of you.

Ultimately, yes, God *is* unfair to us. Placing the punishment we deserved upon the perfect shoulders of Jesus wasn't fair at all. We don't deserve heaven in any way, shape, or form. But Jesus wholeheartedly agreed with this unfair plan for your sake. God doesn't owe you anything on this earth. The blessings He chooses to grant are only because of His great love. It has been said that mercy is when God chooses not to give us what we rightfully deserve (aka, punishment), and grace is when God freely gives us what we don't deserve (eternal life). Thank God that in Christ Jesus we have both. Thank God for His unfairness.

Foolish Giving

October 22, 2018

An adult never would have done it. It wasn't logical. In fact, it was downright embarrassing to offer such a small amount for such a large crowd. Besides, it made more sense to keep it for himself for the journey ahead. Yet the boy didn't think about any of that. He just knew he had some food and other people needed it. So he found Andrew and told him he had five loaves of barley bread and two fish. Perhaps the people around him snickered at how naïve this child was. But Andrew brought the food to Jesus, who multiplied it to feed over 5,000 men, plus women and children. The leftovers alone were astounding. But in order to multiply the food, first the boy had to give it away.

The natural tendency when one is running low on a necessity is to hoard it more closely for oneself. I'm never more mindful of gas mileage, for example, than when I'm running on low fuel and am twenty miles from a gas station. I use every possible trick to extend the use of what little gas I have left—cruise control, putting it in neutral when I'm at a light, accelerating and decelerating slowly, and turning off the heater or air conditioner to conserve energy so I can squeeze every last half mile out of that tank of gas. Or let's say you get to the grocery store and realize you left your credit card at home and only have $20 in cash. Will you donate to the people out front collecting money for the local food bank? We tend to guard what we have, especially when we think we don't have enough.

Yet the account of the feeding of the 5,000 shows us exactly the opposite of what we expect to happen. Rather than the little boy giving up his lunch in vain, going home hungry along with everyone else, everyone left full and satisfied. I can't help but wonder what was going through the disciples' minds as they started out among that huge crowd. Did any of them wonder how that half loaf in his basket was going to help anyone? Were any of them tempted to just eat the small morsel of food rather than give it away? Yet as they gave away the only food they had, miraculously more and more appeared.

It's reminiscent of the widow of Zarephath in Elijah's day. Elijah was sent to her during a three-year drought, and despite the fact that all she had was a handful of flour and a bit of oil, she believed Elijah's promise that God would not allow her to starve. She used the remainder of her flour and oil to make food for Elijah—not just for her son and herself—and day after day, "the jar of flour was not spent, neither did the jug of oil become empty, according to the word of the Lord that he spoke by Elijah" (1 Kings 17:16). It went against human logic, certainly, to feed a stranger the last of the food available in the house, but had this widow followed her original plan to make one last meal for herself and her son, they would have starved. By giving away all she had, she gained so much more.

The Bible is full of examples and promises of God providing for His people. The children of Israel had to trust every morning that God would provide their daily manna and quail. They weren't allowed to keep leftovers as backup. And the widow who gave her two small coins to the temple presumably didn't starve either. Jesus commended her faith to His disciples. He wasn't going to let her down.

Where are you afraid to trust that God will provide? Maybe you're worried about finances and make excuses not to help someone else who is struggling financially as well. Perhaps you're living paycheck to paycheck and tithing seems like a *really* big commitment when you're pinching pennies. Maybe you're stretched emotionally thin, and although you'd like to volunteer, you just don't think you can commit any extra time to it. Whatever your situation, I can almost guarantee that it's not ideal for giving, financially or timewise. You can always find excuses *not* to give. And the devil will do all he can to make you believe giving is foolish. But think about the widow's oil. Remember the boy's lunch. Think of the manna. Remind yourself that God "is able to do far more abundantly than all we ask or think," as Ephesians 3:20 boldly states.

We serve a God who promises to provide. Fear not, for in giving away what little you have, you just might gain everything.

My Guardian Angel, My Grandpa

October 23, 2014

"Heaven gained another angel today in the passing of my aunt."

"My grandpa died five years ago and for these five years I've had the best guardian angel ever."

"Today is the anniversary of my dad passing away. I woke up to a beautiful sunrise and I knew he sent it to remind me he's always with me. Thanks, Dad!"

These kinds of sentiments are very common and often said to help people deal with the death of a loved one. There's a problem with statements like the ones above, however. None of them are even remotely true.

Rather than rely on human emotion, let's check out what the Bible has to say about angels. Angels are mentioned quite a bit throughout Scripture. Yes, God sends His angels to watch and protect us, our "guardian angels," if you will. Psalm 91:11-12 tells us, "He will command His angels concerning you to guard you in all your ways. On their hands they will bear you up, lest you strike your foot against a stone." In Matthew 18:10, Jesus is speaking about children and refers to "their angels in heaven" (NIV). Hebrews 1:14 calls angels "ministering spirits sent out to serve for the sake of those who are to inherit salvation." But angels are separate created beings, completely different from human beings. Jesus came to earth to suffer and die and rise again for humanity, not for angels. 1 Peter 1:12 points out that the plan of salvation, the incarnation and work of Jesus, was revealed to humans, and angels can't even comprehend it—"Even angels long to look into these things" (NIV).

So if we don't turn into angels, what happens to us when we die? Our physical bodies are left behind on earth until the final Judgment Day, but our souls depart. The souls of unbelievers are doomed to hell, while the souls of believers are taken to heaven. In the story of the rich man and Lazarus, both of these truths are shown in Luke 16:22-23. "The poor man died and was carried by the angels to Abraham's side. The rich man also died and was buried, and in Hades, being in torment, he lifted up his eyes and saw Abraham far away and Lazarus at his side." So angels escort our souls to heaven, but we do not become angels ourselves.

Philippians 3:21 tells us that when we are in heaven, Jesus "will transform our lowly body to be like His glorious body." 1 Corinthians 15:35-57 speaks at length about the resurrection bodies we will have in heaven. Revelation 7 distinguishes between the "great multitude...from every nation, from all tribes and peoples and languages, standing before the throne and before the Lamb" (verse 9, NIV) and "all the angels [who] were standing around the throne" (verse 11). Angels and humans are distinct from one another. You will not become an angel when you die.

But isn't it sort of comforting to think that your loved one is watching over you, sending you rainbows and sunsets to remind you of their presence? If you really think about it, that's not comforting at all. Who sends rainbows and sunsets? God Himself. Don't rob Him the honor due His name by trying to attribute those things to a human being. God alone is the Creator. He is the one who deserves the praise. And think about this. I mean, really think about it. As far as deceased relatives watching out for you, would you really want your dead grandfather watching every little thing you do? I wouldn't! Would you want him to look down from heaven where he's worshiping His Savior only to see you yelling at your kids or gossiping about someone or cursing someone who cuts you off in traffic? Would you honestly want your grandpa to see your entire life—the good, the bad, and the ugly? There's only One who sees everything I do and still loves and forgives me, and that's the Triune God. God knows everything I do, say, and think, and He knows full well I don't deserve heaven. But because of Jesus' work on my behalf, I am forgiven. Only God could know every single fault of mine and still love me and want me to spend eternity with Him. That's where real comfort is to be found—in knowing that God knows you completely and still loves you and calls you His own.

Recently a friend wrote to tell me of the death of his grandfather. He wrote, "My grandpa has passed away, certain of his salvation in Jesus Christ." What a beautiful, comforting assurance to believers. No, his grandpa isn't hovering around on earth watching over him. He is enjoying something far better than those of us still on earth can ever imagine—fellowship with his Savior. No offense to my future grandchildren, but when I die I really don't want to hang around to watch them. God's own angels are perfectly capable of that. I'd much rather be singing in the heavenly choir, worshiping "with angels and archangels and with all the company of heaven," seeing my Redeemer face to face. And thanks to Jesus, that's exactly what will happen.

What a Relief

October 23, 2017

It is difficult to explain to someone who has never had poison ivy what a relief it is to replace a used gauze bandage with a clean one. Poison ivy is a rather disgusting thing to have. It blisters and oozes and makes the skin look like it was burned in acid. It needs to be covered with gauze to catch those oozing blisters. But you can't just cover it once and be done with it. It's important to change the dressing frequently and keep the area as clean as possible to optimize healing. I'm getting over a bout of poison ivy myself, and every morning the first thing I do is change my gauze. The old bandage I have on overnight is dirty and crusty and sometimes oozing through, but once I have a fresh, clean bandage on, I feel immediately better. Yes, I'll eventually have to replace that one too, but for the time being, I have relief. In short, I feel clean.

Even if you've never had poison ivy, chances are that you've experienced this sort of relief before. King David did. It was the relief that came from confessing his sin and experiencing God's abundant forgiveness. Here's what he says in Psalm 32:3-4, "For when I kept silent, my bones wasted away through my groaning all day long. For day and night Your hand was heavy upon me; my strength was dried up as by the heat of summer."

David was going through some serious suffering. Although the psalm doesn't say exactly how he was suffering, it's very likely that he suffered both physically and psychologically. He mentions his bones wasting away. That's more than just a guilty conscience. We know from other biblical references that God sometimes did use physical affliction and illness to chastise His children and lead them toward repentance. (See, for example, Psalm 38.) And thankfully, in this case, it worked.

Reading on, David says, "I acknowledged my sin to You, and I did not cover my iniquity; I said, 'I will confess my transgressions to the Lord,' and You forgave the iniquity of my sin" (Psalm 32:5). Ahhh. And there's the relief. David hiding his sin did nothing for him. His sin certainly wasn't hidden from God. And God knew that his sin would eat away at him until he confessed it and received forgiveness. We aren't told exactly what sin David was hiding, although some have speculated that this was after he'd committed adultery with Bathsheba and before the prophet Nathan confronted him about it. Yeah, adultery and murder would eat away at a guilty conscience alright. But any sin can eat away at a person when it goes unconfessed.

What sin have you been hiding? Do you have a pet sin you try to cover up? a nasty attitude toward someone? a grudge you've been holding? Stop carrying that burden. Confess your sin before God as David did. God already knows about it anyhow. You aren't fooling Him. You're only hurting yourself. It's like replacing a dirty bandage. Yes, it's ugly and disgusting and raw underneath, and you may wish to keep it hidden. But if you keep that old bandage on, you're only inhibiting your healing. Bring your wounded conscience before the Lord, confess your sins to Him, and experience firsthand the relief at receiving the healing balm of absolution from the hand of your Great Physician. In short, He will make you clean.

Been There, Done That

October 27, 2014

Being pregnant the fifth time around is a very different experience from being pregnant with your first child. Trust me, I know. Besides the fact that there are four other kids to care for even when all I want to do is sleep, there's the stark reality of the changes in my body. I'm five and a half months pregnant right now, and I'm as big as I was at eight months with my first child. My body has done this multiple times before, so it knows the drill. With my first pregnancy, I hadn't been stretched out in such a way before, so it took longer for the baby bump to appear, and when it did, it was small and cute. No longer. Once a body has gone through these changes, it's easier for it to adjust the next time around. Same for my labor experiences. Each consecutive labor has gotten shorter, which is definitely a good thing. So my body bears witness to the fact that this isn't anything new anymore. It's been there and done that.

I see the same principle at work in our spiritual lives as well. There are a lot of similarities between my body adjusting more quickly to pregnancy and us getting used to a particular sin in our lives. The first time you do anything is a big deal, right? Your first kiss, the first time you drove a car alone, your first paycheck. These are all a big deal at first, but the novelty wears off. Eventually, those things are nothing exciting. Same goes for the trap of sin.

The first time we do something wrong, we may think it's a big deal. Perhaps you used drugs or got drunk or had a one-night stand. And it probably (hopefully) nagged at your conscience. Maybe you vowed you'd never do it again. But the second time temptation comes calling, it's much easier to answer because you've been there and done that. Each consecutive time, it becomes a little less of a big deal, and pretty soon you find yourself trapped in a particular sin. And it doesn't even have to be a "big" sin like the ones I mentioned above. Gossip, lust, mean thoughts about someone, a little compromise of your convictions here and there—all these are things we often gloss over. *Everyone does it, so what's the harm?* we may ask. The danger is that we start to see sin as something minor, and end up getting trapped in it. The writer to the Hebrews exhorts us in Hebrews 12:1 to throw off "the sin that so easily entangles" (NIV). Jesus says in John 8:34 that "everyone who commits sin is a slave to sin." Sin is a big deal. It's easy to get entangled in it and end up as its slave.

But there's good news. Paul tells us in Romans 6:6-7 that we are no longer slaves to sin, "for one who has died has been set free from sin." You see, the very thing that brought you new life also brought you death. "We were buried therefore with Him by baptism into death, in order that, just as Christ was raised from the dead by the glory of the Father, we too might walk in newness of life," Paul says in

Romans 6:4. In your baptism, you died to sin. Your baptism unites you to Jesus' death on that cross, but it also unites you to His resurrection. You have all the benefits of His saving work on your behalf. So now you are freed from slavery to sin.

The entire chapter of Romans 6 is well worth the read, but let me highlight a few verses. Verse 14 encourages us that "sin will have no dominion over you, since you are not under law but under grace," and verse 18 says, "you have been set free from sin and have become slaves to righteousness" (NIV). We also read in verse 22, "now that you have been set free from sin and have become slaves of God, the fruit you get leads to sanctification and its end, eternal life." God has set you free, dear one. You don't have to be a slave to sin. If you have an addiction, seek professional help and a Christian support group to encourage you and lift you up in prayer. If you struggle with a sin, consider private confession and absolution or perhaps an accountability partner. Be careful not to become complacent in sinning.

I can't help what my body does in pregnancy the fifth time around. I'm not thrilled with a larger shape, but I'll take the shorter labor. My body knows the drill. It's been there and done that before. And Jesus has the same assurance for you. He has already paid the consequences of your sin by His death and resurrection. He's been there and done that. And thanks to your baptism, so have you.

A Modern-Day Good Samaritan Story

October 29, 2018

I groaned as I saw the flashing construction vehicles and the line of red brake lights ahead of me. I was taking my son to school, and we hadn't left early enough to allow for delays like this. Some cars were already doing U-turns, presumably to go another route. But our detour option was a much longer way, so I decided to wait a few minutes before making a knee-jerk reaction. Sure enough, a minute later the cars ahead of me slowly started inching forward. Whew. But as I approached the cause of the backup, I could see this wasn't just construction. There was a car with a smashed front end sitting in the middle of the four-lane road, and there was a man lying on the ground next to the driver's side, two construction workers kneeling beside him. Clearly, the accident had happened very recently, since the emergency workers hadn't yet shown up. It was a horrifying feeling to pass right by the man on the ground, not knowing his condition or even if he was alive.

My son and I prayed for him and for the others involved in the accident, and we were fairly silent the rest of the drive, until my son said, "You know, Mr. Smith would have stopped to see if he could help." It was an innocent observation; he didn't mean it as a guilt trip, but I was convicted nonetheless. I should have stopped, but I didn't. It was a modern-day parable of the Good Samaritan, and I was the priest passing by on the other side.

There were a number of reasons I shouldn't have stopped. By now, we really were on the verge of being late for school. The man on the road was apparently already being helped by the construction workers. I didn't want to be in the way. What could I have done, anyhow? Still, the feeling of guilt persisted. *You could have prayed with them,* a voice whispered in my head. I knew that was true. At the very least, I could have stopped to ask if they needed anything. My son's school would have understood if he was late. This was more important.

Perhaps you can recall a time when you could have or should have stopped but didn't. And I'm not just talking about a car accident that just happened. Maybe a friend needed a listening ear, but you were too busy. Perhaps you didn't visit your grandpa in a nursing home because he had Alzheimer's and wouldn't remember if you came anyhow. Maybe your church needed Sunday School teachers and you made lame excuses to get out of volunteering. Or some acquaintances were moving and you didn't offer to help load or unload the moving truck. Serving your neighbor doesn't have to be anything dramatic like giving CPR to an injured man on a busy road. But it is often inconvenient. Serving others requires sacrifice.

Let's look at the actual Parable of the Good Samaritan, found in Luke 10:25-37. After a traveler was attacked by robbers and left for dead, a priest and a

Levite—both of whom would have been expected to help—passed by on the other side of the road. A hated Samaritan then came upon the man and had pity on him. Not only did he stop to bandage his wounds, he took him on his own donkey to an inn and paid the innkeeper to take care of him, promising to stop by at a later time and reimburse any other expenses incurred by the innkeeper. Today, that might look like following an ambulance to the hospital and paying for emergency surgery for someone who doesn't have insurance. Um, yeah, I'm not about to do that.

And that's just it. *None* of us can live up to such high expectations. This is where context is important. Why was Jesus telling this parable in the first place? Because a lawyer had tested Him, asking, "What shall I do to inherit eternal life?" (Luke 10:25). Well, we know the answer to that—there is *nothing* we can do to earn heaven. No matter how "good" we are, we will never be good enough. God demands absolute perfection, and we all fall far, far short of that standard. So the parable of the Good Samaritan is all Law. Jesus isn't telling it to say, "Hey, be like this Samaritan and God will reward you." He's showing that we *can't* be what God expects us to be. Jesus is the real Good Samaritan, who sacrificed His very life to save us from eternal death.

This isn't an excuse not to serve others, however. Jesus only means that we can't earn heaven by our good works. He's not saying we shouldn't help our fellow man. Elsewhere He clearly states that we are expected to serve our neighbors. Matthew 7:12, for example, gives us the Golden Rule, "Whatever you wish that others would do to you, do also to them." Or take Matthew 25:31-46, where He talks about clothing the naked, feeding the hungry, and so on. He explains in verse 40, "Truly, I say to you, as you did it to one of the least of these My brothers, you did it to Me."

I'll never know what would have happened had I stopped at the car accident. Likely, it wouldn't have been anything dramatic. Still, I wish I'd had the courage to stop. But I thank God that the construction workers jumped into action, doing what they could. They turned on their vehicle lights in the darkness to alert people that something was going on. They attended to the injured man while they were waiting for the ambulance. Maybe they even prayed with him too.

As you go through your day, watch for opportunities to serve others. It will rarely be "convenient" for you to do so. But remember, in serving others, you are serving Jesus Himself, the true Good Samaritan.

Why I Will Never Choose God

October 30, 2014

Yesterday afternoon did not start out well. Within ten minutes of my older children arriving home from school, all three were in time outs in separate rooms. Attitudes toward me and toward one another were hostile from the time they walked in the door. Finally I'd had enough and laid down the law. Literally. I slapped a notebook in front of my oldest two who can write, and told them to copy the Fourth Commandment and its meaning three times. Then I went to my own room, upset with all of them and wondering if it was too early to start the bedtime process.

As I fumed in my room, I realized that I could let this sour attitude prevail, affecting our moods for the rest of the day, or I could be proactive and go to them first. Truthfully, I didn't *want* to make the first move. They were the ones who had come home in bad moods, so why should I have to be the peacemaker? Yet as I thought about the alternative, I knew there was only one choice. I had to initiate the reconciliation process. I was still mad at my kids, but my love for them won out. I didn't want us to have a crummy rest of the day, and I wanted to show them how to resolve things. I was concerned for their overall good. So with a prayer, I walked into the room of my eldest, asked what was bothering him, and had a good one-on-one chat. We even prayed together. I did the same for the other kids, and the rest of the day turned out to be very pleasant.

I've often had real-life object lessons demonstrated by my children, and this was no exception. Just as my children came in yesterday determined to be miserable and make everyone else miserable, so we come into this world completely sinful. "None is righteous, no, not one; no one understands; no one seeks for God. All have turned aside…no one does good, not even one," Romans 3:10-12 points out.

The fact is that we *can't* choose God. We don't have some inherent good in us that commends us to God. We can't turn from our sins and choose to follow Him. We'd never do it. If I'd waited for my kids to come out of their rooms on their own yesterday and apologize, they'd still be in their separate rooms right now. Same with us. If God had waited for us to come to Him, we'd all still be lost. We were "dead" in our transgressions, Colossians 2:13 tells us. The Greek word there is "corpse." Powerless. Hopeless. Lifeless. That was us without God's intervention.

But God didn't let us stay that way. He made the first move. His love for us trumped any righteous anger. He had every right to leave us to our sins on the path to destruction and hell. But He didn't. He came to us with the Gospel. He sent Jesus to be one of us, to live a perfect life we could never live, and to die for sins we had committed. Then He rose from the dead to show that He has dominion over sin and even death. His victory is ours.

"And you, who were dead in your trespasses…God made alive together with Him, having forgiven us all our trespasses, by canceling the record of debt that stood against us with its legal demands. This He set aside, nailing it to the cross," Colossians 2:13-14 assures us. Or as Jesus says in John 15:16, "You did not choose Me, but I chose you." The action here is all God's. 100%. And leaving that action up to God is a much bigger comfort than leaving it up to myself. So you see, I don't have to choose God. He already chose me.

How Luther Went Viral

October 30, 2017

By all rights, the Ninety-Five Theses really oughtn't to have had the impact they did. Martin Luther was a relatively unknown professor doing a completely ordinary thing for someone in the academic world of his day. There was nothing unique about him nailing these statements to the door of the local church in Wittenberg. He wasn't looking to start a reformation. He was merely hoping to spark a bit of public debate among his colleagues regarding the practice of indulgences. Yet within a few short months, the Ninety-Five Theses had been reprinted in Nuremberg, Leipzig, and Basel. While the originals were printed in Latin, Nuremberg also reportedly published a German translation of his theses, which was unprecedented. Copies were being widely distributed and read by not only intellectuals, but also commoners. The higher-ups were taking notice of this small-town professor, realizing something had to be done about him before he rallied more people to his cause. He quickly became a household name. Put in today's terminology, Luther went viral.

The practice of posting academic theses was not a revolutionary concept. The printing industry of Luther's day did a fair bit of business by printing theses for universities, although few were noticed outside the academic occasion for which they were posted. Even Luther did not expect his theses to have such an impact, and later admitted in correspondence that had he known the impact they would have, he would have taken more care in writing them.

You see, this was not Luther's first time posting theses for public viewing. He had done so about eight weeks prior, writing ninety-nine theses against Scholasticism, a school of thought that focused on logic and human reason to find universal truth. Ironically, Luther thought the theses on Scholasticism were more bold and controversial than the later ones (the Ninety-Five) regarding indulgences. And as such, he tried his best to promote and distribute the theses on Scholasticism, but few people took note. So when Luther nailed the Ninety-Five Theses to the church door eight weeks later, he could not have believed much more would come of those. Yet now his posting of the Ninety-Five Theses is often pointed to as the event that sparked the Reformation.

But why did these theses provoke such a strong response? Why did his ninety-nine theses slither off into oblivion while the Ninety-Five Theses are still read and studied today? How, when Luther was merely looking to reform some doctrines of the church, did this eventually lead to his excommunication and starting a new denomination that is still going strong 500 years later? There have been all sorts of answers to these questions, from economics to politics to language to personality. Certainly, all these played a role in the Reformation. But the answer is almost too simple. Luther was the first to admit that the main reason the Reformation succeeded was, of course, God.

This is incredibly comforting for us, because it's never up to us to convince anyone of the truths of God's Word. We needn't rely on our own cleverness or intelligence or eloquence (or despair at a lack thereof). I've heard from more than one pastor that some of the sermons they were most proud of elicited little to no response from parishioners, while other sermons they felt were weak or ill-prepared were the ones that most strongly resonated with people. (Ultimately, of course, only God truly knows the impact of any particular sermon upon people's hearts, whether they say anything to the pastor or not.) God uses us as His instruments to spread the Word, but He is the One who brings forth the fruit. As Paul says in 1 Corinthians 3:6-7, "I planted, Apollos watered, but God gave the growth. So neither he who plants nor he who waters is anything, but only God who gives the growth."

This is very good news for Christians today who worry about the state of the Church on earth. The Church is always in need of reform. There will always be false teachings, those who compromise God's truth to appease the world, and even false believers within the Church, but God will not allow His truth to be snuffed out. He has promised to preserve His Word until He returns. Sometimes that means a common monk whose theses go viral. Sometimes it's far less dramatic, as in one person sharing the Gospel with his neighbor. But no matter how God grows His Church, we can be certain He will indeed work through His Word to preserve His saints unto eternity. And so we can sing with confidence the words of "The Church's One Foundation:"

> *The Church shall never perish! Her dear Lord, to defend,*
> *To guide, sustain, and cherish, Is with her to the end.*
> *Tho' there be those that hate her, False sons within her pale,*
> *Against both foe and traitor She ever shall prevail.*
> *(The Lutheran Hymnal 473, stanza 3)*

November

How to Plan a Funeral

November 2, 2014

Yesterday I cried in church. This is not uncommon for me. Whether it's the words of a Scripture reading, a hymn stanza, or even part of the sermon, at some point it hits me how incredible the story of salvation is, how unworthy I am, and how amazing God's love is for me. Yesterday we celebrated All Saints' Day in church, and it was even more of a tear-jerker than usual. It was sort of a mix between Easter and a funeral service, which is really exactly what a Christian funeral ought to be. Yes, we mourn the loss of our loved ones on this earth, but we know that because of Jesus' resurrection, we will see those loved ones again in heaven someday. Death is not final. It does not have the last word. And that's what I want people to know at my own funeral someday. So here are a few things to consider when planning a funeral:

Bible Readings: The Bible is full of references to heaven and eternal life, so don't panic and choose Psalm 23 by default. Sure, that's a wonderful and comforting psalm, and my own Confirmation verse is Psalm 23:1, but it's done so often at funerals that a lot of people tend to gloss over it without really thinking. Consider a reading like Revelation 7:9-17. Can you even imagine that multitude in white robes, standing around the throne of Jesus, singing praises to Him in a loud voice? It gives me chills to think of it. We have no idea what's in store for us in heaven. Imagine singing with every saint that ever lived! And not just the saints, but even the angels will fall down on their faces and worship God. *That's* the God we serve, dear ones. The God whom even the angels adore. We will be in heaven with all the other saints who came before and who will come after us. God will shelter us with His presence so we will never again feel any pain or discomfort. What an amazing promise is ours as Christians. Just thinking about it brings tears to my eyes.

Hymns: As a church musician, I have a different perspective on this aspect than perhaps most people. I've played for a number of funerals over the years, and I see the same hymns resurface at 75% of the funerals for which I play. Again, the hymnal is full of beautiful comforting hymns that speak of the resurrection, so don't choose "What a Friend We Have in Jesus," "Rock of Ages," and "Amazing Grace" just because they're familiar. Pull out a hymnal and look through the Easter section or The Church Triumphant section. I cannot make it through "For All the Saints" without crying. This is somewhat of a drawback, since I sing along with hymns as I accompany them on the organ, and I've found it's difficult to play when one has tears blurring one's vision. Nonetheless, the words are incredible when you think about them:

From earth's wide bounds, from ocean's farthest coast,
Through gates of pearl streams in the countless host,
Singing to Father, Son, and Holy Ghost:
Alleluia! Alleluia!
(Lutheran Service Book 677, stanza 8)

Just like the comforting words of Revelation above, this reminds us of the glory that awaits God's saints from every nation, tribe, people, and language. So don't be afraid to pick hymns above and beyond the old, familiar ones—"Sing With All the Saints in Glory," "By All Your Saints in Warfare," "Behold a Host, Arrayed in White," "Awake, My Heart, with Gladness," "Alleluia! Jesus is Risen," "He's Risen, He's Risen," "This Joyful Eastertide," "If Christ Had not Been Raised from Death"… The trouble for my own funeral won't be which hymns to pick, but which hymns *not* to include! There's such rich theology in the Easter and Church Triumphant sections that bring comfort to those who grieve. Do your mourners a favor and give them that comfort.

Sermon: I'd be perfectly happy if the pastor for my funeral doesn't even mention me in the sermon. Everyone knows why they're there, after all. They have the memories of the deceased in their minds. They don't really need to hear a sermon extolling all those fond memories. I don't want my funeral sermon to be about me. I want people to hear about my Savior and what He did for me, a poor, miserable sinner. I want them to know that I was completely unworthy of the gift of salvation, but that God in His mercy and grace made me His child nonetheless. I want them to hear that He did the same for them. I want them to know that Jesus came to earth to live the perfect life I could never live, to suffer and die for my sins, and to defeat death three days later by rising from the dead. I want them to know that just as death could not hold Jesus, neither can it hold me, and neither will it hold them. Jesus' death and resurrection is ours. His saints will be with Him eternally in heaven. People are seeking comfort at funerals. They actually listen to the sermon, hanging on every word, desperately looking for something that will give them comfort. People don't need to hear about my life at my funeral. They need to hear about my Savior, the only true source of comfort.

I hope people cry at my funeral, but not for me. I want them to get choked up at the incredible love the Father has for His children, that He went to such lengths to win us back. Death is not the end. We do grieve when a loved one dies, but as 1 Thessalonians 4:13 reminds us, not as those who have no hope. In Christ, we will arise!

RUTH E. MEYER

Obsessed with Death

November 5, 2018

A visitor to church might have wondered what was happening on All Saints' Sunday. Granted, it's a unique service as we remember with joy the deaths of those saints who have gone before us. In churches around the world, we took time to list the names of church members who have died within the past year. We even sing in gory detail about the deaths of the saints of old:

A glorious band, the chosen few, On whom the Spirit came,
Twelve valiant saints—their hope they knew And mocked the cross and flame.
They met the tyrant's brandished steel, The lion's gory mane;
They bowed their necks their death to feel—Who follows in their train?
(Lutheran Service Book 661, stanza 3)

Nice thing to be singing with the kids, isn't it? Getting killed by the sword, eaten by lions, burned to death, beheaded… Nothing to see here, folks. Just an ordinary church service, singing about various ways to die. What is it about Christians, that we're so obsessed with death?

Even some holidays are celebrated as a result of death. Valentine's Day commemorates the martyrdom of St. Valentine, who reportedly left a note for his jailer's child on a scrap of paper shaped roughly like a heart. March 17 is the anniversary of the death of St. Patrick, a missionary to Ireland who defended the doctrine of the Trinity. And in the Church Year there are numerous commemorations and feasts that remember the death or martyrdom of a particular saint.

This oughtn't surprise us. After all, one of the pillars of our faith is Jesus' own sacrificial death. Good Friday is our somber remembrance of the suffering and death He endured for our sake. He offered His perfect life as a sacrifice on the cross to appease God's wrath over our sins. Had He not died for us, His life would have meant nothing. It was His death that atoned for our sins, and every Sunday we thank Him for that death on our behalf.

But that's not the end of the story. Yes, Jesus died. But if His death was really the end of it, we would have no reason to celebrate; no cause to remember with joy the death of the saints of old. Paul talks about this in 1 Corinthians 15:17-23: "If Christ has not been raised, your faith is futile and you are still in your sins. Then those also who have fallen asleep in Christ have perished. If in Christ we have hope in this life only, we are of all people most to be pitied. But in fact Christ has been raised from the dead, the firstfruits of those who have fallen asleep. For as by a man came death, by a man has come also the resurrection of the dead. For as in Adam all die, so also in Christ shall all be made alive."

There it is. *This* is why we're obsessed with death. Physical death is but the gate to eternal life with Jesus. All those saints who were martyred firmly believed this and wanted so badly to share this wonderful news with others that they were willing to die for their faith if it meant sharing the Gospel with even one more person.

Dear brother or sister, we have this same hope. Jesus assures us that, "I am the resurrection and the life. Whoever believes in Me, though he die, yet shall he live, and everyone who lives and believes in Me shall never die" (John 11:25-26). When we have this assurance, that death is but the passage to heaven, then we can indeed rejoice in the death of our loved ones. We can celebrate the witness of those who have been martyred for their faith, for we know they are now "obtaining the outcome of [their] faith, the salvation of [their] soul[s]" (1 Peter 1:9).

No, it's not death with which we're obsessed after all. Our eyes are fixed instead on the life to come.

Sine Nomine

November 6, 2017

I love All Saints' Day. The Scripture readings speak of the saints in white robes around God's throne in heaven, we recall the faithfully departed, and we sing some of my favorite hymns. One such hymn is "For All the Saints." I get tears in my eyes every time I sing it. Even the tune name sounds majestic: *Sine Nomine*. Growing up, I knew *nomine* meant "name," so I figured it was something like "A New Name" or "A Holy Name." I didn't realize until I was an adult what it actually meant: "Without a Name." What? Obviously at some point, someone realized the tune wasn't named and (quite originally) named it "nameless." They did at least put it in Latin so it looks more sophisticated, but still. *Without a name?* That's the best we can do?

Yet upon further reflection, I find that this title has a more profound meaning for Christians. Many saints who have gone before us are, to us, nameless. We can name some—those in the Bible, Church Fathers, friends and family members who have passed on before us—but that's a mere fraction of the saints throughout history who are now in heaven. And what about us? To most of the world we, too, are "nameless." Most of us will never achieve great fame. The world will not know our names while we are living, and will forget us soon after we die.

Depressing? Not at all, because there is One who knows each and every one of us by name. Not only has He known you by name since before the world began, He placed His name on you through the waters of Holy Baptism. When you were baptized in God's Triune name, He claimed you as His own and gave you His name. Even the saints of the Old Testament received God's name in the Aaronic benediction, which we still use in worship today. After God gave Moses this blessing in Numbers 6:24-26, He concluded in 6:27 by saying, "So shall they put My name upon the people of Israel, and I will bless them."

Dear one, no matter how insignificant you feel today in the vast scheme of the history of this world, take heart. God, the Creator of the universe, knows you personally. You are not nameless to Him. He loves you enough that He gave you His own name. You are His, now and forever.

Unfaithfully Yours

November 10, 2014

I've played for a number of weddings in my day, and although each wedding was unique, they've all had a few things in common. Every wedding I've ever attended has included vows. In these vows, each spouse pledges to be true to the other. After all the "for better, for worse" stuff comes the solemn statement at the end of the vows, "I pledge you my faithfulness." No one enters marriage with the intention of cheating on their spouse. Nor would anyone marry someone who is known to stray. But let me tell you about someone who did marry a cheater. On purpose.

Some years ago, a faithful believer married an adulterer. He knew before he married her that she would be intimate with other men, but he married her and loved her nonetheless. When she inevitably cheated, he sought reconciliation rather than divorce. He sought her out and wooed her back to him, forgiving her unfaithfulness and working hard to restore the fullness of a husband-wife relationship. Of course everyone knew her reputation, and doubtless he endured plenty of mockery and scorn from others in town, but still he pursued her. He overlooked her infidelity and forgave her. Their relationship was that important to him. Perhaps you've heard of this couple as well. The husband was none other than the prophet Hosea, and his wife the unfaithful Gomer. And here's the real kicker—God was the one who told Hosea to marry Gomer in the first place!

Now let me tell you about another man who wed an unfaithful bride. This man devoted his entire life to his bride, despite the fact that he knew she was unfaithful from the start. He sought his bride and called her back to him again and again. He spent his whole life showing his love for her, and he even made the ultimate sacrifice for her in the end—he died for her. Of course you've probably realized this wasn't *just* a man—this was Jesus, true man and true God. And His unfaithful bride? Well, that's us. We are His Church, His holy bride. And I have to say, we don't make a very good bride, do we? Look at how we run after other gods, other "lovers," if you will. Things that would lead us away from our true love, Jesus. We dishonor His name and sin against Him over and over. On our end, it's a pitiful example of the intimate relationship and commitment between a husband and wife.

Getting back to Hosea and Gomer, why exactly would God command His prophet to marry a known adulterer? Because God wanted Hosea to demonstrate the relationship between Himself and His people. God's Old Testament people, the Israelites, went after other gods time and time again, yet in the end God still loved His people, and sought them out over and over. But that wasn't an ancient example. We may look back at Israel of old and shake our heads as they stooped to pagan sacrifices, but we do much the same thing. They were following the popular culture of the day. We do the same. We compromise our morals for the sake of "peace" in the world. We adopt sinful practices the world has accepted because "everyone's doing it." We try to be relevant to culture by giving in a bit here and there, and all too often, Christians become indistinguishable from the culture around us. Christ's bride isn't terribly faithful to Him at all.

But just as God had Hosea seek reconciliation with Gomer rather than divorce, so does our Bridegroom seek to win us back. He not only forgave us, but took our punishment upon Himself. *The Church's One Foundation* sums it up well: "From heaven He came and sought her to be His holy bride; With His own blood He bought her, and for her life He died" (*Lutheran Service Book* 644, stanza 3).

Jesus had every right to disown us completely, but He chose to forgive. His relationship to His bride was that important to Him. And because of that sacrifice, His bride can stand before Him spotless and pure. Revelation 19:7-8 says, "The wedding of the Lamb has come, and His bride has made herself ready. Fine linen, bright and clean, was given her to wear" (NIV). It's a gift, you see. The bride is *given* this clean linen to wear. That's how faithful our Bridegroom is.

Blue Jean Jesus

November 13, 2014

Who is Jesus, exactly? Specifically, who is He to *you?* There's a big push in Christianity in general to allow everyone to define for themselves who Jesus is, as if that was somehow up to us to decide. Forget what the Bible actually says; just let your feelings tell you who Jesus is. He's kind and accepting, and a personal relationship with Him is more of a buddy system. Jesus is my blue jean buddy, my pal, someone who won't judge me or tell me what I'm doing is wrong. He's someone to hang out with, someone to talk to, someone who will be a casual companion no matter what the activity. But to define Jesus this way is to deny a huge part of who He actually is.

To get a better picture of who Jesus is, let's start in Isaiah 6, where the Triune God appeared to Isaiah. He saw God's glory, and what was his reaction? Absolute terror. He cries, "'Woe is me! For I am lost; for I am a man of unclean lips, and I dwell in the midst of a people of unclean lips; for my eyes have seen the King, the Lord of hosts!'" (Isaiah 6:5). Isaiah saw God with his own eyes, and the very first thing he thought about was his own sin. That's what happens when a sinner stands in the presence of a holy God. Isaiah wasn't thinking, *Gee, this is great! Wait till my pals hear about this one! I actually get to see God face to face!* No, he recognized his own sinfulness in contrast with the holy and perfect God, and He was terrified.

Another instance of this is Simon Peter. After the miraculous catch of fish where Peter summoned James and John to help them, Peter realized that Jesus was no mere man. He didn't give a trite response like *Hey, man, come fish with us whenever you want! You're awesome, dude!* No, he looked at the two boats sinking under the weight of the fish, the nets breaking, and realized, *This guy is holy. And I'm not.* Luke 5:8 tells us, "When Simon Peter saw it, he fell down at Jesus' knees, saying, 'Depart from me, for I am a sinful man, O Lord.'" Again, the first thing he thought about was his sin while in the presence of the sinless Lamb of God.

Some passages in the Bible remind us of just how far short we fall in light of God's holiness. In Amos 5:21-22, for example, God tells His people, "I hate, I despise your feasts, and I take no delight in your solemn assemblies. Even though you offer Me your burnt offerings and grain offerings, I will not accept them; and the peace offerings of your fattened animals, I will not look upon them." This was their worship God was rejecting here, the "good" stuff they did. God wasn't condemning murder or stealing or adultery. He was condemning their very act of worship. Why? Because their hearts weren't right before Him. They thought they could justify themselves merely by going through the actions of worship.

So what do we bring to God? We bring Him our sin. We can't earn His favor in any way. We can only confess our unworthiness before Him. And ironically, it's when we do that that we are freed. When we give up trying to earn His favor and throw ourselves at His mercy, crying, "Depart from me, Lord! I am a sinner!" That's when He lifts our eyes and shows us the cross. Jesus did take what we had to offer. He took our sin upon Himself and in exchange gave us His own righteousness so that we *can* stand before our holy God. "For our sake He made Him to be sin who knew no sin, so that in Him we might become the righteousness of God," 2 Corinthians 5:21 tells us. *That's* the God we worship.

Be careful not to get too casual with God. Yes, He is a personal and loving God, but He is also holy and all-powerful. If you were invited to the White House to meet with the President, you wouldn't go in blue jeans and slap the President on his back saying, "Hey, buddy, how ya doing?" You'd have respect for his office and act accordingly. The same goes for God. Remember that He is the holy God of the universe, who is worshiped by angels in heaven. You can bet that when you see Him in his glory in heaven He won't be wearing blue jeans and a T-shirt. And neither will you. You will stand before Him with a robe that has been washed and made white in His holy and precious blood. I'll take that over blue jeans any day.

Snorkeling in Stormy Seas

November 13, 2017

In retrospect, maybe it wasn't the best move to try snorkeling for the first time in choppy waters. Every time a wave came at me, my instinct was to gasp in a quick breath. Breathing through my mouth into a snorkeling tube was completely unnatural, and immersing my face in the water while breathing through that tube was one of the most terrifying things I've ever done. I was sure I would drown. I fairly hyperventilated into the tube, which as anyone can tell you, is *not* the way to snorkel. I clung desperately to the floatation device our instructor threw out, scarcely daring to let go when I peered underwater. Once when I took my face out of the water, I spit out my breathing tube and promptly sucked in a huge mouthful of water. If snorkeling was scary before, it was nothing compared to the feeling I had after swallowing saltwater. I coughed violently and couldn't take in air. I sounded like I was having an asthma attack (maybe even like I was dying), so much so that our instructor swam over to me, ready to save my life. Nothing to see here, folks. Just your typical novice doing everything the wrong way. The trouble was that I wanted to trust my own instincts rather than trusting the equipment to do its job.

Trusting something or someone else instead of ourselves is difficult for us to do, isn't it? We'd like to think we have all the answers, that we can "fix" any situations that need fixing. Perhaps others have let you down in the past, so it's just easier not to get your hopes up by relying upon someone else. Specifically, it's hard to trust God to provide for us, or to wait for His timing in answering a prayer. We'd rather do things our own way and take matters into our own hands. Perhaps that's why the Bible exhorts us over and over again to trust in God, reminding us *why* we can do so—because He's never let us down before.

"Those who know Your name put their trust in You," Psalm 9:10 reminds us, "for You, O Lord, have not forsaken those who seek You." Isaiah 26:4 asserts, "Trust in the Lord forever, for the Lord God is an everlasting rock." The analogy of a solid, firm rock is also taken up in Psalm 40:1-3, which says, "I waited patiently for the Lord; He inclined to me and heard my cry. He drew me up from the pit of destruction, out of the miry bog, and set my feet upon a rock, making my steps secure. He put a new song in my mouth, a song of praise to our God. Many will see and fear, and put their trust in the Lord." David likely wrote those words when he was fleeing from Saul, but like David, we have all been saved from the "pit of destruction." We were destined for hell, but God saved us from that. He placed our feet upon solid footing: Jesus Himself, the cornerstone of our faith (Ephesians 2:20).

Despite the fact that snorkeling was unnatural for me, a really neat thing happened through the course of my experience. Once I finally realized I could trust the snorkeling gear, I was able to relax a bit, get into the proper rhythm for breathing, and truly enjoy the beauty of the underwater world rather than fretting about getting enough oxygen. I even got to the point that I just kept the snorkel in and breathed through it even with my head above the water, because the waves were such that I could get a faceful of water at any moment. Having the snorkel actually put me at ease in the midst of the waves. I knew I could trust it even when my instincts told me not to.

Similarly, when times are good, it's easy to trust God. But when times get challenging, it's another matter entirely. Consider, then, the words of David from Psalm 56:3-4. "When I am afraid, I put my trust in You. In God, whose word I praise, in God I trust; I shall not be afraid. What can flesh do to me?"

David wrote these words not during a time of calm and peace, but during a time of great personal uncertainty for him, when "the Philistines seized him in Gath," as the introduction to the psalm tells us. Why did David have this confidence? Because God had never let him down before. Neither will He let you down. Even death does not have the final say, for Jesus has defeated death for you. Trust that you are safe and secure in God's loving hands. Even in the midst of stormy seas.

Is Our World the Worst It's Ever Been?

November 18, 2019

People have always believed their current generation was living in the end times, that the world was the worst it had ever been. This is both true and false. The world *is* the worst it's ever been, but it's always been that way. We might have different means of temptation or variations on ways to commit sin, but the sins that exist today have existed since the Fall. In Noah's day, only eight people were saved from the Flood. While the Bible doesn't say how many perished, some estimates range from 750 million to close to four billion (see answersingenesis.org for a more detailed discussion of this). So of all those people on earth, only *eight* believed in God??

Or take the sordid account of Sodom and Gomorrah in Genesis 18:20-19:29. Abraham pleads with God to spare the city if only ten righteous people could be found there. Sadly, there weren't even that many, and the cities were destroyed. (It's a bit harder to find an estimate on how many people lived there, but archeologists have unearthed ruins with a cemetery of half a million people, which indicates these were large cities for their day.)

Paul warns Timothy that in "the last days there will come times of difficulty. For people will be lovers of self, lovers of money, proud, arrogant, abusive, disobedient to their parents, ungrateful, unholy, heartless, unappeasable, slanderous, without self-control, brutal, not loving good, treacherous, reckless, swollen with conceit, lovers of pleasure rather than lovers of God, having the appearance of godliness but denying its power. Avoid such people" (2 Timothy 3:1-5). Every single one of those unpleasant descriptions fits modern-day culture, so we must in the "last days," right? Yes. But so was Timothy, because Paul tells him to "avoid such people," which means they were already doing those things in the first century. Every day between Jesus' ascension and His second coming is part of the "end times."

Murder, theft, homosexuality, gender issues, abortion/child sacrifice, sexual promiscuity, idolatry, drunkenness, persecution, social injustice, prejudice, hatred, rebellion, complacency—these have all existed and thrived in the human race since the beginning. Now, that isn't to say these things aren't serious. They are. Sin is serious and has dire consequences. Dire enough that Jesus had to die for our sins. But that doesn't mean we have no consequences on earth, either. Think of all the people who died in the Flood and in Sodom and Gomorrah. Think of God's own people, the Israelites, who were taken into captivity for turning away from Him. Consider the so-called great civilizations of the world that are no more: Babylon, Assyria, the Roman Empire… Are we any better than they? Will we escape a similar judgment?

Make no mistake, we live in an evil time. And it is the duty of the Christian to speak God's Word even when it is unpopular, even when we are mocked, even when we might risk a lawsuit or harm to our reputation if we refuse to go along with the pervasive tolerance and acceptance that characterize our society. Furthermore, it is the duty of the Christian to pray. We must pray for our country, for its leaders and lawmakers, for our fellow citizens, and for our fellow Christians. It's all too easy to believe that we are alone in the fight, but we are not.

In the days of Elijah, after God's great victory over the 450 prophets of Baal (1 Kings 18:20-40), Elijah ran away after Jezebel threatened to kill him. In despair, he asked God to just take his life, since he was the only prophet left. But God told Elijah that he was not alone. "I will leave seven thousand in Israel, all the knees that have not bowed to Baal, and every mouth that has not kissed him," God promised in 1 Kings 19:18. God will never allow His Church to become extinct. In fact, the Church now is larger than it's ever been. Remember, the number of believers consists not only of those on earth (the Church Militant) but also those in heaven (the Church Triumphant). Every day new believers are being added to the Church Militant through conversion and baptism, and saints on earth join those in heaven every day as well.

So is the world the worst it's ever been? Yes. But the Church is larger than ever before, and it's only going to get bigger from here on out.

The Golden Calf in Your Life

November 19, 2018

The story of the Israelites and the Golden Calf is a ridiculous one, isn't it? C'mon, people. Just a few weeks ago, God performed ten miraculous plagues, then led you through the Red Sea on dry ground but drowned Pharaoh's army after you. On top of that, He fed you with manna and quail in the desert, and yet you forget all this and make an idol to worship? After all God has done for you, *this* is your response? It's laughable, really. This golden calf that Aaron made in front of your eyes is the one who led you out of Egypt? Lame. And yet, all too familiar. Because we are no different today.

The account of the Golden Calf actually reads much like an account from the Christian's week. In Exodus, the man of God (Moses) reminds the people of all God has done for them. He points them to their Savior. But now he's gone, up on this mountain for days on end, and the people are getting restless. They aren't hearing God's Word anymore, and they're doubting this God they can't see. They would much rather have a tangible god; something they can see with their own eyes like the idols of Egypt. So they ask Aaron to make them gods, and he complies by making a golden calf. As if that isn't bad enough, then the people have a big orgy. The Bible is delicate in its language when it says they "sat down to eat and drink and rose up to play" (Exodus 32:6). The word "play" here refers to all sorts of immorality. It wasn't their finest moment, that's for sure.

What about us? We go to church on Sunday and hear God's Word and are strengthened for our lives, but then we leave and go about our daily lives. We aren't surrounded by a sanctuary of fellow believers, the man of God (in this case, the pastor) isn't next to us, reminding us of God's promises, and we start to doubt how relevant our faith really is in these modern times. So we turn to our own idols, whatever they may be. Money, work, sinful pleasures… Perhaps we neglect our own devotional life, leaving us without that strength. Maybe we decide to skip church one week, making it that much easier to skip the next, and the next… But the longer we go without hearing and reading God's Word, the longer we go without partaking of Christ's body and blood, the more we distance ourselves from the fellowship of believers, the more susceptible we are to the devil's attacks and the more vulnerable we are to worship false idols.

But there's more to the story. Yes, the Israelites were punished for their false worship. There was basically a civil war, where the Levites fought against the other tribes in zeal for the Lord. Three thousand people died. On top of that, God sent a plague. Sin really is that serious. But Moses interceded for the people, and God forgave them. He made new tablets to replace the ones Moses had broken, and He renewed His covenant with His people, despite the fact that they clearly couldn't keep it on their own accord. God is faithful even when His people are not. When we return to church, no matter how long it's been, we start the service with confession and absolution. We have sinned—even worshiped false gods—but God forgives.

The story of the golden calf need not be played out every week in your life, dear Christian. Stay in the Word, in corporate worship and in your personal and family devotional life. Remind yourself of all God has done for you. He sent Jesus as the perfect sacrifice in your place. He provides for you every day of your life and blesses you far more abundantly than you ask or deserve. He alone is worthy of your worship and praise. There's no place for dead idols, because we serve the ever-living God.

New Year's Resolutions

November 20, 2014

Happy New Year! Have you started thinking about New Year's resolutions yet? I'm not talking about the ones you make at the beginning of January. I prefer to start thinking about them now, as we get close to the beginning of a new Church year with Advent. I don't make resolutions on diet or exercise. These are spiritual resolutions, and Advent presents the perfect opportunity to instill new traditions in your home. So what are some Advent resolutions you can make? Here are a few ideas to get you started.

Devotions: If you aren't in a regular habit of reading devotions together as a family, Advent is a perfect time to start. There are all sorts of Advent devotionals out there, written for daily use. Most churches give away free copies of such devotionals, so check to see whether your church offers them as well. Establish a regular time when devotions are read. This can vary from family to family. Sometimes it works best to do it at breakfast, while everyone is still (hopefully!) fresh. Dinner is often a good time to read them as well, but if you have evening activities to rush off to, perhaps you could wait for bedtime instead. Find the time that works for your family and try to stick with it as much as you can. Don't beat yourself up if you miss a day here or there, but do try to establish a regular schedule that can naturally continue with daily devotions once Advent ends. (While you're at it, it's a good time to make a routine for your personal devotions as well!)

Music: There's more to Advent than "O Come, O Come, Emmanuel." As a church musician, I get frustrated that there are so many arrangements of said hymn for piano, organ, bells, instruments, and vocal solos, but apparently the world at large doesn't realize there are other Advent hymns out there. In our house, music is a big part of devotions, so one of my resolutions is a "hymn of the week." Last Advent that worked really well. Each of the three and a half weeks before Christmas, our family sang a stanza or two of a different Advent hymn. By the end of each week, our kids had those stanzas memorized. And once you've started this tradition, why not keep it up into the next season of Christmas, and then Epiphany, Lent, Easter…

Bible Verses: Like the hymn of the week idea, we also have a Bible verse of the week during Advent. We memorize Old Testament prophecies like Isaiah 7:14, Isaiah 9:6-7, Isaiah 40:3-5, and Micah 5:2. Copy the verse of the week and hang it on your fridge so everyone can see it. Kids have amazing memories, and honestly can probably memorize this stuff more easily than you can. So during your devotional time, quote the verse together a few times and watch how easily they pick up on the beautiful promises of Scripture.

Unique Family Traditions: All of the things I mention above are generic enough that anyone can adapt them, but each family is unique, and so should have traditions that highlight their uniqueness. One neat idea I've heard is from a family who wraps up 25 Christmas books and opens one each day during December to read together. Ask your spouse or kids for ideas and see what you come up with. I'd never heard of the Advent ribbon tradition until I got married and my husband filled me in. Now we do that with our children rather than a traditional Advent calendar. Each child gets a ribbon hung on the wall, and every day they get a little surprise on their ribbon. Often it's a piece of candy or gum or stickers, but every now and then they'll each get a dollar just for kicks. They love this. (It's a great incentive for getting them out of bed on school mornings, too, for the record…) You can put a Bible verse or hymn verse or an encouraging note on their ribbons for them as well, if you're so inclined. It's a fun family tradition that they look forward to each year.

Service Project: Try as well to include some type of service activity, perhaps even making a resolution to do one service project per month as a family. Some families volunteer at soup kitchens or go caroling to shut-ins or at nursing homes. Growing up, every Christmas Day we went to visit a shut-in who had no family, and although I know we kids complained about having to do it at the time, looking back I realize how much that meant to that gentleman. If you can find a way to include your children in reaching out to others, you will be giving them a gift worth far more than the latest gadget. Squeeze in time during the hectic month of December to help them make Christmas cards for older church members or handmade Christmas gifts for grandparents and teachers. Show them by example that it's better to give than to receive. After all, Advent and Christmas are about giving. God promised to send a Savior, and He did. Your Advent and Christmas celebrations should include giving in some way, and I mean more than just a bunch of toys for the kids. Show them the best gift ever given—Jesus, God's own Son, sent to this sinful world as our Savior. *That's* reason to celebrate—not just during Advent, but all year long.

A Parent's Love

November 20, 2017

Our Saturday started out as a "normal" day, whatever that means in our household. My oldest was off with marching band, I gave the dogs a bath with the assistance of my sixth grader, and the girls were riding their bikes. Nothing unusual thus far. But while I was fixing lunch, my kindergartner burst in to inform me that my third grader had fallen off her bike and was bleeding. Okay, I've patched scraped knees before. I can handle this. But when I saw her, it wasn't just her knees that were scraped. Her lip was bleeding too, and when I wiped the blood away I knew we were looking at a trip to the hospital for stitches. So much for a normal day. My entire afternoon was effectively wiped out by the hour-long trip to the children's hospital and the time spent there, and I'm sure the bill from our ER visit will be exciting when it arrives, but it was totally worth it. After all, she's my daughter.

My experience over the weekend is hardly earth-shattering. Any responsible parent would have done the same thing. When a child needs immediate medical attention, parents drop whatever it is they're doing to help, all at the expense of the parent. Although the injury or illness isn't the parent's fault, the parent is the one who feels the responsibility to fix the problem. So great is a parent's love that he would take the injury in his child's place if possible, just to restore his child to full health again. Hmm. That almost sounds like a blog topic, doesn't it? Because God did the same thing for us, His children.

As God's children, we were in a pretty bad mess, and it was far worse than a split lip. We had deliberately chosen to disobey God, thus alienating ourselves from Him. For our sin, we deserved death and hell. Not a pretty picture at all. And although it was clearly our own fault, God our Heavenly Father took the expense and responsibility upon Himself to fix our sin problem and restore us to full spiritual health. The solution wasn't easy or cheap. It cost Jesus His life. But He did that for us so that we wouldn't be lost forever. So great was His love that He took our place and our punishment, to restore us to full spiritual health. Galatians 4:4–5 spells out what God did for us, His sons and daughters. "But when the fullness of time had come, God sent forth His Son, born of woman, born under the law, to redeem those who were under the law, so that we might receive adoption as sons."

Friend, if you ever doubt how much God loves you, look no further than the cross. Whatever you may be suffering right now, know that God has already provided for your deepest need by sending Jesus to take your sin from you. Yes, it cost Him His very life, but it was totally worth it to Him. After all, you are His precious child.

When You Think God Has Lost Control

November 23, 2015

Have you ever felt like your life was out of control? Have you been tempted to think God couldn't possibly love you if He allows pain and hardships in your life? Or perhaps even—gasp—that *God* had lost control? If so, you aren't alone. And the answer is much easier to understand when you remember that God is our Heavenly Father and that we are His children.

As a parent, I have seen my children at their best and at their absolute worst. I've seen them politely address elderly women in our church as "ma'am" while holding the door open for them, and I've seen them kick their sibling in the stomach just for the fun of it. Sweet hugs one minute can turn into tantrums the next. And one thing I know is that kids *aren't* innately good. I never had to teach my children to lie, steal, whine, hit, or bite. They do these things instinctively. But I would be a terrible parent if I ignored those things or passed them off as childish behaviors they would outgrow. As a parent, I have to do something drastic because I love them too much to allow them to grow up to be spoiled and entitled. I have to discipline them.

The Bible shows us that we too are disciplined by our Father in heaven. Proverbs 3:11-12 tells us, "My son, do not despise the Lord's discipline or be weary of His reproof, for the Lord reproves him whom He loves, as a father the son in whom he delights." Hebrews 12:5-6 quotes that passage and goes on to elaborate:

> *Endure hardship as discipline; God is treating you as sons. For what son is not disciplined by his father? If you are not disciplined...then you are illegitimate children and not true sons. Moreover, we have all had human fathers who disciplined us and we respected them for it. How much more should we submit to the Father of our spirits and live! Our fathers disciplined us for a little while as they thought best; but God disciplines us for our good, that we may share in His holiness. No discipline seems pleasant at the time, but painful. Later on, however, it produces a harvest of righteousness and peace for those who have been trained by it (Hebrews 12:7-11, NIV).*

Discipline is actually a *good* thing when it comes from God. It's proof that He counts you as His child. The reasons may not be evident to you, but He knows what He's doing. When your life seems to spiral out of control and you wonder where God is, He's right there beside you.

Imagine you're in a grocery store and your child starts to throw a tantrum because you won't buy her a toy. Whom do you love more—your child or your fellow shoppers? Your child, obviously. So with that in mind, you (hopefully!) choose what is best for your child in the long run, even though she may scream for all she's worth. You refuse to give in. Outsiders looking in may think you've lost control, but in reality you are shaping your child's future character. So we must ultimately believe that God knows what is best for us, even when it appears He has lost control.

Whatever you're facing, God has not abandoned you or lost control. Trust your Heavenly Father. He knows what is best for you, His dear child. He's looking to your future, not only on this earth, but also a future with Him in heaven.

Come, Lord Jesus

November 27, 2017

Have you ever noticed that the Church Year ends where it begins? The Last Sunday of the Church Year has a strong emphasis on the end times as we wait for Jesus' coming. This flows naturally into Advent, with its emphasis on—you guessed it—waiting for Jesus' coming. Even some of the hymns are interchangeable, equally acceptable for both occasions. "Savior of the Nations, Come," "Lo! He Comes with Clouds Descending," "Come, Thou Long-Expected Jesus," "O Come, O Come, Emmanuel," and "Christ is Surely Coming" show that we're waiting for Jesus, whether His first advent at Christmas or His second advent when He returns. And let's be honest. Waiting is hard for us.

It seems like God's people have been waiting since time began. From the time sin entered the world, God promised a Savior. For centuries, God's people waited. And waited. Many prophets foretold a Messiah that some probably doubted would ever come. There was a 400-year period of prophetic silence before Jesus was born. His people must have thought He would never keep that promise. But then, one otherwise ordinary night in Bethlehem, the promised Savior was born in the most unorthodox of ways—in a humble stable to poor parents. It was exactly the time God was waiting for. "But when the fullness of time had come, God sent forth his Son," Galatians 4:4 tells us. God's timing was perfect.

The promised Savior went about His work on earth in a surprising way too. He didn't rally the troops and rebel against Roman rule. Instead, He suffered and died at the hands of those Romans. And then, most surprising of all, He rose from the dead to prove He had defeated even death for His people. When He ascended into heaven, He promised His disciples He would return. And His followers have been waiting ever since. And waiting. It's easy to get disheartened and think that Jesus is never coming back.

2 Peter 3:9 speaks to us in our impatience. "The Lord is not slow to fulfill His promise as some count slowness, but is patient toward you, not wishing that any should perish, but that all should reach repentance." Do you realize what this means? God is speaking about *you* in this verse. For the past 2000 years, Christians have longed for Christ's return. But if He had returned 100 years ago, none of us would have been born. God is patient until the time when everyone whose names are written in the Book of Life have come to faith. And as His first coming in Bethlehem was a surprise, so will His return be a surprise. No one knows the day or the hour when He will return. So in the meantime, we wait in eager expectation, telling others the beautiful news about Jesus, who has promised in Revelation 22:20, "Surely I am coming soon."

Amen. Come, Lord Jesus!

The Tree of Life

The Church Year isn't the only thing that ends where it begins. The Bible does the same thing. Genesis 2:8-9 tells us that "The Lord God planted a garden in Eden, in the east, and there He put the man whom He had formed. And out of the ground the Lord God made to spring up every tree that is pleasant to the sight and good for food. The tree of life was in the midst of the garden and the tree of the knowledge of good and evil."

Alas, we all know what happened when Adam and Eve ate from the tree of the knowledge of good and evil. Sin entered the world, and has affected every human being since then. One small bite from man, one giant mess for mankind. But God, the master gardener, was not content to leave us in our sin and let us deal with the consequences ourselves. He had the solution, and that was Jesus. Everyone throughout the centuries, from Adam and Eve until those Christians alive when Jesus returns, have another garden, another paradise to look forward to in heaven.

Revelation 22:1-2 sets the scene for us: "Then the angel showed me the river of the water of life, bright as crystal, flowing from the throne of God and of the Lamb through the middle of the street of the city; also, on either side of the river, the tree of life with its twelve kinds of fruit, yielding its fruit each month. The leaves of the tree were for the healing of the nations."

We've come full circle and ended up right back to where we started: in a garden, with the tree of life front and center. If you've ever imagined this tree of life in heaven or seen artist's renditions of it, you probably picture a lush, green tree with juicy fruit, much as you'd picture the tree in the Garden of Eden. But here's one example of how English translations can only get us so far. You see, there are two Greek words for *tree*.

Let's take a look at δένδρον (déndron) first. This is what we generally think of when we hear "tree." It's often used to refer to an oak tree in the Bible, like the oaks of Bashan in Isaiah 2:13. It has branches and leaves and grows lush and green. This is where we get the English word "dendrite," which refers to the nerve cells that branch out. A *déndron* is living and growing. When Jesus speaks about a tree and its fruit in Matthew 7:17-20, He uses *déndron* five times. The sense we get from these verses is a large tree with deep roots, spreading branches, and healthy leaves and fruit.

But now we come to ξύλον (xýlon). Basically, this is a piece of wood. It's timber, a stick, a club, or some other such wooden article. This is used in Acts 5:30: "The God of our fathers raised Jesus, whom you killed by hanging Him on a tree," and in 1 Peter 2:24: "He Himself bore our sins in His body on the tree…" So while *déndron* denotes a healthy tree that is living and growing, the *xýlon* is but an ugly, rough wooden beam. It is the cross!

Given these definitions, I would expect the tree of life in both Genesis and in Revelation to be a *déndron*. But the Greek word is, in fact, *xýlon* in both cases. (The Old Testament was written in Hebrew, but translated into Greek between the third and first centuries BC in a translation known as the Septuagint.) Surprising, isn't it? And yet, it shouldn't be. The cross is where we find life. So it should come as no surprise to us that it would be found in heaven, an eternal reminder of what Jesus has done for us. In other words, the tree of life is the cross of Christ!

Yes, the Bible ends where it began, in a garden, with the tree of life. Everything that happens in between Genesis and Revelation shows us all the trouble God went to just to get us back to paradise. This only makes sense, since Jesus is "the Alpha and the Omega, the beginning and the end" (Revelation 21:6a). Of course the Bible ends where it begins: with Jesus.

What Are You Waiting For?

November 28, 2016

Patience may be a virtue, but it's one I do not possess. Waiting is really difficult for me. Right now I'm waiting for the publication of my first novel, and I'm learning that a lot of writing involves waiting. Waiting to hear whether or not they like my manuscript when I send it in, waiting to receive an edited copy, waiting for a second edited copy, interior design, proofreading… There are a lot of steps, and the whole process takes more than a year from start to finish. While I'm in the middle of the process, that seems like an awfully long time. But all things considered, that's not a terrible wait time. I need to remind myself that it's *good* it takes as long as it does. I don't want to rush through the steps of editing and proofreading only to end up with a sloppy end product. Even though I may wish it was a shorter process, in the end, it's totally worth the wait.

So what is it you're waiting for? A promotion at work? the kids to be out of diapers? test results from a biopsy? Some of these things are weightier than others, and there are times when you may even feel like God has forgotten you as you wait and wait for Him to answer your prayers. If you've ever wrestled with questions of doubt, you aren't alone. People in the Bible wrestled with similar questions—Job, David, and the psalmist Asaph, to name a few.

In Psalm 77, Asaph struggles with despair. The first nine verses are plaintive as he cries out to God. "Will the Lord spurn forever, and never again be favorable? Has His steadfast love forever ceased? Are His promises at an end for all time? Has God forgotten to be gracious? Has He in anger shut up His compassion?" (Psalm 77:7-9). This is serious stuff. I'm not sure what exactly he was going through, but it had to be pretty bad. Have you been there? Wondering if God even cares anymore? Wondering if He really is good and gracious? Waiting for an answer to prayer that you fear may never come?

But now comes a turning point. "Then I said, 'I will appeal to this, to the years of the right hand of the Most High.' I will remember the deeds of the Lord; yes, I will remember Your wonders of old" (Psalm 77:10-11). Asaph decides that even if God isn't gracious and compassionate to him at that exact moment, he will recall His deeds to His people of old. He can rest secure, knowing how God has proven Himself in the past. God led His people out of Egypt and through the Red Sea, leading them "like a flock by the hand of Moses and Aaron" (Psalm 77:20).

Speaking of waiting, the Israelites were in slavery in Egypt for 400 years. Generations of them died without seeing God's promise fulfilled. But when God did intervene, it was with decisive power. This wasn't some slave revolt where the underdogs surprised everyone to win the day. No, God showed His might by the plagues on Egypt, and for added effect, He led the entire band of Israelites through the Red Sea on dry land before drowning the entire Egyptian army in the waters. *That's* how powerful our God is.

Right now we are entering the season of Advent as we *wait* for Christmas. But it's so much more than that. We aren't just waiting for another holiday. We also wait for Jesus' second Advent, when He will return with glory to judge the earth. And as we wait, we can remind ourselves of what God has done in the past. He's never let His people down. After centuries and centuries of waiting, at long last the Messiah was born in the little town of Bethlehem. God fulfilled His promise and sent a Savior to our fallen race. And Jesus lived a perfect life in our place and took our punishment for us. He died for us and He rose for us, assuring us that our future in heaven is secure.

And *that's* a promise that's totally worth the wait.

December

Courageous

December 1, 2014

It's hard to be brave sometimes. As I post this, our family is on the road in the midst of a cross-country move, site unseen by all but my husband. I won't even lay eyes on the house until we pull up to it to move in. We still aren't sure where the kids will go to school, I'm nearly seven months pregnant and have no doctor lined up, and we'll be spending Christmas amongst people we've only known for a couple of weeks. It's a bit daunting, and I'm not feeling all that brave as I look ahead.

The dictionary definition of "brave" is "possessing or exhibiting courage." Franklin D. Roosevelt is attributed the following quote about courage: "Courage is not the absence of fear, but rather the assessment that something else is more important than fear." In our case, what is that "something else"? Faith, of course. Faith that our Heavenly Father has a plan for our good.

My current situation reminds me of Abraham and Sarah (at that time, Abram and Sarai). God appeared to Abram and said, "Go from your country and your kindred and your father's house to the land that I will show you" (Genesis 12:1). God promises that He will make Abraham into a great nation, and just like that, "Abram went, as the Lord had told him" (12:4). Now, *that* took courage. And not just on Abraham's part, but on Sarah's as well. Imagine your husband told you God had spoken to him and told him to move the family to an unknown destination. I can't even imagine what went through Sarah's mind. *God appeared to my husband, but what assurance do I get? After all, Abram's getting old. How does he know for sure this was God and not just some dream? And where exactly are we going, anyhow?*

Abraham and Sarah both must have had their private misgivings, but they went nonetheless. Why? Because their faith in God was more important than their fears. Faith requires courage, because "Faith is the assurance of things hoped for, the conviction of things not seen" (Hebrews 11:1). But here's the thing—God gives us that courage and that faith as a gift. We don't have to muster it on our own. What a relief!

When Moses died and Joshua took over the daunting task of conquering the Promised Land, God gave him a pep talk of sorts. In this speech in Joshua 1, God tells him three times in the span of four verses to "be strong and courageous." In verse 9 He gives the reason we can be courageous: "Be strong and courageous. Do not be frightened, and do not be dismayed, for the Lord your God is with you wherever you go." No matter where your path leads you, God is with you. Even across the country.

Christmas Wouldn't Be Christmas Without the Tree

December 4, 2017

Whether you put yours up the day after Thanksgiving or wait until Christmas Eve, the Christmas tree is one of the most ubiquitous symbols of Christmas. Nearly every household in America has at least one tree. We see them in yards, stores, schools, businesses, and town squares. There are tree lighting ceremonies in many towns. One might say that Christmas wouldn't be Christmas without the tree. And that's entirely true.

People have been using the evergreen as a Christmas tree for at least a thousand years. During winter, it reminds people of the spring to come, and for Christians the sign of growth and life amidst the bare branches of the other trees is an apt reminder of the life we have in Jesus. But let's look beyond that. Let's look back to a time before Christmas even existed; back to one of the very first trees on this earth.

You know the story. Adam and Eve were living in Eden in paradise. There were two specific trees named in this garden: the tree of life, and the tree of the knowledge of good and evil. Regarding these trees, God said, "You may surely eat of every tree of the garden, but of the tree of the knowledge of good and evil you shall not eat, for in the day that you eat of it you shall surely die" (Genesis 2:16-17). But Satan, in the form of a snake, tempted them to eat of it, and they did. Just like that, sin entered the world. Not just sin, but death. God meant what He said. They ate of its fruit and death was the result. But that wasn't the end.

4000 years later, we come to another tree, this one not beautiful. On the rough hewn beams of a cross suffered a man condemned to death for sins not His own. The tree didn't look like much, nor did the man on it. But in this moment of apparent weakness, Jesus earned salvation for everyone who believes in Him. Anyone who eats of the fruit of *this* tree will have life.

Without the message of these trees—one representing death, the other offering life—Christmas would be pointless. Jesus' birth would mean nothing without His perfect life and His death and resurrection for you. So the next time you see a Christmas tree, think of Jesus, who "bore our sins in His body on the tree," as 1 Peter 2:24 reminds us. Indeed, Christmas wouldn't be Christmas without a tree.

To Be Made Whole

December 7, 2015

We met on the elevator. I had noticed him earlier, of course. He was hard to miss. I surreptitiously watched him eat breakfast with his daughter, wondering what their story was. We had a one-minute conversation on the brief ride from the first floor to the second, and then he was gone. I don't even know his name.

This weekend did not go at all how I imagined it would. Saturday we were at a birthday party, the kids happily playing football outside until someone came in to tell me, "One of your boys got hurt." Nothing new there. They're always hurting themselves playing football. But this was different. My eldest was screaming in pain, barely able to move his leg due to excruciating pain. Fearing he'd popped his hip socket out of joint, we loaded him into the van and my husband made the forty-minute drive to the hospital nearest us.

As luck would have it, the X-ray showed a high femur break, and a pretty bad one at that. Now we're talking about surgery. So they consulted with a pediatric surgeon in a town with a bigger hospital. They transported my son via ambulance to a children's hospital there, where they got him ready for surgery to put in a metal brace. The on-call surgeon came in and began the surgery shortly after 11:30 PM. There were a few complications during surgery, so it went longer than expected. By 3:00 they were done, but I still had to wait until my son was over the anesthesia enough to see me. We finally got to the room around 4:30, and I enjoyed a whopping three hours of interrupted sleep on a pull-out hospital couch with a plastic pillow.

I woke up with a terrible headache and a great feeling of self-pity for my son and myself. Of all the kids, it *would* be the one I don't homeschool who has to be immobilized in a wheelchair at first and crutches after that. His basketball season is shot. No more playing outside in the field after school with his friends. And now I get to be nurse to the one who is usually the most independent of my five children. Sigh. Lucky me.

Thinking that some coffee might put me in a better frame of mind, I went to the cafeteria for some breakfast. And that's when I saw them.

The father was ahead of me in line. From the way he spoke to the cook making his breakfast, I knew he'd been there many times before. And when I took my plate out to eat alone, I saw him sitting in the corner with his daughter in a wheelchair, her IV's hooked up on a rolling cart. I couldn't stop watching them as I ate. He took a picture of her on his phone. He put a blanket around her shoulders. His love for her was obvious.

As I looked around the cafeteria, I noticed kids with bald heads, kids getting pulled in wagons with pillows and blankets surrounding them, and kids pulling around IV carts. Suddenly, my own situation seemed very, very insignificant indeed. A broken femur is nothing to sneeze at, certainly, and I don't envy my son in the upcoming weeks and months. But his leg will heal. He may miss basketball, but he'll be okay in time for Little League. My son will live.

Sitting in the cafeteria, I started to cry. I went out onto the patio for some fresh air and the chance to cry freely. And as it happened, when I came back inside, the father and daughter were right there, walking to the elevator with me. He observed that I had been crying, and asked, "How are you holding up?"

That did it. I burst into tears again and confessed, "I'm not crying for me. I'm crying for you. My child is only here for a broken femur." Words I never thought I'd utter.

He smiled sadly and said, "She is dying." No time to mince words.

"I know," I said, tears streaming down my cheeks.

"Her heart—they can't do anything else."

I could only nod.

"I'd gladly have her lose both feet just to have a healthy heart again."

By now we had reached his floor, and he pushed her off, saying, "But God is good."

How could I even respond to that statement? As the elevator doors were closing, I told him, "I'm praying for you." And then he was gone. My parting words to him seemed so trite, so hollow and flippant. I'm sure he's heard those words from other people hundreds of times. But there's so much more I meant when I told him I was praying for him. I pray that God would give him and his family strength and, in time, His perfect peace. I pray that both he and his daughter have the assurance of eternal life in Jesus. I pray that even as they stare death in the face, they know it does not have the last word. For, you see, Jesus already won the final victory.

I reached the nurse's station outside my son's room, and his nurse could tell I'd been crying. She asked if I was okay, and I related the conversation to her. "I never thought I'd be grateful for a broken femur," I concluded as I walked back into my sleeping son's room.

The exchange was over, but I couldn't get it out of my mind. As a matter of fact, I had a burning desire to find that father again, to say the things I hadn't said, to explain what I meant by my assurance I'd pray for them. It became almost an obsession. So I did what I do best. I wrote. I wrote him a letter. I wrote Bible verses of comfort and hope. I wrote hymn verses that speak of the resurrection. I told him I didn't know if I would ever meet him again on this earth, but that my prayer was to see him and his daughter again in heaven someday.

When I finished, I felt much better. But now what? How could I find him again? I went to the morning chapel service hoping to see him there. I scoped out the cafeteria at lunchtime hoping to find him again. I watched for him at the magic show that afternoon. Nothing. So during a slow time at the nurse's station I walked out to our nurse and asked, "Wanna help me go on a wild goose chase?"

Together we called the nurse on the second floor. After our nurse explained what was going on, she handed the phone to me. I described the father and daughter, and the other nurse knew exactly who I meant. She told me to give the note to my nurse, who would deliver it to her, and she would give it to the father. So we did just that.

I still don't know who that man is. I don't know how long he's been here or how much longer his daughter will be with him. I haven't the faintest idea what his name is. Nor does he know mine. But someday, *someday*, I pray that I'll see him again. With his daughter. And if so, we'll be together in heaven praising our Savior. With whole hearts.

Extending Grace

December 7, 2017

One of my fondest Christmas memories is one that, at the time, seemed like a complete disaster. My mom was down with the flu and could hardly get out of bed, much less make the holiday meal she was planning to make. My dad, a pastor, had a funeral the morning of Christmas Eve, besides two evening services, and didn't have time to make anything for us either. So after the funeral we ended up at Taco Bell for our Christmas Eve dinner, my dad wearing his clerical collar and my brothers and I in our play clothes. We still joke about that Christmas, and how people must have thought my dad was a priest taking some underprivileged urchins out for a "gourmet" meal on Christmas Eve. At the time we kids complained, but now we laugh about it and retell the story every Christmas.

That Christmas was hardly perfect by outward standards, but for that matter, neither was the first Christmas. An unfamiliar town? A stable? Dirty, smelly shepherds? I'm sure Mary would much rather have been at home in Nazareth, surrounded by her mother and family for the birth of her baby. But that was the way God chose to send His Son into the world, and it was absolutely perfect. Because Christmas isn't about pomp and pageantry. It's not about the gifts or the feast or how many people are in church. Christmas is all about God's grace.

Let's face it. Christmas is stressful. Although we may lament about how commercialized or secularized the holiday has become, there's little we can do to change that in our society overall. Every year I vow I'm going to "slow down" and enjoy the beautiful season of Advent, but before you know it I'm sucked right back into the mad dash toward Christmas. December is a frenzy to buy presents and attend parties and decorate and bake and send cards and plan children's Christmas programs and... Sigh. You know the feeling, don't you? It's all too easy to get stressed out, to snap at your kids or your parents or that nosy aunt who has an opinion on everything. You may find yourself burned out and even a little bit jaded about Christmas. We all *know* Christmas is about Christ, but how, exactly, does one put that into practice? Let's look to God's Word to answer that for us.

Titus 2:11-14 may not be the first Scripture that comes to mind when thinking about Christmas, but it's the appointed Epistle reading for the Christmas Midnight service in the lectionary. "For the grace of God has appeared, bringing salvation for all people," Titus 2:11 states. So what is "grace," exactly? Put simply, it is God giving us what we don't deserve. We didn't ask for a Savior. We didn't deserve a Savior. But God, in His grace, sent His Son nonetheless.

The Greek word for "grace" is *charis,* which has a slightly different nuance than the English word. There's the added implication of "leaning towards." God leans toward us, even when we turn our backs on Him, wanting nothing to do with Him. He freely extends Himself to get us back to Him. *Freely extends.* Hmm. That sounds almost like…Good Friday? Exactly. On Good Friday, Jesus was extended upon the cross for the sins of the whole world, which brings us right back to Titus 2:11 with God bringing salvation for all people. The Christmas message would mean nothing without the Easter promise.

Brothers and sisters in Christ, *that's* what Christmas is all about. God's gift of salvation, brought to us in the humble form of a newborn. God reconciling us to Himself through His Son. How will this beautiful message affect your Christmas celebration? Are there people with whom you need to be reconciled? Take the first step, even if the other party is the one who wronged you. Extend grace by leaning toward that other person. God doesn't ask of His children what He hasn't first modeled. He sent Jesus to us when we were dead in our trespasses.

Do you find yourself "keeping score" with the number and/or value of gifts? Release yourself from that burden. Remember, through Christ "God was reconciling the world to Himself, not counting their trespasses against them," as 2 Corinthians 5:19 states. If God doesn't keep score, neither ought we. Rather, our gift exchange should remind us of the Great Exchange, where Jesus took our sin upon Himself and gave us His righteousness.

Do you get so busy and stressed out that you don't have time for devotions or worship? Pray that God would show you areas where you can cut back. Maybe you don't absolutely need to send a Christmas letter this year. Maybe you don't have to bake ten different kinds of cookies for the extended family gathering. And maybe, just maybe, that's part of the reason God chose such humble circumstances for the First Christmas—to show us that it's not about the surroundings or the family gathering or the fancy meal or the decorations or the mounds of gifts under the tree. It's about One very special gift to all people of all times. It's about Jesus, the gift of grace.

Lasting Impressions

December 8, 2014

Moving is not for the faint of heart. In the span of our marriage we are on our eighth address. We're averaging less than two years at any given address. Four of those moves have been while I was pregnant. That's a lot of moving. And it's hard, I'm not gonna lie to you. Not just in terms of packing and housing and all those pesky details to work out, but emotionally. And since we just moved a distance of 1300 miles last week, I can say this with a fair amount of authority. But this time around, I learned a lesson from, of all things, vacuuming.

When the movers were clearing out all our boxes and furniture a week or so ago, I realized I could be doing something productive and vacuum out the empty rooms while they were working on others. So dutifully I began my task. I made it through the first three rooms, but when I got to the living room it finally hit me. We were leaving. I passed the section of wall where the kids had peeled a bit of wallpaper off and colored underneath it. I passed the scribbled Sharpie marks my two-year-old had made. I vacuumed the spot where that same two-year-old spilled blue paint that still left a mark no matter how many times we scrubbed it and hit it with the carpet cleaner. I found the yellow Sorry piece we had lost during a family game night. And I started to cry as all the memories of time spent together in that house came flooding back.

You see, a house isn't "just" a house, contrary to what people may tell you. It's a home, made special by the people who live there. And the carpet tells a story. Even after I vacuumed you could still tell where our bed had been in the master room, with like-new carpet underneath and decidedly more worn carpet in the walking path around it. In the living room you could still see the marks in the carpet where the bookshelf and couch had been. You could see the table leg marks in the carpet of the dining room. The pieces of furniture themselves may be gone, but they left impressions behind.

In much the same way, people leave behind impressions. We may have started a new chapter of our lives, but the people we just left behind left strong impressions in our hearts. We don't forget them just because we move away. They live on in our hearts and minds as we remember them with fondness and keep in touch. We, likewise, have made an impression on them. And as we meet new people here now, we have a chance for them to make impressions on us as well.

Believe it or not, you're not only making impressions on those with whom you come into contact. You've already made a lasting eternal impression on God Himself. Don't believe me? Look at this verse from Isaiah 49:16—"Behold, I have engraved you on the palms of My hands." Now that's what I call a lasting impression. God is assuring His people that it is impossible for Him to forget and forsake them. And it's not just an Old Testament promise either. Think about Jesus' palms. They, too, are engraved with the nail marks He endured for our sake. Those marks assure us that He has won our victory. He will never leave us or forsake us. You can count on it. You're engraved on His palms. Eternally.

Why I Don't Do Christmas Anymore

December 10, 2018

I've decided I'm not going to decorate for Christmas anymore. I made the mistake of putting up our tree with the kids last weekend, and it was a disaster. While I'd love to be instilling happy memories for the kids in our annual Christmas decorating, I'm afraid the opposite could well be true. Suffice it to say that there was much fighting, and in the end we had two broken ornaments and two children in tears. So much for quality family time. Who needs this, anyhow? So I'm done. No more decorating for me.

You know, come to think of it, family mealtime is another thing that's not worth it. Our dinner conversations are usually quite loud, often with people shouting over each other to be heard. Our kindergartner slides off her chair to pet the cat. Our two-year-old shrieks for more milk and throws food on the ground. Our middle school boys argue. It's pretty chaotic. Really, why am I bothering? It would be so much easier to just let them eat on the couch in front of the TV and forget about this farce of family meals.

And *church!* Good grief, what about church? Why bother to take young kids to church? My husband is the pastor, so who gets to sit in the pews with them every week? Me. Just me. Yes, the older ones are old enough now to behave and participate on their own, but sakes alive, my toddler gives me a run for my money! By the time church is over, I feel like I've been through a wrestling match with a two-year-old and come out on the losing end. There have been countless services where I've come home mad or feeling like I didn't get anything out of church that day. Why am I doing this to myself?

Sigh. Who am I kidding? Although decorating for Christmas may not be *fun,* it's hardly something I can choose not to do. Putting ornaments on the tree is a family tradition. My kids would be crushed if they didn't get to do that. My toddler would be bummed if he couldn't plug in the lights every evening. Now that it's done, it really does look pretty, with the lights glowing in a semi-dark room. And most important (to the kids), without a tree, where would we put the presents? Overall, while the actual process of stringing lights and hanging ornaments isn't always pleasant and gets sorta messy, the end results are totally worth it.

I suppose I'd better not give up on family dinners, either. Numerous studies have shown the benefits of family mealtime. Eventually (I hope!) we'll be able to have a polite conversation with everyone exhibiting good table manners. But in the meantime, we're establishing the fact that family meals are important for us, even if that isn't always an enjoyable process.

And while we're at it, I'd better not stop taking the kids to church. I know that my two-year-old won't be two forever. Before I know it, he'll be quoting the Lord's Prayer and Apostles' Creed with us. Eventually he'll be able to read and follow along in the hymnal. And yes, the time will come when I'll actually be able to listen to an entire sermon again. He'll grow up knowing that church is a priority to our family. If I'd waited until my kids were all old enough to behave in church, it would be too late. Then my thirteen-year-old still wouldn't be going to church. And by that point, why bother at all?

Fellow parents, there will be weeks, even years, when you might feel dejected and want to give up taking your kids to church. You might be tempted to think it's not worth the hassle; that you aren't getting anything out of church and neither are your kids. But don't fall for that lie! God is blessing your children—*His* children—with the gift of faith, and He has promised that His Word will never return to Him void. So don't give up. Keep bringing your kids to church and Sunday School. Tell them about Jesus often. Make sure they know about His perfect life, His innocent death, and His glorious resurrection. Show them by word and deed that your faith is so important to you that you won't let their bad behavior deter you from hearing God's Word. And eventually, a funny thing will happen. Your kids will grow up and take *their* kids to church.

But for now, I guess I'll go set up the nativities with the kids.

Perpetual Children

December 11, 2017

I'm ready to be done with the toddler years. I love my toddler like crazy, but I've had a baby or toddler in the house for nearly fourteen years now, and it's starting to wear on me. I'm over fun surprises like a fire starting in the bottom of the oven because my toddler thought it would be neat to stuff crayons into those nifty holes down there. I don't particularly relish finding pins scattered across my carpet after my toddler gets into my sewing kit. I'm not keen on finding hot chocolate powder scattered all over the bed and floor during so-called "nap" time. I'm done with temper tantrums and potty training and sippy cups and inane conversations. It sometimes feels like my kids will be children forever.

Anyone who has ever felt this way about parenting might be able to relate to the frustration of the writer of Hebrews when he says, "About this we have much to say, and it is hard to explain, since you have become dull of hearing. For though by this time you ought to be teachers, you need someone to teach you again the basic principles of the oracles of God. You need milk, not solid food" (Hebrews 5:11-12).

Just prior to these verses, he was speaking about Jesus as a priest in the order of Melchizedek. He has more to say on the subject, but knows his readers won't understand it because they haven't gotten past spiritual infancy. Not that they were particularly new Christians, either. They ought to have been teachers by then, but they were still on spiritual milk, not nearly ready for solid food like the order of Melchizedek. The writer of Hebrews wants to have more mature conversations with them, but he can't. Instead, he needs to keep reminding them of the basics of the Christian faith.

Looking ahead a few verses to Hebrews 6:1-2, we read, "Therefore let us leave the elementary doctrine of Christ and go on to maturity, not laying again a foundation of repentance from dead works and of faith toward God, and of instruction about washings, the laying on of hands, the resurrection of the dead, and eternal judgment." It appears that these believers still needed to hear the basics of their faith, as laid out in these verses. They wanted a simplistic faith, without anything terribly challenging. They were content to remain infants in the faith; content to be perpetual children.

Are we any different today? How many times has your pastor heard the complaint that his sermons are too technical or go over people's heads? *Don't confuse us with all that theological jargon, Pastor. Just preach the basics; stuff we can understand.* Maybe we aren't all that different from the readers of Hebrews. Maybe we're content with a simplistic faith too.

So what's the solution? The answer lies in the verses between the two passages above. Hebrews 5:13-14 says, "Everyone who lives on milk is unskilled in the word of righteousness, since he is a child. But solid food is for the mature, *for those who have their powers of discernment trained by constant practice to distinguish good from evil*" (emphasis added). How can we get past spiritual milk and on to solid food? By constant use of the gifts God has given us—His Word, His Sacraments, prayer, and the fellowship of believers.

Adult palates are far more sophisticated than a child's. By experience, they have learned to tell subtle differences in taste. They can tell if a dish has too much or too little salt. They can often sense the addition of an herb or spice not called for in a recipe. Likewise, only spiritually mature people can discern subtle errors and differences in doctrine and Christian living. Many a false teaching has crept into the church, leading those who are not spiritually mature into error.

Brothers and sisters, don't fall into that trap. Dig into God's Word. Go beyond your favorite familiar passages. The Bible is so rich, so complex, that even biblical scholars like pastors admit they can't fathom it all. You will never get to a point where you know everything there is to know about the Bible. Join a Bible study to get into the Word more and help you understand. Faithfully gather with fellow Christians around that Word in church. Feed on Christ in the Lord's Supper. Remember your baptism. Pray that God would grant you wisdom and understanding in your faith. And trust His promise that He will indeed answer that prayer for wisdom and spiritual maturity.

After all, you'll be His child forever.

When Time Stands Still

December 15, 2014

A few weeks ago I went to a symphony performance with my brother. I left in plenty of time to meet up with him and get to the performance hall early. But as I neared the city I saw a sea of brake lights ahead. At first I figured it was just a routine back up, but as I sat there I saw fire trucks, ambulances, police cars, and tow trucks pass on the shoulder and I realized with a sinking feeling that we were there for the long haul. As I was at least a mile from an exit either way, there was nothing to do but wait. I called my brother, who found out that they had actually closed down the expressway for this accident. So my fellow drivers and I turned off our cars and sat there. For an hour and a half. Nothing at all could change the fact that we were stuck. It didn't matter if you were a retiree coming home from a nice breakfast, a businessman who needed to make an important presentation, or even a pregnant lady in labor (thankfully not me)—you were stuck. And you couldn't do anything about it.

One of the hardest things about waiting is that it makes you realize that you aren't in control at all. And that's why I find it curious that the Bible tells us in Psalm 27:14 to "Wait for the Lord; be strong, and let your heart take courage; wait for the Lord!" Anyone who has indeed waited on the Lord's timing knows this is much easier said than done.

Remember, God is eternal. He is patient. He can wait. We, on the other hand, want our prayers answered right away. We live in an age of LTE and next-day delivery and drive-thrus and stores open 24/7. It's hard for us to wait for anything. But God knows what is best for us and He knows sometimes waiting is best. Think of the saints from the Bible and how long some of them had to wait for answers to their prayers. Joseph was in Egypt thirteen years before his purpose became clear. Abraham and Sarah waited twenty-five years for Isaac to be born. Moses spent forty years in the desert before he was even sent to Pharaoh, and then he had to spend forty more years wandering the desert with those stubborn Israelites! Did any of them ever get tired of waiting? I'm sure they did. But here's an interesting insight. The word "wait" and the word "hope" come from the same Hebrew root. So when we are encouraged to wait on the Lord, it's also a reminder to place our hope in Him.

Yes, waiting is hard. It's a helpless feeling. I know. I waited over three years for God to answer a prayer, and when He did it wasn't at all how I expected it to be answered. And maybe that's a good thing. It reminds me that I'm not in charge. I don't have all the answers. But I know the One who is in charge, the One who does have all the answers. And He's the One in whom I place my hope. Even when I'm stuck in a traffic jam.

Santa Sightings

December 17, 2018

I saw Santa Claus in the post office the other day. He ended up in line behind me. Now, my kids don't believe in Santa, but my three-year-old was gawking at him, so I decided to have some fun. "Is that Santa I see here?" I asked my son. "I didn't think Santa mailed stuff from this post office! Isn't he supposed to be in the North Pole?" The pretend Santa smiled, but otherwise remained silent. I have to admit, I was a little disappointed. I'd hoped for an obligatory, "Ho, Ho, Ho!" After all, he *was* wearing the costume. The least he could do was play the part.

The post office wasn't the last time we saw Santa. A day or two later, we saw the same guy, dressed up in the same way, pulling a wagon down the road. On his way to a Christmas party at the day care, maybe? The next day he was at the elementary school's family fun night. This time he wasn't dressed up, but by now, my three-year-old recognized him even without his costume. "What? Santa's here?" he asked, pointing to the man, who was probably there with his grandkids. Whether this guy wanted to be recognized as "Santa" or not, that's how my kid knew him. In that sense, he was never really off-duty.

Neither are you, dear child of God. You might be tempted to think of your "religious life" and your "personal life," as though you only need to be a Christian for an hour a week at church and then put that identity aside as you go about your "real life." This is simply not true. Consider how many people are watching you, even when you don't realize it. I doubt our town Santa Claus went to the family fun night thinking kids would expect him to be Jolly Old St. Nick. Who is watching you? When a neighbor sees you interacting with your family during the week, does he see your identity as a Christian? When you go out to eat with friends, do they hear wholesome talk coming from your mouth, as befits a son or daughter of your Heavenly Father? When you attend sporting events, do those around you raise their eyebrows at your reaction to the refs or umps? Do your children see a parent who practices what he preaches?

You will at some point fall short. Your neighbor will hear you yell at your kids, your friends will hear you gossiping, fellow sports fans will hear a few choice words, and your kids will see you at your worst. When you do mess up, confess it to the Lord and trust that He forgives you and gives you strength to do better another time. But don't allow this to be an excuse. Even though you *know* you'll fail from time to time, remember that you're always "on duty" as a Christian.

The Bible is full of exhortations to holy living. Paul encourages in Ephesians 4:1, "I therefore, a prisoner for the Lord, urge you to walk in a manner worthy of the calling to which you have been called." Peter urges, "Keep your conduct among the Gentiles [unbelievers] honorable, so that when they speak against you as evildoers, they may see your good deeds and glorify God on the day of visitation" (1 Peter 2:12). Philippians 2:14-15 tells us, "Do all things without grumbling or questioning, that you may be blameless and innocent, children of God without blemish in the midst of a crooked and twisted generation, among whom you shine as lights in the world."

So go, dear Christian. Shine that light—*His* light—into the world. After all, you never know who may be watching.

Less-Than-Ideal Circumstances

December 18, 2017

His circumstances were hardly ideal. He'd been beaten and was falsely imprisoned. There was a price on his head and a plot to kill him. Not the sort of situation in which I'd want to find myself. But the apostle Paul didn't complain about the unfairness of it all. Rather, he looked at those whom God was placing in his path: fellow prisoners, Roman soldiers, even the king. God used Paul's circumstances to further the spread of the Gospel. In fact, one might even say God orchestrated those less-than-ideal circumstances.

Put yourself in Paul's place for a moment. He was in Jerusalem to celebrate the festival of Pentecost after having completed his third missionary journey. But some troublemakers stirred up the crowd against Paul. The mob dragged Paul out of the city and started beating him, trying to kill him. He was saved by the Roman tribune and Roman soldiers and centurions. To keep him safe, they kept him in chains in the barracks while they figured out what to do with him. But then Paul found out that a group of overly-zealous Jews had taken a vow that they wouldn't eat or drink until they had killed him. Yikes. Serious stuff. Yet in the midst of all this, God appeared to him and told him, "Take courage, for as you have testified to the facts about Me in Jerusalem, so you must testify also in Rome" (Acts 23:11). You see, this was all part of God's plan.

To escape the plotting of the Jews who wanted Paul dead, the Roman tribune had Paul transported, and as he traveled, he witnessed. He was able to speak about Jesus to Governor Felix, Governor Festus, King Agrippa and his sister, Bernice, many other high-ranking officials, and possibly even Caesar himself. While in Rome, he was under house arrest for two years, but during those years he wrote letters to the churches of his day, letters which we now know as Epistles in the New Testament. The results of his unjust imprisonment were actually very well choreographed. Paul acknowledges this in his letter to the Philippians, where he says, "I want you to know, brothers, that what has happened to me has really served to advance the Gospel, so that it has become known throughout the whole imperial guard and to all the rest that my imprisonment is for Christ. And most of the brothers, having become confident in the Lord by my imprisonment, are much more bold to speak the Word without fear" (Philippians 1:12-14). Paul was able to look beyond his circumstances to see the opportunities God was giving him.

Friend, I don't know what circumstances you face today. Perhaps you're stuck in a job, a town, a situation you don't particularly like. Maybe things in life haven't gone the way you planned them, and you're disheartened or bitter. But take a moment to stop and consider the people with whom God has surrounded you. Pray that God will open your eyes to see the opportunities He is giving you. It was because of a physical ailment that Paul was able to preach in Galatia (Galatians 4:13). While in Rome under house arrest, he was able to witness to Caesar's household (Philippians 4:22). God can use your less-than-ideal circumstances to reach out to those He has placed in your path. From a human standpoint, Paul's life seemed way off course; a once-promising career traded for a life of hardship, beatings, imprisonment, and death threats.

But for God, the circumstances were, quite simply, ideal.

The Weakness of God

December 21, 2014

Have you ever been disappointed in God? Maybe He didn't answer a heartfelt, selfless prayer on behalf of someone else. Perhaps you just get fed up seeing the disarray of the world and wish God would do something to prove Himself. It may be disappointing to realize this, but in this world, God chooses to remain small.

Back in the Old Testament, God had a few really glorious moments. I'm talking Hollywood worthy. The scene with Elijah and the false prophets of Baal was spine-chilling when God sent fire from heaven to burn Elijah's drenched altar. There was also the dramatic rescue of the three men in the fiery furnace, as well as their friend Daniel being spared from the lion's den. Oh, and let's not forget the climactic parting of the Red Sea with Moses and the Israelites. We love that kind of stuff. It shows how powerful our God is. But He doesn't do that very often, does He? Even in the Old Testament He didn't always show His might like this. He didn't always swoop in at the last moment to save them. His prophets were mistreated and He didn't intervene. Some even died for their faithful witness, and to the pagan world, it just proved that God was helpless.

This is a perplexing dilemma. Why does God allow His saints to be persecuted, mocked, and even killed for their faith? Doesn't He have the power to do something about it? And if He does have the power to stop it, why, oh, *why* doesn't He use it?

Lest you despair, consider this: Jesus Himself lived a life of smallness. He, the Son of God, whom angels worship in heaven, chose to become weak for our sake. He entered this world as a single cell inside Mary's womb. He was born as a helpless infant, unable to do anything for Himself. Not only this, but He was born into the most lowly of circumstances. He wasn't born to a wealthy king and queen, laid in a soft bed with silken cloths. He was born to a poor couple in an unfamiliar town in a stable. He laid His head on rough straw in a feeding trough for animals. His welcoming committee was a group of lowly shepherds, dirty and unwashed from being out in their fields. *That*, my friends, is weakness. That's choosing to remain small.

But Jesus didn't stop there. Not only did He have a humble beginning, He chose as well to have a humiliating end: death on a cross, a punishment reserved only for the most vile and wicked criminals. He wasn't the Savior the Jews of His day expected. They wanted a powerful God to swoop in and lead an army to conquer those cruel Romans for them. But that's not what God had in mind at all. He was looking at something far bigger than they could ever imagine—He was looking at eternity. They, on the other hand, just wanted out of their current but temporary earthly situation. God chose to remain small so He could gain for them an eternal victory, where He would indeed reveal His power and might. In heaven, we shall see Him enthroned in all the splendor and majesty due Him. But for now we wait.

This Christmas, take some time to reflect on the "smallness" of God. Think about that helpless baby in the manger. Remember that God often chooses to remain small, because as Paul was assured in 2 Corinthians 12:9, "[God's] power is made perfect in weakness." The infant King in the manger is proof of that.

Overwhelmed at Christmastime

December 23, 2019

December has been brutal to our family this year. We had to put one of our dogs down, which, as any pet owner can tell you, is emotionally draining, to say the least. I've also spent a fair bit of time at the doctor this month. Three of us (myself included) have had or are still dealing with ear infections, one of my sons had a stomach virus, and I lost my voice for more than a week.

Add this to the general chaos of five kids in four different schools with all the gift exchanges, classroom parties, concerts, and programs that go along with the season, and I'm a hot mess. I got the tree up a week ago, but no other decorations until this weekend when my kids asked about the nativities. I'm flying by the seat of my pants for gifts for my kids. I'm all for the idea of "slowing down and enjoying the season," but seriously, how? I know I'm not the only one feeling this way. It's a regular topic of conversation among my friends. It seems like everyone feels overwhelmed.

Mary knew a thing or two about being overwhelmed. Imagine her shock when Gabriel appeared to her to let her know she was to bear the son of God. She had been chosen by God to be the mother of the Savior! What an incredible honor! And yet… Mary was still a virgin. She knew that, but would anyone else believe her? She was a pregnant, unmarried woman in a society that didn't condone pregnancy out of wedlock. This incredible honor God was bestowing upon her came with its own set of challenges.

Joseph was in a similar boat. Thanks to the angel appearing to him in a dream, he knew Mary was pregnant by the Holy Spirit, so he took her as his wife, but he must have known rumors would swirl in Nazareth. People must have whispered behind his back, speculating about how Mary *really* got pregnant. Was the baby his or not? And if not, why on earth would he still marry her? He must be the biggest chump in history.

But there was still more. Thanks to Caesar's decree, they had to travel to Bethlehem for a census. On the one hand, this took care of the rumors swirling about them. People in Bethlehem wouldn't have known the circumstances surrounding the pregnancy. But this trip created new problems. It was a three- or four-day journey on foot (or donkey) from Nazareth to Bethlehem, a challenging trip to make with a pregnant woman. Once they got to Bethlehem, Mary had to give birth in an unfamiliar setting without her family around. She placed the Savior of the world in a feeding trough. Lowly shepherds were the first visitors to the King of kings. In her shoes, I might have been a little miffed. *This* is the best God can do for the arrival of His Son? Yet the Bible records a very different reaction from Mary—she "treasured up all these things, pondering them in her heart" (Luke 2:19).

Mary would need those memories and promises of God treasured in her heart for the days to come. When they presented Jesus at the temple forty days after His birth, Simeon told Mary, "This child is appointed for the fall and rising of many in Israel, and for a sign that is opposed (and a sword will pierce through your own soul also), so that thoughts from many hearts may be revealed" (Luke 2:34-35). Not exactly a ringing endorsement of what would lie ahead for the earthly work of Jesus. Mary must have wondered what exactly that "sword" would be that would pierce her own soul. How could she have imagined the cross?

Within a year or so, Mary and Joseph found themselves stunned by a visit from the Maji, who presented Jesus with gifts fitting for a king. Yet even in the midst of this wonderful event, more troubles surfaced. Mary and Joseph were forced to flee to Egypt with Jesus to escape King Herod's murderous intent to kill the infant King. In their shoes, I know I would have been thinking, "Really, God? Do You even have a plan here? I don't know how much more of this I can handle."

Can you relate? Do you feel so overwhelmed you aren't sure you can handle anything else? Take heart. Mary didn't wait until after Jesus' death and resurrection to treasure up the promises of God. She did it right in the midst of the chaos, surrounded by strangers in an unfamiliar town, having just given birth to the long-awaited Messiah. Overwhelmed? Yes. But she took a moment to "ponder" all those events in her heart. She didn't know how the story would play out. She didn't know what Jesus' earthly ministry would look like. She almost certainly didn't know she would one day watch her Son die on the cross for the sins of the world, including her own. She didn't need to know all that. At that moment, she was content to dwell on God's promises.

Friend, don't wait until life slows down before you "treasure up all these things, pondering them in your heart." In the middle of the chaos is when you need God's promises the most. You have something Mary didn't have: perspective. You know how the story ends. You know God's plan was far bigger than anyone could have imagined. You know the Old Testament prophecies of the Messiah were all fulfilled in Jesus. You've seen God keep His promises in the past, so you know every single promise He makes in the Bible will see its fulfillment, even if some promises won't be fully realized until heaven.

Take a minute today—right now—to find a Bible verse to meditate upon. (Perhaps something like Jesus' promise in Matthew 11:28, "Come to Me, all who labor and are heavy laden, and I will give you rest.") Write it down and stick it in your pocket, or on a sticky note to put on your mirror. Think about it throughout the day and ponder what that promise means for you. Even in the chaos—no, *especially* in the chaos—God is waiting to fulfill every promise to you.

Confessions of a Christmas Hater

December 29, 2015

I hate Christmas. I know, I know, that's a terribly Grinch-y thing to say, but let me explain. I hate the pressure of Christmas and the general entitlement attitude in society regarding the holiday. We're expected to decorate our houses, buy presents, hang lights, buy presents, send Christmas cards, buy presents, bake Christmas cookies, buy presents, and generally spread holiday merriment and cheer everywhere we go. Oh, did I mention buy presents? It's enough to make a person's head spin.

The past two Christmases have been rough for me. Last year we made a 1300-mile move from Michigan to Texas at the beginning of December. We weren't even unpacked when I had to start planning for Christmas. I was also seven and a half months pregnant. Add to that the fact that I was now 1300 miles away from my family and lonely in a new state. I thought this year would be better. I was wrong.

My oldest son broke his femur playing football in a backyard game the first weekend of December. So on top of everything else associated with Christmas, I also had to step up as a nurse to him as he learned to navigate daily tasks with a wheelchair and crutches. It's been a rough couple of weeks. Christmas wasn't even on my radar until mid-December, and I got through the holiday by the skin of my teeth.

The Christmas packages to our families were sent out the week of Christmas, the latest I've ever gotten them out. One arrived on Christmas Eve, one didn't make it by Christmas at all. The Christmas cookies I always make as gifts for local friends were finally baked and handed out the day before Christmas Eve. I realized with horror on Christmas Eve that we only had one gift for our three-year-old from us. Granted, it was a bike, but still, she only got one gift from us while the others got at least three. And I was still wrapping gifts on Christmas Day minutes before the kids ripped into their gifts. Like I said, I made it by the skin of my teeth.

Yet this Christmas was not without its blessings. Despite the rather lopsided gift-giving on our part, each of our children ended up with exactly the same number of gifts to open, a near-impossible feat given the fact that out-of-town relatives and sponsors send gifts as well, which doesn't always equate to equal numbers for the kids. Plus, my oldest two actually bought gifts for other family members this year of their own accord and with their own money. I took my eldest, crutches and all, to Walmart with me one day so he could pick gifts for his younger siblings and for me. My second oldest walked down to our local grocery store one day to buy me a Hershey's bar with his own money. To see my two oldest get excited about buying and giving gifts was a gift in and of itself.

Then, of course, there was the Christmas Eve service. My oldest three kids each had a part. I can honestly say that's the only time I've ever seen Gabriel portrayed on crutches, but he said his lines clearly and confidently, and my shepherd and angel did their parts well too. Part of the service this year included the kids singing certain hymn verses, and hearing my children practice the first verse of "Savior of the Nations, Come" at home was worth a lot to this church musician. And not to be outdone, my three-year-old cheerfully joined my six-year-old singing countless renditions of "Happy Birthday to Jesus" throughout the day on Christmas.

Somehow Christmas worked this year. Despite my seeming unpreparedness for the whole thing, Christmas came anyhow. It didn't matter if certain gifts didn't arrive on time or whether I made cookies or not, or even whether I had an equal number of gifts for everyone. Those things are nice, sure, but they aren't what makes Christmas, *Christmas*. Watching my children sing their praises to the newborn King in the manger humbled me as I realized that they *know* what Christmas is really about. Yes, they get worked up about presents, too. What kid doesn't? But they also know that ultimately, the best gift isn't under the tree. It's in a crude manger in a little town of Bethlehem.

So I guess in the end maybe I don't hate Christmas *that* much after all. I actually ended up enjoying it this year. Maybe even enough to try it again next December.

The Clock is Ticking

Bonus Post

Countless books and blog posts have been written about time management. Clearly, this is a pertinent topic in this day and age, one that many people struggle with. And trust me, I can waste time with the best of 'em. Give me a free day while the kids are in school, and I'll likely look back in the evening and wonder what, if anything, I actually accomplished.

Even the Bible has something to say about managing time, though maybe not exactly in the context we might expect. Ephesians 5:15-16 tells us, "Look carefully then how you walk, not as unwise but as wise, *making the best use of the time*, because the days are evil" (emphasis mine). Likewise, Colossians 4:5 exhorts, "Walk in wisdom toward outsiders, making the *best use of the time*" (emphasis mine). That's the ESV version. The NIV translates the phrase as "making the most of every opportunity," which is a slightly better rendition. An *opportunity* has a different nuance than does *time*. But I like how the KJV puts it even more: "redeeming the time." That carries with it the idea of how valuable time and opportunity is.

Clearly, Paul isn't encouraging us to be more productive at work or in the home. He's talking about opportunities or time spent with those who do not yet know Christ. Make the most of those opportunities. God is not run by the clock the way we are in our society. He doesn't schedule things by the hour. So it's important to look at a distinction in the concept of *time*. To further explore this, we need to look at the two Greek words for "time."

First off, we have χρόνος (*chrónos*). As you might deduce, this is the root word of "chronology." It's a specific, set time, like King Herod asking the Wise Men the exact *chrónos* the star appeared in Matthew 2:7. This is also the word used in Galatians 4:4: "But when the fullness of time [*chrónos*] had come, God sent forth His Son…" At exactly the right *chrónos*, the perfect moment in history, God sent Jesus into the world. Jesus was born on a specific day in a specific year. It's a fixed time, *chrónos*.

Καιρός (*kairós*), on the other hand, denotes a period of opportunity. When the devil leaves after Jesus' temptation, he departs for a more "opportune time," or *kairós* (Luke 4:13). This is the word used in the verses from Ephesians and Colossians above. It's used in places like Galatians 6:10: "So then, as we have opportunity [*kairós*], let us do good to everyone…" As we have *kairós*, we are to do good to others. This concept also implies that at some point there will be an end to this *kairós*. Our period of opportunity will not last forever.

In 2 Corinthians 6:2, Paul says, "Behold, now is the favorable *kairós*; behold, now is the day of salvation." Your period of opportunity for believing the Gospel ends when you die physically (which is a *chrónos* moment!), which is why Paul pleads with the Corinthians "not to receive the grace of God in vain" (v 1). It will be too late to believe in Jesus when you are dead. Make the most of the opportunity not only in your own life, but to spread the Word to others as well!

You have a specific *chrónos* alloted to you on this earth. You were born at a precise time and will one day die at a measurable time. What you do with your *chrónos* is up to you. Make yours a life not lived by the clock, but by *kairós* moments, making the most of every opportunity, redeeming the time to be used to God's glory, because He has most certainly (and literally) redeemed His time for you!

Acknowledgments

As with any book, this one was a long time in the making—seven years, to be exact! When my first book was published, I called my brother and told him, "I need you to talk me down from the ledge. I don't want to do it, but I feel like I *should* start a blog if I'm going to be a published author." Rather than bring me safely down from that dangerous ledge, he said, "Do it." So I did. Anthony, thank you for giving me that push, even if I wasn't all that happy with you at first.

I started my blog in 2014 by posting about two times a week, which eventually lessened to once a week, and then fairly sporadically. I haven't added a proper blog post for over a year now. Blogging used to be all the hype, but podcasts (no, Anthony, do *not* coax me off that ledge!) have taken over as the latest craze, while blogs silently take a back seat.

That might have been the end of it, had I not gotten another push from a friend. Sally told me I should compile my blog posts into a devotional book. I laughed at her suggestion at first. Who would want to buy a book when they could just look on my website and read them for free? But the more I thought about it, the more it made sense to have everything in one handy location, without having to weed through my entire blog online. I could include a Scripture index and topical index to make things easier for readers to find. And call me old-fashioned, but sometimes it's just nice to hold an actual book in my hand. So began the journey of compiling this devotional. Sally, thank you for your suggestion!

But the journey actually began much further back than that with my parents, who brought my brothers and me up in a solid Christian home, taught us about Jesus, and saw to our spiritual development. Mom and Dad, thank you for the invaluable upbringing, for sending us to parochial schools where we learned about Jesus every day, and for modeling your faith to us. You were my first and best teachers.

Thank you to my husband, Jonathan, and our children Benjamin, Timothy, Miriam, Sarah, and Samuel. Your stories are included in the posts in this book. Thank you for allowing me to share them, and for the lessons you have taught me along the way.

Anthony, thank you for your friendship, which means more to me than I can express. Your encouragement and indefatigable enthusiasm for this book are much appreciated. Thank you for the long hours you put into formatting (even during a hospital stay!) so we could get this book published in a timely fashion.

To all my teachers who deepened my understanding of the Bible and gave me the tools to properly interpret Scripture, thank you. To pastors and professors who explained difficult texts and concepts and gave me wonderful insights, thank you as well.

I also thank my pastor friends who endured tedious questions from me and shared with me their knowledge of Greek. Dustin, Jason, and Carl, thank you for patiently answering my random questions along the way. I never once heard any of you complain that I was bugging you *again.*

Dear reader, thank you as well. Thank you for following my blog, for posting comments, for sharing your own stories with me, and for reading this book. I pray that you are encouraged in your own Christian walk.

Above all, I thank my Lord and Savior Jesus, who is the Way, the *Truth*, and the Life. To Him alone be the glory!

Scripture Index

Please note that the verses in parentheses are indirect references

Topical Index

OTHER BOOKS BY RUTH MEYER

CHILDREN'S BOOK

SOLA SERIES

Read the first chapter of each of the Sola books at:
www.ruthmeyerbooks.com/books

Discussion questions for these books are available as well.

CONNECT WITH RUTH

WEBSITES

www.ruthmeyerbooks.com
www.truthnotespress.com

NEWSLETTER

www.ruthmeyerbooks.com/newsletter

BLOG

www.TruthNotes.net

FACEBOOK

www.facebook.com/TruthNotes

AMAZON AUTHOR PAGE

www.amazon.com/Ruth-Meyer/e/B00E6QC2RI

Made in the USA
Middletown, DE
05 May 2023

29571461R00246